SOFTWARE ENGINEERING HANDBOOK

Prepared by
General Electric Company
Corporate Information Systems
Bridgeport, Connecticut

McGRAW-HILL BOOK COMPANY

New York St. Louis San Francisco Auckland
Bogotá Hamburg Johannesburg London Madrid
Mexico Montreal New Delhi Panama Paris
São Paulo Singapore Sydney Tokyo Toronto

NOTICE

Judgements regarding the suitability of information presented herein or in later updates are necessarily the responsibility of the reader. Although reasonable care has been exercised in preparing such information, General Electric Company makes no warranty, either express or implied, including but not limited to, any implied warranties of merchantability and fitness for a particular purpose, regarding such information. In no event shall General Electric Co. be liable to anyone for special collateral, incidental or consequential damages in connection with or arising out of the purchase or use of this handbook, and the sole and exclusive liability of General Electric Co., regardless of the form of action, shall not exceed the purchase price of the Handbook.

Library of Congress Cataloging-in-Publication Data

Main entry under title:

Software engineering handbook.

   1. Computer software — Handbooks, manuals, etc.
I. General Electric Company. Corporate Information
Systems.
QA76.755.S63   1986   005.1   85-15374
ISBN 0-07-023165-6

234567890   HAL/HAL   89876

ISBN 0-07-023165-6

Printed and bound by Halliday Lithograph.

TABLE OF CONTENTS

TABLE OF CONTENTS

TABLE OF CONTENTS

TABLE OF CONTENTS

CHAPTER 7 – SOFTWARE TESTING

CHAPTER 8 – CONFIGURATION MANAGEMENT

TABLE OF CONTENTS

TABLE OF CONTENTS

SOFTWARE
ENGINEERING
HANDBOOK

**Chapter 1
INTRODUCTION TO THE
SOFTWARE ENGINEERING HANDBOOK**

Page 1-1

Software Engineering is a disciplined approach to developing and maintaining software that has evolved from activities generally referred to in the past as "computer programming". The *Software Engineering Handbook,* developed by the General Electric Company and first published internally in 1976, provides both managers and technical contributors with an indepth understanding of each step in the software engineering process.

Throughout the *Software Engineering Handbook,* you are introduced to management and technical methods for software project planning, specification, design, coding, testing and finally, the after project activity, software maintenance. Document formats and review procedures essential to the success of a software project are described in detail. Methods for tracking, reporting and controlling each item produced as part of software development are also defined.

In this chapter, a general introduction to software engineering and suggested uses of the *Software Engineering Handbook* (SEH) are presented. Successive chapters discuss each step of the software engineering process in detail.

1.1 THE PROBLEMS

Over the past decade, computer software has become the pivotal element of computer-based systems. It is software that determines the success of entire systems. Software provides function by tapping the "potential" hardware provides. This in turn leads to the "intelligence" associated with computer-based products.

Unfortunately, development and/or acquisition of computer software has its problems. In the early 1960's software development costs were a small percentage of overall system cost. Hardware was very expensive and (understandably) management effort and discipline were applied to control hardware costs.

As microelectronics evolved, hardware costs plummeted. Cost decreases of two or even three orders of magnitude in a five-year period have not been uncommon. Software costs, on the other hand, being labor intensive have continued to increase with inflation. By 1980, software had become the predominant cost factor in the development of many computer-based systems.

1.1.1 Software Development

The problems associated with software development had their roots in inadequate quality control applied to the programming process during the early days of computing. Because software was a relatively low-cost system element (in 1960), it received scant management attention. Poor management control and flawed technical development frequently occurred. In many organizations these antiquated practices still remain, resulting in the following problems:

1. Software cost and schedule estimates are often grossly inaccurate. Overruns hurt the developer's credibility, and lead to shortcuts that can degrade product quality, invariably causing customer dissatisfaction.

2. Software is not developed systematically even though proven methods for planning, specification, design, coding and testing can be applied.

3. Software is not properly documented. Computer programs should have a suite of documentation that is developed during (not after) the development process with these documents serving as milestones that can help managers to control and assess progress.

4. Software quality is suspect. Proven techniques in software quality assurance—review, inspection and testing—are not consistently applied resulting in quality assurance problems.

5. Software is frequently "unmaintainable". It is difficult to correct latent errors in many programs and practically impossible to adapt those programs to new computers or to provide functional enhancements requested by the customer. Reusable software remains an unachieved, highly-sought goal.

Each development problem noted above can be solved by applying the software engineering techniques discussed in this Handbook.

1.1.2 Software Acquisition

Software, as a product in its own right, has become a major element in the computer marketplace. Many managers, unfamiliar with acquisition techniques for computer software, have been disappointed after purchasing a program which does not satisfy stated requirements. The problems associated with software acquisiton are not unlike the problems associated with the purchase of any product from an external source. However, special care must be taken to assure that the following problem areas are properly addressed:

1. The software product to be acquired meets the stated requirements. The purchaser must adequately understand and *specify* needs and capabilities to be provided by the vendor's product. Methods to do this exist in both situations.

2. If the software product must be modified to "fit" into the purchaser's environment, modification costs must be reasonable and evaluated for cost effectiveness. Often, it is less expensive to modify the purchaser's environment!

3. The vendor must provide adequate support for the software product.

Page 1-2

**Chapter 1
INTRODUCTION TO THE
SOFTWARE ENGINEERING HANDBOOK**

**SOFTWARE
ENGINEERING
HANDBOOK**

Acquisition problems, like development problems, can be avoided. The discipline associated with software engineering can be applied to the acquisition of computer programs or systems.

1.2 A SOLUTION

A solution to the problems described in the preceding section is derived by taking a *life cycle* view of computer software. Like hardware, computer software should evolve through a series of carefully controlled and systematically executed phases.

1.2.1 A Life Cycle View

There are three phases in the life cycle for computer software: definition, development, and maintenance. During the definition phase, the software project is planned; budgets and schedules are estimated; and detailed requirements are analyzed and specified. During the development phase, software requirements are transformed into an operational program using proven methods for design, coding and test. Finally, in the maintenance phase, problems encountered in the field are corrected; adaptations of the software are made for different operational environments; and, enhancements to functional requirements are implemented.

A series of engineering steps occur within each life cycle phase. Each step terminates with a deliverable that can be reviewed.

1.2.2 An Engineering Approach

An engineering approach to the development of any product:

* demands the application of proven methods during each step in definition, development and maintenance;
* requires a series of reviews that serve to assure quality as the product evolves;
* defines specific documentation to be generated at each step;
* encourages the use and development of tools and methods that expedite development; and
* provides a traceable path from preliminary product concept to final product manufacture.

Any discipline develops over many years. In classic fields such as mechanical and electrical engineering, a generally accepted engineering science has evolved. Software engineering is the path toward an engineering science for computer software.

1.2.3 Software Engineering

Software engineering is a set of methods, tools, documents, practices, standards and procedures applied to definition,

development and maintenance of computer software. The software engineering process is quite similar to its hardware engineering counterpart. It exhibits the same characteristics discussed in section 1.2.2.

The remaining chapters of the *Software Engineering Handbook,* describe the following steps:

1. planning—a definition of project scope, resources budget and schedule;

2. requirements analysis—a definition of detailed functional and performance requirements, design constraints and validation criteria;

3. design—a methodical process that transforms requirements into (i) an architectural representation of software and (ii) a detailed procedural representation of software;

4. coding—the use of a programming language to transform the design representation into a machine intelligible form;

5. testing—a series of steps that (i) attempt to uncover latent defects (errors) in the program, (ii) assemble the software into a working package, and (iii) validate the software against requirements.

6. maintenance—the application of steps 1-5 (with additional control procedures) to manage existing computer programs.

Software engineering is a set of disciplined methods. Only through the application of such a discipline can the problems associated with software development be resolved.

1.3 KEY CONCEPTS INTRODUCED IN SEH

The *Software Engineering Handbook* (SEH) describes a number of important concepts for the management and practice of software engineering. This section presents an overview of those concepts.

1.3.1 The Life Cycle

Throughout the *Software Engineering Handbook* the concept of a "software life cycle" is discussed. The software life cycle establishes a chronology of software engineering events. The life cycle begins when software is defined as one element of a computer-based system. Once system engineers associate certain function/performance with software, the definition phase of the life cycle begins.

As previously noted in this chapter, the definition phase concentrates on software project planning and requirements analysis/specification. Using a previously prepared system specification as a definition, software planners and analysts define project scope and develop estimates for budget and schedule. Scope is expanded into a detailed written specification of requirements that is reviewed. The *Software Requirements Specification* becomes the foundation document for all subsequent work during the development phase of the life cycle.

Requirements must be translated to a form that ultimately can be executed by a computer. The development phase begins this transformation of requirements by applying design methods to generate a software architecture and a procedural representation of the software. The architecture and procedural representation drive the coding step that results in the generation of programming language source code — the computer program. Finally, a progression of tests is applied to assure quality and compliance with software requirements.

The maintenance phase of the life cycle involves each activity that occured during earlier phases, but applies software engineering to an existing program. Coupled with maintenance activities is a formal control methodology, called Software Configuration Management, which assures the integrity of the program as it undergoes change.

1.3.2 Software Project Estimating

Software project planning and control are discussed at a number of points in the *Software Engineering Handbook*. Software project estimating provides managers with budgetary and scheduling guidance at the inception of a project. In fact, the "go-nogo" decision for a project may be based on budgets/schedules estimated using historical data, empirical models or automated cost/scheduling tools.

Several estimating techniques are presented in the *Software Engineering Handbook*. Each requires a thorough understanding of the scope of a project; reference to data collected from past projects; logical partitioning of the work to be accomplished; and, the imposition of cross-checks to assure that the estimates make sense.

1.3.3 Requirements Analysis

Software requirements analysis provides a road map for subsequent software engineering work. Each step of the software engineering process must show "traceability" to requirements.

Requirements analysis starts during system definition — when all elements (e.g., hardware, software, information, people) of the system are identified and interfaces between elements are defined. Information structure and flow are modeled using either manual or automated tools; a software specification is developed.

1.3.4 Software Design

Design is the technical kernel of software engineering. The designer begins by mapping software requirements into an architecture whose elements are well-defined modules, each addressing some aspect of requirements. Using one of a number of design methodologies, the architecture, or structure, of the software is refined, documented and reviewed. As the design process continues, the scope of the designer's interest narrows. Once the software architecture has been established, procedural design techniques and tools are applied to each module individually. The resultant detailed design is the basis for structured coding.

1.3.5 Structured Coding

The software design must be transformed into a representation that is machine executable. Structured coding applies a set of programming principles that result in a programming language "source listing" exhibiting good style, clarity of form and documentation. Since the design process has also been structured, there is a general one-to-one match between the design and the source listing.

The source listing is input to a translator that automatically transforms the program into machine executable form.

1.3.6 Testing Steps and Methods

Many sections of the *Software Engineering Handbook* deal with various aspects of software quality assurance. Software testing is one of a number of quality assurance techniques.

Testing begins at the module level. The Software Engineer applies test case design methods and/or automated tools to assure that latent errors have been uncovered. After each module is *unit tested,* it must be integrated with other unit-tested modules to form the complete system. *Integration testing* is a set of strategies and methods for assembling and testing the computer program. Finally, the assembled software must undergo *validation testing* to assure that all requirements have been met.

1.3.7 Software Engineering for Small Projects

Software engineering applies to any size development project. However, when small projects (e.g., less than six person-months of effort, non-critical software, conventional applications) are undertaken, some steps of the software engineering process can be abbreviated; documentation may be shortened and combined; reviews can be less formal — but no less thorough. The *Software Engineering Handbook* provides a set of guidelines for the management of and technical approach to small software projects.

Page 1-4

Chapter 1
INTRODUCTION TO THE
SOFTWARE ENGINEERING HANDBOOK

SOFTWARE
ENGINEERING
HANDBOOK

1.3.8 Software Maintenance

Frequently, computer software is used for 10 or even 20 years after its development is complete. During this time, errors encountered must be corrected; adaptations to new environments must be completed; and, enhancements to the system must be developed. Collectively, these activities are software maintenance—a phase that absorbs up to 60 percent of all dollars spent on computer software.

Ideally, the methods and procedures used during software maintenance are virtually the same as those applied during software development. Unfortunately, programs developed without software engineering discipline are often poorly documented, designed in a manner that resists or defeats change and have undergone haphazard (sometimes unrecorded) changes in the past. Only through a software engineering approach can the burdens of maintenance be reduced.

1.3.9 Software Configuration Management

A variety of documents, reports, listings and data are created throughout the software life cycle. These items comprise a *software configuration*—a set of information that represents software in its many forms. Software Configuration Management (SCM) is a set of activities for the identification, control, auditing and accounting of software items.

The *Software Engineering Handbook,* discusses SCM in a separate chapter, but the activities associated with SCM are applied throughout the software life cycle. Documents must be properly identified for filing and indexing; changes must be audited to assure compliance with standards and procedures; and, management must be apprised of the current status of a project.

1.3.10 Documents and Reviews

Each software life cycle step results in production of a document that becomes part of the software configuration. Documentation develops as a natural consequence of each software engineering step. Documentation reviews mark project milestones.

1.4 PURPOSE OF THE *HANDBOOK*

The *Software Engineering Handbook* has been developed to serve two needs: (1) act as a tutorial text that presents the software engineering process in terms applicable in an industry setting, and (2) act as a sourcebook for procedures to establish the software engineering methodology. The primary objectives of the *Software Engineering Handbook* are:

1. to provide software management with a cohesive set of guidelines, methods and procedures for controlling each step in the software life cycle;

2. to provide software practitioners with a set of methods and tools that apply to requirements analysis, design, coding, test and maintenance;

3. to define documentation formats, review techniques, and configuration control mechanisms that help to assure software quality; and

4. to introduce a software engineering discipline that applies across a broad spectrum of applications and environments.

The *Software Engineering Handbook* is a comprehensive, unified presentation of a discipline that spans many topics in management theory and computer science. It serves the critically important role of introducing what some have called "the most important engineering discipline of the 80s".

1.4.1 A Guide for Managers

As a guide for managers who have direct or indirect responsibility for software development or acquisition, the *Software Engineering Handbook* satisfies a number of needs:

1. The Handbook provides guidance in techniques for software project planning and estimation. It introduces budgeting and scheduling techniques for software projects and defines the important considerations that must be addressed early in a project.

2. The Handbook suggests approaches for the organization of technical staff. Team organizations are discussed in detail.

3. The Handbook defines project milestones and the methods applied to evaluate these milestones. By answering the questions: "What should I expect, how should it be presented, when should it be delivered?", the Handbook provides a manager with reference points throughout a software project.

4. The Handbook identifies specific control mechanisms that can be used to manage the software configuration as it evolves. Control enables the manager to know the status of a project at all times.

5. The Handbook describes a number of quality assurance techniques that include: review procedures, testing methods, configuration control and management.

6. The Handbook provides a foundation for the development of a formal Software Engineering Standards and Procedures Manual.

Although a manager should be cognizant of all topics presented in the *Software Engineering Handbook,* many sections are technical in nature and need not be studied in detail. Section 1.6 of this chapter provides a set of guidelines for the use of the Handbook.

SOFTWARE
ENGINEERING
HANDBOOK

Chapter 1
INTRODUCTION TO THE
SOFTWARE ENGINEERING HANDBOOK

Page 1-5

1.4.2 A Guide for Practitioners

The application of software engineering methods and tools is the responsibility of practitioners (technical staff). The *Software Engineering Handbook* serves as a guide for the practice of software engineering by presenting the following topics:

1. The Handbook describes techniques, tools and representation methods for software requirements specification, design, code and test. Information from many sources has been summarized in the Handbook so that the practitioner can answer the questions: "What methods are available and what are the strengths and weaknesses of each?"

2. The Handbook describes the mechanics of the review process. Each software review is explained and justified.

3. The Handbook introduces a set of tools that include graphical representations (e.g., data flow diagrams, structure charts), and automated tools (e.g., PSL/PSA, PDL).

4. The Handbook describes documentation formats and contents. Each item of the software configuration is described in detail.

Although the practitioner's focus will be on tools and techniques, nearly all of the *Software Engineering Handbook* will be of general interest. (See Section 1.6 for Handbook utilization guidelines.)

1.5 USES FOR THE HANDBOOK

The *Software Engineering Handbook* presents each phase of the software life cycle. Chapters 3-7 describe the software engineering steps in the order that they occur during the definition and development phases. Chapter 9 offers in-depth coverage of the software maintenance phase. Other Handbook chapters consider topics relating to the entire software life cycle.

Chapter 2 is a software engineering process overview that introduces software engineering to one unfamiliar with the discipline. Chapter 8 describes Configuration Management - a set of standards and procedures that are applied throughout the software life cycle. Chapter 10 details modifications in the software engineering approach for small projects. Chapter 11 presents a potpourri of management issues that are relevant to software development.

Finally, Chapter 12 contains a detailed example of a software configuration for an actual project.

The *Software Engineering Handbook* appendices present detailed documentation formats (Appendix A), a discussion of supplementary methods and tools (Appendix B), an annotated software engineering bibliography (Appendix C) and (Appendix D).

1.5.1 A Source for Methods and Procedures

Chapters 3-10 of the *Software Engineering Handbook* are a source of methods and procedures for software development. Chapter 3 presents management planning, estimation methods and the procedures for project tracking and control. Chapter 4 describes software requirements analysis, specification methods and tools. Chapter 5 describes methods, procedures and tools for preliminary and detailed design. Documentation and review procedures are also discussed in Chapters 3-5.

Chapter 6 describes issues associated with coding style and clarity as well as code documentation, portability, and coding tools. Each of the testing steps is presented in Chapter 7. Test strategies, techniques and tools are discussed.

Chapter 8 presents an overview of software configuration management, introducing the procedural and organizational considerations necessary to control the software configuration. Chapter 9 describes software maintenance procedures and documentation.

Chapter 10 presents modifications to methods and procedures that are sometimes warranted for smaller projects. This chapter builds upon material presented in chapters 3-9.

1.5.2 A Source of Document Formats

Appendix A of the *Software Engineering Handbook* contains detailed document formats for each item in the software configuration. Appendices A.1 - A.9 contain outlines of each document and a section by section description of the contents of each document.

Chapter 12 presents an example of completed software documentation. Sample specifications, design documentation, source listings, and test documentation are presented.

1.5.3 A Source of General and Bibliographic Information

General topics related to software management and development are presented at many points in the *Software Engineering Handbook*. Chapters 2 and 11 are primary sources of such information.

Appendix C contains a current, annotated bibliography, organized by topic area, that can also serve as a pointer to further reading in software engineering.

1.6 HOW TO USE THE SOFTWARE ENGINEERING HANDBOOK

The *Software Engineering Handbook* is designed to serve as both a tutorial text and a reference book. Once the overall software life cycle is understood and the steps of the software engineering process have been reviewed, each chapter in the handbook can stand alone.

Page 1-6

Chapter 1
INTRODUCTION TO THE
SOFTWARE ENGINEERING HANDBOOK

SOFTWARE
ENGINEERING
HANDBOOK

Each reader of the Handbook should read Chapters 1 and 2. These chapters introduce the objectives and contents of the Handbook and provide an overview of software engineering. The interests of each reader will guide individual progression from that point. The following sections suggest how to use the *Software Engineering Handbook*.

1.6.1 A Topic-Audience Cross Reference Matrix

Although generalizations always require qualification, certain topics presented in the *Software Engineering Handbook* will be of interest to all readers; other topics are more likely to be of interest to managers, while others of special interest to technical staff. A Topic-Audience Cross Reference Matrix is provided in Figure 1.1. The matrix lists 34 major topics presented in the *Software Engineering Handbook* and suggests audiences for each.

Topics marked by "A" should be of interest to all readers. These topics comprise the minimum subset of Handbook material that should be mastered. Managers should augment "A" topics with all topics denoted by an "M" in the matrix. Technical managers may pursue selected technical categories (denoted by a "T") as well. Practitioners should augment "A" topics with all topics denoted by "T".

1.6.2 Recommended Reading for the Manager

The following guidelines present a recommended sequence of chapter readings for managers at different levels and interests. Chapter sequence is indicated by chapter numbers and appendix letters in the sequence they should be read. Numbers/letters in parentheses (   ) represent optional readings.

Upper level managers: 1, 2, (11), C
Middle level (project) managers: 1, 2, 3, 8, 9, 10, 11, (4-7, A), D
Technical Managers: 1, 2, 3, 4, 8, (5-7), 9, 10, (11), A, (B), 12, D

1.6.3 Recommended Reading for the Practitioner

The following guidelines present a recommended sequence of chapter readings for practitioners at different levels and with different interests. Chapter sequence is indicated by chapter numbers and appendix letters in the sequence they should be read. Numbers/letters in parentheses () represent optional readings.

System engineers and analysts: 1, 2, 4, 8 (3), (5-7, 9-12, A, B), D
Software designers: 1, 2, 4, 5, B, 8, 9 (3), 6, 7, (10-12, A), D
Software engineers: 1, 2, 4-9, (3, 10, 11), 12, A, B, D

1.7 SUMMARY

The *Software Engineering Handbook* serves the needs of a diverse audience. The guidelines presented in this section, coupled with the Table of Contents, Tabs and Index, should provide a useful road map in your study of software engineering.

TOPICS OF INTEREST	1	2	3	4	5	6	7	8	9	10	11	12	A	B	C	D
Software Engineering Overview	A	A														
Development Teams		M														
Cost Estimating Methods			M													
Software Productivity Issues			M													
Automated Tools—Costing			M													
Cost Factors			M													
Project Scheduling			M													
Requirements Analysis Tasks				A												
Characteristics of an Analyst				A												
Specification Formats				A												
Design Issues					A											
Preliminary Design Methodologies					T											
Design Review					A											
Detailed Design Tools					T											
Design Walkthroughs					A											
Structured Programming						T										
Code Style and Clarity						T										
Antibugging						T										
Coding Tools						A										
Software Testing Issues							A									
Software Testing Strategies							A									
Software Testing Methods							T									
The Test Team							M									
Debugging							T									
Test Tools							T									
Configuration Management								A								
Change Control								M								
Software Maintenance									A							
Small Projects										A						
Organization											M					
Standards											M					
Education											A					
Document Formats and Contents												A	A			
Supplementary Methods and Tools														T		
Other Publications															A	
Costing and Estimating																A

Legend:

M = primarily of interest to managers
T = primarily of interest to technical staff
A = of interest to all

Figure 1.1 Topic-Audience Cross Reference Matrix

**SOFTWARE
ENGINEERING
HANDBOOK**

**Chapter 2
SOFTWARE ENGINEERING OVERVIEW**

Page 2-1

Software Engineering is a set of formal techniques for the development of computer software. These techniques apply during each software life cycle phase:

1. definition
2. development
3. maintenance

A well-formulated, orderly approach during each stage is extremely important for both technical personnel and managers. Tasks must be well-defined, schedules must be realistic and progress must be carefully monitored.

The methodology described in this Handbook emphasizes four concepts:

1. Systematic techniques are available to accomplish each task at each phase;

2. Definition and design must be performed prior to implementation and test;

3. Frequent, timely milestones must be established and reviewed;

4. Complete and up-to-date documentation is developed throughout the life cycle.

Figure 2.1 represents the overall flow of events during the software life cycle. It should be noted that major tasks are reviewed during each life cycle phase. However, the definition, development, and maintenance blocks of Figure 2.1 are gross oversimplifications. Each life cycle phase contains numerous tasks and internal review procedures. Each is fully described in later chapters.

Figure 2.2 presents a more detailed breakdown of each stage. It shows each software engineering step and documentation item required by the software engineering process. This Handbook section discusses each activity listed in Figure 2.2. The presentation provides the reader an overview of the entire software engineering process.

2.1 DEFINITION PHASE

The definition phase of the software engineering life cycle is designed to:

1. define overall project objectives that must be satisfied;

2. determine project feasibility;

3. develop a strategy for accomplishing project objectives; and

4. establish project resource costs and schedule.

As shown in Figure 2.2, the definition phase begins with an evaluation of the overall system (hardware and software). System evaluation defines interrelationships and interfaces that must be understood prior to software planning—the first step in the definition phase for software.

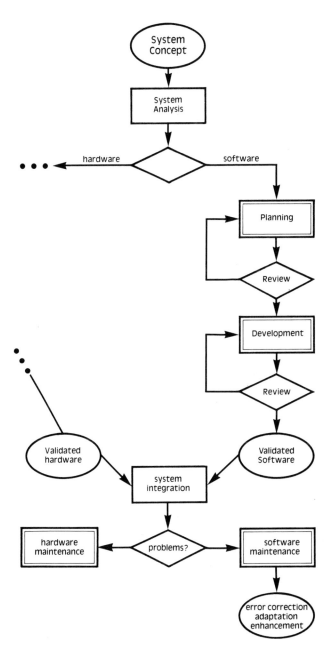

Figure 2.1 Software Life Cycle

Page 2-2

Chapter 2
SOFTWARE ENGINEERING OVERVIEW

**SOFTWARE
ENGINEERING
HANDBOOK**

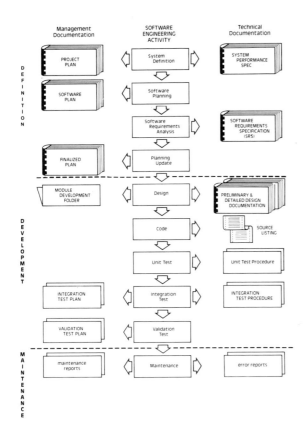

Figure 2.2 The Software Engineering Process

Often, it is not initially clear which functional requirements should be implemented in hardware and which in software. The requirements allocation process (hardware/software trade decisions) usually involves several trade studies to determine an optimal approach. The hardware requirements document is the basis for purchase specifications used for procuring equipment and the basis for performance specifications for design, fabrication and test of special-purpose equipment. These hardware specifications are discussed in this Handbook only to the extent that they interact with various software items to be produced.

The allocation of software requirements is also determined by trade studies. It should be subject to the same make/buy decisions. Software requirements are discussed in the following paragraphs.

For further information on system definition, the following are recommended:

1. Systems Development Management, Auerbach Publishers, 1979
2. Structured Analysis and System Specification, Prentice-Hall, 1979

For other references, see the bibliography in Appendix C.

2.1.2 Preliminary Software Planning

The scope, operating environment and basic functional characteristics of all project software are considered during the preliminary planning step. Required resources and costs are estimated, and a schedule for development is described.

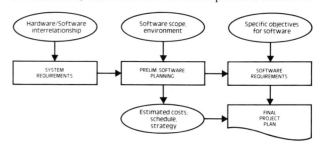

Figure 2.3 The Definition Phase

A software project overview is developed as a result of software planning. This project overview is refined and formalized during software requirements analysis. Once all requirements have been identified, a schedule of personnel, resources and costs may be developed. The final software plan, a combination of preliminary planning based on the overview and detailed estimates established during requirements analysis, is produced.

In the following paragraphs, each definition phase, shown in Figure 2.3, is discussed.

2.1.1 System Requirements Analysis

Much software developed today is part of a larger environment known as a "system". In a system, both hardware and software are integrated to perform a set of functions under a specified set of conditions. The system is defined in a document, the SYSTEM SPECIFICATION (see Appendix A.1 for a suggested format). Figure 2.4 illustrates typical events and considerations for the preparation of a SYSTEM SPECIFICATION. Functional requirements appearing in a SYSTEM SPECIFICATION may be allocated either to hardware or to software.

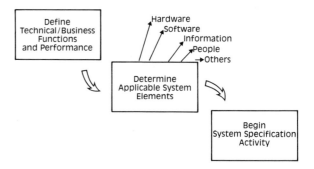

Figure 2.4 System Analysis

SOFTWARE
ENGINEERING
HANDBOOK

Chapter 2
SOFTWARE ENGINEERING OVERVIEW

Page 2-3

The cost and schedule estimates developed during this activity serve as a guideline for subsequent software requirements analysis. The requirements step must be completed before a formal commitment on cost and schedule is made. However, the preliminary estimates should not be exceeded without careful evaluation of the impact. Management concurrence is required to increase these costs. It is entirely possible, for example, that budgets are fixed and that another solution must be found. For example, it may be necessary to reduce project scope or to deliver the total system as a planned series of coordinated releases.

Be aware that the worst possible resolution of a growth in preliminary cost and/or schedule is to ignore it and demand that the preliminary (lower) cost and (earlier) schedule be met. Either they won't and the project will end up "late and overbudget"; or, worse yet, incomplete, low quality software will be delivered to be repaired later at many times the difference in cost with major customer dissatisfaction.

The preliminary planning task yields a planning document that can be evaluated by management relatively early in the overall definition phase. Using this document, the project's feasibility and merit can be evaluated. The initial "go-nogo" management decision can be made.

2.1.3 Software Requirements

Software requirements are defined by a joint effort of the software developer and the user/requestor of the system. The top level SYSTEM SPECIFICATION has defined the overall functional content of the software subsystem. The SOFTWARE PLAN describes software scope more explicitly. The SOFTWARE REQUIREMENTS SPECIFICATION (SRS) details system interfaces, functional details, design, performance and test criteria. It also provides a preliminary user manual for the software.

Documentation

During the software requirements analysis step, a PRELIMINARY USER'S MANUAL is developed. The PRELIMINARY USER'S MANUAL provides a user/requestor with a description of how the software functions from the user's viewpoint. It also forces the software system engineer(s) to consider the software from the user's standpoint. It uncovers inconsistencies and misunderstanding at an early phase if reviewed. Therefore, it is essential that the user/requestor review this document as soon as it is available.

The SOFTWARE REQUIREMENTS SPECIFICATION (SRS) is the requirements baseline for the software subsystem. It is the primary vehicle for management control and technical development. After SRS approval by requestor and developer, each proposed change must be carefully evaluated with regard to cost, schedule and performance. Only those changes deemed to be absolutely necessary are approved. A suggested format for the SOFTWARE REQUIREMENTS SPECIFICATION is given in Appendix A.3. The require-

ments specification may also contain a VALIDATION TEST PLAN. This test plan outlines all tests that the software must satisfy to be completely acceptable to the requestor.

Review

After the requirements document review, the SOFTWARE PLAN is reevaluated. Information developed during requirements analysis may affect required resources, cost and/or schedule. Each modification to the plan must be traceable to a requirements clarification.

The definition phase ends with a software plan review. Successful completion of this final planning review triggers the first step of development: preliminary design.

2.2 DEVELOPMENT PHASE

As Figure 2.2 shows, the development phase of the software engineering process consists of five steps:

1. Preliminary (Top Level) Design
2. Detailed Design
3. Code and Unit Test
4. Integration Testing
5. Formal Validation Testing

It is important at this point to introduce the overall software hierarchy and terminology used throughout the rest of the Handbook. Referring to Figure 2.5, the "software hierarchy" is divided into three levels.

The software subsystem includes all software associated with the project to satisfy all requirements. The software subsystem generally has several functions, each of which satisfies (directly or indirectly) one or more software requirements. Where a function is extensive, it may be desirable to subdivide the function so that the development can be more easily managed.

A module (also called "routine", "procedure" and "subprogram") is executable computer code that implements a functional requirement or part of a functional requirement. A module is normally the smallest item of code known and controlled by the operating system. In the context of an operating system task, modules or groups of modules may be combined to form a task having a given execution priority and frequency.

2.2.1 Preliminary Design

The preliminary design step during software development translates a set of well-defined requirements into a workable SOFTWARE STRUCTURE. The SOFTWARE STRUCTURE defines the relationships among modules and indicates hierarchy of control for the software. This structure is defined by: 1) understanding information flow through the software subsystem; 2) deriving required computer program modules; 3) defining data and control interfaces between these modules; and 4) establishing design constraints such as execution time and storage limits. Preliminary design is done by a design team that performs a top level design of the entire software subsystem.

Page 2-4

Chapter 2
SOFTWARE ENGINEERING OVERVIEW

**SOFTWARE
ENGINEERING
HANDBOOK**

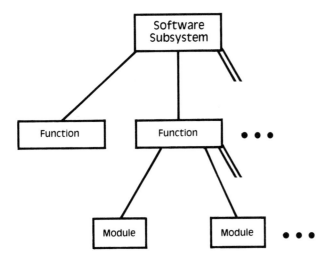

Figure 2.5 Software Hierarchy

Documentation

The tangible output of the software design process is a SOFTWARE DESIGN document. This document evolves from a PRELIMINARY DESIGN description that concentrates on an overall representation of the software to a DETAILED DESIGN description (described in paragraph 2.2.2) that defines discrete procedural elements for each module. The evolution of design documentation is illustrated in Figure 2.6.

The Design Review

Once the PRELIMINARY DESIGN is completed, it is reviewed thoroughly to assure that each requirement is addressed by the design. This design review enables the software manager to formally establish traceability to the REQUIREMENTS SPECIFICATION. The SOFTWARE DESIGN document is the second baseline document for the software subsystem. The design review also evaluates the feasibility and practicality of the intended design. The design review activities are outlined in Figure 2.7. In brief, data flow and software structure are considered; the design description of each program module is evaluated; data base details are considered; interfaces are evaluated.

Design Revision

After review, necessary changes are made to the PRELIMINARY DESIGN. The document must now contain enough information about each module and its interfaces so that detailed design can proceed with a minimum of verbal communication.

When the preliminary design is complete, it is possible to build a skeleton of the software system. This skeleton consists of "dummy" modules (sometimes referred to as stubs) which exercise and test the established interface constraints and the top level flow of control. Building such a skeleton has several advantages:

1. it reinforces confidence in the selected software design;

2. it verifies the highest-level interface specifications very early in the development cycle;

3. it provides a basic vehicle for demonstrating performance at selected points during the development; and,

4. it reinforces management confidence in schedule commitments.

2.2.2 Detailed Design

Detailed design may begin when each required module has been identified and the overall software structure has been established. The PRELIMINARY DESIGN is expanded to include the internal design of each module. The resulting expansion of the PRELIMINARY DESIGN is known as DETAILED DESIGN. It is the basis for coding and unit testing.

The internal design of a module may be specified using a variety of generally accepted techniques. Structured flow charts, HIPO charts, Box Diagrams and a Program Design Language are four common methods used for describing the procedure associated with a given design.

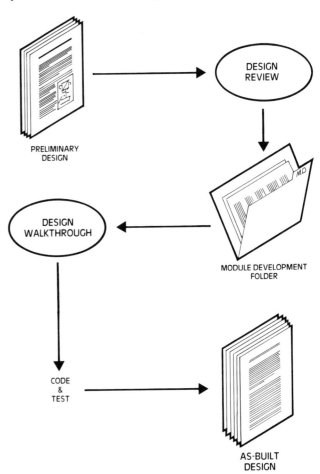

Figure 2.6 Design Documentation

SOFTWARE
ENGINEERING
HANDBOOK

Chapter 2
SOFTWARE ENGINEERING OVERVIEW

Page 2-5

1. Evaluate data flow and software structure.

2. Evaluate module description

    a. functionality

    b. traceability to requirements

3. Consider interaction and flow of control

4. Evaluate data base details

    a. limitations

    b. access

    c. structure

5. Evaluate interfaces

Figure 2.7 Preliminary Design Review

For larger software efforts, it is generally appropriate to assign individual modules to separate software engineers. For smaller efforts, all modules may be assigned to one person. Usually, it is not good practice to assign more than one person to a single module.

The evolving design is continually reviewed by top level technical personnel to assure that budgets are being met and that the design will satisfy specified requirements. Care should be taken to insure that unauthorized modifications or enhancements are not introduced at this stage. Upon completion of detailed design for a module, a DESIGN WALK-THROUGH or DESIGN INSPECTION may be conducted to uncover both functional and logical errors.

As illustrated in Figure 2.8, detailed design often is performed in parallel with other activities. In fact, scheduling priorities may require that later steps in the development stage be performed while other software functions (see Figure 2.6) are undergoing detailed design. This is possible only because top level (preliminary) design establishes each interface and the overall flow of control.

Module Development Folder

As detailed design progresses, documentation for each software module increases in volume and complexity. The Module Development Folder (MDF) is a convenient, readily accessible repository for documentation during the development process. Each MDF contains all development documentation for one or more software modules.

Each MDF contains a cover sheet, illustrated in Figure 2.9, that identifies the program function and may be used to assess the status of the function. Referring to the figure, ten key items are listed on this cover sheet.

The individual with technical project responsibility (the lead software engineer) establishes the due date for the module in consultation with the responsible programmer. The actual completion date is entered by the programmer when the module is completed.

Design Walkthrough

As detailed design progresses, each module is evaluated by an independent reviewer. Usually, another programmer familiar with the project performs the review. When the independent reviewer is satisfied that the module is complete, acceptance is indicated on the MDF cover sheet. The lead software engineer has final technical approval and the authority to resolve differences or conflicts.

An alternative approach is to conduct a more formal design inspection. The inspection involves three or four people, including a trained moderator. The design is assessed using a rigorous format; errors are recorded and corrective action is taken. Inspections provide a highly reliable mechanism for error detection.

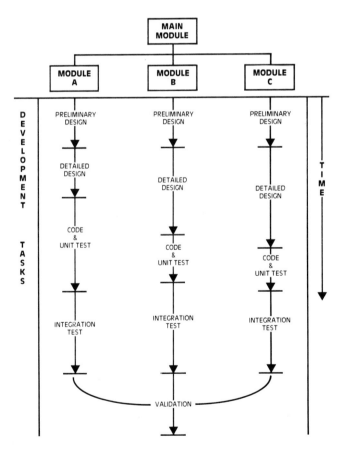

Figure 2.8 Parallel Tasks

PAGE _____ OF _____

PROJECT: _____   REVISION: _____ DATE: _____
MODULE NAME: _____   ISSUE DATE: _____
PROGRAMMER: _____   BUDGET: _____
DESIGN SECTION: _____   SOURCE LINES: _____
                                      OBJ. MOD. SIZE: _____

(MODULE OR ROUTINE NAMES IF APPLICABLE)

DESIGN SUBSECTION					
DESCRIPTION					
CODE TO DESIGN					
SCHED START					
ACTUAL START					
SCHED COMPL					
ACTUAL COMPL					
CODE/UNIT TEST					
SCHED START					
ACTUAL START					
SCHED COMPL					
ACTUAL COMPL					
INTEGRATION					
SCHED START					
ACTUAL START					
SCHED COMPL					
ACTUAL COMPL					
CODE REVIEW DATE/INITIALS					
LISTING DATE					
SOURCE LINES					
BUDGET					
ACTUAL					
OBJ. MOD. SIZE					
BUDGET					
ACTUAL					
CHIEF PROGR. APPROVAL					

**Figure 2.9 MODULE DEVELOPMENT FOLDER
COVER SHEET**

**SOFTWARE
ENGINEERING
HANDBOOK**

Chapter 2
SOFTWARE ENGINEERING OVERVIEW

Page 2-7

2.2.3 Code and Unit Test

Once the DETAILED DESIGN is approved, coding and unit test may begin. Because the detailed design process has explicitly defined the internal structure of a module, coding is merely the translation from the design representation to the appropriate programming language.

Unit testing of a module consists of testing the implementation against pre-established criteria (design) in a stand-alone mode. This step results in a completely tested module using inputs generated by software drivers and producing outputs which are recorded and checked against expected results.

It is not good practice to test a module with other modules until interfaces have been correctly established and the module demonstrates the proper functionality for both "in-bounds", and "out-of-bounds" conditions.

Source code listings are filed in the MDF as they become available. Listings are updated during unit testing and a final source listing, test code and test results are entered once all unit tests are complete.

2.2.4 Integration Testing

The integration testing procedure combines unit tested modules in a manner that allows the entire software package to be assembled and tested in a stepwise fashion. Integration is accomplished using a "top-down" approach in which unit tested modules replace "stubs" in the overall structure.

Figure 2.10a illustrates the philosophy of top down integration. Stubs interfaced with the "main" module are systematically replaced with unit tested modules. The entire package is tested after each replacement. When a build or "functional subset" containing one or more unit tested modules is defined, the build may first be tested independently and then integrated with the overall structure (Figure 2.10b). Although this is a departure from pure top down integration, it is often justified by scheduling requirements.

The time phasing of individual module tests is a factor to be considered when planning the integration test module. For large applications it is not always feasible nor desirable to complete all modules at the same time. Schedule and resource limitations often make this impractical.

Another factor which must be considered is the availability of equipment. In some instances equipment required for testing is available only during a certain time period. Therefore module subsets requiring the equipment must be integrated during this window. This factor must also be considered for equipment components delivered late in the development cycle.

A third factor to consider is the total number of modules to be integrated. An integration test configuration should not attempt to incorporate too many modules at any one time. "Too many" is a function of complexity and comprehensiveness of the tests required.

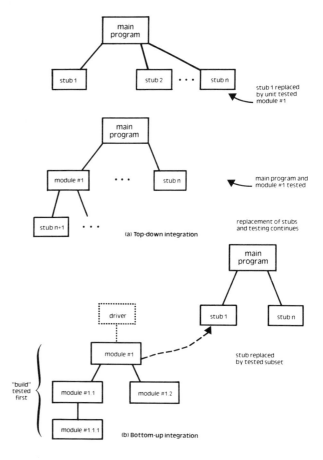

Figure 2.10 Integration Test Techniques

The order of integration testing may also be dictated by the functionality of program routines. For example, all modules associated with some major program function may be integrated during the first segment of integration testing. Other modules would be incorporated in later segments.

Integration testing is documented by a TEST PLAN that tells what is to be tested and how it is to be tested. This document must be traceable to the DESIGN. That is, the integration test plan should identify which aspects of the design are being tested.

Integration testing is complete when all modules have been incorporated and all tests defined in the TEST PLAN have been completed satisfactorily.

2.2.5 Formal Validation Testing

Formal validation testing is one of the most important and difficult steps in the software engineering process. During

Page 2-8

Chapter 2
SOFTWARE ENGINEERING OVERVIEW

**SOFTWARE
ENGINEERING
HANDBOOK**

validation testing, software is evaluated with respect to the specified functions defined for the system. That is, the goal at this testing level is to demonstrate software requirements.

The results of the validation tests are evaluated by the original requestor. Based on test results, the requestor must agree that the software truly meets its system requirements.

The validation process should be a formal one. Check lists of tests to be performed and expected results should be agreed upon before testing commences.

A TEST PLAN is prepared for formal validation testing. In most instances integration test plans and procedures form the base for the validation test plan, thus minimizing documentation effort. In certain instances tests performed during integration may suffice as acceptable validation of requirements. Formal validation testing can be extremely costly. Therefore, the extent of demonstration and validation should be established and costed early in the software life cycle. Ideally, validation costs should be considered during the software planning step or, at the very latest, at the completion of the requirements analysis step.

Part of the validation test procedure may require field-test of a software product. Before being released for general use, it may be desirable to do some controlled testing of the software at selected sites. This type of testing requires close cooperation of both the selected users and the developers. Performance must be monitored closely and corrective actions must be extremely responsive. The mechanics of monitoring and error correction should be established prior to field test so that time lost during testing due to procedural confusion is minimized.

The responsible manager decides at completion of the planned field test if the software is acceptable for general release. This is done by careful analysis of the collected performance data. It should be noted that release of unreliable software always results in excessive maintenance costs.

At the completion of formal validation, the final update to the DESIGN is made. This document now represents the AS-BUILT DESIGN and is the basis for software maintenance, a critically important activity in the final phase of the software life cycle.

2.2.6 System Testing

The software system is only one part of an overall "system" that may also contain hardware, facilities, personnel, etc. Although overall system testing is rarely the responsibility of the software organization, software management should be cognizant of the progress of system tests and be prepared to commit knowledgeable personnel to the overall system test activity.

2.3 MAINTENANCE PHASE

The last phase of the software life cycle begins when software becomes operational and is released to one or more users. The maintenance phase is comprised of two major functions that occur and reoccur until the software becomes obsolete and is retired. The first is SOFTWARE SUPERVISION—the on-going management of the computer program while it is operational. The second is the physical MAINTENANCE—a set of activities that result in modifications to the computer program.

2.3.1 Software Supervision

Even after software has been released for use, activities associated with the control and protection of the software continue to be conducted. Software Supervision—is concerned with (1) continuing control of the software configuration (the documents and executable forms that have been developed during the definition and development phases); (2) communication with users of the software on issues that may affect the use of the program; (3) auditing and tracking of the user community, and (4) protection of the executable software from inadvertent destruction and/or unauthorized use.

Control of all documents, executable forms and data associated with a computer program falls within the bounds of an activity called SOFTWARE CONFIGURATION MANAGEMENT (SCM). SCM is applied throughout the software life cycle and is discussed later in the Handbook.

When software is applied by many users, it is often necessary to provide these users with information relating to the use (and abuse) of the program. For example, minor errors or anomalies in an algorithm may have been detected for unusual input data; changes in the external environment (e.g., a new set of terminals) may require changes in the way a user interacts with the software, or newly developed software may be useful for input preprocessing or output postprocessing. All users of the program must be apprised of such information.

In most large scale computing environments, data are automatically collected (by operating system software) on the use of all computer programs. By auditing software utilization, identification of "frequent" and "casual" users is simplified and communication with the user community is expedited.

Protection of operational programs is accomplished via operating system software and careful auditing by supervisory staff. To protect the software from inadvertent distruction, a computer operations group should make timely backups and maintain archival copies of all production programs at an off-site location. To protect programs from unauthorized use, most systems have "log-on" protection (e.g., passwords, codes, etc.). In addition, SCM serves to limit unauthorized copies of the software and therefore discourages transmittal to unauthorized users.

SOFTWARE
ENGINEERING
HANDBOOK

Chapter 2
SOFTWARE ENGINEERING OVERVIEW

Page 2-9

2.3.2 Maintenance

Maintenance, an extremely important and recurring step in the final stage of the software life cycle, is generally divided into four distinct activities:

1. corrective maintenance—analysis and correction of program errors once the software has been released for general use;

2. perfective maintenance—user requested modification or enhancement of program features;

3. adaptive maintenance—changes to a program that occur because of a change in external environment, e.g. new operating system, different hardware, etc.

4. preventive maintenance—activities that prepare software for any of the above maintenance activities.

Maintenance can be the most costly stage in the life cycle for two reasons. First, the developers are not always available to diagnose problems. Therefore, programmers who are unfamiliar with the software will have to be used, increasing the effort to diagnose and correct problems. Secondly, the maintenance phase is often many times longer than the development period. Several personnel turnovers may occur during this time, and extensive retraining may be required.

"On-site fixes" represent a high cost item associated with software maintenance. This mode of maintenance is extremely costly because it is often very difficult to work at the customer's site. Customer equipment is not always ideal for doing software development and most maintenance work normally has to be scheduled at user convenience. These problems, coupled with unfamiliar surroundings, contribute to the high cost of on-site maintenance.

The costs and effort associated with software maintenance can never be entirely eliminated. However, a well-managed software development program, using the software engineering techniques discussed in this section, is absolutely essential to keep maintenance costs and effort at acceptable levels.

The following documentation, generated during software development, is essential during the maintenance period:

1. The customer accepted requirements specification
2. "As-built" design documentation
3. Fully tested user documentation
4. Internally documented source code
5. Test cases and test results used during development

Items 2-5 must be contained in the MDFs for the software system and on computer storage media. The individual(s) with maintenance responsibility should review and accept these documents before the software is released.

The maintenance effort should be planned in advance. That is, procedures for reporting software problems should be established prior to release; a mechanism for evaluating change and noting "what, who and when" about a change should be established; staff and management responsibilities must be defined. Maintenance efforts should be planned like development efforts. A schedule, cost and required resources should be defined in advance. In addition, the global impact of software modifications must be carefully reviewed before maintenance work begins.

The maintenance effort cycles through the development process and ends with a revised DESIGN document, an update to the user's documentation and a revised source listing with additional test cases and test results, if required. A library should be available for orderly storage and retrieval of software documentation.

2.3.3 Software Configuration Management

An important aspect of software supervision and maintenance is software configuration management, often called software configuration control. For each software product the following items (Figure 2.11) should be formally controlled:

1. DESIGN and TEST DOCUMENTATION
2. USER MANUAL
3. SOURCE CODE
4. EXECUTABLE CODE

A change to any or all of the items can result in a new revision level.

Changes to software should not be made in a random or uncontrolled manner. Proposed changes and possibly groups of proposed changes should be evaluated for cost to implement and impact on performance. Changes are reviewed and approved by a "change control authority" which may be a group for large software products or by the responsible manager for smaller software applications.

ITEMS UNDER CHANGE CONTROL

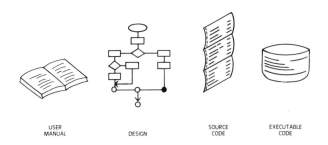

USER MANUAL   DESIGN   SOURCE CODE   EXECUTABLE CODE

Figure 2.11 Software Configuration

Up to this point, changes have been assumed to be of a corrective nature. Other types of changes such as enhancements are also considered during the maintenance period. Some enhancements should be treated as a new development

Page 2-10

Chapter 2
SOFTWARE ENGINEERING OVERVIEW

SOFTWARE
ENGINEERING
HANDBOOK

effort when determining acceptability and cost to develop. Extensive enhancements might well be implemented by a development team, subcontracted by the maintenance responsibility. Other minor enhancements can be handled in the same fashion as corrective changes.

2.4 ORGANIZATION FOR SOFTWARE DEVELOPMENT

The organization of personnel for the software development effort is a controversial topic, and no single approach has universal appeal. However, a team oriented approach to the development of large software systems affords several distinct benefits:

1. tasks may be partitioned and performed in parallel;

2. an informal mode of peer review can improve software quality;

3. backup for critical tasks/individuals is easier to establish; and,

4. progress is somewhat easier to track

One team organization attempted by many software organizations is called the Chief Programmer Team (CPT). The CPT, illustrated in Figure 2.12, consists of a technical supervisor—the chief programmer; a member of the technical staff who acts as the chief programmer's assistant—the backup programmer, and other team members—the technical staff.

The chief programmer is an experienced software professional who has technical responsibility for the efforts of the team. This individual performs top-level design, participates in all reviews and interfaces with project management and other teams. Frederic Brooks, in his classic text, THE MYTHICAL MAN-MONTH, explores Harlan Mills' concept of equating the CPT to a surgical team in a hospital. The chief programmer assumes the role of the chief surgeon, the backup programmer is analogous to a surgical resident and other team members are compared to residents and interns.

Other staff members assist the CPT as they would assist a surgical team. Specialists (e.g. system analysts, data base experts, telecommunications engineers, etc.) support the software team for predefined periods of time. A documentation staff may be called upon to help in the preparation of external documentation such as the USERS MANUAL.

A software librarian generally performs the important task of configuration control during development and also during software maintenance. The definition and development stages of the software life cycle produce extensive documentation that must be cataloged and controlled. The software librarian is responsible for all documentation produced by a software development organization.

The clear separation of skills forces a high degree of "public practice". For example, the software librarian is responsible for picking up computer runs, good or bad, and filing them in the Module Development Folders and for archives of the library where they become part of the public record. Contrast this with traditional programming operations where bad runs go into the wastebasket! Information of value is often lost and information about errors, carelessness or ignorance disappears.

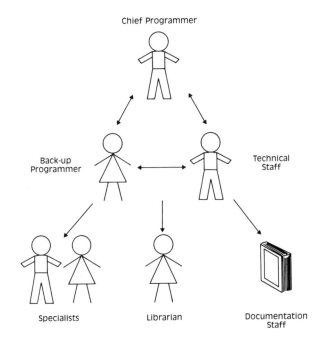

Figure 2.12 Chief Programmer Team

In this regard the software librarian has a management-assigned obligation to account for all design documentation, data and computer runs and is not authorized to pitch bad runs into the wastebasket, even at programmers' request, any more than a controller can ignore costs and expenses, even if requested to do so by the general manager. The identification of program data and computer runs as public assets, not private property, is a key principle in chief programmer team operations.

A worthwhile summary of the CPT is provided by Baker:

"The principal objective of chief programmer team operations is to move software development from a private art to a public practice. The traditional ad hoc mystique of a developing program is very much reduced. The visibility motivates all team members to think more accurately and consistently about their specific jobs. The job structuring in a chief programmer team isolates functional responsibilities between data definition, clerical operations, program design, etc., so that accountabilities are better defined. As a result, communication among team members is sharpened and more precise."[1]

---

[1]Baker, F. T. (Reference 1.1 - Appendix C)

Organizationally, the CPT lies in a hierarchy shown in Figure 2.13. Although many variations are possible, the "project manager" is generally responsible for administrative management tasks while the chief programmer is responsible for technical management.

Several practical reasons make the adoption of the CPT approach very difficult. While Mill's modest proclamation that there are but six Chief Programmers in existence is perhaps an exaggeration, most companies are still reluctant to pay the six-digit salaries required to keep those who are, in fact, members of this small community.

2.5 SUMMARY

Software Engineering applies a set of formal procedures to the definition, development, and maintenance of computer software. Each step in the software life cycle is documented and reviewed. Each procedure is derived from proven techniques. Software development requires both management cognizance and control as well as technical skills. A software development organization can be organized to enhance both.

The next chapter begins the detailed discussion of the steps in the Software Engineering process from definition through development to maintenance.

Chapter 3 discusses Software Planning, and Chapter 4, Software Requirements Analysis. Chapter 5 deals with Software Design, the first of the implementation steps and following that, Chapter 6 discusses Coding with Testing presented in Chapter 7. Chapter 8 discusses Configuration Management, a function applicable to both the Implementation and the Maintenance Phases. Finally, Chapter 9 covers the Maintenance procedures.

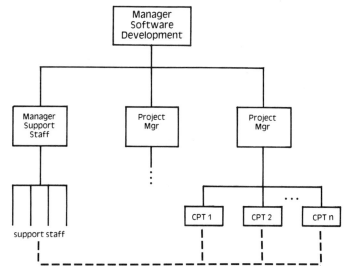

Figure 2.13 An Organizational Hierarchy

SOFTWARE
ENGINEERING
HANDBOOK

Chapter 3
SOFTWARE PLANNING

Page 3-1

Software project definition is one phase of a "system approach" which evaluates a set of interrelated hardware, software, processes and human elements comprising a system. The project planning step of that phase prepares a description of software functional scope, development resources, cost estimates and project schedule.

Since software is only one element of a system, software planning is preceded by a system definition phase in which hardware and software elements are evaluated; a division of tasks is defined; overall system requirements are identified; and, a top level design is established. The complete system requirements analysis topic is beyond the scope of this Handbook. However, before considering the software related aspects, a brief description of this step is given.

3.1 SYSTEM DEFINITION

System analysis defines overall system requirements without regard for the implementation approach. System requirements specify functional characteristics and performance objectives of the system, interface characteristics, environment, overall design concept, reliability criteria, design constraints and predefined subsystems.

System requirements analysis establishes comprehensive specifications which are the baseline for succeeding efforts. Activities include analysis of system requirements, analysis of the user's environment, analysis of similar and/or interfacing systems, preparation of a system specification and design as well as development of a PROJECT PLAN. Appendix A.1 presents a suggested format for a SYSTEM SPECIFICATION.

Analysis of System Requirements

Analysis of system requirements begins with an understanding of the information that a computer-based system must process. Concurrently, information flow and structure (organization) and assessed system functions and performance—the operational requirements—are defined.

The operational requirements of the system are evaluated for completeness, feasibility, and mutual compatibility based on the requestor's statement of requirements. Contact and coordination with requestor personnel is essential during this activity.

Analysis of User's Environment

The user's current environment and operations are studied to determine how the new system will be employed; where any new operations will be located, and what other organizations will interface with the new system.

Analysis of Similar and/or Interfacing Systems

Systems, subsystems, procedures, tools, and techniques already in existence are evaluated to determine their influence on the development of the new system.

Existing systems and subsystems may dictate specific interface requirements and data organization; related procedures and techniques may impose constraints on the design of the system to be developed, and available tools may affect project cost and schedule estimates.

Project Plan

An overall project plan is established in parallel with the SYSTEM SPECIFICATION. Among other topics, the plan shows top level software schedules and cost budgets that are used as "not to exceed" guidelines for the next step, Software Planning.

3.2 PRELIMINARY SOFTWARE PLANNING

Four important objectives must be accomplished during software planning. First, the scope of what is to be accomplished must be defined (derived from the SYSTEM SPECIFICATION). Second, resources (people, hardware and software) required to develop the software must be identified. Third, a software development cost estimate must be made; and fourth, a project schedule (with appropriate milestones and deliverables) is defined. The resulting SOFTWARE PLAN is the basis for a management "go-nogo" decision. Note that both costs and schedule are further refined upon completion of software requirements analysis. Management considerations for software planning are illustrated in Figure 3.1. It is important to realize that a development strategy is a prerequisite to effect cost and schedule definition.

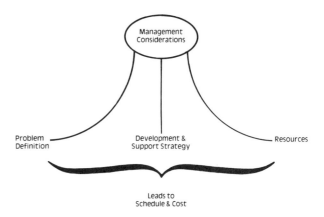

Figure 3.1 Elements of the Software Plan

3.2.1 Scope

In order to develop meaningful estimates for resources, cost, and schedule, a good understanding of software project scope must be obtained. During system definition, the scope of software elements for a computer-based system is defined. Basic elements of scope are illustrated in Figure 3.3. The

Page 3-2

Chapter 3
SOFTWARE PLANNING

SOFTWARE
ENGINEERING
HANDBOOK

planner uses System Specification information to develop *bounded* descriptions of function, performance, interfaces, reliability, and scheduling constraints.

A critical dialogue between requestor and developer occurs at the start of software planning. The software developer assigns a planner (also called system engineer, analyst, senior designer, lead software engineer, chief programmer, etc.) to thoroughly evaluate the SYSTEM SPECIFICATION and/or conduct meetings with the requestor. The planner often simultaneously acts as a consultant, researcher and advisor, communicating with the requestor in language understood by both.

The requestor-planner dialogue is illustrated in Figure 3.2. The planner must understand the software's role within the specified system. The requestor may be asked to justify the need for specific functions and to elaborate upon specified performance characteristics. Scope, resources, cost and schedule can be determined only after the planner has a firm understanding of the software element.

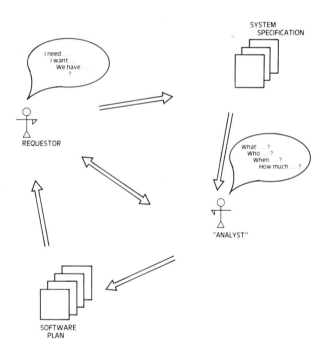

Figure 3.2 Software Planning

In addition to software attributes, the overall objective should be defined. The user's needs should be identified and described accurately in user understandable terminology. Too frequently, the user is almost totally neglected by the planner who often is in a hurry to state the hardware and software aspects of the project.

While determining scope, the planner must exercise great care to assure that characteristics, rather than implementa-

tion details, are stressed. That is, concentration should be on "what" rather than "how". As this step culminates in a management decision, it is essential to understand how management views information gathered and presented.

While it is equally important to *bound* each item discussed, a detailed definition of each item may be postponed until the requirements analysis step. Bounds help establish limits that reduce ambiguity and improve understanding of the scope by all readers.

Proper software bounding almost always requires that exclusions be stated explicitly. To achieve specificity and clarity, it is often necessary to bound in terms of negatives; i.e., to indicate what the software will not accomplish if such indication will help bound the problem.

Whenever the problem definition is fuzzy, (difficult to bound), it may be necessary to first produce a requirements specification then complete the plan. Managers should weigh the costs/benefits of delaying completion of the planning step.

3.2.2 Resource Requirements

The second SOFTWARE PLAN element defines resources required to accomplish the plan. The availability of three distinct types of resources is considered while developing the software plan. It is necessary to identify requirements for. personnel (e.g., system designers, programmers, quality assurance people, technical writers); computer hardware for development testing, validation and special equipment for testing application dependent functions; and existing software that may be used during development or implementation.

Implementation costs are minimized by planning the use of necessary skills and hardware for the shortest feasible time. It is critically important that estimates neither over-utilize nor under-utilize resources. For example, a junior programmer rarely can perform a senior system designer's duties; a designer is not cost-effective doing work that can be performed by a junior programmer.

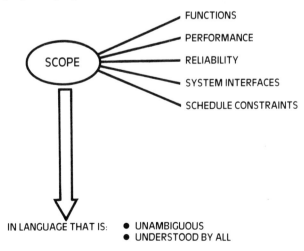

Figure 3.3 Software Scope

**SOFTWARE
ENGINEERING
HANDBOOK**

**Chapter 3
SOFTWARE PLANNING**

Page 3-3

Determine Human Resources

Most software projects are managed so as to apply personnel only when there is need for their specific talents. However, it is essential that one person be responsible from beginning to end. This person, referred to in Chapter 2 as the lead software engineer, directs software definition and development.

Staff size and skill mix depends on the software project's nature. Organization for software personnel, encompassing software designers, programmers, specialists, and documentation personnel, was discussed in Chapter 2. The interaction of personnel is illustrated in Figure 3.4.

Sometimes it is necessary to subcontract either to fill a technical void or to balance resource loading. For example, very few software engineering groups have programming language designers. Usually, this special knowledge is best subcontracted, unless language development is to be a continuing effort. In summary, it is important to match the resource and the task. Overkill can be expensive; underkill can be a disaster.

Determine Hardware Resources

Computer hardware is required some time during most software projects. The computer type, as well as the timing and duration of computer usage must be forecast. Several different computing services are available; each must be evaluated with respect to cost, developmental characteristics and availability.

If a computer for software development is among equipment to be procured, lead times for benchmark preparation and evaluation, equipment order, shipping, installation and "settling time" should be anticipated. On average, delivery is 120 days or more after receipt of order.

Often, special equipment may be needed. It is usually neither possible nor economically feasible to have special equipment available for duration of a project. Optimal scheduling of equipment utilization is very important.

In summary, the required resources must be quantized and phased consistently with availability and schedule constraints.

Determine Software Resources

Software itself is often not considered an important, and often critical, resource in the development of new software. Through proper use of existing software, development schedules can be dramatically reduced; reliability of developed programs can be enhanced; and overall costs reduced.

Software resources divide into the two generic classes shown in Figure 3.5. Support software includes the operating system and all software development tools available to the project development team. By providing powerful design aids, editors and compilers, test tools and word processing systems, management can greatly reduce time spent in each step of the development process.

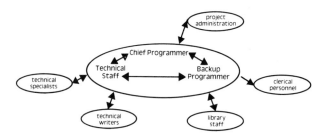

Figure 3.4 Chief Programmer Team

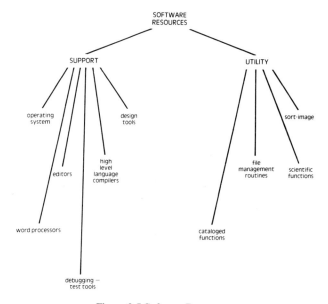

Figure 3.5 Software Resources

Appendix B.2 provides an overview of the classes of software tools that are available during the software life cycle.

Utility software includes all existing packages and routines either embedded in the system to be developed or used in the process of developing the application. Reliable utilities improve consistency, reduce both design and implementation time, and eliminate redundant effort.

Each software resource must be evaluated for portability, adaptability, reliability and cost. Careful evaluation and screening of supplementary documentation and vendor/developer supplied support is also important.

3.3 COST ESTIMATION

Prior to the evolution of the Software Engineering discipline, cost estimation for computer software was a highly subjective procedure. As little historical data was collected, costing was extremely dependent on the "experience" of the estimator—order of magnitude errors were common!

Page 3-4

Chapter 3
SOFTWARE PLANNING

SOFTWARE
ENGINEERING
HANDBOOK

The initial steps of software planning have identified and bounded the scope of the effort and have defined the required resources to accomplish development tasks. Costing, a follow-on to these steps can be rationally initiated only after the above steps are complete.

A systematic approach to software costing follows, however, before specific techniques are considered, several preliminary concepts must be introduced.

3.3.1 Software Categories

Unquestionably, software development cost is a function of the type of software being produced.

Brooks, in his book, *The Mythical Man Month,* divides software into four categories:

1. the basic program
2. the program product
3. the programming system
4. the programming system product

The *basic program* is designed and implemented for the author's exclusive use. There is generally little need for detailed documentation; there is no need to interface with other software or people. These programs are usually very specific in function. Ease of maintenance or enhancement are, at best, secondary considerations.

The *program product* is a basic program intended for use by persons other than the author; it must be supported and maintained. This type of software requires complete and accurate documentation. It should be modularized to ease maintenance and update. The *program product* also requires more extensive testing since the impact of errors can be substantial, depending upon the extent of its distribution.

The *program product* can cost three times as much as a *basic program.* This substantial cost increase is due to the software's use by other individuals without the author's help. Frequently, a *basic program* is costed when a *program product* is desired; considerable cost overruns result.

The *programming system* is a set of *basic programs* integrated and tested as a single program to perform a set of predefined functions. This type of software costs three times more than the *basic program* because there are both software and possibly human interfaces which must be designed and tested.

Programming system documentation must be rigorous, especially where more than one programmer is involved. Interface specifications must be written and formally controlled. The development can be further complicated by organizational responsibility and/or geographical separation. Each of these qualifiers must be considered when costing this type of software.

The *programming system product* combines the effort involved in producing a formal product with the complexity imposed by the *programming system.* This type of software requires the most sophisticated planning, development and maintenance effort; it often costs nine times more than a *basic program.*

3.3.2 Software Productivity Data

To establish a quantitative, systematic approach to software cost estimation, hard data on end-to-end software development costs* must be collected and categorized for historical reference.

Table 3.1 lists a minimal set of productivity data that is easy to collect once a Software Engineering approach is in place. Unfortunately, collecting such data on completed projects may be difficult or impractical. There is absolutely no reason such data cannot be collected for new projects.

TABLE 3.1
SOFTWARE PRODUCTIVITY DATA

1. Software Type (e.g. real time, scientific, process control, etc.)

2. Machine Configuration (processor type/memory available)

3. Requirements Analysis Effort (person-months)

4. Major Functions (one entry for each function)

    a. function category (e.g. data base update, terminal I/O, etc.)

    b. design effort (person-months)

    c. lines of validated source code

    d. coding effort (person-months)

    e. test effort (person-months)

5. Actual/Estimated Cost

6. Actual/Estimated Completion Dates

7. Total Lines of Code

8. Total Effort (person-months)

9. Implementation data

    a. special development tools

    b. programming language(s) used

    c. stability of requirements (subjective)

* In this discussion, all development costs, from planning through validation testing, are considered. These end-to-end costs include generation of all the associated documentation.

SOFTWARE
ENGINEERING
HANDBOOK

Chapter 3
SOFTWARE PLANNING

Page 3-5

The use of quantitative historical data to supplement experiential "feel" is critical for accurate cost estimation. A means for collecting software productivity data is essential to long range success using the costing techniques presented in the next section.

Even though detailed historical data on past projects is unavailable, it is possible to collect rudimentary data: prepare lists of past software development projects; use budget records from past years, to determine the dollars and effort expended on each project (e.g., via relevant charge or project numbers or other accounting mechanisms); use the number of lines of code produced as a result of each project to compute average cost per line of code ($/LOC) and "productivity" (LOC/person-month). These values provide coarse historical data for use in cost estimation until more recent project data become available.

Where no such organization-dependent data are available, industry trends have been observed and may be used until a sufficient data base is established. These averages (Figure 3.6) can serve as inexact guidelines for software estimating. However, it is important that each organization develop and refine parameters that reflect the kind of software it produces. The data provided in Figure 3.6 should be used with discretion.

Referring to the Figure, the complexity characteristics reflected in the TYPE category include both functional and structural complexity (number of routines, number of interfaces, etc.). Real-time implies a performance response requirement such as "ten transactions per second" or "temperature control 10 degrees centigrade around a base setting".

Extremely critical applications often involve severe penalties for failure to meet performance requirements such as large financial loss or even loss of life. These applications require exhaustive testing which can increase any TYPE cost by a factor of two.

3.4 COSTING TECHNIQUES

Software cost estimation is not an exact science. Therefore, several different techniques should be applied to serve as a cross-check against one another. Comparison of results help to uncover inconsistency.

Three techniques for software cost estimation are presented. The objective of each technique is to estimate labor effort associated with software development. After the three approaches have been presented, methods for comparison and a discussion of the costs follows.

-Industry Trends-
(1976 dollars shown)

TYPE I—Simple, non-real time

e.g., square root, simple I/O

$5–$9 per source line

TYPE II—Simple, real-time

e.g., digital input/output driver

$12–$24

TYPE III—Moderately complex, non-real time

e.g., fast Fourier transform

$7–$25

TYPE IV—Moderately complex, real time

e.g., disk driver

$20–$40

TYPE V—Complex, non-real time

e.g., process simulation

$15–$40

TYPE VI—Complex, real time

e.g., closed loop control of a process

$25–$60

TYPE VII—Complex, real time, extremely critical

e.g., weapon control systems

over $100

(These dollar amounts reflect industry ranges and should be used for comparison purposes only, recognizing that individual variances by factors of 10 or more continue to be reported.)

Figure 3.6 Cost Per Coded Line

3.4.1 The Lines-of-Code Technique

The Lines-of-Code (LOC) technique is a relatively simple, quantitative procedure that associates the cost of developing

Page 3-6

Chapter 3
SOFTWARE PLANNING

**SOFTWARE
ENGINEERING
HANDBOOK**

each software function with the number of source lines projected for that function. The source line estimate is based on experience of senior staff (if a software productivity data base does not exist) or historical data. That is, the proposed software is compared to a similar completed program and line counts are then adjusted to reflect significant functional differences. This method is most effective when historical data from previous, similar projects is available. For example, a line editor designed and coded for project X performs functions similar to a proposed line editor. Therefore, the proposed software will probably require a similar number of lines.

A second estimating method for required lines of code is to actually do some trial coding to get a better feel for the size of the program. As this can be extremely time consuming and costly, it is recommended only for very critical programs where there is no clear understanding of source code volume and the impact of errors on overall cost would be considerable.

The LOC technique does not differentiate between high level language (e.g. FORTRAN, PASCAL, PL/M) source lines and assembler language source code. Historical data show the cost per source line is constant regardless of language level. It follows that a high level language that results in 5 to 10 lines of equivalent assembler code provides an automatic productivity gain*.

Once the number of lines of source code has been estimated, cost is determined by multiplying number of lines by average cost per line. Average cost per line can range from

$5.00 to well over $100.00 per line depending upon the complexity of the software and salary level. Most industry applications fall within the $16 to $50 per line range based on a burdened labor cost of $250/day.

As an example of the lines-of-code technique, consider a process control system with the functions shown in Table 3.2. The functions, derived from the software system scope, have been estimated to require the number of lines of code in the column "EST. # LINES". Historical data provides the productivity data in lines produced/person-month. Cost accounting provides $/line based on current labor rates. Using the information contained in columns 2,3 and 4, cost and effort are calculated and shown in columns 5 and 6.

3.4.2 The Task-Costing Technique

The task-costing technique determines software development cost by summing the projected cost of each individual development task. Task effort (person-month) is multiplied by cost per person-month to yield cost/task.

When estimating software costs using this technique, six tasks are assumed. Five are almost exclusively software effort; one, Validation Test, requires participation of other disciplines. Table 3.3 shows the tasks, steps and effort associated percentages:

* The advantages and disadvantages of high level languages vs. assembler language are discussed in Chapter 6.

Table 3.2 EXAMPLE–LINES OF CODE COSTING TECHNIQUE

FUNCTION	HISTORICAL LINES/MO.	EST. # LINES	CURRENT	$	MO.
REAL TIME DATA ACQUISITION	92	840	36	30240	9.1
DATA BASE UPDATE	102	1210	18	21780	11.8
OFF LINE ANALYSIS	134	600	24	14400	4.4
REPORT GENERATION	145	450	11	4950	3.1
REAL TIME CONTROL	80	1100	45	49500	13.8
				$120870	42.2

**SOFTWARE
ENGINEERING
HANDBOOK**

Chapter 3
SOFTWARE PLANNING

Page 3-7

**Table 3.3 Distribution of Software Project Effort
by Task**

Task Of	Typical Percentage Overall Effort
Software Planning	5
Software Requirements	10
Design	25
Code and Unit Test	20
Integration Test	25
Validation Test	15
Total	100

Each task should include documentation. Costs are then determined by applying labor rates appropriate for skill level assigned each task (e.g. senior personnel should be involved in planning and design, while junior people can be applied to the coding task).

Software Planning

Generally, software project planning (preliminary and final) should not exceed 5% of the software budget allocation. In cases where software is similar to past efforts, planning may require only 1% of the budget. On the other hand, when it is necessary to do extensive trade studies or feasibility studies, the software planning effort can easily approach 10% of the total effort.

Requirements Analysis

The requirements analysis task as a whole can be estimated as the sum of six subtasks namely:

1. conduct fact-finding and research
2. define information flow and structure characteristics
3. identify system interfaces
4. define all software functions explicitly
5. consider design and test constraints
6. conduct reviews and iterate

Functional definition is the most time-consuming requirements analysis subtask. While definition of a function can vary widely depending on complexity, criticality and the skill of the analyst, it is safe to assume that one person-week is required to specify the requirements for each major function. This time includes analysis, enough design to establish credibility, documentation, review and iteration. Based on a person-week per major function guideline, the percent allocation for software requirements analysis varies with the size and complexity of the software to be produced. In general, requirements analysis accounts for 10% to 20% of the total software effort.

Software Design

The design task divides into preliminary and detailed design subtasks. Design cost is estimated by considering the effort to:

1. refine data flow and/or data structure
2. develop software structure
3. identify input, processing, output, interfaces, constraints for each module
4. define modular procedure in detail
5. conduct reviews and requisite iteration

As with requirements analysis, the design cost is related to the number of software functions, the number of modules required to accomplish each function, and their complexity and/or criticality.

Code and Unit Test

The code and unit test step is estimated by projecting the number of modules to accomplish each software function; the number of source lines/module and the amount of effort required to produce one unit tested line. Historical data is extremely helpful if this approach is taken. Additionally, test software and data base creation (if required) should be considered in the final estimate.

While productivity varies with skill and experience, it is unlikely that a proficient programmer can deliver more than 20 validated source lines per day (100 source lines per week) over the entire project duration. As an approximation lacking historical data, determine the number of person-weeks required for the project by dividing the total number of lines of code by 100. Of this, code and unit test should account for about 20%.

Testing

Integration test, the assembly of the software system, systematically incorporates routines into *builds* in a top-down manner. This process is defined in the TEST PLAN. In addition, custom test-software may be needed simply to exercise the software to be tested. Depending on the exhaustiveness of testing, test-software costs can be extremely high. In some cases the development of test software costs more than the software being developed.

Although there is no easy way to estimate the cost of integration testing, a quantitative approach may be used as a guideline. The effort to test a build is roughly 50% of the effort required to design, code and unit test the individual routines which are being combined in the build.

Page 3-8

Chapter 3
SOFTWARE PLANNING

**SOFTWARE
ENGINEERING
HANDBOOK**

Validation test validates the fully integrated and tested software against requirements. This task's effort depends on the number and complexity of the requirements to be validated and demonstrated. Special software may have to be developed to conduct the validation test. As with the previously mentioned custom, throw-away test software, this special software may have considerable impact on project cost. As this task relates directly to requirements, a guideline for estimating its effort is to use 50% of the effort expended on the software requirements and system design.

Incorrect estimates of the software testing effort are the primary cause of cost and schedule overruns. In general, 40 percent of the overall project defintion and development effort is spent in testing. Therefore, estimates that result in a significantly lower percentage of time should be reviewed carefully.

Example

Use of the techniques and guidelines, discussed in the preceding paragraphs, is applied to the process control system (discussed in Paragraph 3.4.1) to derive Table 3.4. Notice that appropriately different labor rates have been used for each software engineering step.

EXAMPLE–LABOR COSTS/TASK COSTING

TASK	EST.# OF PERSON-MONTHS	LABOR RATE/ PERSON MONTH	COST
REQUIREMENTS	5.0	$3400	$17000
DESIGN	15.0	3200	48000
CODE & UNIT TEST	8.0	2650	21200
INTEGRATION	13.0	2900	37700
VALIDATION	3.5	2900	10150
	44.5		$134050

Table 3.4

Summary

This technique estimates the cost of each task of the software engineering methodology. Each task's cost is highly sensitive to complexity, skill levels (cost) of people, and utility of available tools.

Guidelines must be made to reflect each organization's situation. Accurate historical data is a must if dependable estimates are expected. Cost estimation for each of the above tasks must allow time for reviews and iteration. In all cases, estimates of effort include the time to produce documentation.

3.4.3 Automated Cost Estimation

Automated cost estimation tools provide a productive method for the generation of estimates for many project efforts. However, all tools must be evaluated for specific business applicability. They all require long term data collection and good data bases to be effective. The other important aspect of such tools is their usability—ease of use is a prime and legitimate concern for all evaluators of software packages. A more detailed discussion of automated management tools can be found in Section 2 of Appendix D.

3.4.4 Comparison of Results

The costing techniques presented in paragraphs 3.4.1, 3.4.2 and 3.4.3 provide a means for estimating labor costs associated with software development. Before "other costs" are added a comparison of the results obtained from each technique must be made.

It is unrealistic to expect exact agreement among the cost estimation techniques. Even with accurate productivity data, a 5 to 20 percent variance can be expected. The primary objective of cost estimating is to obtain fairly consistent estimates by more than one method. Management must understand why differences exist and resolve them as required.

Estimate inconsistency can normally be attributed to one or more of the following causes:

1. poor understanding of project scope (lack of communication between requestor and planner);

2. overly optimistic projections by software development staff;

3. incorrect or misinterpreted historical data or worse, no historical data at all;

Management's review of cost estimates must also consider the experience of the planner with the class of software to be developed; e.g. a person with broad experience in microprocessor software might have difficulty with a large mainframe application.

In each case, estimates must be reviewed thoroughly; assumptions should be carefully evaluated; if possible, two independent sources for each estimate should be used.

3.5 THE "MAKE-BUY" DECISION

In the preceding section, each cost estimate assumed that software was to be developed "from scratch". In reality, many projects can make use of packaged software to satisfy part or all of the functional requirements for the software element of the computer-based system.

A "make-buy" decision is needed whenever a vendor can supply software that meets (in whole or in part) the functional requirements outlined in the software scope. The real purchase cost of the software must be weighed against the development costs estimated as part of the planning step. Among the questions that must be answered as part of the decision making process are:

1. Does the vendor-supplied software meet all functional requirements defined in the scope of the SOFTWARE PLAN? If not, what percentage of function/performance will have to be enhanced or added locally? What costs are associated with the enhancements?
2. Has the vendor-supplied software been developed using software engineering methods? Is it maintainable? Does a good documentation base exist? What documentation is supplied with the package?
3. Does the vendor-supplied software meet human interface requirements for the system to be developed?
4. Does the vendor-supplied software already have a user base? How many users are working in an environment identical to the local environment (hardware, operating system, database, etc.)? Are current users happy with the package; with vendor support of the package? Is there a user's group?
5. What is the vendor's policy on software maintenance; on error correction and reporting? What are the vendor's rates for future adaptation or enhancement of the software? Does a maintenance contract exist? Is the vendor the original developer of the package?
6. Will the vendor supply source code or will the source code be placed in escrow?
7. Have adequate benchmark and validation tests been conducted on the vendor software?
8. Is there more than one candidate vendor package? Have all candidates been evaluated? Have benchmark tests been conducted?
9. How are new releases of the package handled? How long are older releases supported? What is the frequency (based on past performance) of new releases?
10. Is special training required to use the package; to operate the package? Is the training conducted at the local site? Is there any cost associated with training?

Each of these questions should be answered as a first step in the make-buy process. Purchase price alone, no matter how low, should not be the sole criteria for the make-buy decision.

3.5.1 A Make-Buy Example

To illustrate the make-buy decision making process, consider software that must be developed/purchased for manufacturing shop floor control. The scope of the software element of the shop floor control system has been established, and a cost estimate of $220,000 has been developed (11,000 LOC at $20/LOC). An outside vendor offers a shop floor control system that seems to meet the scope established in the plan. discussions with vendor representatives indicate that the

vendor software contains 9,500 LOC (a good substantiation of local estimates) and licensing cost is $75,000 with $5,000 yearly "update fee". The cost per LOC to purchase the source code is far below local development costs ($7.90/LOC versus $20.00/LOC); the continuing yearly fee is less than in-house maintenance estimates. The set of questions noted above used to reach a decision about purchasing from the vendor. Further analysis and benchmarking suggest that between 1,000 and 1,500 source lines in the vendor's package must be modified to meet local requirements; 500 source lines must be added for special database interfacing. The vendor, reluctant to make the necessary modifications, suggests that local development staff can "make the changes with little or no difficulty".

A vendor-supplied software documentation review uncovers a superficial design document and informal test information. The User Manual is excellent.

The *real* cost of the vendor supplied software is itemized below. Notes following the itemization explain some of the entries:

vendor-supplied software purchase price	$ 75,000
cost to modify 1,500 LOC locally (note a)	$ 90,000
cost to add 500 LOC locally (note b)	$ 20,000
update fee (5 years)	$ 25,000
Total	$210,000

Notes:

a. The local cost associated with maintaining (in this case modifying) someone else's program will be considerably more expensive than "from scratch" development costs. A factor of 3 cost multiplier is applied to the $20/LOC for development.

b. The local cost of enhancing (in this case adding to) someone else's program will be considerably more expensive than "from scratch" development costs. A factor of 2 cost multiplier is applied to the $20/LOC for development.

In this example, the estimated cost to develop ($220,000) and the estimated cost to buy ($210,000) are very close. Answers to the other questions in the make-buy decision making process must be used to make a final decision. All things being equal, there is probably less risk associated with the purchase of a *proven, existing* package than with the development of equivalent software. However, any maintenance work, whether done by the local development staff or the vendor can increase the real cost substantially.

3.5.2 Software Selection from Multiple Packages

For many applications, there are literally hundreds of potential software packages that meet system requirements (e.g., over 150 inventory control systems, 80 order entry systems, 60

Material Requirements Planning systems, 100 database management systems are available for evaluation). When many candidate packages exist, it is necessary to develop a systematic technique for software evaluation. The following evaluation characteristics are recommended:

1. Cost—the real cost of the vendor-supplied software as computed in Section 3.5.1.

2. Service and Support—based on other users with identical operational environments.

3. Documentation—for users and for local maintainers.

4. Expandability/Flexibility—to address future applications or changes in environment.

5. Reputation—of the vendor and the vendor-supplied software.

6. Stability—based on the age of the package and the number of releases over the past two years.

7. Machine or Operating System Dependency—based on programming languages used; special features tied to specific hardware.

8. Completeness—of function and performance based on software scope.

Candidate vendor packages may be comparatively evaluated by using each of the above characteristics to develop a SOFTWARE EVALUATION MATRIX. First, establish a weight factor (based on local importance) for each characteristic. Grade each candidate package on a scale of 1 to 10 for each characteristic listed above. The final grade for each package is:

$$\text{SUM} \mid (\text{characteristic})_k (\text{weighting factor})_k \mid$$

Where $k = 1$ to 8

Each package's final grade is compared and used as an input to the make-buy decision.

3.6 OTHER COSTS

Labor is unquestionably the largest cost in most software development efforts. However, other costs often become a significant fraction of overall project expenditures. These costs include:

1. computer costs
2. travel and living expenses
3. material and miscellaneous hardware costs

Each of these costs must be estimated as a function of software scope and resources.

3.6.1 Computer Costs

Computer costs divide into two distinct areas: 1) cost of computers to be acquired—hardware cost, and 2) cost of CPU time and secondary expenses when using existing equipment—computer time costs.

Hardware Cost

Organization accounting procedures determine whether hardware costs are part of the software budget. If hardware cost is included, a fixed price quote from a vendor(s) provides fairly accurate cost data.

Hardware costing can be complicated by lease vs. purchase trade-offs. Time value of money, hardware depreciation, periodic upgrade, hardware and software maintenance may each effect the ultimate decision in this area.

Computer use charges are estimated by 1) determining the number of hours needed to develop, test and code; and 2) multiplying by current rates. However, actual computer time costs may be complicated by a "bundled" or "unbundled" rate structure. Unbundled rates include only the cost of CPU processing and appear to be much cheaper than bundled rates that include listings, magnetic storage, extra copies and related costs. It is also difficult to equate a single comprehensive rate to the quantity that is easiest to estimate—programmer terminal time.

Time Sharing

Time sharing service is used most frequently when software testing does not require access to a machine with the same architecture as that of the target machine (the computer for which the application is intended). Applications developed via time sharing are usually coded in a higher level language such as COBOL, FORTRAN or PASCAL. Time sharing service rates variances are difficult to analyze. However, certain generalizations can be made:

1. On-line, immediate (foreground) service during prime hours is most expensive. Savings can be realized by doing more things in the "background" with delayed service and by working during non-prime time periods.

2. Data base storage on-line (instantaneous access) can also be expensive. Requirements should be analyzed to determine the extent to which the data base must be maintained on-line.

3. Special services such as preparation and/or mounting/dismounting of magnetic tapes, cards or multiple copies may incur additional charges and should be identified and evaluated prior to any commitment.

Batch or Background Processing

Another type of computer service is commonly called batch mode or background processing. This service allows

SOFTWARE
ENGINEERING
HANDBOOK

Chapter 3
SOFTWARE PLANNING

Page 3-11

the vendor to schedule work for efficient utilization of computer resources. Programs are executed according to a schedule that takes job priority and system resources into account. Program response or turn-around time is considerably longer than time sharing mode but batch time can be obtained at comparatively low rates.

A programmer testing a program using batch processing may wait several hours before getting the results of a test run. So long as there is other useful work to be done during this wait period, the progress of a programmer using batch processing need not be adversely affected.

Certain programming tasks, such as assemblies and compilations, lend themselves well to batch mode. While editing and certain types of testing are more efficiently done on-line (timesharing mode). For example, batch mode does not allow interactive debugging, a technique costly in terms of computer service, but extremely productive with respect to programmer utilization. An appropriate balance between batch and timesharing must be determined for each project. Often this balance is poor because management has not properly planned and scheduled it.

Dedicated Computer Service

A third mode of computer service is the dedicated or block mode usage. Here, the entire computer is dedicated to one project or one programmer. This can be the most expensive type of service, especially when the computer facility is not owned by the group that needs the computer.

A certain amount of dedicated time is required for implementation of most real time applications. If at all possible, this should be confined to the final stages of integration testing.

3.6.2 Travel and Living Costs

Travel and living costs should not be overlooked since some projects incur substantial expenditures. When the requestor is in a different city from the developer, travel and living expenses are usually incurred during the following steps:

1. requirements analysis
2. requirements specification review
3. design review(s)
4. final integration test
5. validation test

Software development should be planned to minimize travel and living requirements for software staff. Often, the decrease in productivity attributed to work in a 'foreign' environment and lack of local support facilities can have a far greater impact on the success of a project than the explicit T&L costs themselves. The costs of work at a customer site can be more than three times the costs for the same work at the factory.

3.6.3 Material and Miscellaneous Hardware

The material cost (e.g., paper, disk packs, magnetic/paper tape) and miscellaneous hardware (e.g. PROM programmer, CRT display) are often included in the software budget. Material and other hardware are essential resources for software development.

3.7 FACTORS INFLUENCING SOFTWARE COST

In his 1981 book, Barry Boehm (*Software Engineering Economics,* Prentice-Hall, 1981) describes factors that affect the ultimate cost of computer software. The factors fall into four broad categories —product, computer, personnel and project—and are assigned quantitative values in Boehm's Constructive Cost Model (COCOMO).

In COCOMO, software development effort (and therefore, software cost) is modeled as a nonlinear function of the number of estimated lines of code to be developed. COCOMO equations take the form:

$$m = c_1 * KLOC^a * PROD \, |f_i|$$

Where:

m = number of person-months for development effort
c_1 = model coefficient
a = model exponent
f_i = cost factors noted above (i=1 to 16)

Each model cost factor is assigned values based on the degree of its importance and impact. As Boehm's cost factors affect all projects, it is worth noting these factors even if the COCOMO model is not applied. Each cost factor is described below:

Product Cost Factors

Required Software Reliability: the degree to which effort will be expended to assure software reliability. For example, the formality and number of software reviews; formal application of quality assurance and configuration management procedures; the overall impact of software failure during operation.

Data Base Size: the size and complexity of the database to be developed or integrated. Consideration should include database design, number of information elements, access methods, query techniques, etc.

Software Product Complexity: the logical and structural complexity of the software to be developed.

Computer Cost Factors

Execution Time Constraints: the degree to which program execution time is tied to successful accomplishment of software requirements. Generally, time constraints are encountered in real-time applications and some interactive systems.

Page 3-12

**Chapter 3
SOFTWARE PLANNING**

SOFTWARE
ENGINEERING
HANDBOOK

Memory Constraint: the limitation of available memory for program storage and data structures.

Environmental Volatility: the frequency and extent to which the environment external to the software (e.g., computer hardware, operating system, database system) will change during the software development effort.

Computer Turnaround Time: the responsiveness of the programming environment.

Personnel Cost Factors

Analyst Capability: experience and expertise of personnel performing analysis functions.

Applications Experience: experience of development personnel with the application area to be addressed.

Programmer Capability: experience and expertise of personnel performing programming functions.

Environment Expertise: experience and expertise of personnel working in the environment for software development.

Language Experience: experience and expertise of personnel in application of the programming language(s) chosen for the project.

Project Cost Factors

Programming Practices: use of modern programming practices (top-down design methodologies, top-down testing techniques, structured coding, etc.) during the project.

Software Tools: the availability of software tools for each of the software engineering steps.

Schedule Constraints: the degree to which scheduling constraints will affect the application of software engineering techniques.

Other Cost Considerations

In addition to the cost factors noted above, Boehm has outlined other software cost considerations (for further information, see B. W. Boehm, "The High Cost of Software", Practical Strategies for Developing Large Software Systems, E. Horowitz, ed., Addison-Wesley, 1975, pp.4-14).

Language. In general, experience indicates that the cost per source instruction in assembly language or Machine-Oriented Language (MOL) is about twice the cost per source instruction in a Higher-Order Language (HOL) such as FORTRAN.

Real-time applications. The cost/instruction of real time software is about five times that of conventional programs.

Type. Per instruction, the Operating System (OS) component of a system tends to cost about 2.5 times the cost per instruction of the applications or utility program components.

Point on learning curve. Experience shows an experienced programming group requires 50-100 percent more effort to develop an unfamiliar program than some variant of a familiar program.

Application area. Another cost variation source is the ultimate application for the software. For example, a management information system, an avionics package and an industrial process control system all require different planning and skills.

Amount of documentation. Experience indicates that documentation costs run about 10 percent of the total software development cost. For nonautomated documentation (e.g., excluding listings and automatically generated flowcharts), typical costs are about $35-150 per page, depending primarily on the amount and complexity of the analysis involved.

Amount of previous software used. The cost of adapting existing software into a new project may be determined by objectively estimating the modification and interface costs for the new application.

Stability of requirements and stability of development environment. These factors are important determinants of software cost, but their influence can only be estimated subjectively. Their effect tends to be proportional to the length of time it takes to complete the project.

Representations of development environment. The added cost required to adapt software to actual operational conditions (different computer configurations, operating procedures, etc.) can be quite significant (up to 95 percent in some instances) but can only be estimated subjectively.

Management. Like personnel, this is another extremely important factor. However, cost estimates can only be subjective.

It is important to account for the above factors when estimating software costs. There are, however, many additional factors (e.g., particular programming language, number of input and output items, frequency of operation, in-house versus contract, absolute hardware characteristics such as memory size and word size). In general, such factors tend to be less well correlated to cost, although in particular situations they may be both significant and clearly correlated with cost.

3.8 SCHEDULING

The last element of the plan involves scheduling of resources and tasks. This implies that an implementation approach (development scenario) has been conceived and will be used as the basis for both scheduling and costs. Scheduling is always related to a specified or derived completion date. However, in order to obtain a realistic schedule, an iterative approach that considers both time required and completion date should be used.

Two common scheduling pitfalls are: 1) the arbitrary addition of projected task times without regard to end-date objectives: or, 2) forced adherence to an unrealistic end-date. A thorough understanding of what is to be accomplished and some first hand knowledge of the people expected to perform the tasks is the only way to avoid these difficulties.

Scheduling activities are iterative by nature. Although described in step-by-step presentation, in many instances a decision made in one place causes a rethinking of previously determined approach. Figure 3.8 illustrates the scheduling flow schematically.

The objective of scheduling is to establish well-defined milestones for the project. Each milestone exhibits the general characteristics, illustrated in Figure 3.7

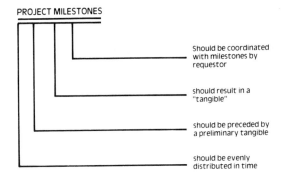

Figure 3.7 Milestone Characteristics

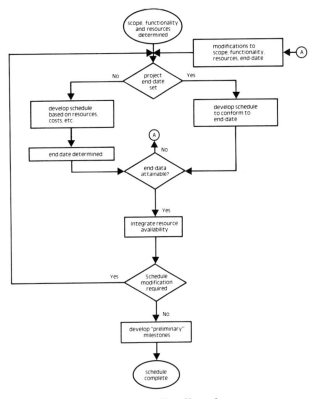

Figure 3.8 Scheduling Chronology

Milestone accomplishment should be accompanied by availability of a tangible; i.e., something that can be audited, reviewed, demonstrated or tested. "Concept determined" is a poor milestone; "concept document ready for review" is a good milestone.

Each critical milestone should be preceded by a "preliminary" tangible. For example, completion of the DESIGN document should be preceded by the availability of a preliminary copy. This allows technical management to assess direction and progress prior to the milestone deadline. Preliminary versions of tangibles provide lead time that may be used to recover from any technical deviations or impending schedule slippages. Preliminary review also allows constructive feedback prior to formal review.

3.9 SOFTWARE PLAN REVIEW

Software plan review occurs twice during the planning stage of the software life cycle. Once the preliminary software plan has been prepared, management reviews budgets and schedule for feasibility, cost estimates are reviewed for consistency and schedules are checked against available manpower. The scope and basic requirements are evaluated with the requestor.

The second plan review occurs after the final software requirements have been established. Changes to the preliminary plan are evaluated by management, preliminary user documentation must be reviewed by the requestor, and the revised scope (if required) is re-evaluated. Although changes to the plan may be required, this review is not a license to expand the scope.

3.10 SUMMARY

The SOFTWARE PLAN is a management document that establishes project scope, resources, cost and schedule. Communication between the planner and requestor is essential to the success of this step in the Software Engineering process.

During preliminary planning, overall software characteristics were defined and bounded, and a strategy including scheduling and cost data was developed. Software requirements analysis refines this earlier work to produce a detailed specification which concentrates on four important aspects of the software:

1. information flow and interfaces
2. functional requirements
3. design requirements/constraints
4. testing criteria/quality assurance

A SOFTWARE REQUIREMENTS SPECIFICATION (SRS) documents these aspects. The SRS, described in Appendix A.3, is the document generated by the software engineer or analyst which defines in detail each of the four aspects listed above. The SRS is often supplemented with a Preliminary User's Manual which provides a direct description of the user interface and is invaluable during the requirements review.

The SOFTWARE REQUIREMENTS SPECIFICATION should be traceable to the SYSTEM SPECIFICATION and SYSTEM DESIGN documentation. That is, every software requirement that is described must have a basis in system documentation. A global view of the software requirements task, indicating its position in the sequence of events of the definition phase, is shown in Figure 4.1.

Software requirements analysis and the resultant specification are key to the success of the software development process. Detailed requirements provide a means for transforming management objectives into a tangible product, therefore the SRS is a key management reference to which all subsequent work can be traced. In addition, the SRS is the basis for design and provides important data for validation.

4.1 SYSTEM REQUIREMENTS

The SYSTEM SPECIFICATION, derived earlier in the definition phase, forms the basis for all software requirements work. In this section, the system definition procedure is examined so that the procedures that result in a basis for software requirements work may be understood.

The procedure for system specification is illustrated in Figure 4.2. Once the system concept is defined, the definition phase begins with a consideration of functional and performance requirements for the system. Some of these requirements may be satisfied by hardware, others by software and still others by remaining system elements (e.g., people, information, documentation, procedures). Existing hardware and software are examined and the "information environment" of the system is examined. Finally, human engineering and interaction characteristics are defined.

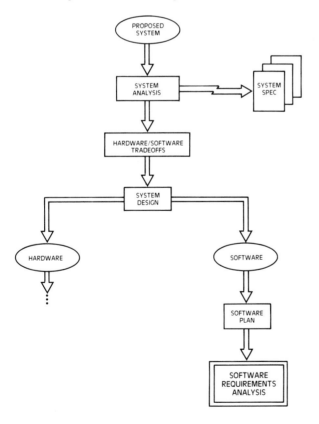

Figure 4.1 A Global View of Software Requirements

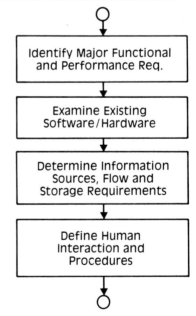

Figure 4.2 System Specification-Procedure

A detailed presentation of system specification activities is beyond the scope of this *Handbook*. However, Figures 4.3a—4.3g provide a general description of the flow of events that occur during system specification. Note that the flow charts shown in the Figures represent a simplified view of complex analysis and definition activities.

Page 4-2

Chapter 4
SOFTWARE REQUIREMENTS ANALYSIS

**SOFTWARE
ENGINEERING
HANDBOOK**

Figures 4.3a — 4.3c indicate the decisions and tasks that are applied during the analysis of hardware elements for a system. Initially, functions are defined and a determination of "off-the-shelf" availability is made as shown in Figure 4.3a. If hardware must be developed, the use of existing components or subassemblies is explored. For "off-the-shelf" hardware, appropriate vendor comparisons are made.

Once all functions have been considered, interfaces to the hardware (from other system elements) are examined (Figure 4.3b). Finally, other characteristics of the hardware are analyzed to assure that it will meet reliability and validation requirements (Figure 4.3c).

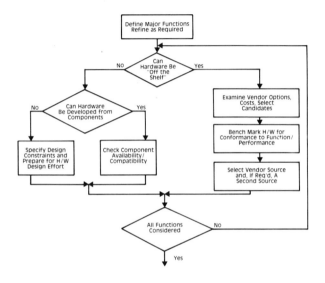

**Figure 4.3a System Specification – Hardware
Fuctions & Performance**

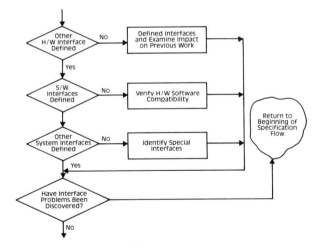

Figure 4.3b System Specification – Examining Interfaces

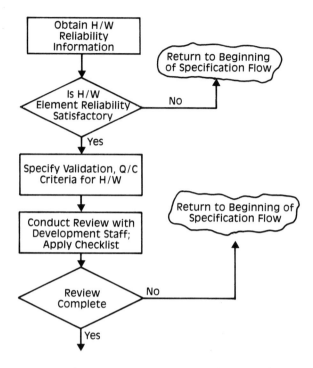

Figure 4.3c System Specification – Other Characteristics

Specification activities for software-related system elements are described in Figures 4.3d and 4.3e. Again, functions are defined, algorithm development commences and the use of existing software to satisfy all or part of the software requirement is examined.

The information element is extremely important for all computer-based systems. Figure 4.3f illustrates the activities that must be conducted to analyze overall information flow and structure (discussed later in this chapter) and related database requirements. Finally, in Figure 4.3g ergonometric and operational characteristics are examined to provide a "user's view" of the system.

Information obtained as part of the system definition activities described above will be used as a basis for software requirements analysis. In fact, thorough work during system definition will serve to bound and expedite the requirements analysis step.

4.2 REQUIREMENTS SUBTASKS

Software requirements analysis is a particularly difficult step in the Software Engineering process because both the requestor and developer are forced to exhibit a fairly detailed understanding of the system at an early stage. Unfortunately, details are often nebulous at this time.

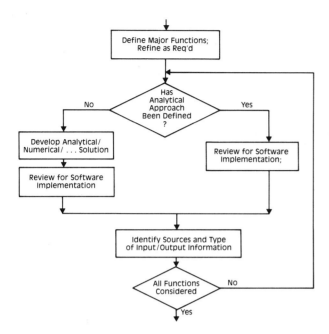

Figure 4.3d System Specification – Software Functions

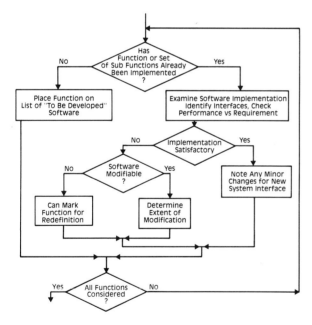

Figure 4.3e System Specification – Example of Existing Software

Requirements analysis must be tailored to meet the special needs of each effort. However, a number of subtasks, common to all analysis work, are described in the following paragraphs.

4.2.1 Study the Software Plan

Requirements analysis can commence only after major functions and interfaces are understood. The SOFTWARE

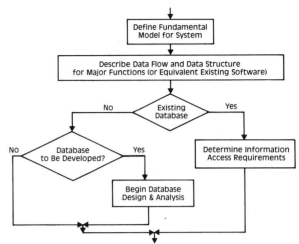

Figure 4.3f System Specification – Information Characteristics

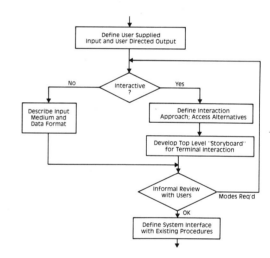

Figure 4.3g System Specification – Human Interaction

PLAN provides bounded descriptions of the proposed system and is a necessary point of departure for other work. The "analyst"* should establish a checklist of functions and quantitative bounds so that requestor concurrence can be established during analysis interviews.

4.2.2 Establish Communication for Analysis

Software requirements analysis is a process of communication as well as a rigorous examination of a problem. The analyst must establish a framework upon which all communication can be built. Users/requestors must be identified; topics must be outlined; and an interview format must be planned.

---

* The role and characteristics of the "analyst" are presented in Section 4.3.

Page 4-4

Chapter 4
SOFTWARE REQUIREMENTS ANALYSIS

**SOFTWARE
ENGINEERING
HANDBOOK**

In general, the analyst usually encounters three classes of users/requestors:

1. The manager with ultimate responsibility for system implementation, who provides guidance on top level objectives.

2. Technical staff of the requestor organization including technical managers and senior project staff. These individuals provide technical details for both functions and interfaces.

3. Hands-on users who work with the system once it has been fully validated and accepted. These individuals provide important interface information and dictate the sophistication of user documents.

Each user/requestor "interview" must be carefully planned in advance. Since the requestor's technical staff may be large, guidance on "who-knows-what" about specific functions and interfaces must be obtained. Ideally, a single person provides all information required by the analyst. Realistically, a number of people with sometimes contradictory viewpoints must be interviewed.

4.2.3 Build an Information Flow Model

The key to a complete understanding of software requirements begins with the definition of information flow in a system. All software can be viewed as a transform that accepts input information and produces output information. The job of the analyst is to develop a set of information flow models—called DATA FLOW DIAGRAMS—that depict the flow of information through the software. The DATA FLOW DIAGRAMS, described in detail in Section 4.4, are defined in increasing detail and provide the following benefits early in the analysis step:

1. The set of information flow models provides a structured approach to early requirements work. The software is described in a series of steps that begin with an abstract "fundamental model" (see Figure 4.4) and moves through a series of refinements achieving greater and greater detail.

2. The data flow diagram provides a template for the generation of the SOFTWARE REQUIREMENTS SPECIFICATION.

3. The graphical nature of data flow diagrams makes them an ideal tool for early review with the user/requestor.

4. The information flow model leads directly to a definition of software functions and subfunctions and a description of all internal interfaces between functions as well as external interfaces with other system elements.

The information flow model will also be used as a mechanism for mapping requirements directly into a software design. This provides traceability between requirements and design and forms the starting point of a software design methodology.

4.2.4 Define Functional Details and Interfaces

The goal of each software requirements analysis interview is to expand upon or corroborate functional details and interface characteristics.

The analyst must determine the output produced by a function; the input data that drives the function and the processing steps that must be accomplished to transform input to output. Additionally, the use of externally defined data structures must be stipulated.

Using the information flow modeling technique, the analyst may subdivide complex functions by refining relevant data flow diagrams (see Section 4.4).

The following topics should be addressed for each software function:

1. Interfaces
   a. human
   b. hardware
   c. software
2. Functional
   a. input data
   b. processing steps
   c. output data
3. Data Structure Characteristics

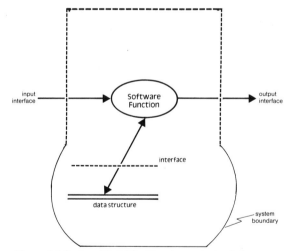

Figure 4.4 System Model for Requirements Analysis

It is vitally important to provide an unambiguous description of the functional processing steps. This "processing narrative" is the basis for design and is a major source of misinterpretation. A number of techniques including decision tables, HIPO charts and specification language may be used to remove ambiguity. These techniques are discussed in detail in Chapter 5.

4.2.5 Establish Design Constraints

The design of software may be affected by outside world influences external to the system. Cost, schedule, hardware limitations, processing or performance criteria, available development tools, destination and resources are only a few of many potential influences on design.

The analyst must identify design constraints and attempt to verify that each constraint is legitimate and can be justified on the basis of top-level system objectives.

4.2.6 Specify Validation Criteria

During communication with users/requestors, the analyst must continually pose the question:

"HOW WOULD YOU RECOGNIZE A SUCCESSFUL SYSTEM (FUNCTION) IF IT WERE DELIVERED TO YOU TOMORROW?"

This question and corresponding answers form the set of validation criteria for the software.

Validation criteria should be as specific as possible. Tests that can be used to validate each major software function should be defined; criteria for successful system integration must be established, and performance characteristics defined.

The user/requestor may frequently attempt to satisfy the preceding question with broad generalities. The analyst must pursue exact validation criteria and recognize that an inability to specify such, indicates an ill-defined concept of the software by the user/requestor. Validation criteria form the foundation of test planning and are omitted at the developer's peril!

4.2.7 Develop a Preliminary User's Manual

The PRELIMINARY USER'S MANUAL plays a key role in review of requirements. The manual provides the hands-on user with a view of the software as it will be used and demonstrates that requirements analysis has uncovered all important input and output for the software. Finally, the manual allows the external interface to be evaluated for human engineering factors.

The SOFTWARE REQUIREMENTS SPECIFICATION must provide a detailed description of software. It is sometimes difficult for the end user to recognize problem areas unwittingly hidden in necessary detail. The PRELIMINARY USER'S MANUAL often elicits the following reviewer's comment: "Gee, I didn't think this was the way we were going to invoke this function...it won't work because...". Better that such comments are made during the definition phase, rather than at system validation!

4.2.8 Review Software Requirements

The first analysis iteration culminates with the SOFTWARE REQUIREMENTS SPECIFICATION. The SRS must be reviewed by the developer and the user/requestor. Information flow, each interface and function must be carefully evaluated for correctness, completeness and clarity.

The following topics should be considered:

1. have existing systems been carefully evaluated?

2. does each function remain within the scope defined in the SOFTWARE PLAN?

3. do inconsistencies or redundancies exist?

4. have all levels of management and technical user/requestor personnel been interviewed?

5. does the developer's technical staff foresee problems during design or implementation?

6. are design constraints justified, realistic?

7. have validation criteria been defined in detail?

8. have alternative approaches been considered?

9. has a format for user/requestor review of the SRS been established?

The requirements review almost always results in modification or redefinition of some requirements. This iterative step in requirements analysis is to be expected and even encouraged. Ultimately, a completed SRS, acceptable to both developer and user/requestor, sets the foundation for software design, implementation and validation.

4.2.9 Review the Plan

Information determined during requirements analysis may result in necessary modifications to software scope as defined in the PLAN. The analyst must review the planning document to verify that resources, costs and schedule are still valid. If changes to the plan are required, a management review must be conducted to isolate causes for changes and to approve any increase/decrease in resources, cost or time.

4.3 THE ANALYST

The job description of an "analyst" varies from organization to organization and from project to project. J. W. Atwood, in his book, *The Systems Analyst* (Hayden, 1977) proposes a number of duties and characteristics of the analyst.

Page 4-6

Chapter 4
SOFTWARE REQUIREMENTS ANALYSIS

SOFTWARE
ENGINEERING
HANDBOOK

In general, the analyst performs the following duties:

1. acts as a consultant to management and the user/requestor;

2. collects data from many sources and synthesizes problem solutions;

3. analyses new systems and evaluates existing systems;

4. prepares documentation and management reports;

5. understands hardware and software interfaces;

6. performs research as required to formulate the SRS;

7. conducts "interviews" to develop the SRS; and

8. keeps abreast of advanced techniques.

Each of the above duties combines art and science. The analyst must rely on experience and must understand the roles of other individuals involved in the software effort.

The above duties indicate that an analyst must be a senior level person. Atwood identifies the following characteristics that may be observed in a successful analyst:

1. ability to think logically, symbolically, abstractly, and creatively;

2. works well as part of a team;

3. has a good knowledge of the capabilities of computer hardware and software;

4. works within the constraints of time tables and schedules and is conscientious in meeting deadlines;

5. seeks the ideas of others and involves them in the analysis and design of a system;

6. considers himself/herself both a teacher and a student, willing to train others but also constantly keeping up-to-date through night classes, personal reading, and short seminars;

7. listens attentively but does not depend upon the opinions of others, rather determining for himself/herself what the real facts are;

8. familiar with organizations and especially the principles of business and/or government administration.

The analyst often encounters problems that include communication difficulties, requirements that change during the analysis step, the pressure of tight schedules, and organiza-tional politics. To circumvent problems the analyst must speak the user/requestor's language; develop the SRS so that late changes can be incorporated; plan the analysis step carefully, and understand the organization of the user/requestor and the software developer.

4.4 DATA FLOW DIAGRAMS

The key to successful analysis of computer software is an understanding of the information that the software will process. The Data Flow Diagram (also called a data flow graph or bubble chart) provides a graphical approach for describing the information flow characteristics within a system.

A simple data flow diagram is illustrated in Figure 4.5. Input information is changed into output information by three simple transforms (the circles in the figure) that modify data as it moves through the software. Each arrow in the Data Flow Diagram (DFD) represents information, thereby providing an indication of the interfaces between internal software functions and the interfaces to the external environment. An "information store" (represented by double lines in the Figure) may be used to represent active files or a database that is used by the software.

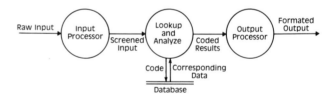

Figure 4.5 Simple Data Flow Diagram

The DFD is a relatively simple graphical tool that has the following characteristics:

1. Information (data flow) is represented by labeled arrows.

2. Transformations (processes) are represented by labelled circles.

3. An information store (e.g., files) is represented by a labelled, double line.

The DFD is developed beginning with a fundamental model (Figure 4.4) that represents the software as a single transform. The fundamental model (sometimes called level 1 transform) is then refined through a series of DFDs until sufficient detail is developed. The process of DFD refinement, shown in Figure 4.6, expands each transform by maintaining information continuity—that is, information into and out of a transform remains fixed regardless of the level of refinement. Referring to the figure, information items A and B do not

SOFTWARE
ENGINEERING
HANDBOOK

Chapter 4
SOFTWARE REQUIREMENTS ANALYSIS

Page 4-7

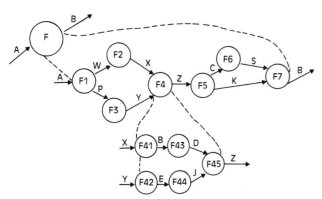

Figure 4.6 Information Flow Refinement

change for the level 2 expansion of F. Similarly, X, Y and Z are unchanged for the level 3 expansion of F4.

To illustrate the use of the Data Flow Diagram, a simple example is presented in Figures 4.7a, b and c. Software to solve a system of equations is to be developed. The level 1 DFD (Figure 4.7a) indicates the overall input and output to the software and represents an engineering database as an information store.

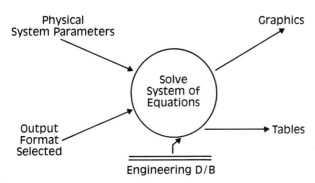

Figure 4.7a Example – "System Solver"; Level 1

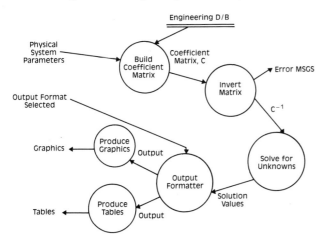

Figure 4.7b Example – "System Solver", Level 2

Refining "Build Coefficient Matrix" Transform:

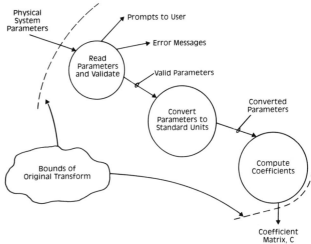

Figure 4.7c Example – "System Solver", Level 3

The "system solver" is expanded into a level 2 DFD in Figure 4.7b. Note that important functions (e.g., invert matrix, solve for unknowns) are shown at this level. In Figure 4.7c, a level three expansion of the "build coefficient matrix" transform is shown. Throughout the levels of expansion, information continuity is maintained and intermediate data are defined. The Data Flow Diagram is intended to represent information flow. It is not a flowchart and is not intended to indicate decision making, flow of control, loops and other procedural aspects of the software.

The DFD is a useful graphical tool that may be applied during early stages of requirements analysis. It may be further refined during preliminary design and is used as a mechanism for creating a top level structural design for software. The techniques for achieving a design from the DFD are discussed in Chapter 5.

4.5 SOFTWARE REQUIREMENTS SPECIFICATION

The SOFTWARE REQUIREMENTS SPECIFICATION (SRS) is the primary deliverable of the requirements analysis step. The SRS serves as a reference document for software design and validation testing. All phases of development must ultimately be traceable to the requirements document.

As mentioned at the very beginning of this chapter, the document is divided into four sections.

1. information flow and interfaces
2. functional/requirements
3. design requirements constraints
4. test criteria/quality assurance

Page 4-8

Chapter 4
SOFTWARE REQUIREMENTS ANALYSIS

SOFTWARE
ENGINEERING
HANDBOOK

Information flow is described using the data flow diagram. In general, a number of levels of refinement are shown. Interfaces are data entry or exit points. Data may be supplied by human, hardware, or software system elements, and may be transmitted from an external environment or among internal functional elements of the system.

Functions are a set of procedures that accomplish the processing requirements of the system. Each function has input, processing and output. Each function is normally subdivided so development may be more easily accomplished. Data structures may be associated with functions and are discussed in this section.

Design constraints are usually keyed to performance or environmental considerations. That is, software must be designed to execute at a specified speed or reside within a predefined amount of memory. Other constraints may be derived from available resources.

Test criteria indicate the set of conditions that must be satisfied for successful validation of the software. Specific criteria for each function are described and system integration tests are defined.

A graphical representation of the software is crucial to understanding. Block diagrams refer to a broad spectrum of graphical aids that help to clarify the preceding four sections.

4.6 AUTOMATED TOOLS FOR REQUIREMENTS ANALYSIS

An experienced analyst performing each of the analysis subtasks described in Section 4.2 can produce a Software Requirement Specification that forms the foundation for development. However, because the SRS is a written document, a number of inherent problems exist:

1. functional requirements or other segments of the SRS may be difficult to verify;

2. redundancy, omission and inconsistency can remain undiscovered;

3. beyond review procedures, there is no method of "testing" the specification;

4. it is extremely difficult to assess the global impact of modifications.

Automated tools have been developed to mitigate the problems discussed above. The tools have been designed with the following criteria:

1. a formal syntax (form) must be developed so that contents of the specification may be "processed" automatically;

2. detailed documentation may be derived using the automated tools;

3. a means for analyzing (testing) the specification for inconsistency and redundancy must be provided and a set of reports may be generated to indicate completeness;

4. communication should be enhanced through the use of automated tools.

Figure 4.8 illustrates the family of "tools" for software development. As noted in the Figure, automated tools for specification and analysis have high short-term potential to improve software quality.

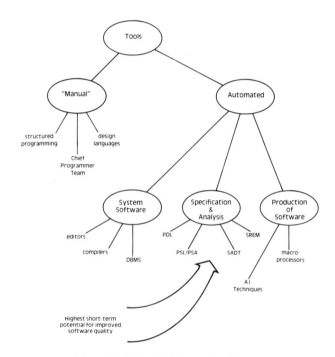

Figure 4.8 Tools for Software Development

PSL/PSA is one of a number* of automated tools that are currently being evaluated by government and industry for software requirements specification. PSL/PSA, an acronym for Problem Statement Language/Problem Statement Analyzer, is the product of a on-going research and development conducted at the University of Michigan.

PSL is a formal language for describing systems. PSA is an analysis package that processes the PSL description. A complete description of PSL/PSA is beyond the scope of this Handbook. However, the following general capabilities should be noted.

* for an overview of other tools, see: Davis, C. and Vick, C. The Software Development System, Journal of Software Engineering, IEEE, January, 1977.

**SOFTWARE
ENGINEERING
HANDBOOK**

**Chapter 4
SOFTWARE REQUIREMENTS ANALYSIS**

Page 4-9

PSL/PSA provides automated facilities for the complete description of information systems, regardless of application area. Using PSL descriptors, attributes of the system are placed in a computerized data base that contains detailed information about:

1. system input/output
2. system structure
3. data structure
4. data derivation
5. system size and volume
6. system dynamics
7. system properties
8. project management

Once the data base has been created, information may be added, deleted or modified in a consistent manner. PSA processes the data base to produce a variety of reports that cross reference information, test for inconsistencies or omissions, and produce documentation.

For further sources of information on PSL/PSA, the reader is urged to reference the Software Engineering Bibliography, Appendix C.

4.7 SUMMARY

The SOFTWARE REQUIREMENTS SPECIFICATION forms a foundation for all software development steps that follow. Analysis is a detailed, often difficult, procedure that is predicated on communication between an experienced analyst and one or more user/requestors. The requirements document must be reviewed by the development staff and the user/requestor. Justifiable cost and schedule changes are incorporated at this point in the software life cycle.

Once requirements have been approved, the software development staff has a well defined "target" for design work. The SRS serves the primary document for management review of traceability, and technical review of functionality.

Software design has evolved from an intuitive art dependent on experience to a science which provides systematic techniques for software definition. This chapter introduces methods and tools applicable to preliminary and detailed design.

Preliminary design is a process that generates a description of software structure, i.e., an architectural view of the elements that comprise a software system. By having a complete description early in the development stage, the reviewer may more easily evaluate a software configuration and suggest improvements.

Detailed design uses tools which assist in defining the procedural detail for the software structure described. A variety of tools are available, each relying on a disciplined approach to the specification of procedural detail.

Design efforts yield formal documentation which must be carefully reviewed to assure traceability and correctness. Reviews and reviewed materials are also discussed in this chapter.

5.1 A DESIGN CHRONOLOGY

Software design is the first step in the development phase of the software life cycle. During the definition stage (discussed in Chapters 3 and 4), some implicit design has already been performed. It would be impossible to produce a meaningful SOFTWARE PLAN and SOFTWARE REQUIREMENTS SPECIFICATION without visualizing a conceptual design.

Design is performed by one or more software engineers who refine the functions allocated during requirements analysis. Using the SRS as a guide, these engineers establish overall software structure; the procedural detail for each module is then described.

A software design chronology is illustrated in Figure 5.1. Preliminary design concentrates on defining the flow of data through the software subsystem and determining a logically consistent structure for the software. Each module that defines a function is identified; interfaces between modules are established; and, constraints/limitations are described. Preliminary design also defines the data base items, formats, sizes and access mechanisms. It concentrates on those aspects which are "global" by nature; that is, those data items used in more than one module.

The first design deliverable is a preliminary DESIGN document. This document (discussed in Section 5.6) receives a Preliminary Design Review (PDR) to assure traceability to requirements, technical clarity and correctness. Aspects contributing to the successful generation of this document are discussed in Section 5.3.

Once the PDR is complete with required corrections made and approved, detailed design may commence. Effort now focuses on the specification of individual modules while holding preestablished structure and interface descriptions constant.

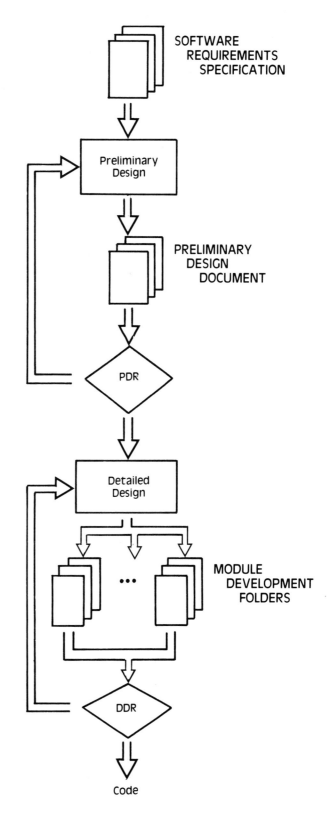

Figure 5.1 Design Chronology

Page 5-2

Chapter 5
SOFTWARE DESIGN

SOFTWARE
ENGINEERING
HANDBOOK

The goal of the detailed design step is a complete written procedural description of each software system routine. Module internal design may be specified using various accepted techniques. Detailed structured flowcharts, box diagrams or a Program Design Language (PDL) are common methods used for describing procedure. The Module Development Folder (MDF) is established at the beginning of detailed design and acts as a repository for all design, (and later) code and test data associated with a software module.

Upon completion of module detailed design, a detailed design review (DDR) or "design walk-through" is conducted by the lead software engineer or his designee. This review procedure should verify that: 1) the detailed design faithfully accomplishes the module functionality that was described in the PRELIMINARY DESIGN DOCUMENT; 2) the algorithm will perform the required function; 3) the design is complete, unambiguous and well documented.

5.2 PRELIMINARY DESIGN

A systematic approach to preliminary design is absolutely essential to the success of the software development process. As design is the basis for all subsequent development, decisions made here have a profound impact on the cost of detailed design, coding, and all phases of testing.

The ideal design methodology provides the software engineer with:

1. well-defined measures that may be used to assess the "goodness" of a design;

2. straightforward rules that relate information obtained during requirements analysis to a distinct software structure;

3. a practical approach that is amenable to a wide variety of software applications.

Several important design methodologies have been proposed in the literature. Structured design, a technique described by Yourdon and Constantine, relies on a consideration of data flow through a system. Other design methodologies, notably the Jackson, Orr and Warnier techniques (see Appendix B-1), are based on data structure. Less widely used techniques, such as higher order software (Hamilton and Zeldin) and meta-stepwise refinement (Ledgard) combine a process and data orientation.

The Handbook methodology for software design is based on Yourdon's structured design approach. It provides guidelines for software structure evaluation; it introduces a data-flow-oriented approach to determining structure. Alternative approaches, easily adapted to a wide variety of problems encountered in the application of special purpose computers, are also presented.

The chapter considers the following topics:

1. software concepts
2. structured design
3. other design methodologies
4. summary

This material is presented to introduce a rapidly evolving "science" of software design. Further readings (e.g., E. Yourdon and L. Constantine, Structured Design, Yourdon Press, 1978) and study are recommended to supplement the introductory information contained here.

5.3 SOFTWARE CONCEPTS

Until recently, the software engineer had few measures of software quality and fewer characteristics through which a design might be described. In order to produce a workable design, measures of "goodness" are established and considered during preliminary design process. Earlier it was noted that the primary goal of preliminary design is to establish software structure and to define the modules and data that the structure implies. The concepts presented have been published in texts by Myers, Yourdon, Constantine, V. Weinberg and others. Specific terminology has been adopted from *Structured Design* by Yourdon and Constantine.

5.3.1 Structure and Procedure

A hierarchical software structure is used to establish relationships between the functional elements of a software system, that is, the manner in which the program is partitioned and organized. Referring to Figure 5.2a, the relation and interaction between individual software modules is given without regard to time or sequence. In this figure, it can be seen that module M invokes ("calls") modules A, B and X. However, the sequence in which A, B and X are called and the conditions (if any) under which each is called are not indicated.

By contrast, procedure (Figure 5.2b) represents both the sequence and conditions under which a process occurs. It can be seen that process P1 or P2 is invoked based on a condition and that P3 precedes the processing indicated by P4.

During preliminary design, software structure is identified without regard for procedure. A consideration of the sequence and conditions of processing inherent within a module are postponed until detailed design.

5.3.2 Subordinate and Superordinate Relationships

The relative location of a module in the software hierarchy can be specified in terms of the module(s) that invoke it and the module(s) invoked by it. A module is directly subordinate to another module if it is invoked by that module. For exam-

**SOFTWARE
ENGINEERING
HANDBOOK**

Chapter 5
SOFTWARE DESIGN

Page 5-3

ple, module C of Figure 5.2a is directly subordinate to A and ultimately subordinate to Module M. Conversely, Module M is directly superordinate to A, B and X and ultimately superordinate to C, D, E, F and other unnamed modules.

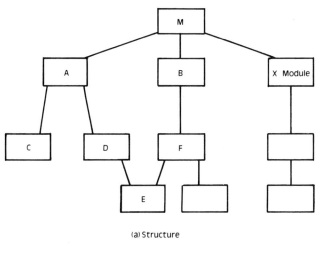

(a) Structure

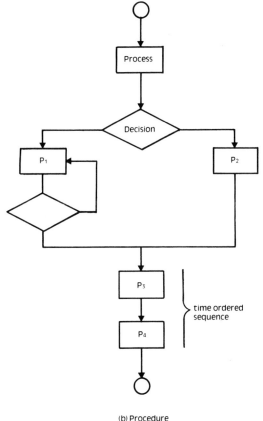

(b) Procedure

Figure 5.2 Structure and Procedure

5.3.3 Afferent and Efferent Characteristics

The software system model, illustrated by Figure 4.4, implies data being transformed from an external form (input) to an internal representation and then changed back to another external form (output). Therefore, information flow through software can be categorized as: (1) incoming or *afferent* flow; (2) outgoing or *efferent* flow, and (3) flow that occurs at the transition of incoming and outgoing data—called *transform* flow. Afferent and efferent data flow characteristics will determine the software structure developed. A step-by-step software design technique, using data flow characteristics, is discussed in Section 5.4.

5.3.4 Coupling

The complexity of any mode of communication is proportional to the amount, frequency, and variety of data flow. A software module is coupled to the "outside world" via the flow of data and control. Coupling is a qualitative measure of a module's interaction with other modules and/or data.

Ideally, modules would be independent of outside influences. Unfortunately, real-world software requires interconnection between modules. Coupling is determined by: 1) the type of connection; 2) the complexity of the interface; 3) the type of information flow; and 4) the time at which interconnections become final (called the 'binding time'). These are illustrated in Figure 5.3. The goal in defining software structure is to minimize coupling.

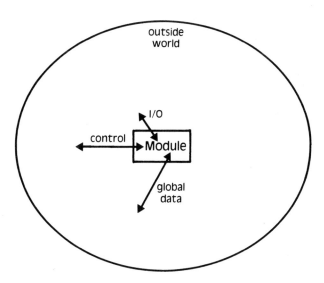

Figure 5.3 Coupling

Page 5-4

Chapter 5
SOFTWARE DESIGN

SOFTWARE
ENGINEERING
HANDBOOK

Modules are normally connected by call-type statements which pass data between modules. This data should be kept clear and simple; the use of control flags (i.e., variables that dictate conditional operations in the called module) should be minimized.

Input/Output should be isolated within a few modules, rather than being dispersed throughout the system. Branches from the middle of one module to the middle of another module (called "pathological" branches) should be discouraged. The way data affecting the interface is defined can also affect coupling.

A subtle form of coupling, that is a major source of "intermodular noise" and software errors, is use of global data (e.g. FORTRAN COMMON). When two modules having no direct subordinate relationship refer to the same global data, each module is coupled to the data and to each other through that data. Use of global data should be limited.

In summary, the degree of coupling is a measure of module independence. Reducing coupling within software reduces complexity. Lower complexity eases design, testing and debugging of modules.

5.3.5 Cohesion

Cohesion is a measure of the integral unity of the task performed by a module. Unlike coupling which is concerned with the relationship among modules, cohesion measures the single-mindedness of a module.

In an ideal software system, each module performs a single well-defined task; e.g., the absolute value function. In actuality, an individual module may perform tasks that have been combined because:

1. the designer has arbitrarily decided to group a set of unrelated tasks together (coincidental cohesion);

2. each task must be executed at the same point in time (temporal cohesion);

3. the tasks form a special purpose procedure (procedural cohesion);

4. the tasks all reference the same data (communicational cohesion);

5. the output data of one task is the input to the next task (sequential cohesion); and

6. all tasks contribute to the execution of only one well-defined function (functional cohesion).

The benefits of a highly cohesive module are obvious: error isolation is simplified as each module performs a small number of related tasks; design and coding are simplified because complexity is reduced; maintenance is greatly improved since tasks are unified. In his text Weinberg provides

useful guidelines to identify categories of cohesion. These are reproduced in Figure 5.4. The functionally cohesive module is the ideal. The coincidentally cohesive module represents the lowest (worst) mode of cohesion.

Using a SENTENCE to describe internal processing for a module:

IF a sentence is a *compound sentence,*

    or contains a comma,
    or contains more than one verb.

    THEN the module probably has *communicational, sequential, or logical cohesion*

ELSE IF

    sentence contains time-oriented words such as

    first, last, next, after, start, initialize,

    cleanup, terminate, etc.

    THEN the module probably has *sequential,*

    procedural, or temporal cohesion

ELSE IF

    sentence contains a plural or collective object,

    THEN the module probably has *logical or*

    communicational cohesion

ELSE IF

    sentence makes no sense or contains no continuity

    of function,

    THEN the module probably has *coincidental cohesion*

ELSE   (none of the above)

    then the module has *functional* cohesion

Figure 5.4 Guidelines for Cohesion

5.3.6 Modularity

The measures of software discussed above are predicated on a modular software structure. Modularity is a measure of the number of individual modules that have been defined to implement a system. Because size and complexity are di-

SOFTWARE
ENGINEERING
HANDBOOK

Chapter 5
SOFTWARE DESIGN

Page 5-5

rectly proportional, it follows that dividing a system into a number of modules lowers complexity and subsequently, reduces software cost. Figure 5.5 shows that complexity reduction obtained by reducing module size can be offset by the increased interface complexity (and cost). That is, some number of modules will result in minimum cost. As additional modules are added, cost increases.

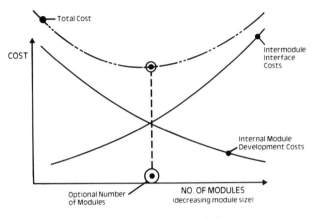

Figure 5.5 Cost of Modularity

5.3.7 Morphological Features

Yourdon and Constantine define the shape, or morphology of a software structure in terms of four features: depth, width, fanout and fan-in. These features are illustrated in Figure 5.6.

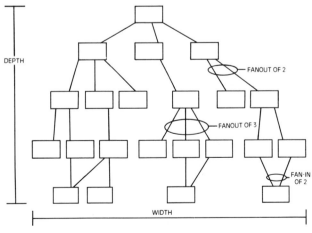

Figure 5.6 Morphology

A well-designed structure often has the shape of an inverted urn (Constantine). That is, top-levels of the structure have relatively high fanout, middle levels have less fanout and bottom levels exhibit fan-in to general utility modules.

5.3.8 Scope of Effect/Scope of Control

Decisions at one level of the software structure may affect processes or data at other levels. The scope of effect of a decision is the set of all modules that are in some way affected by that decision. The scope of control of a module is the set of all subordinate modules and the module itself.

Referring to Figure 5.7, the scope of control of module A is the set of modules A, B, C, D, E, F. If a decision in A affects all modules subordinate to it, then the scope of effect is the same as the scope of control.

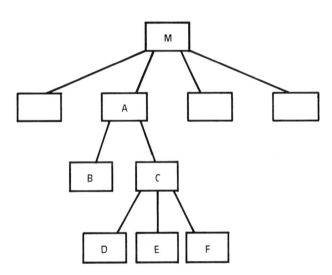

Figure 5.7 Scope of Effect/Control

Yourdon and Constantine propose two design guidelines:

1. the scope of effect should be a subset of the scope of control

2. a decision point can often be moved upward in the structure to assure guideline 1 is satisfied.

If a decision made in module C affects processing in modules D and E (Figure 5.7), the above design guidelines are accomplished. However, should a decision in C affect module B, a violation has occurred as B is outside the scope of control of C. Moving the decision to A (if practical) remedies this situation.

Page 5-6

Chapter 5
SOFTWARE DESIGN

SOFTWARE
ENGINEERING
HANDBOOK

5.3.9 Summary

The preceding paragraphs present an overview of important measures of software structure. By providing a means of measurement for software structure evaluation, the stage for systematic design, review and corrective action has been set.

System complexity is reduced by minimizing intermodular coupling, maximizing module cohesion, and following scope of effect/control guidelines. A common sense approach to the above goals must be applied, potential complications must be weighed and tradeoffs considered.

The concepts introduced in this section provide software measures where none have previously existed. The designer should consider ease of software implementation, testing and maintenance as guiding criteria in the application of these concepts.

5.4 STRUCTURED DESIGN

Structured design is a step-by-step methodology that produces a software structure using data flow information as a starting point. The methodology can be divided into the following steps:

1. analyze and refine the Data Flow Diagram (DFD);

2. examine DFD information flow characteristics;

3. determine a structure based on step 2;

4. refine the structure to establish preliminary design.
A flowchart representing the important steps in the structured design method is given in Figure 5.8.

To illustrate the methodology, a continuing example will be used throughout this section. A brief processing narrative for the example follows:

Microprocessor-based software must be developed to support a Manufacturing Facilities Control System (MFCS). The system monitors energy consumption obtaining periodic data on fuel oil consumption and electrical requirements. MFCS evaluates total energy consumption against monitored pollutants and derives a facilities profile that represents consumption efficiency and pollutant index.

Prior to this point, a complete SOFTWARE REQUIREMENTS SPECIFICATION would have preceded design. The design shall reflect data obtained as a consequence of requirements analysis.

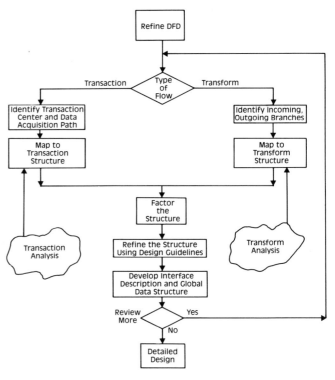

Figure 5.8 Data Flow Oriented Design

5.4.1 System Data Flow

As part of software requirements analysis, a set of data flow diagrams has been developed for MFCS. During derivation of the DFDs, the following suggestions can aid the analyst. In general, the DFD is easiest to develop if the designer works consistently in one direction of data flow (primary input toward primary output or vice versa) without regard to detail implicit in any bubble. Control logic is never shown. Simple error paths are omitted in the interest of clarity. The flow in large systems is developed separately for each major function. Finally, the DFD is not a flowchart—it is a representation of data transformation and not procedure.

Applying the above guidelines, the DFD for the MFCS example can be developed. The initial graph is shown in Figure 5.9a and a first level refinement is shown in Figure 5.9b. It should be noted that data and bubbles are labeled with meaningful descriptors.

Figure 5.9a Initial DFD

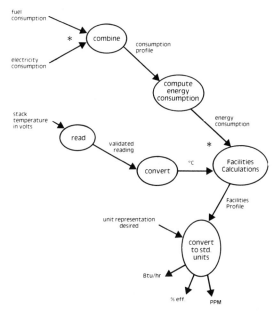

Figure 5.9b Refined DFD

5.4.2 Define Information Flow Boundaries

The second design step is identification of afferent (incoming) and efferent (outgoing) data flow paths. Data entering a system is transformed from its "outside world" representation to some internal representation. This transformation, often accomplished in a number of steps, is the afferent (incoming) data flow path. Similarly, as data leaves the core of the system the internal representation is step-at-a-time transformed back to an outside world representation. Figure 5.10 illustrates the above concept.

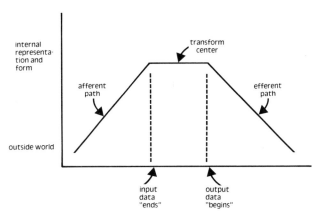

Figure 5.10 The Transform Center

5.4.3 Transform-Centered Analysis

By defining the afferent (incoming) and efferent (outgoing) paths, the transform center of the software is identified. Evaluating the DFD for the example system (Figure 5.9b), the transform center may be isolated as shown in Figure 5.11.

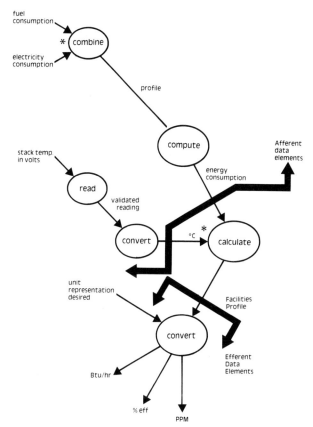

Figure 5.11 Isolating the Transform Center

It should be noted that for large DFD's, the precise location of the transform center boundaries (heavy arrows) may be subject to individual interpretation. By varying the location of flow boundaries, alternative designs may be generated. Hence, the "final" design may be selected from two or more candidates.

The third step is to perform first level factoring, i.e., to define the top two levels of software structure. Factoring identifies a control module that will perform all functions of the system by accessing subordinates that control all afferent, transform, and efferent processing and these immediate subordinates. The DFD is translated into a top level structure as shown in Figure 5.12.

Page 5-8

Chapter 5
SOFTWARE DESIGN

**SOFTWARE
ENGINEERING
HANDBOOK**

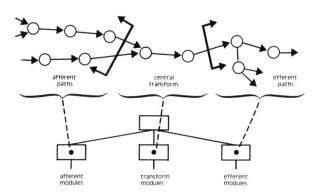

Figure 5.12 First Level Factoring

The factoring procedure is driven by an important premise: top level modules in the software structure serve to control processing but do little actual processing themselves. Each level of subordinate modules performs less control and more processing. At the bottom levels, modules should have high cohesion, a trait manifested by little, if any, external control.

The final step continues the factoring process by mapping transforms along the afferent, transform, and efferent paths into modules in the software structure. Working from the central transform outward, individual bubbles or combinations of bubbles are represented as modules in the structure. The resultant structure, illustrated in Figure 5.13, has three distinct substructures that reflect input, processing and output.

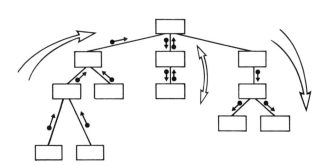

Figure 5.13 Resultant Structure

As factoring proceeds, it is often necessary to refine the DFD so that more detailed flow and structure may be represented. When large multifunction central transforms are encountered, each function may be assigned its own branch from the main control module. Factoring is terminated along any branch when it is not practical to define additional subtasks. The goal is not to generate "very small" modules, but rather to develop the smallest number of distinct modules that satisfy functional requirements and design measures such as coupling and cohesion. The factoring process is

illustrated in Figure 5.14a-f. Using the MFCS example data flow diagram as a basis, factoring begins with the specification of top level control modules, Figure 5.14a. Good design techniques demand using module names that avoid ambiguity and communicate function. The afferent branch is factored in Figure 5.14b. Although the VALIDATE module has transform characteristics, the flow of data (as illustrated by the arrows) is unquestionably afferent.

The DFD is refined (Figure 5.14c) and forms a transform substructure as shown in Figure 5.14d. Factoring of the efferent branch is straightforward (Figure 5.14e). The resultant software structure, combining all modules, is shown in Figure 5.14f.

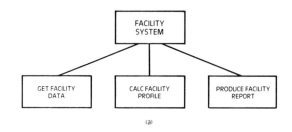

(a)

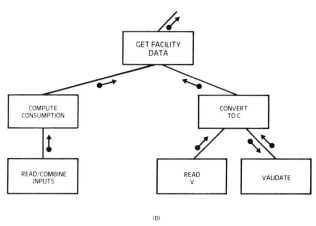

(b)

Figure 5.14a-b Example Problem—MFCS

5.4.4 Transaction-Centered Analysis

When a DFD has a configuration similar to that shown in Figure 5.15, the data flow is "transaction-centered". That is, data or control information passes to a bubble that initiates one of several alternative actions or sequences of actions based on the incoming data. The transaction center, denoted as T in Figure 5.15, performs the following tasks:

1. receives incoming data (called 'transactions') in raw form;

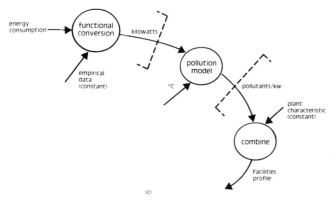

(c)

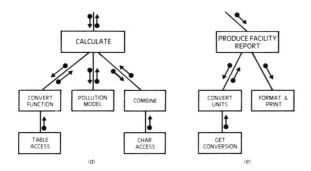

(d)   (e)

Figure 5.14c-e (continued)

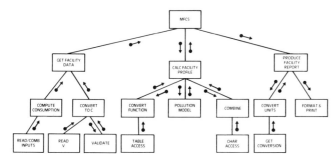

Figure 5.14f

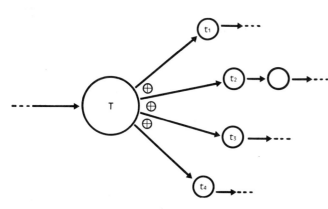

Figure 5.15 Transaction Centered DFD

2. analyzes each transaction to determine its type;

3. selects an action path based on the transaction type;

4. serves as a top-level control module for the process.

A transaction-centered DFD maps into a software structure that takes the form shown in Figure 5.16.

The design strategy for transaction centered flow differs somewhat from transform analysis. As the DFD is developed, transaction sources must be identified and the actions resulting from a given transaction must be defined. Using the structure in Figure 5.16, the DFD is factored into a "get-and-analyze-transaction" branch and a "dispatch" branch. Detail for subordinate modules along each path is developed from the transaction center outward.

Continuing the MFCS example, consider a subsystem that

...processes real-time inputs from various machinery, lighting, exhaust and process control equipment. Each input is preceded by an identification code (a letter) followed by packed data corresponding to the input source...

Using the above processing narrative (and data contained in the SRS), a data flow diagram (Figure 5.17) may be developed. The characteristic transaction center is immediately evident. The corresponding structure, partially completed, for this DFD is shown in Figure 5.18.

An important property of data flow analysis is that transform and transaction centered structures may be combined to form building blocks for the overall software structure. For example, a transform centered structure may occur on an action path of a transaction processor, or a transaction processor may comprise the afferent branch of a transform centered structure.

5.4.5 Summary of Structured Design

Using guidelines for the application of a structured design methodology system data flow is defined and a software structure—the cornerstone of a preliminary design—is derived. Two independent methods of analysis have been described to accommodate transform and transaction centered data flow. The techniques and resultant structures may be combined to accommodate large or complex systems as well as small, compact systems.

This section presents guidelines for structured design. However, as in any discipline, common sense and practicality must be applied. Design constraints such as critical timing or memory requirements, may require modification of derived structures. However, the techniques presented above provide a systematic approach which results in modular software which is morphologically good.

Page 5-10

Chapter 5
SOFTWARE DESIGN

**SOFTWARE
ENGINEERING
HANDBOOK**

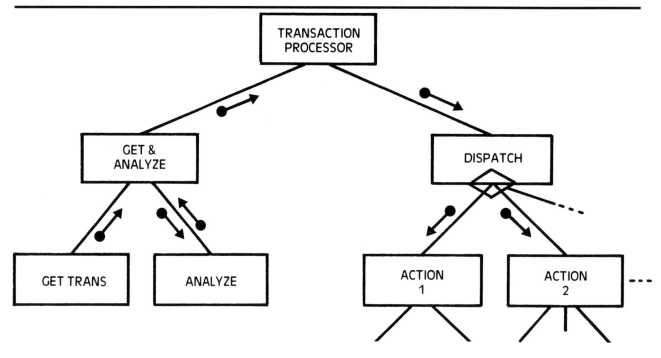

Figure 5.16 Transaction Structure

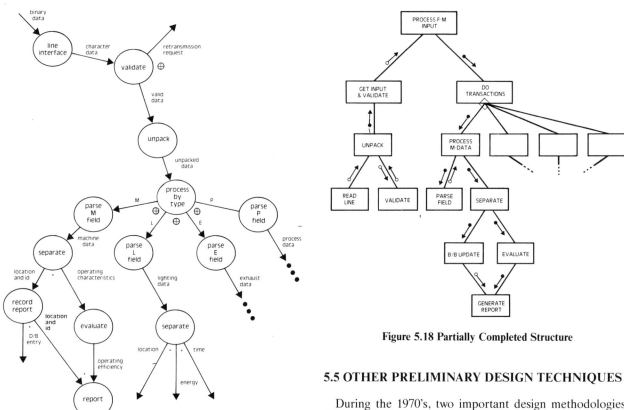

Figure 5.17 Example DFD

Figure 5.18 Partially Completed Structure

5.5 OTHER PRELIMINARY DESIGN TECHNIQUES

During the 1970's, two important design methodologies have been developed that emphasize the relationship between data structure (rather than data flow) and software structure.

SOFTWARE
ENGINEERING
HANDBOOK

**Chapter 5
SOFTWARE DESIGN**

Page 5-11

Each methodology is applicable when data structure is well-defined and hierarchical in nature—attributes frequently found in commercial data processing. An overview of these methods is presented in Appendix B.1.

5.6 DELIVERABLES—PRELIMINARY DESIGN

The preliminary design approach described in Section 5.4 is the first step in the development of the DESIGN document. Each module in the software structure is described in detail; interfaces are defined; limitations and restrictions are identified; and data structure characteristics are determined.

PRELIMINARY DESIGN documentation is produced according to the format shown in Appendix A.4. It is not necessary to complete all sections of the design document at this time. However, structural characteristics, data flow/structure and basic interface specifications must be completed in detail because they will be placed under formal change control after review and approval.

Sections of the design document (Appendix A.4) which constitute preliminary design are listed below:

1.0 Scope
2.0 Applicable Documents
3.0 Design Description (all paragraphs)
4.0 Modules (paragraphs indicated below)
    4.X.1 Processing Narrative of Module X
    4.X.2 Interface Description (preliminary)
    4.X.3 Procedural Description
    4.X.4 Comments
5.0 File Structure and Global Data
6.0 Requirements Cross Reference
7.0 Test Provisions
8.0 Packaging
9.0 Special Notes
10.0 Appendices

5.7 PRELIMINARY DESIGN REVIEW

The preliminary design review (PDR) is a formal, technical and management review of the software development effort. The review concentrates on top-level structural design of the software and design traceability to requirements.

A PDR is scheduled after PRELIMINARY DESIGN documentation has been completed. Participants in the review are:

1. designer—individual(s) responsible for structure definition and authors of design document;

2. manager—individual with project responsibility and administrative control;

3. chief software engineer—the technical supervisor with development responsibility;

4. technical specialists—senior technical staff with specialities relevant to the software development effort;

5. observers—representatives from other project development teams, requestor personnel, operations staff and others.

Each PDR participant is interested in specific review criteria. Figure 5.19 indicates some of the more important concerns of each participant.

A design review is an extremely useful, yet potentially volatile, procedure. The reviewers should review the design, not the designer. It is extremely important that the PDR be carefully planned and thoughtfully managed.

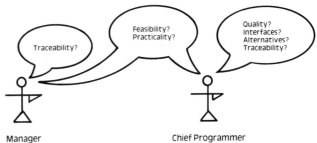

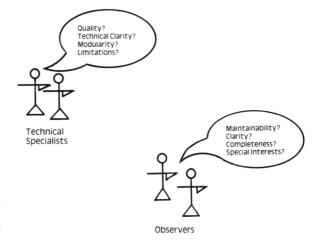

Figure 5.19 Review Criteria

Review Content and Procedure

The precise form of a PDR varies among organizations; however, common content and procedure are normally present. At least one week prior to the review date, all PRELIMINARY DESIGN documentation should be distributed to review participants. Written comments are requested and are to be submitted on the day of the PDR.

The designer(s) prepares an audio-visual presentation highlighting each important element of the design. The presentation should include 1) a discussion of objectives, 2) a

Page 5-12

Chapter 5
SOFTWARE DESIGN

SOFTWARE
ENGINEERING
HANDBOOK

requirements precis, 3) data flow, 4) derived structure, 5) discarded alternatives (if applicable), 6) a description of important modules, 7) data structure presentation, 8) design constraints and limitations, 9) requirements cross reference, and, 10) management considerations.

A review agenda is established by the designer(s) in consultation with the manager and chief software engineer. The agenda should be distributed at the start of the PDR.

PDR Guidelines

Careful management of the PDR is essential. Mis-managed reviews often degenerate into useless debates, personal inquisitions or worse! Since the review is so important to the software development success effort, careful control must be established. The following guidelines are recommended:

1. The tone of the review must be constructive. All comments are directed at the software. Abusive or hostile individuals should be counseled and/or excluded from the PDR.

2. A written record of all important comments should be made during the review to serve as a checklist for action items. Someone should be assigned this role prior to the PDR.

3. The review raises issues; it shouldn't try to resolve them. Although limited problem solving and suggestions are useful, the agenda should be enforced.

4. An antagonistic atmosphere should be discouraged; rebuttal must be minimal.

5. The number of PDR participants should be limited. Otherwise, since each participant is encouraged to contribute, total review time becomes excessive.

6. The review should be scheduled at a time and place that assures no outside interruptions.

7. The manager or software engineer is the arbiter who must control the flow of the review. The designers should never be required to assume this role.

The conduct of a PDR requires a delicate balance between constructive criticism and "now I've you, you SOB (software-oriented bumpkin). Conducted correctly, the PDR assures technical clarity and management traceability—two issues essential for a successful development effort. If major discrepancies exist upon completion of the PDR, the manager and technical supervisor must decide what corrective measures to take. This may lead to scheduling another design review of the module(s).

5.8 DETAILED DESIGN

The goal of detailed design is development of a software representation directly translatable into a programming language. Each module is considered individually during detailed design with emphasis placed on a description of procedural detail.

The PRELIMINARY DESIGN documentation (Appendix A.4) and methodology concentrate on a definition of software structure, data flow/structure, interface characteristics and the processing narrative for each module. The processing narrative is a structured-English description identifying the inputs to a module; the actions, conditions and limitations that occur during processing and the outputs of that same module.

Detailed design is traceable to the preliminary design description. Special tools are used to transform the preliminary design text into a systematic, structured, unambiguous representation of processing.

This section presents a number of design tools that can be used to prepare the detailed design description. Three tool categories are considered:

1. graphical tools
2. design language
3. tabular tools

Each tool category provides a means for an unambiguous description of procedure.

5.8.1 Graphical Tools

Graphical techniques depict module processing in pictorial form. Each graphical tool makes use of a distinct symbology that promotes representation of structured programming constructs (Figure 5.20 and 6.1) and in some cases, data description and access.

Two graphical tools are discussed in this section: structured flowcharts and box diagrams. The flowchart is a well-known graphical tool; the box diagram is less widely used. It, however, has significant representational and control advantages.

Flowcharts

The ubiquitous flowchart is a design tool that is known to nearly every individual involved in computing and engineering. Although the flowchart can be used to represent any combination of conditions, actions and branches (a disadvantage to be discussed later), the fundamental structured constructs are illustrated in Figure 5.20. These flowcharts con-

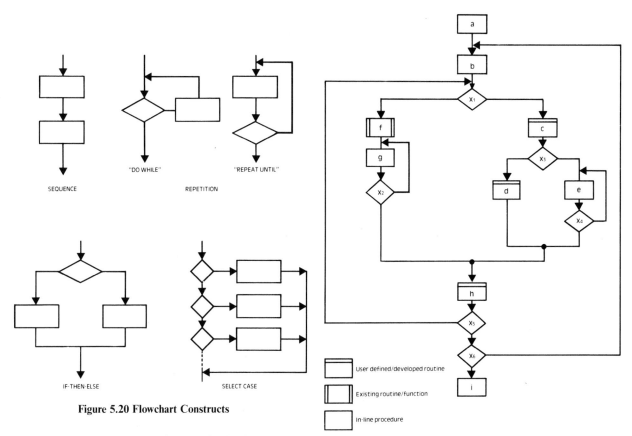

Figure 5.20 Flowchart Constructs

Figure 5.21 Example of a Structure Flowchart

structs are discussed in detail in Chapter 6. The flowchart is assembled by concatenating or nesting individual constructs to form the processing algorithm. Figure 5.21 illustrates a typical example.

The benefits of the flowchart are universal familiarity, wide usage and general acceptance. However, the flowchart does not inherently enforce use of structured constructs. The ready availability of "the arrow" continually tempts the designer to make branches outside the functional domain of a process. When used correctly, the structured flowchart is an easily readable, flexible and readily understood. When used incorrectly, it precipitates "spaghetti-bowl code" that is difficult to understand and impossible to maintain.

Box Diagrams

Box diagrams, a graphic alternative to the flowchart, enforces the use of *only* structured constructs. Also called Nassi-Shneiderman or Chapin charts, the box diagrams provide symbology for each construct as illustrated in Figure 5.22. All processing is contained within a "box" that may be refined to include smaller boxes as processing needs dictate. However, there is no representation for a branch from within a box to some location outside the box (a violation of functional domain). Therefore, structured constructs are guaranteed.

The representation of sequence, if-then-else, and repetition are fairly straightforward. The example illustrated in Figure 5.23 is the exact functional equivalent to the flowchart in Figure 5.21.

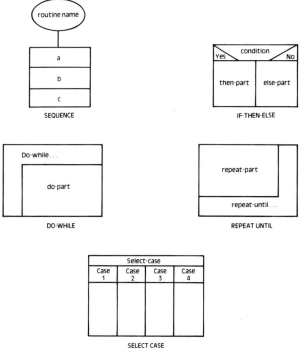

Figure 5.22 Box Diagram Constructs

Page 5-14

Chapter 5
SOFTWARE DESIGN

**SOFTWARE
ENGINEERING
HANDBOOK**

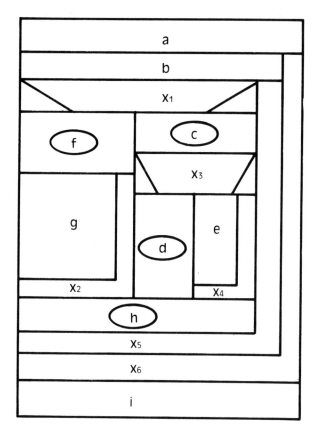

Figure 5.23 Example of a Box Diagram

(Identical to flowchart structure of Figure 5.21)

The reader is urged to study these figures until the box diagram technique is understood.

When used as a detailed design tool, the box diagram often incorporates a separate box that contains a data description for the module to be defined. Illustrated in Figure 5.24, the "data box" describes interface arguments, local and global data (variables) and relevant data structures that are accessed or created by the module.

The main benefits of the box diagram are structure enforcement and a concise mode for representing functional domain. Disadvantages to the use of the box diagram are difficulty in manually modifying an existing diagram (without complete redraw) and relatively limited usage to date. The box diagram forces the designer to think in terms of structured constructs. For this reason alone, it is a worthwhile detailed design tool.

5.8.2 Program Design Language

The primary intent of detailed design tools is to provide an unambiguous design description that may be directly trans-

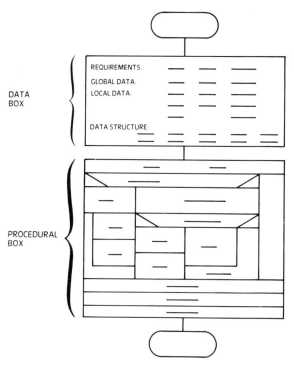

Figure 5.24 Detailed Design Representation

lated into code. Therefore, a representation whose constructs are isomorphic to those of the programming language) provides a straightforward medium for translation.

A Program Design Language (PDL), also called pseudo-code or structured-English, provides a means for representing data and processing (the structured constructs) in a text format. A PDL has formal syntax that indicates processing and data constructs, but incorporates free-form English language descriptions to explain details. Although a design language is not directly executable, automated techniques for design evaluation and even "code to" conversion have been implemented by Hitachi, IBM and others. PDL statements may be grouped into three major categories:

1. data declaration
2. process description
3. I/O

In addition, special constructs and statements may be developed for particular applications, such as statements for multitasking or real-time applications.

The design language statement normally contains a keyword followed by English language for pseudo-code phrases that qualify the keyword. For example, the design language description for a portion of a SORT module would be:

.
.
.

```
IF        first item of list › second item of list THEN
          interchange both items
ELSE      replace first item with buffer entry 1 replace
          2nd item with buffer entry 2
              ENDIF
```

.
.
.

In the previous example, all design language keywords are upper case, while lower case English is used to describe processing. Conversion to a programming language is relatively straightforward. In FORTRAN, the SORT implementation becomes:

```
IF (LIST(I).GT. LIST (I+1)) THEN
          TEMP = LIST(I)
          LIST(I) = LIST(I+1)
          LIST(I+1) = TEMP
ELSE
          LIST(I) = BUFFER(1)
          LIST(I+1) = BUFFER(2)
ENDIF
```

It should be noted that THEN, ELSE and ENDIF are part of the program code. This is the case with structured languages FORTRAN or PASCAL. In less useful languages, IF-THEN-ELSE must be simulated using other language constructs (principally GO TO).

A typical design language subset for the structured constructs is given in Figure 5.25. Note that design language constructs may be nested within one another; i.e., in the following example, both an IF construct and a CASE construct are nested within the WHILE construct.

```
WHILE latch is set
  IF buffer not empty
        select buffer entry
        process entry
  ELSE
        switch buffer pointer
        reset latch
  END IF
  CASE OF latch setting
      CASE latch = priority 1
          *
          *
          *
      CASE latch = priority 2
          *
          *
          *
```

```
      CASE ELSE
          *
          *
          *
          write error message
  END CASE
END WHILE
```

Continuing the example begun with the flowchart in Figure 5.21, a design language description equivalent to the flowchart and the box diagram in Figure 5.23 is presented in Figure 5.26.

The design language is the most flexible of all detailed design tools. It is relatively easy to learn. It can be edited at a computer terminal. It is amenable to automated processing and is most easily translated to code. The only drawback to design language is a lack of graphical representation. Some tools such as the Integrated Software Design System (Chapter 6) are able to generate flowcharts from PDL and vice versa.

Appendix B.3 contains a detailed description of the Integrated Software Design System PDL—an automated design language.

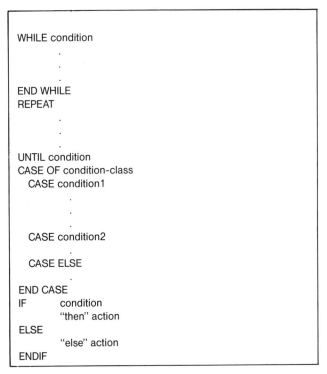

```
WHILE condition
    .
    .
    .
END WHILE
REPEAT
    .
    .
    .
UNTIL condition
CASE OF condition-class
    CASE condition1
            .
            .
    CASE condition2
            .
    CASE ELSE
            .
END CASE
IF        condition
          "then" action
ELSE
          "else" action
ENDIF
```

Figure 5.25 Design Language Subset

Chapter 5
SOFTWARE DESIGN

```
perform calculations "a"
REPEAT
  perform operation "b"
  REPEAT
    IF condition "x1"
      perform "c"
      IF condition "x3"
          REPEAT
             perform calculation "e"
          UNTIL condition "x4"
        ELSE
             perform "d"
        END IF
      ELSE
        perform "f"
        REPEAT
          perform operation "g"
        UNTIL condition "x2"
      END IF
      perform "h"
    UNTIL condition "x5"
  UNTIL condition "x6"
perform operation "i"
EXIT
```

Figure 5.26 Design Language Example

(Identical to flowchart structure in Figure 5.21)

5.8.3 Tabular Tools

The procedural description of a module often requires the execution of one or more actions based on a set of conditions. A decision table is a tool that provides a systematic technique for the representation of actions and conditions and their relationship to one another. The basic format of the decision table is illustrated in Figure 5.27.

The table is divided into four sectors: condition and action stubs that contain a list of all conditions and all actions, respectively; a condition entry that indicates one of all possible states of a condition; an action entry that defines what action(s) is selected for a given set of conditions. A "rule" is a column passing through both 'entry' sectors.

As an illustration of the use of decision tables, consider the following excerpt of a processing narrative:

... a machine with a capacity of more than 1000 pieces/hr which has a poor maintenance record or that is more than 10 years old should receive priority treatment ...

It is assumed that "poor maintenance record" and "priority treatment" have been quantitatively defined elsewhere.

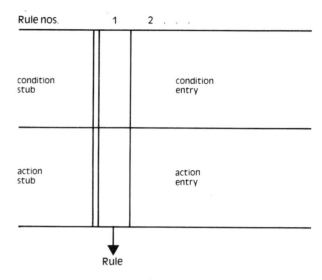

Figure 5.27 Decision Table

The decision table is constructed in the following manner:

1. Determine the number of rules by calculating the product of all condition permutations. For example, for the processing narrative above:

condition 1	capacity › 1000	2 possibilities
2	poor maintenance record	2 possibilities
3	› 10 years old	2 possibilities

Therefore, there are 2x2x2 = 8 possible rules

2. List all conditions and all actions and draw columns for each rule. (See Figure 5.28a)

3. Develop all possible combinations of conditions by first alternating each possible state along the bottom condition row; next, repeat the alternation on each succeeding row where the number of equivalent entries, N, is defined:

$$N = n * \exp(r)$$
where: n = number of possibilities (states)
r = number of condition rows
See Figure 5.28b

4. Once the condition entries have been established, indicate the appropriate actions for each rule.
See Figure 5.28c.

5. Collapse rules that result in equivalent actions. For example, rules 1 and 2 of Figure 5.28c are 'indifferent' to condition 3.

6. Rearrange the table so that rules that result in similar actions are grouped together. See Figure 5.28d.

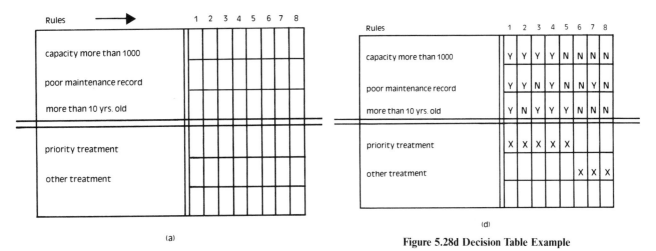

(a)

(d)

Figure 5.28d Decision Table Example

The above steps will result in a decision table that provides no ambiguity with regard to processing conditions and their consequences.

Although the decision table can be automatically translated into code without error, it may be somewhat more difficult to work with manually than other tools discussed. Decision tables are ideal for describing modules with distinct action-condition processing or for finite state machines; it is highly recommended for use in such cases.

In his text dedicated to decision tables, Montalbano describes procedures for assessing completeness and consistency of decision tables. The tabular format of this detailed design tool is directly amenable to automated evaluation and has been used to automatically generate flowcharts and even programming language code. A major advantage of decision tables is that they are easily validated by humans and present complex logical relationships on a single page which would require a large number of pages in any other representation.

5.8.4 A Comparison of Tools

The goal of detailed design is development of a concise, unambiguous procedural description of a module that can be translated directly into code. Any of the tools presented in this section, if used properly, is worthwhile for detailed design specification. However, criteria may be specified to aid in a comparison of techniques and tools.

The following criteria for comparison of detailed design tools are defined:

1. ease of use—Is the tool relatively easy to learn, easy to understand and is the procedural description easy to read?

(b)

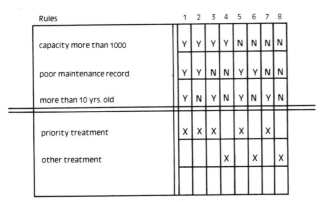

(c)

Figure 28a-c Decision Table Example

Page 5-18

Chapter 5
SOFTWARE DESIGN

SOFTWARE
ENGINEERING
HANDBOOK

2. logic representation — Are conditions and actions represented in a concise, understandable manner?

3. code-to — How difficult is the translation from detailed design description to a programming language?

4. machine readable — Is the design description amenable to automated processing?

5. changeability — Can the design be modified easily?

6. structure enforcement — Does the design tool enforce structured programming by providing only structured constructs?

7. frequency — How frequently is the tool used for software development?

8. data representation — Is there a means for representing data type and structure?

Table 5.1 contains a comparison of four detailed design tools using the criteria discussed above. Examination of the table indicates that design language is the tool that provides the greatest benefit. Referring to the table, each tool shows strength in particular categories. Decision tables have very strong logic representation and verification capabilities; flowcharts are relatively simple and are used widely; box diagrams enforce structure explicitly. Project design documentation is most effective when a single detailed design tool is used consistently. For this reason, one technique should be selected for use in a project. Different projects may deliberately choose different design representation.

5.9 DELIVERABLES–DETAILED DESIGN

The goal of the detailed design step is to produce a complete, detailed description of each module in the software system. To this end, a Module Development Folder (MDF) is prepared for each software module.

The MDF, described in detail in Appendix A.6, contains the majority of Sections 4 through 10 of the DE-SIGN document (Appendix A.4). All internal data and data structure are defined; procedure is specified using a structured approach; one of the tools described in paragraphs 5.8.1, 2 or 3 is used throughout; files and global data are described, and applicable unit test guidelines are established.

Table 5.1 A Comparison of Detailed Design Tools

	DECISION TABLES	FLOW-CHARTS	BOX DIAGRAMS	DESIGN LANGUAGE
EASE OF USE	fair	good	poor	very good
LOGIC REPRESENTATION	very good	fair	good	good
LOGIC VERIFICATION	very good	poor	fair	fair
CODE TO	good	fair	good	very good
MACHINE READABLE	very good	poor	poor	very good
CHANGEABILITY	good	poor	poor	good
STRUCTURE ENFORCEMENT	not applicable	poor	very good	good
FREQUENCY OF USE	low	high	low	medium
DATA REPRESENTATION	poor	poor	poor	fair

The schedule committed to after the Requirements Review establishes the end dates for development tasks, and the responsible software engineer determines the dates for the intervening items, making entries on the MDF cover sheet. Each item is reviewed and signed-off by an independent reviewer as it is put in the folder. A design which necessitates a change in an interface or exceeds a budgeted allocation must be brought immediately to management's attention.

The MDF exists throughout the life of the product (including the maintenance phase). The entire MDF should be easily accessible to all project personnel.

5.10 DETAILED DESIGN REVIEWS (DDR)

Upon completion of a module's detailed design its logic, data structure and interface must be reviewed for correctness and maintainability.

A Detailed Design Review (DDR) is conducted for each software structure module. This review is a milestone in the software development phase. The Detailed Design Review is conducted by the responsible software

SOFTWARE
ENGINEERING
HANDBOOK

Chapter 5
SOFTWARE DESIGN

Page 5-19

engineer and generally involves a small number of technical people. The results of each review are reported to the lead software engineer.

The DDR may be accomplished using one of three formats:

1. an informal desk "walkthrough" conducted with another staff member;

2. a more formal "structured walkthrough" that is conducted by a small team of reviewers—each with a specific role to play during the review;

3. a formal "design inspection" that is conducted by an inspection team and results in a rigorous assessment of design quality.

Industry data indicates that a formal DDR can be as effective as testing in uncovering some classes of design errors! Because errors are uncovered much earlier in the development process, the chance for error amplification (one error in design can grow to become n errors due to amplification through the coding step) is reduced. In addition, the number of errors released to the field will also be reduced. As the DDR format becomes more formal, the likelihood of detecting design errors also rises. The format that is chosen for a project is generally dictated by staffing, the organization of teams for software development and past practice.

A general attitude, proven productive to adopt, is that the DDR must not be considered a "defense" of the design, but rather a design disclosure. To this end, great care should be taken in selecting and training reviewers so that the DDR fosters understanding, not hostility.

5.10.1 The Informal Walkthrough

An informal walkthrough is normally conducted by one high level technical person who has familiarity with the overall design. The reviewer meets with the designer; reviews all module design documentation (which has been provided beforehand); and recommends modifications or additions to the design. However, the DDR is not the point at which alternative designs should be recommended. Alternatives should be carefully considered during the PDR.

The project software engineer acts as a mediator when the reviewer and designer have different opinions and has ultimate authority to recommend design changes. Once design changes based on the walk-through have been made, the CODE TO DESIGN document is released and the unit code and test step begins.

5.10.2 The Structured Walkthrough

The structured walkthrough involves several people and is characterized by a planned set of activities. The design is

described by a *presenter* (who may or may not be the designer). The presenter reads through the design, one logical process at a time, while other DDR participants assess it for correctness. The DDR is controlled by a *coordinator* who serves as a moderator by maintaining an agenda, mediating differences of opinion and frequently serving as a *secretary/scribe* to record all findings of the review team.

Other participants in the DDR may include a *maintenance oracle* whose primary purpose is to foretell maintainability; a standards bearer who checks for design and documentation standards violations; a *user representative* who takes the users' perspective and other *technical personnel* with expertise relevant to the design at hand. Each of the preceding roles need not be filled by separate people. In fact, a good structured walkthrough can be accomplished with three or four people.

The format and activities that occur during a structured walkthrough take the form outlined below:

1. the objectives of the DDR are described by the coordinator;

2. the designer presents a brief overview of the design;

3. the presenter reads the design (line by line if PDL is used) as other participants follow and raise questions/errors as appropriate.

4. the secretary/scribe records all questions and errors;

5. violations of standards are noted;

6. final recommendations are made and the design team votes to accept the design or return it for corrective action.

7. results of the walkthrough are entered into the MDF;

8. a list of action items is produced after the review;

9. the designer begins the process of correction/modification dictated by the review.

10. the responsible software engineer monitors the activities to note any effect on the schedule.

5.10.3 Design Inspections

A design inspection performs all the functions of a structured walkthrough, however the inspection is a more formal procedure moderated by staff specifically trained in the technique. Originally developed by IBM, the inspection technique is characterized by specific review team responsibilities (a trained moderator, readers, etc.) and activities (formal preparation, use of formal check-lists, formal error reporting, follow-up, etc.).

Page 5-20

Chapter 5
SOFTWARE DESIGN

SOFTWARE
ENGINEERING
HANDBOOK

Either structured walkthroughs or inspections can be applied during both detailed design and coding. Either technique, properly applied, guarantees higher software quality. For more detail see "Design and Code Inspections to Reduce Errors in Program Development", M.E. Fagan, *IBM Systems Journal,* Volume Fifteen, Number 3, 1976. It is usually counterproductive to use both procedures on a single module.

5.11 MANAGEMENT OF DESIGN

Control and scheduling of the software design effort is difficult because of the "creative" nature of the design process. However, techniques, deliverables and reviews discussed in the previous sections provide a worthwhile framework for effective design management.

The modular nature of software advocated in this chapter allows the design manager to partition effort; review and develop incrementally, and distribute responsibility for the design task among members of the software team.

The design manager must perform the following tasks:

1. organize the design team

2. establish standards

3. schedule design tasks

4. define modes of user/requestor interaction with the design team

5. specify documentation format

6. establish review procedures

Tasks 1,2,5 and 6 have already been discussed in other sections of the Handbook. Design task scheduling and guidelines for user/requestor contact are discussed below.

5.11.1 Design Task Scheduling

The schedule developed during software planning indicates the time boundaries for the design effort. Within these boundaries, the manager must partition effort on individual design tasks. The following *preliminary design tasks* must be estimated: SRS review and clarification, DFD preparation, development of software structure, description of modules and interfaces, document preparation, PDR and iteration.

Although typical data are not readily available, the above tasks normally comprise between 20 and 40 percent of the overall design effort.

Detailed design tasks may be estimated in two ways. The time required to specify procedure and data description for each module may be estimated. As a cross-check, the manager can estimate the effort required to develop all detailed design for afferent, transform and efferent processing functions and the software data base. Estimates for DDRs and iteration also must be made and incorporated within the overall time constraints defined in the Software Plan.

5.11.2 User/Requestor Interaction

User/requestor involvement in software design is a controversial subject. Advantages of user/requestor involvement include a distinct user orientation in the final software; better understanding of delays if technical problems arise; and few surprises at system validation. Disadvantages include the potential for constantly evolving requirements; additional communication paths that can complicate design; and friction between personnel. The ultimate decision must be based on the user/requestor's technical competence, the "user orientation" of the software and contractual or political obligations.

The manager must establish a format for handling formal suggestions made by the user/requestor during design. Although informal suggestions and 'review' can be constructive, a 'look-over-the-shoulder' atmosphere must be discouraged. Many organizations compromise; that is, the user/requestor receives the DESIGN documentation and is asked to participate in the PDR. This happens quite frequently in government related contracts but it should be discouraged when company-proprietary products are being developed.

5.12 SUMMARY

Software design is a manageable process that may be performed using systematic techniques and tools. Preliminary design leads to a description of the overall structure. This structure may be evaluated using distinct measures of good design. The detailed design phase uses a set of tools that encourage a disciplined procedural specification.

The design task requires distinct documentation that is reviewed first at the preliminary design level and later as each module's details are specified. Documentation is the foundation for all subsequent development steps. It is essential to software maintenance. Reviews provide both management and technical control and establish traceability to software requirements.

**SOFTWARE
ENGINEERING
HANDBOOK**

Chapter 6
STRUCTURED CODING

Page 6-1

Once detailed design is complete and appropriate documentation has been generated and reviewed, software is coded. Coding is the translation of the design description into a predetermined programming language.

The coding language for each module is established during planning. Unless severe performance constraints are encountered, all routines should be coded in a high level language (e.g. FORTRAN, PL/M, PASCAL, Ada*). When it can be demonstrated that a performance goal cannot be achieved, assembler language coding may be required. Usually, a change of algorithm will improve performance far more than recoding in assembler language.

The coding process itself follows guidelines established for structured coding. By using a limited number of flow-of-control constructs, readability, testability and maintainability of the software can be dramatically improved.

6.1 STRUCTURE IN PROGRAMS

Since the early 1970s several related software techniques, known collectively as "structured programming", have received much attention in the Software Engineering field. Structured programming is based on two premises:

1. that programs must be designed and written in a manner that is understandable and maintainable;

2. that reliable software can be created by refining a problem (and its solution) into manageable elements.

The concepts of structured design, presented in Chapter 5, are outgrowths of the structured programming philosophy. In this section, the elements of structured programming that are applicable to the coding task are presented.

6.1.1 Importance of Structure

The presence of recognizable patterns at the source code and subroutine levels greatly simplifies both manual and automatic validation of software. The meaning of programs can be understood by programmers in larger, more convenient logical units and automatic tools can be used to aid in the development process.

When software is unstructured, validation is complicated as each statement must be treated as a unique case. That is, the meaning and validity of a module is determined only by examining each of its statements individually. Except for the patterns enforced by language syntax, no other easily recognizable patterns can be assumed to be present.

* Ada is a registered trademark of the United States Department of Defense.

The absence of internal structure is a burden on the programmer, requiring a statement-by-statement examination of execution paths during debugging. In order to understand the software, the programmer must simulate a computer. This technique is tedious and error-prone.

The structured coding approach uses a limited number of logical constructs. The constructs combine groups of program statements into easily recognizable "chunks". Each logical "chunk" is a self-contained procedural element that has a single entry and a single exit.

Structured programs are better than unstructured ones in three areas: increased reliability, easier verification, and easier modification. During design and coding of a program, the programmer converts specified functional requirements into a solution. During the verification of a program, the programmer correlates differences between the 'true' function and the actual characteristics of the program. Finally, during software maintenance, a programmer must understand the program text and then proceed with corrections, adaptations or enhancements.

6.1.2 Structured Coding

Structured coding is a technique that enables program control logic to be represented by a limited number of control structures. Each control structure has a single entry and a single exit, thereby supporting the functional refinement used in top down design.

Each control structure performs a unique operation and may be combined or nested with other control structures. Sequence, repetition and conditional selection are used to build an algorithm with any level of complexity.

Referring to Figure 6.1, the structured constructs are presented in flowchart and box diagram form. SEQUENCE indicates procedural steps that are executed one after another unconditionally. Repetition is accomplished using DOWHILE or REPEAT-UNTIL. Conditional execution is accomplished with the IF-THEN-ELSE construct, and optional selection is performed using the CASE construct.

It should be noted that the GOTO construct (an unconditional branch) is conspicuously absent. In structured coding, GOTOs are strictly controlled and should be used only under the following circumstances:

1. to implement a structured construct in an unstructured programming language (e.g., FORTRAN pre ANSI '77),

2. when elimination of the GOTO will obscure rather than clarify functionality.

By eliminating unconditional branches, "spaghetti-bowl" code—named for the twisted, winding paths that processing takes—is eliminated. Stated more formally, structured coding allows functional domain to be maintained hence, each block of code has a single entry and a single exit.

Page 6-2

**Chapter 6
STRUCTURED CODING**

**SOFTWARE
ENGINEERING
HANDBOOK**

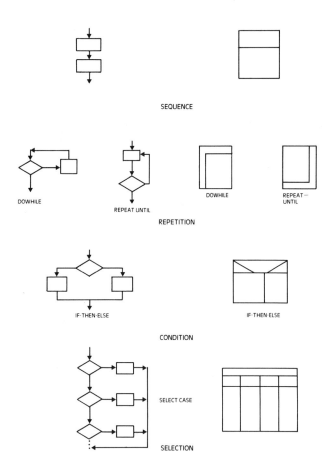

SEQUENCE

DOWHILE

REPEAT UNTIL

REPETITION

DOWHILE

REPEAT— UNTIL

IF-THEN-ELSE

IF-THEN-ELSE

CONDITION

SELECT CASE

SELECTION

Figure 6.1 Structured Constructs

The described constructs improve program "readability" since program structure is developed in a predictable manner, enhancing clarity and emphasizing logical flow. Program readability is also enhanced through modularity. If the size of a single software module is limited to one or, at most, two printed pages, individual subfunctions can be rapidly identified and understood.

6.1.3 Code Format

In addition to the constructs themselves, the coding format (e.g., indentation, commenting conventions) should be defined to provide maximum clarity and readability. Figure 6.2 illustrates possible indentation and commenting conventions. For clarity and understandability, the contents of repetitive loops and the else-part of IF statements should be indented. For example:

```
            DO 20, I = 1, NM
                NP = I + 1
                DO 10, J = NP, N
                    IF ( A(I).GE.A(J) ) THEN
                        T = A(J)
                        A(J) = A(I)
                        A(I) = T
```

```
            ELSE
                CONTINUE
            ENDIF
    10      CONTINUE
    20  CONTINUE
```

Referring to the above Fortran-77 code fragment, it is easy to discern the contents of both DO loops and the THEN-part of the IF statement. Indentation enhances clarity by showing the logical structure of the code.

The importance of software modularity has already been stressed. Each routine should be limited in length - one or two output pages is recommended. In general, one executable statement should occupy a printed line.

6.2 CODE DOCUMENTATION

Internal software documentation (documentation that is part of the source listing or is implied by the code itself) is considered in this section.

Internal documentation begins with a prologue for a module. The prologue serves as an introduction to the module and should contain:

1. a statement of the routine's purpose or function
2. a reference to design documentation
3. a brief description of the algorithm used
4. a list of arguments and their meaning
5. a list of error conditions and branches
6. a list of called routines
7. identification of author, reviewer and date
8. a list of dated modifications that occur during maintenance phase.

The prologue may also contain any general information that can be of use to the reader.

Once the prologue has been written, internal documentation begins with the selection of variable names and labels. Variable names and labels should be self explanatory whenever language constraints permit. For example, WIDTH is a better variable name than XX1 when a dimension is described. Similarly, labels should be identified when language rules permit.

The final and most important level of internal software documentation is the source level comment. Comments should be used to clarify—not reword or repeat—what a segment of code does and why. For example, the comment

```
        .
        .
        .

C           IF DATE LESS THAN 15 SET I to 6
```

24-Jun-1982 17:01:55
30-Oct-1981 10:32:26

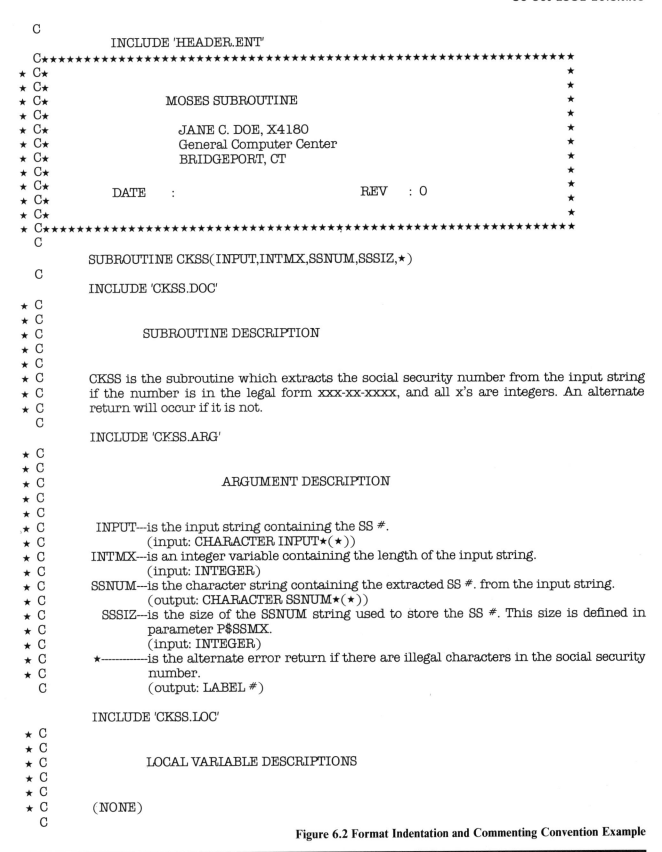

```
      C
                INCLUDE 'HEADER.ENT'
      C***************************************************************
  *   C*                                                          *
  *   C*                                                          *
  *   C*           MOSES SUBROUTINE                               *
  *   C*                                                          *
  *   C*              JANE C. DOE, X4180                          *
  *   C*              General Computer Center                     *
  *   C*              BRIDGEPORT, CT                              *
  *   C*                                                          *
  *   C*                                                          *
  *   C*       DATE    :                    REV   : 0             *
  *   C*                                                          *
  *   C*                                                          *
  *   C***************************************************************
      C
              SUBROUTINE CKSS(INPUT,INTMX,SSNUM,SSSIZ,*)
      C
              INCLUDE 'CKSS.DOC'
  *   C
  *   C
  *   C           SUBROUTINE DESCRIPTION
  *   C
  *   C
  *   C   CKSS is the subroutine which extracts the social security number from the input string
  *   C   if the number is in the legal form xxx-xx-xxxx, and all x's are integers. An alternate
  *   C   return will occur if it is not.
      C
              INCLUDE 'CKSS.ARG'
  *   C
  *   C
  *   C               ARGUMENT DESCRIPTION
  *   C
  *   C
  *   C    INPUT---is the input string containing the SS #.
  *   C            (input: CHARACTER INPUT*(*))
  *   C   INTMX---is an integer variable containing the length of the input string.
  *   C            (input: INTEGER)
  *   C   SSNUM---is the character string containing the extracted SS #. from the input string.
  *   C            (output: CHARACTER SSNUM*(*))
  *   C    SSSIZ---is the size of the SSNUM string used to store the SS #. This size is defined in
  *   C            parameter P$SSMX.
  *   C            (input: INTEGER)
  *   C   *------------is the alternate error return if there are illegal characters in the social security
  *   C            number.
      C            (output: LABEL #)

              INCLUDE 'CKSS.LOC'
  *   C
  *   C
  *   C           LOCAL VARIABLE DESCRIPTIONS
  *   C
  *   C
  *   C    (NONE)
      C
```

Figure 6.2 Format Indentation and Commenting Convention Example

Chapter 6
STRUCTURED CODING

Page 6-4

**SOFTWARE
ENGINEERING
HANDBOOK**

24-Jun-1982 17:01:55
30-Oct-1981 10:32:26

```
        IMPLICIT INTEGER (A-Z)
        INCLUDE 'SYSIO.CM'
★ C
★ C    This commom defines the system input and system output logical unit number. This is set
★ C    in BLOCK DATA IGLOBK.
★ C
★ C    /SYSIO/
★ C      SYSIN-----is an integer variable containing the logical unit number for system input.
★ C      SYSOUT--is an integer variable containing the logical unit number for system output.
★ C
★        COMMON/SYSIO/SYSIN/SYSIN,SYSOUT
★        INTEGER SYSIN,SYSOUT
         LOGICAL CKNUM
         CHARACTER INPUT★(★),SSNUM★(★)
         SSNUM = ''
         DSFLG  = 0
         DO 100 II = 1, INTMX
                  L = II
  C---
  C---CHECK IF ZZZ OF ZZZ-XXX-XXX ARE NUMERIC
  C---
                  DO 500 I = 1,3
                           K = I
                           IF(.NOT.CKNUM(INPUT(L:L))) GO TO 1000
                           SSNUM(K:K) = INPUT(L:L)
                           L = L + 1
   500                CONTINUE
  C---
  C---CHECK IF THE '-' OR ' ' OR A NUMERIC :XXX-XX-XXXX OR XXX XX XXXX OR
  C---XXXXXXXXX
  C---IF THE STARTED THE SS# IN THE FORM XXX-XXX THEN IF MUST CONTINUE
  C---IN THE FORM XXX-XX-XXXX
  C---
                  IF(INPUT(L:L) .NE. '-' .AND. INPUT(L:L) .NE. ' ') THEN
                           IF(CNNUM(INPUT(L:L))) THEN
                                    K = K + 1
                                    SSNUM(K:K) = '-'
                           ELSE
                                    GO TO 1000
                           ENDIF
                  ELSE
                           K = K + 1
                           SSNUM(K:K) = '-'
                           L = L + 1
                           DSFLG = 1
                  ENDIF
  C---
  C---CHECK IF ZZ OF XXX-ZZ-XXXX ARE NUMERIC
  C---
                  DO 600 I = 1,2
                           K = K + 1
                           IF(.NOT.CKNUM(INPUT(L:L))) GO TO 1000
                           SSNUM(K:K) = INPUT(L:L)
                           L = L + 1
   600                CONTINUE
```

Figure 6.2 (continued)

**SOFTWARE
ENGINEERING
HANDBOOK**

**Chapter 6
STRUCTURED CODING**

Page 6-5

24-Jun-1982 17:01:55
30-Oct-1981 10:32:26

```
C---
C---CHECK IF THE '-' OR ' ' OR A NUMERIC :XXX-XX-XXXX OR XXX XX XXXX OR
C---XXXXXXXXX
C---IF THE STARTED THE SS# IN THE FORM XXX-XX THEN IF MUST CONTINUE
C---IN THE FORM XXX-XX-XXXX
C---
                IF(INPUT(L:L) .NE. '-' .AND. INPUT(L:L) .N.E. ' ') THEN
                        IF(DSFLG .EQ. 1) GO TO 1000
                        IF(CKNUM(INPUT(L:L))) THEN
                                K = K + 1
                                SSNUM(K:K) = '-'
                        ELSE
                                GO TO 1000
                        ENDIF
                ELSE
                        K = K + 1
                        SSNUM(K:K) = '-'
                        L = L + 1
                ENDIF
C---
C---CHECK IF ZZZ OF XXX-XX-ZZZZ ARE NUMERIC
C---
                DO 700 I = 1,4
                        K = K + 1
                        IF(.NOT.CKNUM(INPUT(L:L))) GO TO 1000
                        SSNUM(K:K) = INPUT(L:L)
                        L = L + 1
 700            CONTINUE
C---
C---IF DO NOT HAVE TRAILING BLANKS THEN ERROR MESSAGE AND RETURN ELSE
C---JUST RETURN
C---
                IF(L .GE. INTMX) RETURN
                IF(INPUT(L:INTMX) .NE.' ') GO TO 1000
                RETURN
 100            CONTINUE
C---
C---ILLEGAL CHARACTER IN SS #
C---
 1000           CONTINUE
                WRITE(SYSOUT,2000) K
 2000             FORMAT('***ILLEGAL CHARACTER IN SS NUMBER NEAR COLUMN ',
     +                  I2,'***')
                RETURN
                END
```

Figure 6.2 (continued)

Page 6-6

Chapter 6
STRUCTURED CODING

SOFTWARE
ENGINEERING
HANDBOOK

IF(DATE.LE.15) I = 6

adds no useful information. A better comment might be

C   FOR 1ST HALF OF MONTH, INDEX IS 6

The frequency of comments depends upon the complexity of the code. The software engineer must consider the situation of a reader who is totally unfamiliar with the code. Enough explanatory information must be produced to provide clarity. However, too many comments can hinder readability, thus, the right mix must be established.

6.3 ANTIBUGGING

In his text on software development, Yourdon* defines antibugging as "the philosophy of writing programs in such a way as to make bugs less likely to occur - and when they do occur (which is inevitable), to make them more noticeable to the programmer and the user". This implies conducting as much error checking as is practical and possible in each routine.

Some tests which should be incorporated into all software are:

1. input data checks
2. interface data checks, i.e., tests to determine validity of data passed from calling routine
3. data base verification
4. operator command checks
5. operating system checks (difficult)
6. output data checks

Although all tests are not required in every routine, error-checking is an essential part of all software. Generally, antibugging is specified during detailed design, and implemented during the coding step.

6.4 CODING STYLE

Computer programming is a human activity and a description of a "good" program can only be made qualitatively. However, certain guidelines for coding style can be established that result in efficient, adaptable, easily understood code.

The following style guidelines, suggested by Yourdon, should be applied by all software professionals:

1. Use structured coding techniques
2. Don't misuse language features
3. Don't write programs that modify themselves
4. Avoid multitasking unless absolutely necessary

---

* Yourdon, E., Techniques of Program Structure and Design, Prentice-Hall, 1975.

5. Avoid unnecessarily complicated arithmetic and logical expressions
6. Parenthesize to avoid ambiguity
7. Be simple and direct

Programming style is a combination of the above guidelines and the use of common sense. Good style results in efficient, easily read code that requires little or no external documentation to be understood.

A detailed discussion of programming style would be out of place. For the reader interested in further discussion of this topic, Kernighan and Plauger's *The Elements of Programming Style* is recommended. This short (132 pp.) text gives an excellent overview of programming style and provides many examples in FORTRAN, COBOL and PL/1. Table 6.1 summarizes the many rules presented in Kernighan and Plauger's text.

TABLE 6.1

RULES FOR GOOD PROGRAMMING STYLE
(From Kernighan and Plauger)

Write clearly—don't be too clever.

Say what you mean, simply and directly.

Use library functions.

Avoid temporary variables.

Write clearly—don't sacrifice clarity for "efficiency".

Let the machine do the dirty work.

Replace repetitive expressions by calls to a common routine.

Choose variable names that won't be confused.

Avoid unnecessary branches.

Don't use conditional branches as a substitute for a logical expression.

If a logical expression is hard to understand, try transforming it.

Use data arrays to avoid repetitive control sequences.

Choose a data representation that makes the program simple.

Write first in an easy-to-understand pseudo-language; then translate into whatever language you have to use.

Use IF...ELSEIF...ELSEIF...ELSE...ENDIF to implement multi-way branches.

Modularize. Use subroutines.

Make sure comments and code agree.

SOFTWARE
ENGINEERING
HANDBOOK

Chapter 6
STRUCTURED CODING

Page 6-7

Don't just echo the code with comments—make every comment count.

Don't comment or patch bad code—rewrite it.

Use variable names that mean something.

Use statement labels that mean something.

Format a program to help the reader understand it.

Document your data layouts.

Use GOTOs only to implement a fundamental structure.

Avoid GOTOs completely if you can keep the program readable.

Write and test a big program in small pieces.

Use recursive procedures for recursively-defined data structures.

Test input for plausibility and validity.

Make sure input doesn't violate the limits of the program.

Terminate input by end-of-file or marker, not by count.

Identify bad input; recover if possible.

Make input easy to prepare and output self-explanatory.

Use uniform input formats.

Make input easy to proofread.

Use free-form input when possible.

Use self-identifying input. Allow defaults. Echo both on output.

Make sure all variables are initialized before use.

Don't stop at one bug.

Use debugging compilers.

Initialize constants with DATA statements or INITIAL attributes; initialize variables with executable code.

Watch out for off-by-one error.

Take care to branch the right way on equality.

Be careful when a loop exits to the same place from side and bottom.

Make sure your code "does nothing" gracefully.

Test programs at their boundary values.

Check some answers by hand.

10.0 times 0.1 is hardly ever 1.0.

Don't compare floating point numbers solely for equality.

Make it right before you make it faster.

Make it fail-safe before you make it faster.

Make it clear before you make it faster.

Don't sacrifice clarity for small gains in "efficiency".

Let your compiler do the simple optimizations.

Don't strain to re-use code; reorganize instead.

Make sure special cases are truly special.

Keep it simple to make it faster.

Don't diddle code to make it faster - find a better algorithm.

Instrument your programs. Measure before making "efficiency" changes.

6.5 PORTABLE SOFTWARE

Software "portability" or "transferability" may be defined as a measure of the ease with which a computer program may be moved from one computing environment to another. Among the factors that affect portability are: the computers involved, the software application, programming language(s), and special techniques used during software development.

Although the transfer of software from one computer to another can rarely be accomplished without some conversion effort, a number of techniques may be used to increase portability. During software design, modules should not be highly coupled to operating system characteristics; standard data manipulation should be used; packaging should be considered; and standard languages must be specified.

Modular software design is essential to good portability. Software features that will require conversion (e.g. operating system dependent I/O) should be isolated in separate routines whenever possible. This strategy facilitates the conversion effort by enabling techniques to be concentrated on manageable elements. During software coding, transferability should be considered with regard to language selection, availability of translators/compilers, and special coding features.

The most important consideration for generating portable code is use of a standard-defined, higher-level programming language available on a majority of hardware configurations. Conversion of assembler language code can be at least ten times more difficult than conversion of the same module coded in a high level language.

Page 6-8

Chapter 6
STRUCTURED CODING

**SOFTWARE
ENGINEERING
HANDBOOK**

Other coding considerations that may enhance transferability are: 1) parameterization and 2) code constraints. Parameterization is a programming technique that allows important numeric and symbolic data to be altered via a single statement. As a simple example, consider a routine that contains FORTRAN I/O to the card reader and printer. If each READ/WRITE contains the unit number in explicit form (Figure 6.3(a)). All I/O statements in the routine must be changed when unit numbers change. Figure 6.3(b) illustrates a parameterized version of the above example. Note that only the definitions of KR and KP need be changed, allowing for easier and less error-prone conversion.

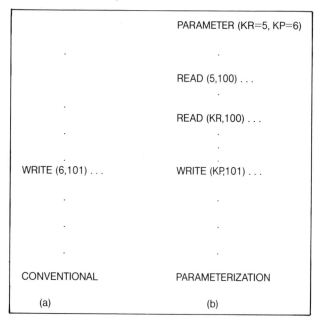

Figure 6.3 Code Parameterization Example

Coding constraints can enhance portability by avoiding language features that are difficult to transfer. Such features are the exotic or little used constructs that may yield different results when compiled on a different machine.

Finally, software portability is greatly enhanced by complete documentation, a natural result of the Software Engineering process. If software transfer is likely, a formal transfer plan should be developed as part of software requirements. The transfer plan indicates conversion techniques that will be required.

6.6 IMPLEMENTATION TOOLS

Implementation tools may be defined as a set of techniques and automated methods that facilitate various phases of the software engineering process. Some tools, such as editors and diagnostic software, are provided as part of most operating systems. Other tools must be purchased or developed to supplement the software development process.

In this section an overview of the basic types of implementation tools is presented. In addition, an introduction to the specific tools that are part of General Electric's Software Development Environment (SDE) is presented. Each software organization must evaluate specific tools to determine which will best serve individual development requirements. In fact, it is often necessary to develop or purchase specialized tools to meet local requirements.

Implementation tools are used to facilitate the generation and verification of source code, and may be generally divided into three categories:

1. detailed design source code preparation
2. language processing
3. program evaluation aids

During *source code preparation* a number of facilities should be available to enable the programmer to enter and format language statements. Once source code has been entered, *language processing* tools, such as macroprocessors and optimizing compilers are often invoked. *Program evaluation aids* may be used to complement documentation tools and to insure that programming standards are maintained.

6.6.1 Source Code Preparation

The editor is probably the most important source code preparation tool. Almost every operating system contains an editor, but there is great variation in the usefulness of these tools. An editor must be "human oriented", that is, its command structure should be easily learned and easily used.

Most good editors can work at both the source line and character level (current efforts are focused on full screen — 24 lines by 80 characters — editor development). Most have powerful "find" and "insert" commands that can be applied globally or to some set of source lines. A good editor allows commands to either be very brief (i.e., a single character when possible) or fully spelled out and understandable. The expert prefers the former, the novice the latter. Error messages should be self explanatory. Finally, an automatic backup facility should be available so that source files cannot be destroyed inadvertently.

Other source code preparation tools include indentation and reformatting aids. Indentation aids are generally applied to existing software. These tools provide loop and logical indentation. Reformatting aids are used to restructure existing code (e.g., renumber FORTRAN labels in ascending order) for better understanding.

6.6.2 Language Processing

A number of software tools have been developed to complement and extend programming language compilers. Among these tools, the precompiler, macroprocessor and special compilers provide the most significant benefit.

SOFTWARE
ENGINEERING
HANDBOOK

**Chapter 6
STRUCTURED CODING**

Page 6-9

The precompiler or preprocessor accepts as input source level code with extended constructs that are unacceptable to the programming language compiler. The precompiler is executed immediately before the compiler and generates syntax that is acceptable to the compiler.

The purpose of the precompiler is to provide structured constructs where none exist; to provide a method for substituting variable names and code groupings at compile time; and to extend the programming language without modifying the compiler itself.

A typical precompiler for FORTRAN-77 might provide the following constructs:

DO WHILE; REPEAT UNTIL; CASE.

These constructs are used by the programmer and translated by the preprocessor into analogous FORTRAN code.

A macroprocessor is often part of precompilation software. It allows access to a "macro library" that contains tested code for frequently encountered operations or procedures. By using an INCLUDE construct, the programmer can incorporate blocks of source level statements into previously generated source code. The macroprocessor is extremely useful for debugging because diagnostic operations may be simply included.

Special compilers include the checkout compiler and the optimizing compiler. The checkout compiler executes source code "semi-interpretively"; that is, the programmer can direct the progress of program execution and examine memory and register contents. The optimizing compiler enhances object code generation by applying techniques that result in extremely efficient executable code.

6.6.3 Programming Evaluation Aids

Programming evaluation aids perform two distinct functions: 1) to analyze source code for conformity to programming standards and semantic clarity; 2) to provide data for later software documentation. Tools in this category include automatic testing software and automatic flow charting and cross reference programs.

6.6.4 A Generic Development Environment

The tools discussed in the preceding paragraphs are examples of automated tools which should be part of any practical, productive setting for application development. Such environments should include vendor specific packages as well as additional software developed by the user for a specific local need. All tools require integration into the user setting to help increase productivity and improve software quality. The tool box should be hosted on a machine capable of supporting the people doing the development as well as those managing the software effort.

An environment for software development must encompass tools for design, coding, testing, documentation, and configuration management. Examples of tool categories are listed below:

* design definition
* code generation
* product evaluation
* product control
* management report generation
* utilities

A generic development environment should support all phases of software development with automated methods. Utilization of the tools provided not only enhances the ability to develop systems more efficiently, but also relieves and automates many of the burdensome tasks associated with development such as documentation of code, coding comments, and configuration management.

6.7 DELIVERABLES AND REVIEWS

The primary deliverable for the coding step is an internally documented, syntax-error-free "source listing". Obviously, a module that is correct syntactically is not necessarily correct semantically. That is, a lack of compiler errors does not mean that the module will function properly. A unit test procedure, discussed in the next chapter, is used to verify the semantic correctness of the source listing.

The source listing for each module is reviewed at a code walkthrough or code inspection. The coder, software engineer responsible for detailed design, and another team member desk-check the module code. The walkthrough format has been described in Chapter 5. An indication and sign-off may be established as part of the Module Development Folder (MDF) cover sheet.

The code walkthrough should stress three review criteria:

1. traceability of the code to detailed design and a recheck of correctness;

2. internal documentation and readability;

3. maintenance of structured coding standards and proper language usage.

Because coding is an implicit review of detailed design, minor design errors may be uncovered. It is absolutely essential that the detailed design representation and code correspond to each other; therefore, if code changes are required, modification begins with the corresponding design update.

A number of software organizations embed the detailed design description (design language) as part of the internal documentation of a module. In this way, code changes and the resultant detailed design update can be accomplished simultaneously.

Chapter 6
STRUCTURED CODING

Page 6-10

**SOFTWARE
ENGINEERING
HANDBOOK**

6.8 MANAGEMENT CONSIDERATIONS

Coding is the software development process step that is furthest removed from management cognizance. However, the software engineering manager must:

1. establish guidelines or standards for structured coding and internal documentation;

2. encourage code walkthrough as a review of the coding step;

3. provide coding tools that will improve productivity and software quality;

4. strive for a coding environment (i.e., enough terminals, computer availability, memory, support software) that does not frustrate human efforts;

5. provide training for all software staff.

The software manager must remember that even after code has been successfully reviewed, as much as 40 percent of the development effort (testing) remains.

6.9 SUMMARY

Structure within a module is specified during detailed design and implemented during the coding step. A limited set of coding constructs is essential to improve software readability, testability and maintainability. Code must be internally documented as coding progresses, not after the fact. Standard language features should be used so that software portability is maintained. Every attempt should be made to code in a high level programming language. Empirical evidence indicates that high level languages improve both productivity and software quality.

The deliverable of the coding step - the source listing - is reviewed during a code walkthrough. Modifications to code must be reflected in the detailed design representation.

The coding step is particularly sensitive to tools and resources that aid the programmer. Software management must establish guidelines and provide necessary resources to assure the success of this step in the software life cycle. Good structured code is a natural consequence of good structured design.

Testing accounts for 40-50 percent of the development effort for a typical software project. In fact, for critical human-rated software systems testing can consume 80 percent of the overall development effort.

Unfortunately, software testing is the least understood of the steps in the Software Engineering process. However, because of the high cost associated with testing, research in software "quality assurance", automated testing, and test procedures is being conducted at an ever-increasing rate.

In this chapter specific procedures for test of a software system are presented. Three levels of testing, unit integration, and validation provide quality assurance for the individual module; for the system as it is being constructed; and for the software as a complete entity.

7.1 TEST OBJECTIVES AND DEFINITIONS

Software testing is a quality assurance function with the following objectives:

1. verification of the software design by evaluating structural interfaces and procedural elements;

2. validation of software requirements;

3. to provide a method for systematic assembly of the software; and

4. definition of a quality baseline to which maintenance can be traced.

Test objectives are satisfied by a series of tests that begin with design reviews and culminate with validation testing of the software subsystem.

All objectives must be designed to satisfy one overriding goal:

The goal of software testing is to force the software to fail so that errors may be uncovered.

In other words, a successful test is one that uncovers an error, rather than one for which no errors are found.

7.1.1 Software Reliability and Failures

Definitions of software reliability and failure are interdependent and somewhat controversial. A software failure is the occurrence of a fault that may be categorized as:

1. nonconformity to specification
2. nonconformity to documentation
3. violation of design constraints OR
4. "a situation in which the software does not do what the user/requestor reasonably expects it to do!"

A simple definition of software reliability may be stated as "the probability that a program will operate without failure for a given period of time."

7.1.2 Test and Debug

The terms "test" and "debug" are often used interchangeably. However, in the context of this chapter, test and debug are viewed as entirely separate tasks.

Testing is a systematic process that may be pre-planned and explicitly verified. Test techniques and procedures may be defined in advance and a sequence of test steps may be specified.

Debugging is an "art" used to isolate and correct the cause of an error. The symptoms exhibited by a fault in software are not always directly traceable to the fault. Debugging combines a systematic search with an intuitive feel for the nature of the error and program.

7.2 THE TEST CHRONOLOGY

Software testing is the most tedious, unpredictable and expensive phase in software development. To ease this situation, a distinct test chronology may be defined. The test chronology is illustrated in Figure 7.1. The time sequence of events may be viewed top to bottom in the Figure.

Software "testing" actually begins with the preliminary and detailed design reviews and the code walk-through. These manual pre-implementation "tests" can isolate a significant percentage of all faults in the software. In addition, the cost and effort associated with pre-implementation test (i.e., reviews) is far less than computer based tests that would be used to isolate the same errors.

Once the code walkthrough is completed and the code approved, a module undergoes unit testing. The unit test verifies input and output for the module; indicates validity of the function or sub-function performed by the module, and shows traceability to design.

As modules are successfully unit tested, an integration test plan is developed to incorporate each module into the overall software structure. Integration testing accomplishes two tasks:

1. provides a means for assembling the software;
2. tests each step in assembly to isolate errors introduced by newly incorporated modules.

Formal deliverables are developed for integration testing and a two-part test review is conducted during this step.

Page 7-2

Chapter 7
SOFTWARE TESTING

**SOFTWARE
ENGINEERING
HANDBOOK**

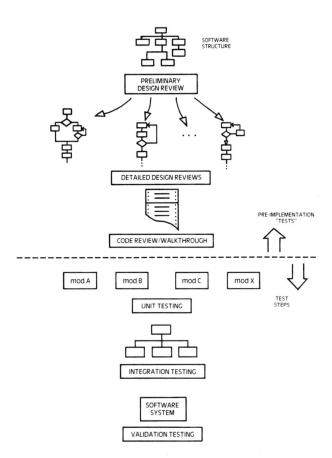

Figure 7.1 Test Chronology

The last step in the testing phase verifies that the assembled software system meets all requirements defined in the SOFTWARE REQUIREMENTS SPECIFICATION. This step, called validation testing, is the last before software is released from the development organization for system test.

Each step in the test phase has distinct deliverables, reviews and technical considerations. The following sections present each of the three test steps in detail.

7.3 UNIT TESTING

During unit testing, each module is tested individually and the module interface is verified for consistency with the design specification. All important processing paths through the module are tested for expected results. All error handling paths are also tested. The unit test procedure is represented schematically in Figure 7.2.

Unit testing starts with an informal test plan that describes specific classes of tests and test data. Once the test plan is prepared, test cases are generated. Test data should be care-

fully designed to exercise in-bounds and out-of-bounds conditions. Expected results for all test cases must be defined in advance. In many cases, programs known as "drivers" are used to exercise the module and record and report results. Many testing procedures incorporate combinations of these techniques.

If timing is an important characteristic of the module, tests should be generated that measure time critical paths in the worst case situation and the average case. This information is essential for performance measurement.

Although unit testing is generally considered the responsibility of the implementation programmer, the project leader should be aware of the unit test results. All unit test cases and results become part of the Module Development Folder. The test cases used for unit testing may become a subset of tests during the next step—integration testing.

7.4 INTEGRATION TESTING

The software system is assembled and tested in a systematic manner during the integration testing step. Integration testing is a formal procedure that must be carefully planned and coordinated with the completion dates of unit tested modules.

Integration testing begins with a software structure that has been defined using stubs. A stub, illustrated in Figure 7.3, is a dummy module that allows testing of superordinate (i.e., calling program) control and interface correctness. Stubs are replaced by unit tested modules or builds (described on page 7-3) as integration testing proceeds.

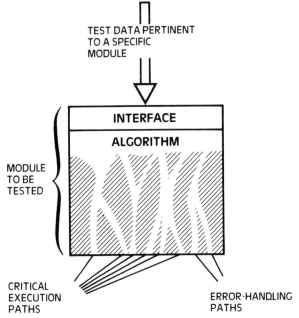

Figure 7.2 Unit Test

**SOFTWARE
ENGINEERING
HANDBOOK**

**Chapter 7
SOFTWARE TESTING**

Page 7-3

| SUBPROGRAM NAME |
| INTERFACE DESCRIPTION |
| CODE TO INDICATE ENTRY |
| CODE TO INDICATE PROPER TRANSFER OF INTERFACE DATA |
| RETURN |

Figure 7.3 The Stub

Integration testing may be performed using "bottom-up" or "top-down" techniques. The bottom-up approach incorporates one or more modules into a build; tests the build, and then integrates it into the software structure. The build normally comprises a set of modules that perform a major function of the software system. Initially, the function may be represented by a stub that is replaced when the build is integrated.

In the top-down approach, individual stubs are replaced so that top-level control is tested first, followed by stub replacements that move downward in the software structure (Figure 7.4). Using top-down integration, all modules that comprise a major function (e.g., a specific input algorithm) are integrated, thereby allowing an operational function to be demonstrated prior to completion of the entire system.

Most practical integration test plans make use of both bottom-up and top-down techniques. Scheduling constraints and the need for parallel testing dictate the compromise approach. The techniques are summarized in Figure 7.5.

7.4.1 Integration Planning and Scheduling

The number of integration levels the classes of tests to be performed, and the order in which routines and builds are incorporated into the overall software structure are considered in the INTEGRATION TEST PLAN. Several factors should be considered:

1. Are routines to be integrated in a pure top-down manner or should builds be developed to test subfunctions first?

2. In what order should major software functions be incorporated?

3. Is the scheduling of module code and test consistent with the order of integration?

4. Is special hardware required to test certain routines?

Once these questions are answered, a list of all modules is developed. Associated with each module are its unit test completion date, date of first integration, destination (e.g., build into which it will be incorporated or functional level) and a reference to required test data/results for that module.

When equipment not present is needed for testing the software, the test schedule must be checked for consistency with that hardware's delivery schedule. For example, if three display terminals are needed for checking display software, tests must be scheduled during a period when the terminals will be available. Leeway (schedule slack) should be allowed for hardware installation and possible late delivery.

Another important consideration during integration test planning is the amount of test software (e.g., drivers, test case generation) that must be developed to adequately test the required functionality. For example, it may be cost effective to delay testing of a communication function until hardware is available rather than generate test software to simulate communication links. Similarly, it may be better to include certain completed modules in the software structure in order to avoid having to develop software drivers. These decisions are made on the basis of cost and risk.

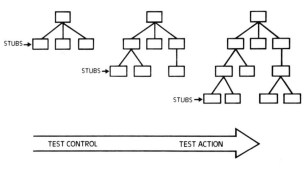

Figure 7.4 Top Down Testing

Page 7-4

Chapter 7
SOFTWARE TESTING

SOFTWARE
ENGINEERING
HANDBOOK

```
TOP-DOWNTESTING      BOTTOM-UP TESTING

• highest level (control)    • low level (work) modules
  modules tested with          are incorporated into
  "stubs"                      functional subsystem

• next level stubs           • subsystems combined
  replaced by unit
  tested modules

• continue until all         • overall system assembled
  stubs replaced

                             • methods may be combined
```

Figure 7.5 Integration Test Procedure

The format of the INTEGRATION TEST PLAN is described in Appendix A.5. An abbreviated outline of integration test documentation is given in Figure 7.6.

7.4.2 Integration Procedure

The integration test procedure describes all technical details for tasks defined in the INTEGRATION TEST PLAN. Each test phase is explicitly addressed with emphasis placed on test techniques, test data and expected results. A detailed description of all test software is included.

The integration test procedure must be designed to uncover errors that result from:

1. incorrect interface implementation
2. intermodular "noise" caused by access to global data
3. file and data structure integrity violations
4. improper control and sequencing of modules
5. inappropriate/incorrect error-handling

The stated purpose of each test should include the class of errors that the test hopes to uncover.

Each time a module or build is incorporated into the overall structure, tests are generated for the new addition and old tests are rerun to assure that intermodular "noise" has not caused problems in other (already integrated) modules. Initially, interfaces are retested, followed by in-depth testing of the module or build.

All integration tests are performed by a test team and are demonstrated to a reviewer. Ideally, the test team should contain a mix of experienced and junior personnel and should be independent of the development team.

7.4.3 Test Report

At completion of a predefined integration level, a test report is written. The report documents test results and lists any discrepancies which must be resolved before the tested components can be used as the foundation for another inte-

gration level. A final test report is generated at the completion of testing indicating any unresolved difficiencies that require management attention.

```
1.0   SCOPE
2.0   APPLICABLE DOCUMENTS
3.0   PLAN
3.1     Test Phase Description
3.2     Test Schedule
3.3     Test Software
4.0   PROCEDURE
4.N     Phase N Test Procedure
4.N.1     Purpose
4.N.2     Technique
4.N.3     Modules to be Tested
4.N.4     Test Software
4.N.5     Test Data and Expected Results
5.0   SPECIAL PROVISIONS.
6.0   APPENDICES
```

Figure 7.6 Integration Test Documentation

```
1.0   SCOPE
2.0   APPLICABLE DOCUMENTS
3.0   PLAN
3.1     Test Segments
3.2     Schedule
3.3     Test Software
4.0   PROCEDURE
4.N     Test Description
5.0   VALIDATION CRITERIA/VARIANCE BOUNDS
6.0   SPECIAL PROVISIONS
7.0   VALIDATION CHECK LIST
```

Figure 7.7 Validation Test Documentation

7.5 VALIDATION TESTING

Validation testing demonstrates that the software is operational and conforms to all functional and performance requirements contained in the SOFTWARE REQUIREMENTS SPECIFICATION. Testing is guided by a VALIDATION TEST PLAN (Appendix A.5) based on these requirements. The generation of this Test Plan can begin when the SRS has been completed and approved. Validation testing serves to demonstrate that all functional and performance characteristics of a software specification have been achieved. Both the development organization and the requestor are involved in validation testing.

Ideally, validation testing is performed by an independent test group that has not been involved in design or implementation of the software. This independent test group should include top-level personnel and should approach testing from the ultimate user's viewpoint. Whenever possible, the user should be allowed to participate in validation testing, establishing the credibility of the tests.

SOFTWARE
ENGINEERING
HANDBOOK

Chapter 7
SOFTWARE TESTING

Page 7-5

7.5.1 Test Plan

Unlike other testing activities, a VALIDATION TEST PLAN defining functions to be tested and expected results has been prepared long before testing starts. TEST PLAN inputs are derived from two primary sources: the SYSTEM DESIGN and SOFTWARE REQUIREMENT SPECIFICATION.

An outline of validation test documentation is given in Figure 7.7. The test plan defines: "segments" that validate each software function, a schedule for testing each function, and any software that must be developed to simulate hardware or software not available to the developer. In addition, special provisions for hardware, personnel and other validation resources are specified.

7.5.2 Test Procedure

The goal of unit and integration testing is to uncover latent errors by making the software fail. The goal of validation testing is demonstrating software traceability to requirements. The validation test procedure consists of the following steps:

1. execute test cases that exercise a software function or performance requirement;

2. document and review all results;

Testing is complete when all tests have been executed correctly and reviewed. If one or more validation tests fail, the deficiency is recorded on a "deficiency list" and passed to the development organization for evaluation.

The deficiency list is reviewed by development management and the user/requestor; corrective action is scheduled as required.

7.5.3 System Test

Software is but one part of a system that can include hardware and personnel. Therefore, software must be incorporated into the overall system and tested as each function of the system is integrated.

System testing requirements and the system role of software are defined in the SYSTEM SPECIFICATION. The software organization is rarely responsible for system testing. However, software development and/or maintenance personnel should be available to diagnose problem reports that have been attributed to software. The level of involvement in system testing is directly related to the importance of software within the system. If large manpower requirements are foreseen, these should be allowed for in the testing budget and schedule.

7.6 THE TEST TEAM

There is a growing trend within large software development organizations to establish a Software Quality Assurance (SQA) suborganization. One element of the SQA organization is the *test team* whose chief responsibility is integration and validation test planning and execution.

The rationale for a separate test team is supported by the following arguments:

1. A test team can embrace the test philosophy stated in Section 7.1; i.e., the team has succeeded when thorough testing uncovers errors.

2. Because the test team has not worked on software development, errors that might be "invisible" to a developer are likely to be uncovered by the tester.

3. Better records of the type, frequency and cause of errors are maintained. The test team is not concerned with masking the occurrence of errors to "look good".

The relationship between the development and test organization is illustrated in Figure 7.8. A mild adversary relationship between the teams is to be expected, but cooperation must be strongly encouraged by management. Both teams have a vested interest in assuring the quality of software is high.

7.7 TEST PRINCIPLES

This section is devoted to a number of worthwhile test concepts, principles, guidelines and checklists proposed in The Art of Software Testing, Glenford Meyers, Wiley-Interscience, 1979. This software testing text is highly recommended for all Software Engineers.

7.7.1 General Guidelines

Meyers states the following "principles" of software testing:

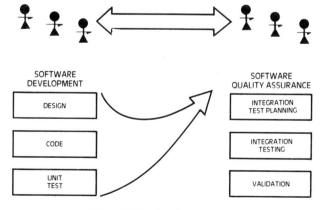

Figure 7.8 Testing Organization

Page 7-6

**Chapter 7
SOFTWARE TESTING**

**SOFTWARE
ENGINEERING
HANDBOOK**

1. Testing should not be performed by the person or team that developed the software.

2. Testing should not be planned under the tacit assumption that no errors will be found.

3. A necessary part of test documentation is the specification of expected results.

4. Test for invalid and unexpected input conditions as well as valid conditions.

5. The probability of the existence of more errors in a module or group of modules is directly proportional to the number of errors already found.

6. Testing is the process of executing software with the intent of finding errors.

Meyers maintains that "... testing is an extremely creative and intellectually challenging task". When testing follows the above principles, the creative element of test design and execution rivals any of the preceding software development steps.

7.7.2 Test Case Design Techniques

Proper test case design is critically important to the success and thoroughness of the testing process. During the period 1965-75, a number of test case design methods were proposed in the literature. Myers summarizes many of these in his book on software testing.

Two philosophies are applied to test case design. The first, *black box-testing,* uses only the software requirements specification to generate test cases. That is, the software is viewed as a black-box transform—inputs are varied and output is examined for correctness. If a good SRS exists, black-box testing can be successful, but it is not enough. The second testing philosophy, *white-box testing,* uses the logical flow of the detailed design (or code) as a driver for test case design. White-box testing examines specific paths in a module to determine if non-executable paths exist; infinite loops are present; incorrect results accrue for executable paths; and, logic is consistent and correct. Finally, a combined approach, *gray-box testing,* incorporates elements of both philosophies.

The test case *design* can be conducted systematically using published techniques. An overview of the most common test case design techniques follows. For a complete description, see Myers' text.

A number of white-box test case design methods make use of a "flowgraph" (also called a program graph or directed graph) representation of a module. The flowgraph (not to be confused with a data flow diagram) represents program statements and nodes (circles) and flow of control as arrows (called edges) connecting the nodes. A simple flowgraph for the Pascal program in Figure 7.9a is shown in Figure 7.9b. Node numbers are shown in both. Using a flowgraph as a guide,

"basic path testing" may be applied to develop a set of independent test cases that exercise each linearly independent path in the flowgraph. This method assures tests that cover all logic flow have been derived; that all statements have been executed at least once.

In addition to having a reasonable probability of finding an error, a well-designed test case has two other properties:

1. It reduces by more than a count of one, the number of test cases that must be executed to achieve "reasonably complete" testing;

2. It covers a large set of other possible test cases; that is, it uncovers a general class of errors rather than one discrete error associated with a specific input case.

A black-box test case design technique, "equivalence partitioning", provides a systematic approach to the definition of test cases that have a high probability of uncovering a class or errors. "Boundary value analysis" is a test case design method that uncovers classes of errors at the limiting boundaries of a module or program (i.e., the limiting size of data structures, maximum and minimum values).

Other test case design techniques, such as "cause effect graphing" provide a graphical approach to the generation of decision tables that may be used to generate test cases. "Error guessing" hypothesizes specific classes of errors (based on intuition and experience) and leads to test cases that are designed to expose these (possibly non-existent) errors.

In addition to test case design methods, mathematical proofs of program correctness have received considerable attention in the literature. Proofs of correctness, if applied manually, are not applied after the program is written, but during the process of detailed design and coding. For further information, see Anderson (*Proving Programs Correct,* Wiley, 1979).

7.7.3 An Error Checklist

Although it is impossible to enumerate all software errors encountered during testing, seven error classes may be defined:

1. Data reference errors—those which occur when data-items are referenced improperly.

2. Data declaration errors—conflicts between intended and actual usage.

3. Computation errors—the result of improper analysis or computational precision.

4. Comparison errors—the result of improper or imprecise condition expressions.

5. Control-flow errors—the result of incorrect branching targets.

SOFTWARE
ENGINEERING
HANDBOOK

Chapter 7
SOFTWARE TESTING

Page 7-7

```
PROGRAM AVERAGE(INPUT. OUTPUT):
*******************************************************************
*                                                                 *
*              This program reads a series of integers from the   *
*              standard input device and computes their average.  *
*                                                                 *
*******************************************************************
CONST
   MAXVALUE = 300;               {MAXIMUM VALID INPUT VALUE}
   MINVALUE = -300;              {MINIMUM VALID INPUT VALUE}
   MAXRECORDS = 100;             {MAXIMUM NUMBER OF RECORDS READ}
VAR
   TOTALREAD,                       {TOTAL INTEGERS READ}
   TOTALVALID,                      {TOTAL VALID INTEGERS READ}
   SUM,                             {RUNNING TOTAL OF VALID INTEGERS}
   NUMBER    :    INTEGER:       {INTEGER VALUE READ FROM INPUT}
   AVRG       : REAL:            {AVERAGE OF ALL VALID INTEGERS}
BEGIN
(1) TOTALREAD := 0:
(2) TOTALVALID := 0:
(3) SUM := 0:

(4) READLN(NUMBER):
    WHILE NOT EOP AND (5) (TOTALREAD<MAXRECORDS) (6) DO
      BEGIN
        (7) TOTALREAD := TOTALREAD + 1;
          IF (NUMBER>=MINVALUE) (8) AND NUMBER<=MAXVALUE) (9) THEN
            BEGIN
            (10) TOTALVALID := TOTALVALID + 1;
            (11) SUM : = SUM + NUMBER
            END
          ELSE:
        (12) READLN(NUMBER)
    (13) END:   {WHILE-LOOP}

(14) IF TOTALVALID>0 THEN
       (15) AVRG := SUM / TOTALVALID
     ELSE
       (16) AVRG := 0.0;

(17) WRITELN('TOTAL RECORDS READ = ', TOTALREAD);
(18) WRITELN('TOTAL VALID RECORDS READ = ', TOTALVALID);
(19) WRITELN('AVERAGE OF VALID INTEGERS = ', AVRG:7:1)
END
```

Figure 7.9a. Pascal Program Sample

Page 7-8

**Chapter 7
SOFTWARE TESTING**

SOFTWARE
ENGINEERING
HANDBOOK

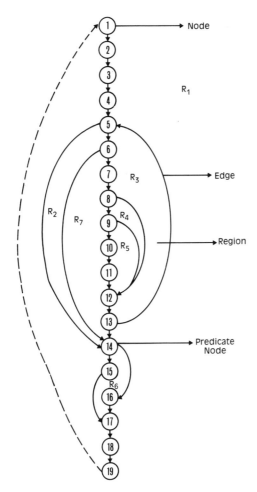

Figure 7.9b Flowgraph for Program in Figure 7.9a

6. Interface errors—the result of improper passage of data between modules (see Section 5).

7. Input/Output—the result of incorrect file formats or erroneous file specification.

Glenford Meyers in his text, "The Art of Software Testing", provides a good checklist that may be used during testing. If a test procedure addresses each question posed in the checklist, the probability of a successful test, one that finds errors, is improved substantially.

7.7.4 Debugging

Section 7.1.2 of this chapter defined debugging as the art of isolating and correcting error causes. Three basic approaches to software debugging are encountered in practice.

Brute-force debugging is the most inefficient technique. Nevertheless, it is a frequently used one. The brute force approach may be performed inductively: 1) locate error data;

2) organize data and evaluate; 3) devise an error hypothesis; 4) prove the hypothesis; 5) iterate from (1) or (3), as required. So long as the tester does not jump to conclusions, make partial corrections to errors, or yield to time pressures, the brute force approach works.

Debugging by deduction is a process of elimination and refinement. All possible causes and hypotheses are stated after the error is examined. Error data is used to eliminate some possibilities. The remaining hypotheses are evaluated for most probable cause. This cause is refined in an attempt to pinpoint the error source. The refined hypothesis is proved or another of the remaining ones is selected.

The final debugging approach is backtracking. This technique is extremely useful for small programs that can be mentally "executed in reverse". From the point at which the error symptom appears, the tester works backward examining the path to the symptom in reverse. Somewhere on this backward track, the error cause will be encountered.

The primary cause of debugging difficulty is time pressure and/or the refusal of the tester to seek help. Upon reaching an impasse, another person should be asked immediately to examine the problem. Days, even months of effort have been wasted by "glaring errors" invisible to one person but immediately obvious when another person was finally asked to help.

7.8 AUTOMATED TOOLS FOR TESTING

Software testing tools are automated aids that help the tester determine whether or not performance and design criteria have been satisfied. The following discussion, adapted from Reifer*, presents an overview of the more common testing tools.

7.8.1 Program Flow Analyzer

A program flow analyzer is software that provides statistics on source code statement usage and timing data. Each software routine is evaluated during test case executions in order to isolate errors in the code.

7.8.2 Test Drivers, Scripts, Data Generators

To run tests in a controlled manner, it is often necessary to work within the framework of a "scenario"—a description of a dynamic situation. To accomplish this, tools are used to load the input data files for the system with data values representing the test situation or events. Output data are recorded and used to evaluate expected results. These aids reduce errors introduced during retesting.

7.8.3 Test Bed

A test bed includes all computer and interface hardware required for a software system, thus permitting evaluation of

**SOFTWARE
ENGINEERING
HANDBOOK**

**Chapter 7
SOFTWARE TESTING**

Page 7-9

hardware/software interfaces and actual input/output. The reliability of the software system is increased by executing the program to confirm the actual timing characteristics.

7.8.4 A Typical System

A typical automated test system for FORTRAN programs** is presented below. The functions that this system performs are found in most test software.

The test system described by Clarke has the following characteristics:

1. Generates test data to drive execution down a program path. By automatically generating input data for a comprehensive set of program paths and then executing the program with the generated input data, the user is assured that the code has been well tested.

2. Detects nonexecutable program paths. Not all program paths are executable and, therefore, the system attempts to recognize nonexecutable paths. Detection of executable and nonexecutable paths is useful for subsequent program analysis.

3. Creates symbolic representations of the program's output variables as functions of input variables. Symbolic representations of the output variables aid in program validation by concisely representing a path's computations. The symbolic representation is in a human readable form that facilitates error detection.

4. Detects certain types of program errors. To further aid in program validation, an attempt is made to generate data that will detect some of the more common run time errors, such as subscripts that are out of bounds.

7.8.5 Performance Analysis Tools

Software performance characteristics are measured by automated tools called monitors, analyzers, timers, maps and traces. The following discussion, adapted from Pomeroy*, provides an overview of such techniques.

Program measurement and evaluation are most often used as adjuncts to system testing. In addition to establishing that performance specifications have been met, these tools are used to calibrate software and provide useful information to designers of similar systems.

* Reifer, D. J., Automated Aids for Reliable Software, Report No. SAMSO-TR-75-133, U.S. Air Force, August, 1975.

** Clarke, L., A System to Generate Test Data and Symbolically Execute Programs, Univ. of Colorado, Report No. CU-CS-060-75, February, 1975.

System characteristics are not always quantifiable. Performance is a quantitative statement of how well a computer program does its job. Performance characteristics such as throughput, resource utilization, reliability, job turnaround and response time, availability, capacity, and effectiveness are measurable. However usability characteristics such as human factors, serviceability, and maintainability, which express the effect a program has on its environment and the people who use it, are not measurable. They assist in establishing the ease of use of a program relative to other programs.

Performance characteristics are measured by monitors, analyzers, timers, maps, and traces. The organization of these measurement and evaluation tools is depicted in Figure 7.10.

Hardware monitors are devices that count and time the intervals between selected voltage pulses in a running computer without degrading the system. Accomplished by attaching probes to the target system, these measurements can be used to assess hardware usage such as wait and channel times. System activity is then recorded in the monitor's registers or on magnetic media. Most hardware monitors have reporting and/or data reduction programs supplied with them. Some of these programs provide plots as an option.

Whereas hardware monitors are used to measure the internal processing activities of a computer system, software monitors indicate I/O activity or the processing activity within the CPU. A software monitor is a program that provides detailed statistics in a production processing environment, recording usage of system software and hardware components by counting frequency of use and by recording the amount of use over some sampling period. Statistical output resulting from these measurements can be reported immediately or can be saved as a chronological trace for postprocessing. Software monitors are generally programmed in machine language to minimize degradation of normal system processing. The timing source used can be a standard computer interval timer or some other suitable high-resolution timer. Desirable features of a software monitor are the ability to add and remove the monitor without disrupting normal system processing and the ability to selectively request statistical options.

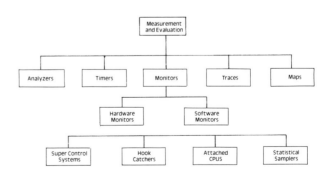

Figure 7.10 Performance Analysis Tools*

* Pomeroy, J. W., A Guide to Programming Tools and Techniques, IBM Systems Journal, v.1.12, no.3, 1972, pp. 234-254.

Page 7-10

Chapter 7
SOFTWARE TESTING

SOFTWARE
ENGINEERING
HANDBOOK

There are four basic approaches to software monitoring:

1. **Super control system monitoring** treats the operating system being measured as a problem-state program. The monitor operates in supervisor-state; it receives control whenever an interrupt occurs. It records detailed information about the target system, but in doing so, such

   a monitor usually causes target-system performance degradation. Special hardware, such as a high-resolution timer, may be required for super control system monitoring.

2. **Hook catching monitoring** relies on instructions ("hooks") placed at strategic points in a system being measured. These instructions cause a transfer to a catching routine that records appropriate data for later processing and then returns control to the measured program.

3. **Attached-CPU monitoring** uses standard hardware to feed data to the system being measured and to analyze the response time of that system. A primary use of an attached CPU monitor is to analyze teleprocessing systems.

4. **Statistical sample monitoring** records events occurring at specific points in time. This technique has less impact on normal system processing than the techniques previously discussed, yet produces equally valid measurements when optimum sampling intervals are selected correctly.

An *analyzer* provides source-language or execution-frequency statistics to assist in performance evaluation. It normally runs in problem-program state and requires no modification to the target program. Source-language analyzers are used to optimize individual programs.

A *timer* time-stamps and/or computes elapsed time between target program events. It executes in supervisor or problem-state; it may require target program modification. A timer normally depends on the interval timer for its timing information. Timer span may range from one instruction to an entire program. Many tools combine timing, monitoring and tracing functions.

Maps provide location and/or size information about all or selected parts of the target system or about device-resident data.

A *trace* records the chronological sequence of events taken by a target program during its execution. All or selected segments of the program may be traced. Output from a trace may then be used to drive models of the system to be measured.

7.9 SUMMARY

Software testing represents a significant percentage of overall development effort. Yet, as the least understood Software Engineering step, it is often given too little management and technical attention.

All testing is divided into three parts (levels): unit test, integration test and validation test. Each level represents an expansion in the scope of testing. Test planning is more formal as each succeeding level is encountered.

Although each software system has its own unique series of tests, general testing principles can be stated. Above all, it is important to note that "testing shows the presence of software errors—it can never show their absence".

SOFTWARE
ENGINEERING
HANDBOOK

Chapter 8
CONFIGURATION MANAGEMENT

Page 8-1

The software configuration consists of all documents produced during the software engineering definition, and development phases and various machine readable forms (e.g., listings, executable code, tests/results) of the software itself. These elements of the software configuration are the only tangibles produced during the project's definition and development phases.

As individual Software Engineering steps are completed the software configuration evolves. Reviews and walkthroughs generate changes that result in modification of configuration "items"; development tasks can generate updates to documents produced previously, and testing often results in changes propagating through most elements of the software configuration.

Because the software configuration is the only tangible representation of a program or software system, it must be controlled to preserve accuracy, to maintain up-to-date information, and to impart clear, concise information for each succeeding software engineering step. This chapter presents organizational and management guidelines for Software Configuration Management (SCM).

8.1 THE SOFTWARE CONFIGURATION

The software configuration is an instantaneous snapshot of the physical representation of software at some point in time. This representation takes two forms;

1. non-executable material generated to document or complement the computer program; this includes written documents, program listings and test data/results.

2. executable material processed directly by a computer, i.e. machine readable code and data base information stored on machine accessible media.

Written material, accounting for most of the overall software configuration, includes some documentation developed by definition and development staff intended only for internal use.*

Publications and manuals, written either by development personnel or technical writers is generally intended for use by the user/requestor of the software. Reference material (e.g., test results) is generated internally and finds use in the software maintenance phase.

The software is usually packaged as machine executable material stored on magnetic media. Since many versions of the executable material may exist before the software is validated, control of this segment of the configuration is essential.

---

* The SOFTWARE REQUIREMENTS SPECIFICATION and/or the DESIGN DOCUMENT may be disseminated to the user/requestor of the software.

Configuration management consists of four tasks:

1. establishment of documentation standards and a document identification scheme;

2. evaluation and recording of all changes to the software configuration—change control;

3. accurate tracking and controlled access to completed documents; and

4. continuous audit of the software configuration.

Each of these tasks is discussed in Sections 8.3 to 8.6.

The responsibility of configuration management generally lies outside the development team, and is ideally suited to coordination by a software librarian.

8.2 DELIVERABLES AND BASELINES

The deliverables included in the software configuration are illustrated in Figure 8.1. At the nucleus of the configuration is machine executable software, transported from the developer to the user/requestor. Each "copy" of machine executable software must be logged so that all software in the field may be tracked. Listings and test data, assigned appropriate identification, are coupled with the machine executable software.

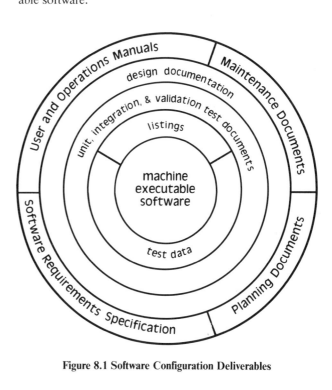

Figure 8.1 Software Configuration Deliverables

Page 8-2

Chapter 8
CONFIGURATION MANAGEMENT

SOFTWARE
ENGINEERING
HANDBOOK

Moving outward from the validated software, the configuration encompasses all documents produced during the software engineering process. INTEGRATION and VALIDATION TEST SPECIFICATION, the DESIGN documentation, SRS and PLAN become part of the configuration as each is completed, reviewed and approved. In addition, the USER and/or OPERATION MANUAL and MAINTENANCE documents are also included.

Baselines are defined as points during the software life cycle at which configuration control is applied to a specific deliverable. If stringent controls are applied too early in the document development stage, frustration, poor productivity and possible customer dissatisfaction are likely to result. Configuration control should be imposed only when formal review and approval for the specific software engineering step has been achieved.

Software configuration baselines are shown in Figure 8.2. If succeeding steps generate changes to a document preceding a baseline, formal review and justification of all document modifications (change control) is required.

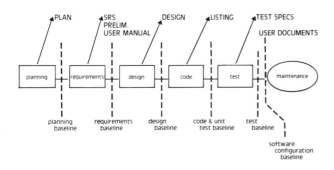

Figure 8.2 Software Configuration Baselines

8.3 CONFIGURATION IDENTIFICATION

As each baseline is reached the software configuration hierarchy of documents grows. The SRS "begats" the Design Document which "begats" detailed design descriptions of each module. Ultimately, source listings are produced, test specifications are generated, while changes (due to review and testing) are carefully assessed and incorporated.

The SCM identification task has the following objectives:

1. define an organized documentation structure in an understandable, predictable manner;

2. provide methods to accommodate revisions and aid in tracking those changes as they occur;

3. correlate changes with "who, what, when, why and how" to facilitate control.

The identification task begins with the definition of "software configuration items" representing deliverables required as each baseline is established. The format, content and control mechanisms for all documentation are defined to trace information as the configuration hierarchy evolves. Appropriate identifiers are assigned to all products, documents, and media, using a numbering scheme that provides information about the software configuration item. Finally, the identification should facilitate change control — to accommodate additions and modifications.

The software configuration is maintained for the life of a software system. Library and referencing aids are established to support the configurations generated.

Three fundamental approaches to documentation control can be applied:

1. All software documents and other elements of each configuration are maintained as part of an already established engineering drawing/documentation library.

2. A special software library is established for all software configurations.

3. An on-line software library is established supported by word processing and document retrieval facilities accessed via secure computer terminals.

Any one of the above options can be successfully implemented.

Regardless of the approach to documentation control, a referencing system should be established. Guidelines for a document numbering system are presented in Figure 8.3 with each document referenced by a unique number containing:

1. a unique project identifier
2. a configuration element item identifier
3. a revision level number
4. an attribute code

The above data appears in each element of the configuraton and should be used whenever cross-referencing is conducted. Figure 8.4 contains examples using the guideline.

8.4 CHANGE CONTROL

Change control is a mechanism for the evaluation and approval of changes made to Software Configuration Items (SCI) during the software life cycle. Three distinct types of control may be established:

1. individual control
2. management control
3. formal control

DOCUMENT REFERENCE NUMBER
XXX-YYY-Z-RL-NNN

where
XXX-YYY	is a common identifier for each software project where:
	XXX—is a component identifier
	YYY—is a project identifier
Z	is an item identifier
	P—plan
	R—requirements specification
	D—design document
	S—source listing
	T—test documentation
	U—user manual
	I—installation guide
	M—maintenance manual
RL	is the revision level
NNN	is an attribute code (such as date) defined by the developer to reflect important attributes of the configuration element

Figure 8.3 Document Reference Numbering

SPC-001-P-0-3/80— This is a Special Purpose Computer Center Plan for project 1. It is the original document. It was placed under change control in March 1980.

SPC-001-P-1-5/80— This is revision 1 to the Plan. It was placed under change control in May 1980.

SPC-005-R-3-9/81—This is revision 3 to the Requirements Specification for SPCC project number 5. This document was placed under change control in September of 1981.

Figure 8.4 Document Reference Number Examples

Each control level represents a higher degree of formality. However, provision must be made at all levels for "the quick-fix" (discussed later).

When an element of the configuration is under *individual control,* the responsible technical person makes changes to documentation as required. Although an informal record of revisions is maintained, such records are generally not placed in the document itself. Individual control is applied during the formative or draft stages of document development and is characterized by frequent changes.

Management control implies a review and approval procedure for each proposed change to the configuration. As in individual control, management control occurs during the development process, but is used after an element of the software configuration has been approved. The software librarian maintains all copies of documents under management control and a designated reviewer (often the responsible manager) must evaluate and approve changes. This level of change control is characterized by fewer changes than individual control. Each change is formally recorded and is visible to management.

Formal change control occurs during the software maintenance phase of the life cycle. The impact of each maintenance task is evaluated by a Change Control Board (CCB) which approves modification to the software configuration. Formal change control is imposed after validation and is strictly enforced by the software librarian.

As change control becomes more formal, review and approval procedures can become rather lengthy. Practicality often dictates that some mechanism for a "quick-fix" be established. The quick-fix change procedure should not be used to circumvent other levels of change control, but rather to provide a temporary means for rapid modification of the software configuration in emergency situations. This is especially important when a major error occurs in the field and a customer is severely hampered by the problem.

8.4.1 The Control Process

As noted in the preceding section, change control is applied whenever a Software Configuration Item (SCI) undergoes change (Figure 8.5). However, the degree and formality of control will vary depending upon the status of the SCI.

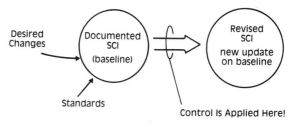

... throughout the software life cycle ...

Figure 8.5 Where Is Control Applied?

The overall flow of the SCM control process is illustrated in Figure 8.6. A change request (discussed in Chapter 9) asks for modification(s) to correct an error or deficiency, adapt to a new environment, or enhance operating software and is submitted for analysis by the software organization. After both technical and management issues are considered, a change report is issued and passed to the Change Control Board (CCB) for evaluation. The request is either approved or rejected and the requestor of the change is notified.

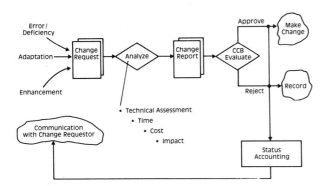

Figure 8.6 The Control Process

8.4.2 The Change Control Board (CCB)

The Change Control Board (CCB) is the "governing body" for all issues associated with SCM. The make-up and size of the CCB will be dictated by the size and criticality of the software development project. In general, the CCB is comprised of members from the user/requestor, and developer organizations. For small projects, the CCB may be comprised of one representative of the user, requestor and developer. For large projects, the CCB itself may be organized in a hierarchy that addresses system issues, hardware and software separately.

The CCB becomes involved with a software project at its inception and performs the following tasks:

1. analyzes the impact of "revolutionary" changes to the system, calling upon technical disciplines for recommendations as required;

2. categorizes and prioritizes changes as they are requested and approved;

3. mediates conflicts between disciplines and organizations that arise due to change;

4. assures that proper record keeping and accounting are conducted.

In Chapter 9 the role of the CCB during the maintenance phase is discussed in detail.

8.5 CONFIGURATION AUDITING

Software configuration audits verify the SCI traceability to preceding baselines and validate that it correctly reflects software requirements.

The objective of the auditing function is to (1) establish the technical and administrative integrity of the baseline; (2)

assure that changes made to the SCI are within the scope of requirements, and (3) serve as a prerequisite for CCB approval of a SCI.

In their book on SCM, Bersoff, Henderson and Siegel (*Software Configuration Management,* Prentice-Hall, 1980) recommend a series of applicable auditing checklists as each of the software baselines is completed. Each audit addresses technical issues (e.g., "Are there unanswered questions concerning technical options, trade-offs, interfaces?"), management issues (e.g., "Do the user, buyer and seller agree on system requirements and the interpretation thereof?") and SCM issues (e.g., "Is each SCI identified in the design baseline identified per SCM identification standards?").

The configuration auditing function is applied on a continuous basis throughout the software life cycle, rather than after the fact. Software reviews (discussed throughout the *Handbook*) may be used as the technical audit, but separate management and SCM auditing must also be conducted.

8.6 CONFIGURATION STATUS ACCOUNTING

The goal of Configuration Status Accounting (CSA) is to answer the questions "What happened?" and "When did it happen?" As illustrated in Figure 8.7, CSA takes information from each of the SCM tasks and builds a database from which reports may be generated. The CSA function provides a "history" of the development process. Project staff can determine (by reviewing CSA records and reports) when specific changes were made, what elements were added to an approved baseline, and what the status of the configuration is at a given time.

A prime source of information for the CSA function is the minutes of CCB meetings. These minutes contain information about baseline status, audits, approved/rejected change requests, and other information important for historical reference. In addition, information contained in the Software Problem Report and Software Change Report (discussed in Chapter 9) can be useful for CSA reporting.

8.7 SUMMARY

Software configuration management is an essential supplement to Software Engineering definition, development and maintenance phases. The configuration is comprised of written documents and executable material. Since documents are the external-world representation of software, review and controls are necessary to assure that a document accurately reflects the functions and characteristics of the program.

Configuration change control is initially conducted by the individual software engineer. After a task baseline has been passed, management control, and ultimately, formal control are established.

**SOFTWARE
ENGINEERING
HANDBOOK**

Chapter 8
CONFIGURATION MANAGEMENT

Page 8-5

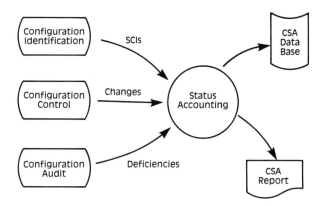

Figure 8.7 Status Accounting

**SOFTWARE
ENGINEERING
HANDBOOK**

Chapter 9
SOFTWARE MAINTENANCE

Page 9-1

Typically, a software organization spends over 50 percent of its budget maintaining old software; typically, the percentage increases each year. When software resources are expended on maintenance, economic constraints and lack of the sufficient technical personnel limit the development of new systems. First priority must be given to keeping existing software "up and running". For these reasons, software maintenance must be performed efficiently when required; development must be aimed at cost-effective maintenance.

Software maintenance can be to a software organazation what an iceberg was to the Titanic! Maintenance is the most time consuming and important activity in the software life cycle. Maintenance demands more management attention, technical planning and systematic review than that spent in the Definition and Development phases.

This chapter presents a Software Engineering approach to program maintenance. The concept of maintainability is introduced; maintenance organization, reporting and procedures are discussed; software reliability is reviewed and management considerations are described.

9.1 MAINTENANCE CATEGORIES

A precise definition of software maintenance is difficult because different organizations attach different meanings to the term. However, three distinct categories of maintenance can be defined:

1. corrective maintenance—correction of errors introduced to the software during development left undiscovered during testing (i.e., errors due to a failure in testing).

2. adaptive maintenance—modification of software due to changes in its external environment (the vendor changes the host operating system).

3. perfective maintenance—enhancements that extend function or improve performance.

Corrective maintenance results when software fails. In general, such failures are precipitated by a combination of input data that has never been previously encountered or by an incorrect interface between hardware or other system software. Faults encountered after software release range from trivial, bothersome problems that can be corrected in a scheduled fashion to critical errors that halt operation of a business. Critical errors are corrected "under-the-gun"; nevertheless these corrections must still be planned, reviewed, and controlled.

Adaptive maintenance occurs as the external environment that interfaces with software changes. Software conversion efforts from one operating system release to the next or one computer to another are common adaptive maintenance tasks. Another reason for adaptive maintenance is change in "data environment". That is, modification to a data base; new data access methods; or a change in physical media. In most cases, adaptive maintenance should be planned, scheduled and implemented in an identical manner to new software development.

Perfective maintenance enhances an existing software system to provide functions and/or performance characteristic not defined in the SOFTWARE REQUIREMENTS SPECIFICATION. In addition to the development of new features, perfective maintenance encompasses improving processing efficiency, decreasing program size or enhancing software maintainability.

Some define a fourth maintenance category, work performed on the software configuration in order to reduce or avoid future corrective, adaptive or perfective maintenance. Called "preventive maintenance" after its analogous activity for hardware, this maintenance work can cost-effectively reduce later maintenance effort and time.

A study by Lientz and Swanson (*Software Maintenance Management,* Addison-Wesley, 1980) indicates perfective maintenance accounts for just over 50 percent of all effort expended on software maintenance while corrective and adaptive maintenance account for approximately equal shares (21 and 25 percent respectively). This data confirms that software will be changed. A clear conclusion stands out— design, implementation and testing should be conducted with an eye toward the inevitable modifications that will be requested.

It should be noted that all maintenance categories are applied to the entire software configuration. Maintenance of software documentation is equally as important as maintenance of executable software.

9.2 MAINTAINABILITY

The maintainability of software is a qualitative measure of the following factors:

1. ease of understanding
2. ease of diagnosis and testing
3. ease of change

Each factor relates to the entire software configuration, although emphasis is placed on the program.

Ease of understanding is reflected by the ability of an outside auditor to understand the structure, interfaces, functions and internal procedure of the software. Modularity, detailed design documentation, internal source code documentation and structured design all contribute to ease of understanding.

Ease of diagnosis and testing depend upon ease of understanding. Again, good documentation is essential. Additionally, software structure, availability of "debugging tools" and previously defined test procedures are very important. Software test cases developed and used during implementation should be available to the maintainer. The software should be designed to facilitate location of faults and allow diagnosis of subsequent modifications to correct existing faults.

Page 9-2

Chapter 9
SOFTWARE MAINTENANCE

SOFTWARE
ENGINEERING
HANDBOOK

Ease of modification is directly related to design criteria discussed in Chapter 5. Coupling, cohesion, scope of effect/control and other criteria affect ease of modification.

All maintainability factors are closely interrelated. It is impossible to modify a program not understood by the maintenance staff. An apparently correct modification may cause other errors whenever complete diagnosis and testing is difficult.

Although maintainability is a qualitative attribute, a number of quantitative (i.e., measurable) characteristics that relate to maintainability have been proposed:

1. problem recognition time
2. administrative delay time
3. maintenance tools collection time
4. problem diagnosis time
5. change specification time
6. active correction time
7. local testing time
8. regression/global testing time
9. change review time
10. distribution time

These characteristics, proposed by Gilb*, are directly measurable and are a bottom-line indicator of software system maintainability.

9.3 MAINTENANCE PROCEDURES

Maintenance procedures include: establishment of a maintenance staff organization; definition of error reporting modes; provision for maintenance evaluation, implementation and review; change control, and maintenance record keeping. These topics are included in this chapter.

9.3.1 Organization

A staff organization for software maintenance must be adopted to the local software environment. An idealized organization (Figure 9.1) can be used as a point of departure.

Referring to the Figure, requests for maintenance ("reports") are submitted to a maintenance controller who has responsibility for the coordination of the maintenance task. Each report is evaluated by technical staff, called system supervisors, responsible for one or more existing software systems. A preliminary estimate of problem cause and correction time is established and communicated to the maintenance controller. The controller, in conjunction with a Configuration Control Board (CCB) or a Change Control Authority (CCA), establishes priority, evaluates the change impact and establishes a preliminary schedule. Maintenance is then performed by appropriate staff personnel.

* Gilb, T., "A Comment on the Definition of Maintainability", ACM SIGSOFT, Software Engineering Notes, vol. 4, no. 3, July, 1979

Depending upon the size of a software organization, the maintenance controller and CCA may be one person or (for large projects) a committee of management and technical personnel. Regardless of size, evaluation, review and control is essential for efficient maintenance.

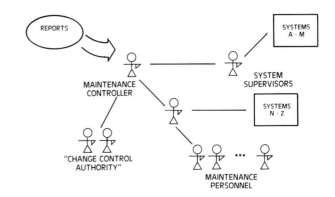

Figure 9.1 Organization

The primary CCA function is impact assessment of a proposed change. Design changes in one software module often generate changes in other modules. This snowballing affect must be determined before approving a maintenance task.

After the required technical data has been collected and the overall impact of modifications has been reviewed, the CCA establishes priority and approve the maintenance effort. The CCA, or its technical designee, should review the modification upon completion. Responsibility for assuring consistent software design and meeting all original requirements is the CCA's.

9.3.2 Planning

The maintenance planning approach is similar to the software planning approach. Software maintenance tasks should not be directed toward haphazard correction of "one bug at a time". Rather, software revision should be evaluated with regard to criticality (to user and developer) with resultant revision priorities established by management.

The maintenance plan should include:

1. scope of current maintenance task
2. resources required
3. validation requirements
4. cost
5. schedule

The plan may be cross-referenced to other documents in the software configuration and will ultimately become a baseline document within the configuration.

SOFTWARE
ENGINEERING
HANDBOOK

Chapter 9
SOFTWARE MAINTENANCE

Page 9-3

9.3.3 Implementation

The maintenance task, parallels the design, code and test steps for new software development. However, it can be affected by time pressures causing legitimate abbreviation of some steps. Nevertheless, the basic concepts of development, review and test remain unchanged.

9.3.4 Error Reporting

Maintenance requires a systematic technique for reporting errors. The Software Problem Report (SPR) provides the means for reporting errors (and other requests for maintenance) in operational and test software including documentation. The Report, shown in Figure 9.2, is completed by the individual who uncovers the error or desires a modification and is sent to the maintenance organization. In general, the SPR originator should complete items D, F, G, H, I, K, N, and O as a minimum. Items J, L, and M should be completed if known or applicable. If the SPR is used to report a software error, supporting documentation generated from an actual run (e.g. system dump) should be included with the report. Each entry of the SPR is discussed in detail in Appendix A.7

Items A, B, C, E, and P are completed by maintenance personnel with change control responsibility. The completed SPR is used by the CCA to make a decision regarding the acceptance or rejection of corrective action.

The SPR provides a formal means for recording all software faults and modification requests. However, in order to properly evaluate the SPR, the user must also provide supplementary information:

1a. a printout depicting the error occurrence

1b. a "spec" indicating the requirements for the requested modification

2. a listing of input data

3. a termination memory dump (if required)

4. a description of the hardware environment

5. an indication of the software release (version and revision number)

Error reporting instructions must clearly list the essential information for SPR completion.

9.3.5 Evaluation of Change

Once a complete SPR has been received, a Software Change Report (SCR) is completed by maintenance personnel. Incomplete SCRs are returned to the sender with a notice of missing data. The change report indicates (1) the error category (see Appendix A.7.3), repair strategy, and the status of the repair; or (2) the nature of the modification. A typical SCR document is shown in Figure 9.3. The Software Change Report, is the only means for obtaining change approval from the Change Control Authority. (which is also required for documenting a proposed change to software.

Each SCR submitted to the CCA will have the following items completed: A, B, C, D, E, F, G, H, I, J, K, L, or O, M, Q (if applicable), T, U (if applicable), V and W. Items N, P, R, and S will be completed by the maintenance organization for approved SCRs after the work is completed. Item X will be completed by the originator either after the SCR is rejected by the CCA, or upon completion of work for an approved SCR. Each entry of the SCR is discussed in detail in Appendix A.7.

The Change Control Authority evaluates each SCR and assigns a priority (relative to unprocessed SCRs) and change class to the requested modification. The priority is based on the importance of the error or modification. The change class is used to differentiate between corrective, adaptive or perfective maintenance. Within an error class, three possible types may be encountered:

1. Scheduled maintenance must be performed to correct the error. Scheduling is based on priority.

2. Error can be circumvented without software modification.

3. Correction for the error already exists.

After this evaluation is completed, the CCA estimates the resources required to effect a change and schedules the task based on priority.

9.3.6 Error Correction

As a result of the formalized reporting and evaluating procedures discussed above, similar (related) errors may be scheduled for correction at the same time. By addressing groups of errors, redundant maintenance tasks can be eliminated.

Error correction begins with an evaluation of the relevant Module Development Folder (MDF). Corrections are designed in the same manner as new functions. The preliminary and detailed design reviews are as essential to maintenance as they are to new software development.

A test plan and procedure, incorporating old test cases and new tests predicated by the change, is developed. It is important to establish that a change will not create problems in other software modules.

Page 9-4

Chapter 9
SOFTWARE MAINTENANCE

**SOFTWARE
ENGINEERING
HANDBOOK**

S	OFTWARE	LOG NO: Ⓐ
P	ROBLEM	LOG DATE: Ⓑ
R	EPORT	TIME: Ⓒ

| Ⓓ DEV ☐ INTEG ☐ VAL ☐ SYS ☐ | STATUS: Ⓔ | 1 | 2 | 3 | 4 | 5 | 6 | 7 |

ORIGINATOR: NAME
               ADDRESS   Ⓕ   TELEPHONE

PROBLEM WITH: Ⓖ   ROUTINE ☐   DATA BASE ☐   DOCUMENT ☐

ROUTINE/ELEMENT/SS: Ⓗ	REV. Ⓘ	TAPE Ⓙ
DATA BASE: Ⓚ	DOCUMENTS: Ⓛ
TEST CASE: Ⓜ	HARDWARE UNIT: Ⓝ

PROBLEM DESCRIPTION/IMPACT: Ⓞ

NOTES:

Ⓟ

Figure 9.2 Software Problem Report

SOFTWARE
ENGINEERING
HANDBOOK

Chapter 9
SOFTWARE MAINTENANCE

Page 9-5

S	OFTWARE	ERROR CATEGORY Ⓧ	LOG NO: Ⓐ
C	HANGE		LOG DATE: Ⓑ
R	EPORT		TIME: Ⓒ

ORIGINATOR Ⓓ	SS: Ⓔ	ROUTINE: Ⓕ

RESPONSE TO SPRS: Ⓖ				

Ⓗ RESPONSE INCLUDES:
ROUTINE MOD ☐   DOC. UPDATE ☐   DATA BASE CHG ☐   EXPLANATION ☐

RESPONSE: Ⓘ

APPROVAL: _____ Ⓙ

CHANGE:

CODE TYPE: Ⓚ   I/O ☐   COMP ☐   LOGICAL ☐   DATA HAND ☐

ROUTINE: Ⓛ	OLD MOD: Ⓜ	NEW MOD: Ⓝ

REF DATA BASE: Ⓞ	DBCR Ⓟ	REF DOCUMENT Ⓠ	DUT: Ⓡ

HAS FIX BEEN TESTED? Ⓢ	YES NO NA	YES NO NA	YES NO NA	YES NO NA	YES NO NA
REMARKS:	_____ ELEMENT	_____ SS	SS INTEG.	VALID.	OPERATIONS

WAS PROBLEM CORRECTLY STATED ON SPR? Ⓣ   YES ☐   NO ☐

REMARKS: Ⓤ

PROBLEM SOURCE: Ⓥ   SYS SPEC ☐   REQ SPEC ☐   DES SPEC ☐   DB ☐   CODE ☐

ESTIMATES RESOURCES: Ⓦ   MANHOURS _____ COMPUTER TIME _____

Figure 9.3 Software Change Report

Page 9-6

Chapter 9
SOFTWARE MAINTENANCE

SOFTWARE
ENGINEERING
HANDBOOK

9.3.7 Maintenance Procedure Summary

The maintenance process is essentially a modified and abbreviated version of the definition and development stages. The SPR provides the initial input from which a maintenance plan (the SCR) and strategy must evolve.

Figure 9.4 illustrates the maintenance chronology. It should be noted that management involvement is required to determine costs/schedules and ultimate action on every "request for maintenance". In addition, every completed maintenance task must precipitate an updated MDF and DESIGN document.

Maintenance reports (SPR and SCR) should be filed by project so that

1) historical data indicating types and causes of errors can be developed;

2) error trends may be identified and preventive maintenance may be planned (if required);

3) and test procedures may be evaluated to determine strategies to uncover similar errors in other software.

9.4 MANAGEMENT CONSIDERATIONS

Management and technical responsibility for the maintenance task should be established prior to release of new software. The maintenance controller must consider the following topics:

1. acceptance of validated software
2. amended software release criteria
3. configuration control, auditing and accounting
4. coordination of personnel
5. maintenance record keeping

The publication of software maintenance guidelines (or standards) will provide a consistent management approach throughout the software organization.

9.4.1 Acceptance of Software for Maintenance

Before validated software is released, the maintenance controller must verify that:

1. all software documentation is complete and up to date;

2. all test cases and test results have been properly recorded;

3. procedures to record and track all copies of the configuration have been established;

4. maintenance procedures and responsibilities have been defined.

The software configuration is placed under formal change control (Chapter 8) and all subsequent modifications must be reviewed by CCA.

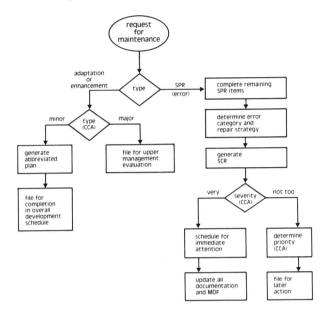

Figure 9.4 Maintenance Chronology

9.4.2 Amended Software Release Criteria

After a software modification has been made, the maintenance controller conducts a review to verify that regression testing* has been conducted; all documentation has been updated, and accurate record-keeping data (see paragraph 9.4.5) has been collected. Modifications, with appropriate documentation, are packaged for dissemination to all users of the software.

9.4.3 Configuration Management

The basic characteristics and procedures for software configuration management have been discussed in Chapter 8. The configuration must allow for the release of modified documentation and executable software in the form of revisions and versions.

Revisions

A software revision is generally used to correct one or more classes of errors encountered after the original software was released. The revision may also be used to add simple functions, improve performance and implement an adaptation to a new environment.

* using a series of tests to validate the modification and provide assurance that new errors have not been introduced.

SOFTWARE
ENGINEERING
HANDBOOK

Chapter 9
SOFTWARE MAINTENANCE

Page 9-7

When critical (as determined by CCA) software errors are encountered, the maintenance organization may release a Temporary Software Fix (TSF) to enable the user to circumvent or correct the problem. Each revision incorporates all preceding TSFs.

A software revision must be compatible with earlier revisions. This implies that the complete series of validation tests performed for the previous revision(s) are used to validate the revised software

Versions

A new software version generally incorporates all modifications made in preceding revisions and can be used to introduce major enhancements that extend the scope of the original SOFTWARE REQUIREMENTS SPECIFICATION.

Because new and sometimes different functions may be incorporated in a new version, complete compatibility with previous versions may not always be possible. If compatibility

cannot be guaranteed, special documentation must be released with the new version, outlining functional differences and their impact on the user. When the software is a product, it may be necessary to develop an emulation package so that existing software and data may be accommodated by the new version.

A typical chronology of maintenance releases is illustrated in Figure 9.5. The initial release, Version 1, is usually followed by some number of TSFs. Revisions follow as time passes, with a second version of the software appearing after approximately 2.5 years in the example shown.

If support for the initial version is continued, maintenance planning becomes more complicated. As noted in the figure, revisions of Version 1 (rev. 1.4 and 1.5) are continued while early revisions of version 2 (rev. 2.1 and 2.2) are also conducted.

Support for early versions of most software is discontinued after a pre-specified time or when error reports decline substantially. As shown in Figure 9.5, the software is considered "stable" and further maintenance work is planned only for later versions.

9.4.4 Coordination of Personnel

Coordination of technical personnel to work on new software development and maintenance of old software is a difficult task. The maintenance function may be a permanent part of the organizational structure or a transient task within a development group. The correct approach is dictated by 1) the size of the software organization; 2) the number of programs to be maintained, and 3) the nature of the software (product or internal use).

Regardless of the maintenance organization, at least one technical person (the "system supervisor") should have a working knowledge of all software configurations. In addition, a back-up should be established for the system supervisor.

9.4.5 Maintenance Record-Keeping

Collecting historical data provides management information needed to evaluate software maintenance efficiency. A maintenance register is one means of establishing a formal mode for maintenance record keeping. An outline for register entry is shown in Figure 9.6.

Items 1-4 (Figure 9.6) are self explanatory and can be acquired from SPR and SCR data. Maintenance statistics, item 5, can cover a broad spectrum of data. The following list of maintenance measurements has been proposed by E. B. Swanson* and covers all maintenance conducted by a software organization:

S1: Number of programs maintained, as of end-of-period. (This is simply a count of the number of programs installed and covered by open orders for maintenance).

Year	Version	Revision
TSF		
1 release version 1		
TSF 1		
TSF 2		
.		
.		
.		
Rev 1.1		
TSF i		
TSF i+1		
.		
.		
.		
2 Rev 1.2		
TSF j		
TSF j+1		
.		
.		
Rev 1.3		
release version 2		
.		
Rev 1.4		
Rev 2.1		
.		
3 Rev 2.2 .		
.		
Rev 1.5		
stable		
Rev 2.3		
.		
.		

Figure 9.5 Maintenance Releases

* Swanson, E. B., The Dimensions of Maintenance, Proc. 2nd Intl. Conf. on Software Engineering, IEEE, 1976.

Page 9-8

Chapter 9
SOFTWARE MAINTENANCE

SOFTWARE
ENGINEERING
HANDBOOK

S2: Total number of source statements maintained, as of end-of-period.

S3: Total number of machine instructions maintained, as of end-of-period.

S4: Average number of source statements per program maintained, in each programming language.

S5: Average number of machine instructions per program maintained, in each programming language.

S6: Percent of number of programs in each programming language.

```
MAINTENANCE REGISTER

1. SOFTWARE IDENTIFICATION
2. NATURE OF REQUEST
   A. REPORTED BY:
   B. DESCRIPTION
   C. REPORT DATE
   D. COMMENTS
3. ACTION
   A. AUTHORIZATION
   B. TECHNICAL STAFF
   C. MODULES EXAMINED/AMENDED
   D. CAUSE OF ERROR
   E. REGRESSION TESTS
4. CONTROL
   A. ESTIMATED EFFORT
   B. BUDGETED/ACTUAL COMPLETION DATE
5. MAINTENANCE STATISTICS
```

Figure 9.6 Maintenance Record Keeping

S7: Total number of program runs undertaken. (The sum of the run counts associated with the programs maintained, over the interval of measurement).

S8: Total number of processing failures occurring during program runs undertaken. (The sum of the failure counts associated with the programs maintained, over the interval of measurement).

S9: Average number of processing failures occurring per run undertaken. (This is computed as S8/S7, and may be termed the "processing failure rate". An increase may be due either to external cause (e.g., the installation of new programs not sufficiently debugged) or internal effects (e.g., hasty modifications in maintenance, introducing new bugs).

S10: Average age of programs maintained.

S11: Number of maintenance orders initiated, in each basic category.

S12: Number of maintenance orders closed, in each basic category.

S13: Number of maintenance orders open, in each basic category, as of end-of-period.

S14: Total net benefits associated with perfective maintenance completed. (Maintenance is said to be completed when the associated maintenance order is closed).

S15: Total person-hours spent in perfective maintenance completed.

S16: Average net benefits associated per person-hour of perfective maintenance completed. (This is computed as S14/S15, and is one rough indicator of the "productivity of a person-hour of perfective maintenance".

S17: Number of program changes made. (A simple count of the number of program changes made over the measurement interval).

S18: Number of program changes made, in each maintenance basic category.

S19: Average number of program changes made per program maintained. (S17/S1)

S20: Total number of source statements added by program changes made.

S21: Total number of source statements deleted by program changes made.

S22: Net addition to total number of source statements maintained, due to program changes made. (S20-S21)

S23: Total number of person-hours spent in program change.

S24: Total number of person-hours spent in program change, in each maintenance basis category.

S25: Average number of person-hours spent per processing failure correction. (This is computed from those components of S18 and S25 which correspond to changes made due to processing failures. It is one indicator of the maintainability of the software, in the given maintenance environment.)

S26: Average number of person-hours spent per source statement added by program changes made. (This is computed as S20/S23, and is an alternative indicator of software maintainability, in the given maintenance environment).

**SOFTWARE
ENGINEERING
HANDBOOK**

**Chapter 9
SOFTWARE MAINTENANCE**

Page 9-9

9.5 MAINTENANCE REVIEW

Record-keeping provides information for the maintenance review process. The maintenance controller, system supervisor and maintenance staff must address the following questions:

1. Given the current situation, what aspects of the design should have been done differently?

2. Is preventive maintenance indicated by the SPRs we're seeing?

3. Does this SPR reflect an error introduced during preceding maintenance?

4. What resources should have been available (and weren't)?

5. Are we recording the correct maintenance statistics?

In addition to these general questions, the maintenance measurements listed in paragraph 9.4.5 and the maintainability characteristics given in Section 9.2 can be used to provide a quantitative indication of maintenance efficiency.

9.6 SUMMARY

The last phase of the software life cycle—maintenance—consumes more budget dollars than all steps in the definition and development phases combined. To a very great extent, software maintenance overload has been caused by poor definition and development. Software engineering provides a means for improving the definition and development phases and thereby precipitating a reduction in required maintenance effort.

Maintenance categories include: corrective, adaptive, perfective as well as preventive maintenance, each addressed by a maintenance organization with well-defined responsibilities. The software maintenance procedure requires planning, review and control.

Many projects undertaken by a software organization require less than six person-months of effort. Often, only one, or at most, two individuals are involved throughout the definition and development phases. Such "small" projects must be approached using Software Engineering discipline. However, the degree of formality may be dictated by the nature of the requestor, the size of the development organization, the software category and the useful life of the software.

10.1 THE NATURE OF SMALL PROJECTS

The software project "size" cannot be judged solely by the effort required to complete it. Recalling the software categories proposed by Brooks (paragraph 3.3.1):

1. the basic program
2. the program product
3. the programming system
4. the programming system product;

a small "programming system product" require considerably more formal software engineering than a small "basic program".

The nature of small software projects can be determined by four factors:

1. user/requestor
2. size of the development organization
3. software category
4. projected life of the software

The *user requester* has a significant bearing on the degree of software engineering formality in a small project. Software developed for in-house use by individuals interfacing directly with the software development staff need not be treated with the formality of product software. However, the user/requestor must always receive sufficient user documentation. As a minimum, an abbreviated design document and internally documented source listing should exist regardless of the user/requestor.

The *size of the software development organization* may also have some bearing on the way small projects are treated. Initial user/requestor contact, development, and subsequently, maintenance may be performed by different people in a large organization. In this case, all software engineering steps and deliverables should be used. In a small organization (e.g., five or fewer technical staff), all phases of the software life cycle may be performed by one person; therefore, less formal procedures and abbreviated documentation can be used for small projects.

As previously noted, *software category* is normally the determining factor for small project formality. All software products, regardless of size, should be developed with rigorous adherence to each software engineering step and deliverable. Software for a small local audience may be developed using less formal procedures, however, the review and test processes should still be applied to assure acceptance by the user community.

The *projected life of software* resulting from a small project may dictate the software engineering approach. If long term usage is expected, sufficient design documentation and test data must be generated for maintenance support.

The following sections describe a software engineering approach for "small projects". That is, the nature of the software as defined by the four factors discussed safely allows a modified software engineering process.

10.2 SMALL PROJECT DEFINITION

A SOFTWARE PLAN is essential for any project regardless of size. Since planning is often performed by the same individual performing the design, code and test, there is a tendency to move immediately to development. This must be discouraged!

The SOFTWARE PLAN for a small project should include the scope (often dictated by a PROJECT PLAN), related costs and schedule. The PLAN often becomes part of the SRS and is reviewed by the responsible manager during that document's review.

A SOFTWARE REQUIREMENTS SPECIFICATION (SRS) should be prepared for all software efforts regardless of size. The SRS is the only way to measure design implementation adequacy and to establish validation/acceptance criteria. Once the requirements document has been completed, software costs and schedule contained in the PLAN are reviewed for consistency.

10.3 SMALL PROJECT DEVELOPMENT

Preliminary and detailed design steps and documentation for small projects are similar to those discussed for large projects. For small projects, design reviews can present difficulties since other software personnel may not be familiar with the project. Nevertheless, a design review is critical; it should be performed by one or more high-level technical personnel and the responsible manager. The technical personnel need an opportunity to review planning documentation to familiarize themselves with project objectives.

Both the code and unit test step and the development of the Module Development Folder (MDF) are unchanged. Where only one software engineer is involved, there is often a tendency to "underdocument". This must be discouraged. All coding and testing standards must be maintained.

Depending upon project complexity, formal test plans for integration may not be required. However, all software drivers, test cases and results must be thoroughly documented and saved for maintenance. Each change surfaced by testing should be reflected in the AS-BUILT DESIGN document and applicable source listing(s).

Traceability to design and requirements documents is essential. Test results must be reviewed to assure that both function and performance have been satisfied.

Formal validation should be performed for every software project. At the very least, the software manager should be assured by software demonstration and personal review of program documentation that the requirements originally specified have been achieved.

10.4 SMALL PROJECT MAINTENANCE

Whenever a single individual works alone on a small software project, there is a possibility no one else may understand the software when maintenance is required. For this reason, it is critically important to emphasize preparation of complete, accurate documentation during the development phase.

Change control applies to all software used by individuals other than the developer. Although small software efforts may have less formal maintenance procedures (i.e., no SPR or CCA), maintenance must be monitored using the same cost-benefit criteria for larger projects.

10.5 SOFTWARE CONFIGURATION FOR SMALL PROJECTS

A software configuration must be established and maintained for any program used outside of the software development group. The following paragraphs describe the documents to be developed for small projects. A complete description of all document formats is given in Appendix A.

10.5.1 Definition Documents

The SOFTWARE PLAN and SOFTWARE REQUIREMENTS SPECIFICATION may be combined as one document or may be developed separately. An outline for the PLAN follows:

1. Scope
2. Resources
3. Cost
4. Schedule

For a small project, the planning document may be as short as two or three pages.

The SRS is developed in its entirety for all software products (regardless of size), but may be abbreviated for local development efforts. The following outline is recommended:

1. Project Overview
2. Information Description
3. Functions
4. Design Constraints
5. Validation Criteria
6. Block Diagrams

The SRS is a formal document and must be reviewed by software management and the user/requestor.

10.5.2 Development Documents

Although design documentation for small projects contains the same elements of a "large" project design many sections are abbreviated. Data flow and structure as well as software functions are defined. Procedural descriptions may be incorporated directly into source listings, thereby combining detailed design documentation with internal program documentation.

Source code follows software engineering standards. In fact, additional source level documentation may be required to offset abbreviated versions of other documents.

Test documentation may be abbreviated for small software projects. Integration testing is documented as an overview that concentrates on planning and procedural elements of the test sequence. The Validation Criteria section of the SRS may be used for validation test documentation.

10.5.3 Maintenance Documents

By virtue of the nature of a "small" project, maintenance is often mistakenly assumed to be minimal concern. Contrary to this assumption, all software products require complete maintenance, record-keeping and documentation.

10.5.4 Configuration Management

Configuration management procedures remain unchanged for small projects. All documents are filed in the software library and configuration control is used to manage modifications to documents and executable materials.

10.6 SUMMARY

Small software projects can be approached using a modified Software Engineering methodology in which documentation is abbreviated; reviews are less formal, and a team approach is unwarranted. However, the philosophy of Software Engineering remains unchanged.

A "small" project must be evaluated to determine whether less formality is an advisable alternative. Four factors—user/requestor, development organization, software category, and projected life—may be used to support the evaluation.

A "small project" designation neither relieves management of responsibility for definition and development control, nor does it allow the developer to use unsound techniques or produce erroneous/incomplete documents. The designation is used to expedite software life cycle phases without adversely affecting software quality or reliability.

SOFTWARE
ENGINEERING
HANDBOOK

Chapter 11
MANAGEMENT ISSUES

Page 11-1

Although software engineering provides a systematic approach for software development project management, planning inconsistencies, procedural complications and tracking difficulties can still arise. To minimize these problems, a manager with software responsibility must understand the relationships between software engineering and its associated management issues.

This chapter discusses several management issues and supplements topics discussed in Chapters 1-10 of the *Handbook*. An organizational framework for software management is proposed; reasons for software project failures are discussed; software engineering standards and education are described; and, an implementation approach for the methodology is recommended.

11.1 AN ORGANIZATIONAL FRAMEWORK

The overriding organizational objective for effective software development is establishment of an environment that facilitates communication among development staff, user/requestor staff, and most importantly, between developer and user/requestor. Communication between developer and user/requestor is crucial to the success of a project in the definition phase. This requires lines of communication be established early and used often.

Figure 11.1 illustrates an organizational framework for software development. The unshaded circles represent three tiers of management control for the development organization. The user/requester organization (for purposes of managing system development) is indicated with shaded circles. Lines of communication are shown for internal (solid) and external (dot-dashed) paths.

The development organization has three management functions; namely: system management, software manager and software project manager.

The system manager is responsible for overall system development and has responsibilities that include:

1. coordination of hardware and software definition, development and integration;

2. identification of resources required for system development;

3. approval authority for costs and schedule; and

4. interfacing with top level management of both requestor and developer.

The software manager is responsible for day-to-day planning and control of the software effort. The software manager develops a detailed plan and establishes resources, cost and schedule associated with software development. The Software Project Manager is a senior software analyst responsible

for technical aspects of project development. By directing requirements analysis; managing development effort; conducting reviews, and establishing adherence to software configuration standards, the senior software engineer coordinates all technical aspects of software development.

The system manager should insist that the user/requestor organization establish a requestor manager whose primary responsibility is to coordinate all communication between developer and requestor. The requestor manager should appoint individuals to act as contacts for technical aspects of each system element.

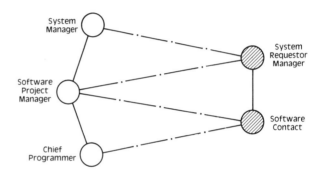

Figure 11.1 Organizational Framework

If suitable user/requestor management is not assigned to the project and adequate software contact not established, the overall management framework is weak. Software development should not be initiated until this weakness is rectified.

11.1.1 Planning, Analysis and the Management Framework

A good management framework promotes communication during this phase of the software life cycle. User/requestor managers and technical contacts have the following responsibilities during the definition phase:

1. schedule meetings with software development staff;

2. provide a detailed description of desired software scope (preferably written);

3. conduct repeated reviews of the developer's perception of scope and function;

4. become actively involved in the definition phase, recognizing it to be critical to project success.

The definition responsibilities of software development managers have been discussed in Chapters 3 and 4. Within the management framework, the software development manager must:

Page 11-2

**Chapter 11
MANAGEMENT ISSUES**

SOFTWARE
ENGINEERING
HANDBOOK

1. establish and maintain contact with the user/requestor;

2. include the user/requestor in definition and review of project scope; and,

3. accurately communicate the collected information to the development team;

4. oversee development of the SOFTWARE PLAN and SOFTWARE REQUIREMENTS SPECIFICATION.

The importance of the framework to project success cannot be overemphasized. Both management domains must take an active role to assure the success of planning and problem analysis.

11.1.2 Management Problems During Definition

Four primary problem areas are encountered by software managers during the definition phase of the software life cycle:

1. communication problems
2. lack of planning tools
3. requirements that change over time
4. political problems

Most communication problems arise during software definition since the system being discussed exists in concept only. That is, it is often difficult to discuss concept in the absence of a tangible model. This leads to preoccupation with irrelevant physical, outward details of the software.

Person-to-person communication can be complicated by a lack of common language between analyst (developer) and user/requestor. Maximum use of diagrams coupled with minimum use of jargon tends to create an atmosphere that encourages the comment—"I don't understand this aspect of the system"—tends to improve interpersonal communication.

Other communication problems arise from poorly written planning documents. Information initially understood often becomes muddled or ambiguous when committed to writing. Conversely, well-written documentation can be misinterpreted by a reader.

A lack of definition tools can create major problems for resource, cost and schedule estimation, and detailed requirements analysis. The primary planning "tool" is historical data used to guide software estimates. Lacking such data, it is extremely difficult for a manager to review estimate accuracy. Other tools, e.g. PSL/PSA (see Section 4.6), can assist the software engineer in developing specifications and evaluating the impact of changes in requirements.

Changing requirements are a fact of life in most large software projects. Although the SRS is reviewed by the user/requestor as the "final" statement of software functions,

modifications may be necessary as development progresses. Planning documents must be developed so that the impact of change can be ascertained.

Changes should be encouraged during the definition phase. An alternative approach or a "second-thought" proposed during analysis can be easily accommodated. A change requested after system integration can increase cost by two orders of magnitude as compared to the same change requested during the requirements step.

Politics is a problem easy to recognize but extremely difficult to solve. If politics are allowed to short circuit communication during the definition phase, the software project is very likely to fail. Although political problems can never be eliminated, the software manager can reduce their impact by:

1. understanding the organizational structure of the user/requestor;

2. establishing contact with all cognizant user/requestor managers;

3. defining documentation standards and review guidelines;

4. recognizing that managers and staff in both the development and user/requestor organizations may feel "threatened" by a new system and must be apprised of effects and changes precipitated by the system.

11.2 SOFTWARE PROJECT FAILURE

A software project fails when requirements defined during the definition phase are not met; when cost and/or schedule are exceeded by a significant margin; and when the user/requestor is dissatisfied with the software. Fortunately, there are a series of controls to alert a manager to potential problems long before "failure" occurs. The software manager should watch the following signals of impending trouble:

1. Little or no communication occurs between developer and user/requestor. PLAN and SRS are developed without advice/consent and are not thoroughly reviewed.

2. Software engineering step reviews are behind schedule; completed with no modifications required; or iterating endlessly at a specific step.

3. No schedule or budget changes occur after software requirements analysis or preliminary design.

4. Code is available after 20 percent of schedule is complete.

5. Development staff are reassigned.

These danger signals are listed in order of priority. The successful manager must learn to recognize these signals early in a project.

SOFTWARE
ENGINEERING
HANDBOOK

Chapter 11
MANAGEMENT ISSUES

Page 11-3

11.2.1 Excuses for Failure

Regardless of application a number of "generic excuses" are often espoused when a software project fails. The following list of excuses (with commentary) has been developed by Stephen Keider* for Auerbach:

The Specifications Changed. Regardless of project complexity, all project specifications change to some degree. What the manager is really saying is:

1. The front-end analysis was incomplete or poor.

2. The project estimate was incorrect.

3. The plan was incomplete or nonexistent.

4. The user never reviewed the functional specifications.

5. The actual impact of budget or schedule changes was never anticipated.

The User Did Not Know What He Wanted. This is the classical excuse; it attempts to justify poor project implementation. What the manager is really saying is:

1. The user was never asked what he needed.

2. The developer decided to do the project because it was interesting.

3. An incompetent analyst worked with an incompetent user.

4. Communications between developer and the user never existed.

Lack of Machine Time Hampered Development. With the abundance of computer power available and the ready accessibility of terminals and/or minicomputers for development, this excuse is becoming less plausible. What the project manager is often saying is:

1. I did not plan well for test time and was caught in the machine crunch at year-end closing.

2. I was not very imaginative addressing this problem; I really did not look at such alternatives as scheduling night shift or weekends or using a service bureau.

Vendor Slippage of Equipment and Software. This was an excellent excuse in 1965 when CPU and operating system architecture was in the infant stage. Today, what the manager is probably saying is:

* Keider, S.P., Why System Development Projects Fail, Systems Development Management Auerbach Publishers; pamphlet no. 34-02-01.

1. The vendor said the first shipment would be during third quarter. I unthinkingly assumed that the first machine would be delivered to me.

2. I was so excited about working with a new machine that I forgot about making the system work.

3. I really do not have a valid reason for the project being behind schedule except for poor management, so I decided to blame the vendor.

We Built a Cadillac and All They Wanted Was a Volkswagen. This common excuse is often applied to a first-time application of computers or to a user attempting to operate the system with semi-literate help (e.g., the use of a sophisticated production control system in a foundry). What the manager is really saying is:

1. We never asked the user what was needed.

2. I am more interested in what I learned and implemented than with the usability of the system by the user.

We Were Given a Poor Estimate. This is a good excuse when all else fails. However, it is only good once. When used, it should be met with the response, "Well, what is your estimate?" This invalidates any future use of the excuse. What this excuse really means is:

1. I have not estimated or planned this project.

2. I did not track or manage the project; if I had, I could have told you months ago that the estimate was inaccurate.

The Slippage is the Result of a High Turnover Rate. Obviously, staff turnover will affect a project. What the project manager is saying, however, is that he does not know whether:

1. This is a poor project because people are leaving, or

2. People are leaving because this is a poor project.

There Has Been a Lack of Commitment by Top Management. Lack of commitment can cause problems for all concerned with the project. What the project manager is probably saying, however, is:

1. Top management does not have confidence in the staff's ability because of past performance.

2. The potential impact of our project was never really explained to top management.

11.2.2 Reasons for Failure

Commentary on each of the excuses discussed in the preceding paragraph provides some insight into the real reasons for software project failure. Three classes of problems exist:

Page 11-4

**Chapter 11
MANAGEMENT ISSUES**

SOFTWARE
ENGINEERING
HANDBOOK

1. **Inadequate planning**—poorly defined development organization; nebulous definition of project scope; seat-of-the-pants estimates; inappropriate resources; vague statement of requirements; lack of anticipation.

2. **Cursory or non-existent reviews**—no timely, reviewable milestones; poor documentation; staff unavailable to conduct review, no follow-up of review suggestions; no involvement of user/requestor.

3. **Lack of a well**-structured method—ill-defined or non-existent design approach; unstructured design and code; no formal testing; lack of standards; "reinvent the wheel" for each project.

Throughout the Handbook, techniques to avoid each problem class have been presented. Judicious implementation of the software engineering methodology provides a major safeguard against most software project failures.

11.3 STANDARDS

The development and promulgation of software engineering standards is strongly debated. One group feels that every document, technique, review and organization must be formally standardized; another group views any standard as an unnecessary restriction to creative management and technical efforts. The answer falls between these highly polarized outlooks.

The following guidelines can be used by the manager considering development of software engineering standards:

1. If standards are developed, they must be enforced; therefore, don't publish standards that cannot or will not be enforced.

2. Start with standard document formats; a standard document format often "forces" use of other standard techniques.

3. Develop standard checklists and document cover sheets (e.g. the MDF cover sheet) to guide reviews and establish traceability.

4. State a policy on reviews—how, when, by whom they are to be conducted.

5. Do not standardize techniques until they are proven by use on one or more actual projects.

6. Since software engineering is evolving, expect standards to change over time as greater experience is gained.

Published standards promote a common approach to software development. A common base of understanding is essential for management control, technical development and maintainability. The introduction of software engineering standards need not be a chaotic process. Gunther* proposes the following points to govern introduction of standards:

1. Provide a reason for following every rule, one that can be understood and appreciated by those who must follow it.

2. Introduce each new member of the organization to established standards during an orientation discussion; explain how following them benefits all in the organization. Cite several examples to show where following standards paid off and where not following standards led to problems.

3. Introduce each new standard orally. It is preferable to do this during a monthly communications meeting or other settings not specifically staged for the presentation of standards so that participants will not anticipate the meeting with aversion.

4. Encourage discussion of each new standard, particularly to bring out any objections to it or doubts about its effectiveness.

5. Keep all standards up-to-date. Never criticize a worker for following an obsolete standard unless you are sure the individual is aware of the new one and has had time to adopt it. Conversely, never fail to communicate new standards, in writing. Always allow time for them to be phased in.

6. Make sure all standards are understood, not only in terms of what is to be done but in terms of how it is to be done.

11.4 SOFTWARE ENGINEERING EDUCATION

Disciplines embodied in software engineering are unknown to many software professionals and their managers. The General Electric *Software Engineering Handbook* provides important information about the methodology. Supplementary training is also essential. Education is the vehicle for implanting any new technology; software engineering is no exception. To prepare any company to move forward in this area, five major training areas must be considered:

1. General Business Managers
2. Technical Managers
3. Technical Staff
4. Entry-level Staff
5. Other Retraining Efforts

General Business Managers

Business managers must find out that software engineering exists; that systematic techniques for computer software management and development are available; that productivity measures are available; that tools are available to develop better cost and schedule estimates; that management cognizance of the software development process needs to be improved; and that a vast array of resources can be provided to improve software quality and reduce software cost.

* Gunther, R. C., Management Methodology for Software Product Engineering, John Wiley, 1979, pp. 318-19.

**SOFTWARE
ENGINEERING
HANDBOOK**

Chapter 11
MANAGEMENT ISSUES

Page 11-5

The manager need not be technically sophisticated to understand the increasing costs involved in software development. Recognition that an investment in procedures and resources can provide significant payoff in the long term should be the immediate result of this effort.

Technical Managers

Technical managers must also be educated; the details of the software engineering process must be understood. As the technical manager often has project responsibility, organization, planning, cost estimation and scheduling are major concerns. The technical manager, able to recognize the resources and controls required for software engineering must communicate those needs to business managers. At the same time the technical manager must communicate with technical staff establishing guidelines and review procedures for computer software development. Education at this management level is crucial since; there is a critical shortage of top technical managers versed in modern software engineering technology.

Technical Staff

Technical staff must be trained in a broad array of software engineering techniques. Analysis approaches, design methods, structured coding, and testing techniques are among the training topics relevant to the technical staff. However, before and/or during training the technical staff must be convinced that software engineering methods will work and enhance their job stature.

Resistance to change, to the implementation of new techniques in the software development area, is typical throughout industry. Resistance, irrational or reasoned, must be countered by education, not coercion, to produce a healthy, effective working environment. A set of dictated standards will not result in an improved software development picture. Until the technical staff is convinced that behavioral changes are justified and will result in better quality software, nothing will happen.

Entry-Level

Entry level training is a key element of any training program. Entry level people readily accept new modes of control and are eager to apply new techniques provided they are involved in meaningful work. A well designed, formal entry-level program can also improve recruiting results by demonstrating a commitment to software as a discipline. Such programs can provide intensive training and "accelerated experience" that cannot be achieved in any other manner.

Other Retraining Efforts

The last facet of a comprehensive training program to address the software issues is retraining. As technologies change, talented individuals move rapidly toward technical obsolescence. Many people can be retrained to satisfy the dramatic need for additional software staff. A retraining curriculum can be carefully designed to complement existing knowledge of the participants and provide a fundamental background in software engineering methods.

11.5 HOW TO ESTABLISH SOFTWARE ENGINEERING

The Software Engineering Handbook provides a foundation for establishment of software engineering. But before the methodology can be put into place, management and technical staff must be convinced that it will:

1. improve the effectiveness of software development;
2. lead to better control over the development process;
3. not lessen the "creativity" of technical staff;
4. justify increased effort required to document and review.

In effect, software engineering must be "sold" to each level in an organization. Section 11.4 answers the question, "what's in it for me", for business managers, technical managers, technical staff, and entry-level people.

Education is the first step toward establishing a software engineering methodology. To quote Yourdon*:

"First convince your audience that current techniques still leave much to be desired. Second, convince them that new techniques are demonstrably better than any of the approaches currently being used."

"... you need ammunition—some statistics, case studies and documented evidence ..."

Education must be tailored to the audience, e.g. emphasize productivity with managers, emphasize design/quality issues with technical staff.

One of the best studies that provides detailed evidence in favor of software engineering has been developed by Walston and Felix**. The authors consider a broad range of variables that support the need for up-front analysis. Software engineering techniques are shown to improve productivity by a factor of 1.5 to 2.0!

11.5.1 An Implementation Approach

A step-by-step approach to implementation of a software engineering methodology is difficult to define. Organizational structures, project size and application, and the degree of management support and technical acceptance can all affect an implementation approach.

---

* Yourdon, E., *Managing the Structured Techniques,* 2nd edition, Prentice-Hall, 1979.
**Walston, C. and Felix, C., *A Method of Programming Measurement and Estimation.* IBM Systems Journal, 16.1, 1977, pp. 54-73.

Page 11-6

Chapter 11
MANAGEMENT ISSUES

**SOFTWARE
ENGINEERING
HANDBOOK**

The following steps are provided as a point of departure:

1. Do some preliminary research to get internal and external statistics on software development. These data can be used to justify the following steps for top level management.

2. Educate managers and technical staff. Options include internally produced courses (these require considerable effort to develop); or a wide range of external offerings provided by consultants, professional societies and universities.

3. Establish informal standards by defining document formats, review procedures and recommended techniques. The "guidelines" should be written and reviewed prior to step 4.

4. Select a prototype project. Criteria for selection are discussed in Section 11.6.2.

5. Establish a method for collection of software productivity data. The type of data to be collected has been discussed in other sections of the Handbook. Collection method must be simple and require relatively little staff effort.

6. Decide upon a development organization that is workable within the local environment.

7. Initiate the project.

8. Expect time spent on the learning curve. Progress on the prototype project may be hampered by unfamiliarity with techniques and some degree of confusion about documentation and reviews.

9. Demand technical and management reviews; track progress carefully. Since the prototype project is also used to test the efficacy of a software engineering approach, successes and failures at each step should be reviewed.

10. Encourage critiques of methods and/or documentation format from development staff. All critiques should be accompanied by suggestion for improvement.

11. At project completion, evaluate all information collected.

12. Modify "informal" standards as required by insights gained in step 11.

Don't let informal standards become formal standards unless each worked successfully and has been accepted by development staff.

11.5.2 Selecting a Prototype Project

A software engineering prototype project is really an experiment that is to be conducted during the development of a software subsystem. Does the software engineering methodology work? Can it be adapted to the local environment? Can local staff apply new methods successfully? These questions, and others, can be partially answered after the prototype project is complete.

Yourdon specifies three primary attributes of a prototype project:

1. the project should not be too large;

2. the project should be useful, visible, but have relatively low risk;

3. the project should be measurable.

In general a project that will require from 6 to 18 person-months is ideal for the prototype. High risk efforts should be avoided because of uncertainty inherent in the application of any new approach. Productivity data acquired from the prototype should be compared to data collected (often, after the fact) from other projects.

11.6 SUMMARY

Management of software engineering requires a consideration of issues that supplement concrete documentation, technical and review procedures. A well defined organizational framework, coupled with the lines of communication between developer and user/requestor, is essential for successful software development. Reasons for project failure must be studied in an attempt to recognize excuses and underlying causes.

Software Engineering requires education and training for all levels of management and technical staff. The training approach will vary with the audience, but the basic philosophy remains the same. Once training is complete, a step by step approach to implementation of the methodology follows.

**SOFTWARE
ENGINEERING
HANDBOOK**

Chapter 12
COMPREHENSIVE EXAMPLE

Page 12-1

INTRODUCTION

This chapter of the Handbook presents an example that illustrates the important activities and documents produced during the software engineering process. The example is based on an actual software development project performed by students in General Electric's Software Engineering Program who are all primarily recent college graduates.

The example depicts the definition and development of a software tool for FORTRAN language scource code manipulation. A project description is contained in the following section.

The example is intended to be comprehensive. That is, each step in the process is considered. However, documents presented have been abbreviated to conserve space and to promote easier comprehension of the concepts.

The example documents conform closely in content and format to those outlined in Appendix A. It should be noted that specific characteristics of a project or the software itself may dictate slight variances from guideline. When necessary, the example documentation departs from the guidelines so that pertinent information may be stressed or detailed descriptions expressed more clearly. In the interest of brevity, all Table of Contents for each document have been omitted.

SYSTEM DESCRIPTION
PART I

Requestor: John W. Smith
Title: Manager Advanced Software Engineering
Component: Software Engineering Tool Center
Phone: (203) 999-5599
Project Supervisor: Jane F. Doe
Phone Extension: 9987

Project Description:

The FORTRAN Prettyprint module will accept a FORTRAN source program as input, will reformat the program by properly indenting its flow-of-control structure and will write the reformatted program to file. It is anticipated that this program will process the output of preprocessors such as RATFOR which typically generate many unneeded CONTINUE statements. The Prettyprint module will eliminate redundant CONTINUE statements.

Objectives:

The objective of this project is to provide a design and documentation tool. Using this tool in conjunction with structured coding techniques, the programmer will be able to quickly check flow-of-control structures. The automatic provision of an indented source program will improve the self-documenting properties of the program.

Input:

The input to this module will be a FORTRAN source program from a disk file.

Output:

A new reformatted file will be the output. The original input source will be saved in the original file.

Constraints:

The software for this project will be written in FORTRAN with a major consideration being portability from one vendor's equipment to another's.

SYSTEM DESCRIPTION
PART II

Requestor: John W. Smith
Title: Manager Advanced Software Engineering
Component: Software Engineering Tool Center
Phone: (203) 999-5599
Project Supervisor: Jane F. Doe
Phone Extension: 9987

Project Description:

The Declaration Formatting Module processes the declarative statements of a FORTRAN source program to format them in a uniform manner. It alphabetizes the variable names in each statement and rewrites each type declaration statement as a series of one or more statements consolidated by type.

Objectives:

Provide a generally useful tool for reformatting a FORTRAN source program to assist in improving its self-documenting properties.

Input:

A FORTRAN source program is the input to this module.

Output:

A new file will be created with the declarative statements formatted as described above. The original file is saved.

Constraints:

The software for this project will be written in FORTRAN with a major consideration being portability between vendor's equipment.

Page 12-2

Chapter 12
COMPREHENSIVE EXAMPLE

SOFTWARE
ENGINEERING
HANDBOOK

SOFTWARE PLAN
FORTRAN FORMATTER

1.0 SCOPE

This plan outlines the scope, tasks, deliverables, resources, costs and schedule for a FORTRAN Formatter as requested by the Manager of Advanced Software Engineering in the Software Engineering Tool Center.

1.1 OBJECTIVES

The FORTRAN Formatter (FORTFORM) is a software package that is used as a documentation tool for ANSI FORTRAN '66 source program development. This package produces a reformatted program based on the source flow-of-control statements. Another feature of FORTFORM is the declaration formatting module which recognizes the declarative section of a FORTRAN source program. This software can also accept the output of a RATFOR preprocessor which converts source code into FORTRAN.

1.2 FUNCTIONS

FORTFORM is divided into five major functions defined below:

1.2.1 Declaration Reformatting

1. Reorder declarative statements by type.

   This function groups together similar type declarative statements and puts them in a prescribed order to be defined in the Requirements Specification. The declarative statements which do not conform to ANSI FORTRAN '66 standards will be flagged.

2. Alphabetize variable names within groups of similar type declarative statements.

   FORTFORM reorganizes the variable names within statements alphabetically. An exception will be made for "COMMON", "EQUIVALENCE" and "DATA" statements where alphabetizing will not be done since variable position is meaningful.

1.2.2 Program Body Reformatting

1. Reformat flow-of-control structure.

   Indentations in the source code are made to show logical structure in the program.

2. Eliminate redundant "CONTINUE" statements.

Excess "CONTINUE" statements created by the RATFOR pre-processor are removed.

1.2.3 Box Comments

Three or more consecutive comments are displayed in a more readable fashion. This will be achieved by boxing the comments in asterisks.

1.2.4 Line Fetch

The Line Fetch function reads lines from the user source file and selects information needed for reformatting. This information will be specified in the Requirements Specification document.

1.2.5 Line and Error Store

The newly reformatted source program will be saved in a separately created file. The original sourced file will remain untouched. Error messages will be stored in a second output file generated by FORTFORM.

1.3 PERFORMANCE

No special timing characteristics are required, however FORTFORM will be limited to 32K works of memory. System dependent features will be confined to those modules that handle I/O and will be explicitly documented. Conformity to the ANSI FORTRAN '66 Standard will be maintained.

1.4 RELIABILITY

Standard integration and validation test procedures will be conducted in accordance with the **Software Engineering Handbook.** Hardware failure will not be critical, since the original user file will be kept intact.

1.5 SYSTEM INTERFACES

FORTFORM will be developed on the HP3000 computer, operating under the MPE III Version 3 operating system. A terminal with the standard ASCII character set will be the user interface.

1.6 SCHEDULE CONSTRAINTS

The FORTFORM software package will be implemented in the six week period beginning with Fiscal Week 30 of this year.

SOFTWARE
ENGINEERING
HANDBOOK

Chapter 12
COMPREHENSIVE EXAMPLE

Page 12-3

2.0 TASKS AND DELIVERABLES

The following tasks and deliverables will be required:

TASKS	DELIVERABLES
1. Planning	Software Plan
2. Requirements Analysis	Requirements Specification
	Preliminary User Manual
3. Preliminary Design	Preliminary Design Document
4. Detailed Design	Detailed Design Document
5. Code	Source Listing
6. Unit Test	Test Results
7. Integration Test	Test Plan/Procedure/Results
8. Validation	Test Plan/Procedure/Results
9. Release	Controlled Software Documents
	Final User Documentation
	As-Built Source Code Listings
	Test Software/Results

3.0 RESOURCES

3.1 PEOPLE

The following technical personnel will be required during FORTFORM development.

1. Project Manager
   Requirements, design and test supervision.

2. Four Junior Software Engineers
   Requirements, design, code and test.

3.2 HARDWARE

FORTFORM will be developed on the HP3000 computer. During this development, HP3000 disk drives will be used for file and program storage. Terminals with standard ASCII character sets will be used for input and output. Line printers will also be available for output testing.

3.3 SOFTWARE

The FORTFORM software package will be developed under the MPE III Version B operating system using its standard features and utilities. The RATFOR preprocessor Version 1 and the HP3000 compiler, FORTRAN/3000 Version 01 will be required.

4.0 COST

The cost of the FORTRAN FORMATTER development is projected using a "Task Costing Technique". See Table 1.

5.0 SCHEDULE

A task schedule for the FORTRAN FORMATTER software package development is shown in Figure 1. Deliverables and reviews are denoted by asterisks.

REQUIREMENTS SPECIFICATION
FORTRAN FORMATTER

1.0 SCOPE

This specification defines software requirements for the FORTRAN Formatter (FORTFORM). FORTFORM is a software package that is used as a documentation tool for ANSI FORTRAN '66 source program development. This package produces a reformatted program based on the source flow-of-control statements and reorganizes the declarative section of a FORTRAN source program. The scope and project resources, costs and schedule are defined in the FORTFORM Software Plan Version SEP004P.0-79/7.

The requirements specification will present the interfaces, functions, design considerations, testing procedures and a block diagram of the FORTRAN Formatter Software Package.

2.0 INTERFACES

2.1 HARDWARE

FORTFORM will be developed and executed on the Hewlett-Packard 3000. Interface is through a teletype-compatible terminal with a standard ASCII character set. A total memory capacity of 32K (see Appendix III Glossary) words will be used. FORTFORM will operate within 24K words leaving an approximate 8K words for operating system usage and FORTRAN library routines.

2.2 SOFTWARE

FORTFORM will execute under control of the MPE III Version B operating system on the HP3000. FORTFORM will be written in RATFOR (see Appendix III Glossary), therefore the RATFOR preprocessor will be necessary to convert FORTFORM to Hewlett-Packard Extended FORTRAN 3000. The HP3000 compiler will be used for FORTFORM development. Operating system tools to be used are Trace/3000, Edit/3000, and Debug (see Hewlett-Packard 3000 User Manuals).

2.3 HUMAN

FORTFORM will be a tool for FORTRAN programmers. To access this software package, the user will run FORTFORM from an ASCII terminal. The user will be required to specify the following:

Page 12-4

Chapter 12
COMPREHENSIVE EXAMPLE

SOFTWARE
ENGINEERING
HANDBOOK

TABLE 12.1 TASK COSTING TECHNIQUE

TASK	LABOR/ PERSON WEEKS	PERSON- WEEK COST	TOTAL
Plan and Requirements	6.5	$1820	$11830
Preliminary Design	3.0	1780	5340
Detailed Design	6.8	1780	12100
Code and Unit Test	4.2	1780	7480
Integration	3.2	1810	5790
Validation	2.0	1850	3700
Release	.8	1750	1400
Totals	26.5		$47640
ADDITIONAL COSTS			
Computer time			750
Supplies			500
GRAND TOTAL			$48890

WEEKS	1	2	3	4	5	6	7	8	9
TASKS									
Plan and Requirements	%%%%%%%*								
Preliminary Design		%%%%%%%%%%%%%*							
DETAILED DESIGN				%%%%%%%%%*					
CODE AND UNIT TEST						%%%%%%*			
INTEGRATION TEST							%%%%%%%%%%%%*		
VALIDATION TEST								%%%%%%%*	
RELEASE									*

Figure 12.1 Fortform Development Schedule

1. An input file containing the user's FORTRAN source code.
2. An output file where the user wishes the newly reformatted source code to be placed.

3. An error file for FORTFORM error messages to be written.

When FORTFORM has finished processing the user's file, the user will receive a message from the terminal indicating the status of the program execution. The user can then list the new source output file and error file (if errors have occurred).

2.4 PACKAGING

The FORTFORM Software Package may be transported by 800 B.P.I. (see Glossary) 9-track tape.

3.0 FUNCTIONS

FORTFORM Software will implement five major functions: (see Figure 12.2)

1. Line Fetch (FETCH)
2. Declaration Reformatter (DCL)

SOFTWARE
ENGINEERING
HANDBOOK

Chapter 12
COMPREHENSIVE EXAMPLE

Page 12-5

3. Program Body Reformatter (BOD)
4. Boxing Comments (BOX)
5. Line and Error Store (STORE)

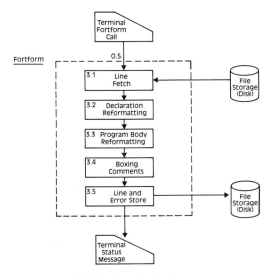

12.2 Fortform Block Diagram

Upon the user's request, FORTFORM will perform the following:

1. Reorder declarative statements by type (see Appendix III Glossary).

2. Alphabetize variable names within statements.

3. Indent Flow-of-Control structures.

4. Eliminate redundant "CONTINUE" statements (see Appendix III Glossary, page 12-11).

5. Box Comments.

3.1 LINE FETCH

Input

The Fetch function receives one statement (see Appendix III Glossary) at a time of the user's source program file.

Processing

The Fetch function reads one source statement and selects the following information:

1. Program Section: Declarative block (see Appendix III Glossary, page 12-10) or Program Body Indicator.

2. Statement Type: FORTRAN Statement Category Indicator.

3. Statement Number: Indicates presence of a statement label.

4. Statement Beginning: First non-blank character position after column six.

5. Statement Termination: Indicates the position of the last non-blank character in a statement.

6. "DO" Loop Terminal Statement Number: A number found in the "DO" statements. This number indicates the statement label of the terminal statement in a "DO" loop.

Output

The applicable information is passed to the Declaration Reformatting, Program Body Reformatting or Boxing Comments Functions (see functions following).

3.2 DECLARATION REFORMATTING

The Declaration Reformatting Function accepts source statements from the Line Fetch Function. Statements are grouped together and ordered by type. Variable names within similar type statements are alphabetized. "COMMON", "EQUIVALENCE", and "DATA" statements will be output with no processing of variables due to the special positional requirements in those statements.

Input

Input to the Declaration Reformatting Function consists of declarative statement types and their associated variable names. This information comes from the Line Fetch Function (see Section 3.1).

Processing

The Declaration Reformatting Function collects and saves variable names by type in a symbol table. When the end of the declarative statement block has been reached, the Declaration Reformatting Function alphabetizes all variable names for each declarative type. New statements are constructed from the symbol table. No statement continuations will be made. The "COMMON", "EQUIVALENCE", and "DATA" statements will be grouped by type, but variable names within them will not be alphabetized. After alphabetizing by type, declarative statements will be grouped together in the following order:

INTEGER
REAL
DOUBLE PRECISION
COMPLEX
LOGICAL
"NON-ANSI DECLARATIVE STATEMENTS"

Page 12-6

Chapter 12
COMPREHENSIVE EXAMPLE

SOFTWARE
ENGINEERING
HANDBOOK

DIMENSION
COMMON
EQUIVALENCE
EXTERNAL
DATA

Non-standard FORTRAN declarative statements (see Glossary) will not be processed. They will be flagged, grouped, and placed after data type statements and before the other declarative statements. Error messages will be generated for variable name overflow and non-standard declarative statements. (See Appendix I, Section 3.1, page 12-8), for specific examples.

Output

Output from the Declaration Reformatting Function is written to a temporary file and error codes are sent to the Error Store Function. The temporary source file will later be combined with output from the Program Body Reformatting Function. Output consists of:

Declaration statements
Error codes.

4.0 DESIGN CONSIDERATIONS

For transportability, a maximum 32K words will be used. Approximately 8K of the 32K will be available for operating system usage. The remaining 24K will be a sufficient memory size for FORTFORM execution and data storage.

Up to 6 files can be opened to be used as work space.

FORTFORM will be coded in RATFOR on the HP3000.

FORTFORM will process ANSI FORTRAN '66 statements.

The user's program should be compiled under the ANSI FORTRAN '66 compiler and checked for errors before using FORTFORM.

The user's input file must be one program segment: one subroutine, one function, or one block data subprogram.

Non-ANSI FORTRAN '66 declarative statements will be grouped together and placed between data type statements and other declarative statements. (See Section 3.2.)

A maximum program size of 500 total source lines will be accepted by FORTFORM. Of these, 150 executable statements, excluding declaratives and comments will be accepted. Upon exceeding either of the two above limits, reformatting will terminate. The remainder of the user source file will be output as it appeared originally. However, If the limit of 500 total source lines is exceeded within the declarative section, FORTFORM will terminate and no output file will be created.

No more than 300 variable names may appear in the declarative block. This will include "EXTERNAL" subroutine names, but exclude "COMMON", "EQUIVALENCE", and "DATA" statements. If this limit is exceeded, processing will terminate and the user's specified output file will not exist.

ANSI FORTRAN '66 standard allows up to 19 continuation lines. Thus, if due to FORTFORM indentations more than 19 continuation lines are generated, FORTFORM will terminate and no output file will be created.

Line-length of seventy-two (72) characters will be accepted by FORTFORM.

All statements excluding comments and continuation lines must start in column 7 or greater. Comments will begin in column 1 with a "C". Line continuations will begin in column 6. This is done in accordance with ANSI FORTRAN '66 standards. Any FORTRAN sequence numbers in the user's source file will be eliminated.

Nesting of up to five levels will be allowed for "DO" loops. Upon reaching this limit, no indentations will be made for succeeding levels.

A "DO" statement must be completed on one line.

If the user attempts to specify an already existing output or error file, or an input file which does not exist, the user will be asked to respecify the file.

Design and coding is aimed at minimal conversion effort for transportability. Input and output functions may have to be modified to accommodate other system's I/O features. An effort will be made to group and comment system-dependent features for ease for conversion to another system.

5.0 DATA BASE

FORTFORM does not make use of an existing data base. A program data structure will be defined during the design phase.

6.0 QUALITY ASSURANCE

Validation of the FORTFORM Software Package will consist of four test classes: error message testing; bounds testing; parallel logic tests and user document validation.

6.1 TEST REQUIREMENT

This section combines a discussion of test requirements and specific tests to be conducted. Subparagraphs address each of the test classes listed in Section 6.0.

SOFTWARE
ENGINEERING
HANDBOOK

Chapter 12
COMPREHENSIVE EXAMPLE

Page 12-7

6.1.1 Error Message Test

All error logic will be tested. To assure that any one of the following tests is testing only one aspect, all other restrictions will remain in bounds.

FILE ALREADY EXISTS—FORTFORM will be run specifying an output or error file that already exists.

FILE DOES NOT EXIST—FORTFORM will be run specifying an input file that does not exist.

SOURCE SIZE EXCEEDED—Two source files containing 501 lines each will be used as input to FORTFORM. One file will consist of only declarative statements and comments. The other file will have executable statements in addition to declarative statements and comments.

EXECUTABLE STATEMENT LIMIT EXCEEDED—A source file containing 151 executable statements will be input to FORTFORM.

6.1.2 Bounds Test

Out of bounds and limit testing are conducted during this phase.

OUT-OF-BOUNDS TEST—This is accomplished by the test specified by the test specified in Section 5.1 ERROR MESSAGE TEST.

WITHIN BOUNDS TEST—A first test will be made using a file which contains all maximum limits. These are 500 source lines, 150 executable statements, a statement with 19 continuation lines, 300 variable names and "DO" loops nested 5 deep.

Four additional tests will be made. These will be done using files with the following characteristics:

500 source lines;
145 executable statements
19 continuation lines
295 variable names
4 nested "DO" loops
---
495 source lines
150 executable statements

6.1.3 Parallel Logic Test

Two FORTRAN programs that are output from the Ratfor processor and two ANSI FORTRAN '66 programs will be used as input files to FORTFORM. The results of FORTFORM will be checked visually. The files will be compiled and executed. The results will be compared to the results of the original programs to assure that original logic was not modified by FORTFORM processing.

6.1.4 User Documentation

User documentation will be turned over to the requestor to review for ambiguities.

Expected results of the tests are listed in Appendix II.

APPENDIX I
PRELIMINARY USER MANUAL

Fortran Formatter
(FORTFORM)

FORTFORM is a tool to aid the FORTRAN programmer in documenting ANSI FORTRAN '66 source programs. The following types of functions are performed by FORTFORM.

—Alphabetically sorting variables in FORTRAN Declarative Type statements and grouping Declarative statements by type.

—Indentation of Flow-of-Control structures.

—Elimination of redundant "CONTINUE" statements.

—Boxing of Comments.

(See PROCESSING Section 3.0.)

1.0 USER INTERFACE

After logging on, to use FORTFORM, type:
:FORTFORM

The user will then be prompted for file names:
PLEASE ENTER INPUT FILE NAME—? ifn
PLEASE ENTER OUTPUT FILE NAME—? ofn
PLEASE ENTER ERROR FILE NAME—? efn

where: ifn is the user specified input file name;
ofn is the user specified output file name; and
efn is the user specified error file name.

When FORTFORM has finished processing the user's file (see HUMAN Section 2.3), the user will receive a message indicating the status of the program execution. Execution is either successful or unsuccessful and one of the following messages will appear on the terminal.

"FORTFORM NORMALLY TERMINATED"

or

"FORTFORM ABNORMALLY TERMINATED-LIST ERROR FILE", efn

Two files will have been created. One will contain the reformatted ANSI FORTRAN '66 source code and the other will contain error messages (see ERROR MESSAGES Section 4).

Chapter 12
COMPREHENSIVE EXAMPLE

2.0 FILES

2.1 FILE NAMES

A file name is a designator which contains 1 to 8 alpha-numeric characters, beginning with a letter (see HP MPE Command Reference Manual).

2.2 INPUT FILE

To use FORTFORM, the user is required to specify a file containing the ANSI FORTRAN '66 source code to be reformatted. The following limitations are imposed on the input file:

—The user's ANSI FORTRAN '66 source code should be compiler error free.

—The user's input file must be one program segment: one subroutine, one function, or one block data subprogram.

—It may not exceed 500 lines of source code. Of these, 150 executable statements will be the upper limit.

—The number of variable names appearing in the Declarative block may not exceed 300. This includes "EXTER-NAL" subroutine names, but excludes "COMMON", "EQUIVALENCE", and "DATA" statements.

—Line-length of 72 characters will be accepted by FORTFORM.

—All statements, excluding comment statements and continuation lines must start after column 6.

—Comments will begin in column 1 with a "C".

—Line continuations will begin in column 6 according to ANSI FORTRAN '66 rules.

—A "DO" statement must be contained on one line.

—Nesting of up to five levels of "DO" loops will be processed.

—Any FORTRAN sequence numbers in the user's source file will be eliminated.

2.3 OUTPUT FILE

The user is responsible for specifying an output file in which the reformatted source code is to be placed. If the user attempts to specify an already existing file, the user will be asked to respecify the output file. The user should check both, program execution status and the error file, before assuming output file completeness.

2.4 ERROR FILE

The user is responsible for specifying an error file in which generated error messages are to be placed. If the user attempts to specify an already existing file, the user will be asked to respecify the error file. For further explanation of errors see ERROR MESSAGES in Section 4.

3.0 PROCESSING

3.1 DECLARATION REFORMATTING

The Declaration Reformatting Function will group together declarative type statements in the following order:

INTEGER

REAL

DOUBLE PRECISION

COMPLEX

LOGICAL

After the above data type statements have been grouped, variable names within the type statements will be alphabetized. If more than 300 variable names, including "EXTER-NAL" subroutine names appear in the declarative block, FORTFORM will terminate and an error message will appear in the error file. The output file will remain empty.

Any non-ANSI FORTRAN '66 declarative statements found will be grouped together and placed after the above data type statements. Variable names will not be alphabetized in these statements.

The remaining declarative statements will be arranged in the following order:

DIMENSION

COMMON

EQUIVALENCE

EXTERNAL

DATA

Variable names will not be alphabetized in "COMMON", "EQIVALENCE" and "DATA" statements.

SOFTWARE
ENGINEERING
HANDBOOK

Chapter 12
COMPREHENSIVE EXAMPLE

Page 12-9

Examples:

Example 1

INPUT
  DIMENSION Z(1),Y(5),A(7),I(10)
INTEGER M,L,Q(7),B(10)
DOUBLE PRECISION D
REAL F,H(5),G

OUTPUT
  INTEGER B,L,M,Q
  REAL F,G,H
  DOUBLE PRECISION D
  DIMENSION A(7),B(10),H(5),I(10),Q(7),Y(5),Z(1)

Example 2

INPUT
  COMMON Z(1),A(4)
  EXTERNAL SIN,COS,TAN,SQRT
  COMPLEX M,N,L,K(15)
  LOGICAL T,F
  DATA T/1/,F/0/
  INTEGER Q(5),H
  EQUIVALENCE (B,D)
  DATA Q/1,2,3,4,5/,A/2,3,4,5/

OUTPUT
  INTEGER H,Q
  COMPLEX K,L,M,N
  LOGICAL F,T
  DIMENSION K(15),Q(5)
  COMMON Z(1),A(4)
  EQUIVALENCE (B,D)
  EXTERNAL COS,SIN,SQRT,TAN
  DATA T/1,F/0/
  DATA Q/1,2,3,4,5/,A/2,3,4,5/

Example 3

INPUT
  INTEGER Q,A,R,B,C(5)
  REAL*4 P,Z,Y
  INTEGER D,E,F,T(2)
  LOGICAL U(2)
  REAL*8 X,N,M(2)
  COMMON I(10),J(20),H(30)

OUTPUT
  INTEGER A,B,C,D,E,F,Q,R,T
  LOGICAL U
  REAL*4 P,Z,Y
  REAL*8 X,N,M(2)
  DIMENSION C(5),T(2),U(2)
  COMMON I(10),J(20),H(30)

3.2 PROGRAM BODY REFORMATTING

The Program Body Reformatting Function identifies logical levels. "DO" structure indentation will be three spaces per logical level. Previously indented logic will be rearranged according to the FORTFORM indentation specification. If indenting causes a line overflow, line continuations will be generated. Processing will also delete redundant "CONTINUE" statements. Redundant 'CONTINUE" statements are those "CONTINUE" statements that have no statement number.

Executable statements will be counted to check the 150 statement limit.

4.0 ERROR MESSAGES

The following is a list of error messages generated by FORTFORM. Below each is an explanation of the error.

1. file name FILE ALREADY EXISTS

The user has specified an output or error file that is already in existance. The user will be asked to respecify the file.

2. file name FILE DOES NOT EXIST

The user has specified an input file that is not in existence. The user will be asked to respecify the file.

3. SOURCE SIZE EXCEEDED

The source input file contains too many lines. The limit of 500 lines will be processed. The rest of the input file will be placed in the output file with no further processing. However, if the 500 line limit is exceeded within the declarative section, FORTFORM will terminate processing and no output will be created.

4. EXECUTABLE STATEMENT LIMIT EXCEEDED

The source input file contains too many executable statements. The limit of 150 executable statements will be processed. However, the remaining input file will be written to the output file without further processing.

5. STATEMENT CONTINUATION LIMIT EXCEEDED

The source input file contains a statement that has too many continuations. (The limit is 19 continuations.) No processing will occur. FORTFORM will terminate.

6. VARIABLE-LIMIT EXCEEDED

The input source file contains too many variable names in the declarative section. (The limit is 300 variable names.) No prcessing will occur. FORTFORM will terminate. No reformatted source code will be placed in the output file. The reformatted source output file will not be created.

Chapter 12
COMPREHENSIVE EXAMPLE

Page 12-10

SOFTWARE
ENGINEERING
HANDBOOK

7. EMPTY INPUT FILE file name

The user specified input file was found empty. No processing could be done.

8. NESTING LIMIT EXCEEDED

The input source file contains a nested "DO" loop structure that exceeds the five level depth limit. Only five levels of indentations will occur. FORTFORM will continue execution.

9. NON-ANSI FORTRAN '66 DECLARATIVE STATEMENTS USED

The input source file contains non-ANSI FORTRAN '66 declarative statements. All occurances of these will be grouped and placed after ANSI FORTRAN '66 data type statements. No variable alphabetizing will occur. FORTFORM execution continues.

10. DECLARATIVE SECTION SYNTACTICALLY INCORRECT

The input source file contains syntactically incorrect variables in the declarative section of the program. No processing will occur. FORTFORM will terminate. No reformatted source will be placed in the user output file.

11. NON-ANSI FORTRAN '66 VARIABLE NAME USED

The input source file contains non-ANSI FORTRAN '66 variable names in the declarative section. These variable names will be put in a newly created statement and added to the non-ANSI declarative section. FORTFORM execution continues.

APPENDIX II
EXPECTED TEST RESULTS

The following appendix is the expected test results from FORTFORM validation tests. The numbering of the paragraphs is set to follow the paragraph numbering in the test section of the requirements specification.

A.1 ERROR MESSAGE TEST

The following section of tests is to insure that the error messages are written in the appropriate place.

A.1.1 file name FILE ALREADY EXISTS

PLEASE ENTER NEW FILE NAME

This message should appear on the user log-on device when the user output or error file name already exists in the directory.

A.1.2 file name FILE DOES NOT EXIST

This message should appear on the user log-on device when the user input file name is not listed in the directory.

A.1.3 file name FILE DOES NOT EXIST

PLEASE ENTER NEW FILE NAME

This message should appear on the user log-on device when the user input file name is not listed in the directory.

A.2 Source Size Exceeded

This error message should appear in the user error file when the 501st source line in encountered in the FORFFORM.

A.3 Statement Limit Exceeded

This error message should appear in the user error file when the 151st executable statement is found by FORTFORM.

APPENDIX III
GLOSSARY

B.P.I:

Bits per inch.

Declarative Statement Section:

Section of ANSI FORTRAN '66 program where the following statements appear:

INTEGER	DIMENSION
REAL	COMMON
DOUBLE PRECISION	EQUIVALENCE
COMPLEX	EXTERNAL
LOGICAL	DATA

Declarative Type:

The declarative type categorizes declarative statements according to their variable types. For example: INTEGER, REAL, DOUBLE PRECISION, DIMENSION, etc.

Flow-Of-Control Structure:

ANSI FORTRAN '66 "DO" loop structure.

**SOFTWARE
ENGINEERING
HANDBOOK**

Chapter 12
COMPREHENSIVE EXAMPLE

Page 12-11

In-Bounds:

Within specified limits. (‹=)

K:

1024 or 2**10.

Line:

72 character string

Logical Level:

Associated with each "DO" statement is a range that is defined to be those executable statements from and including the first executable statement following the "DO", to and including the terminal statement associated with the "DO". This range constitutes one logic level. Another situation occurs when the range of a "DO" contains another "DO" statement range. This would constitue a second logic level.

Non-Ansi Declarative Statements:

Those declarative statements not found in the ANSI FORTRAN Standard X3.9-1966.

Out-Of-Bounds:

Outside of specified limits. (›)

Program Body:

Section of a program following the declarative statement section.

RATFOR:

RATFOR, Rational Fortran preprocessor used for development, which follows standards according to University of Arizona Version 1.

Redundant "CONTINUE":

Those "CONTINUE" statements which have no statement numbers.

Statement:

A statement may be classified as executable or nonexecutable. Executable statements specify action; nonexecutable statements describe the characteristics and arrangement of data, editing information, statement functions, and classification of program units.

Transportable Program:

A program that can be moved from one computer to another vendor's computer with a minimal amount of conversion effort. Areas requiring conversion will be modularized and commented where possible.

**DESIGN DOCUMENT
FORTRAN FORMATTER**

1.0 SCOPE

This document identifies all design characteristics of FORTFORM. A complete description of scope and requirements is provided in the FORTFORM Plan and Requirements Documents.

2.0 APPLICABLE DOCUMENTS

1. FORTFORM Software Plan, SEP004P.0-79/7

2. FORTFORM Requirements Specification, SEP004R.0-79/8

3. ANSI FORTRAN, ANSI X3.9-1966

4. RATFOR-A Preprocessor For a Rational Fortran

   Kernighan, Brian W.; Bell Laboratories

5. Software Tools

   Kernighan, Brian W.; Bell Laboratories

   Plauger, P.J.; Yourdon Inc.

   Addison-Wesley Publishing Company; 1976

6. HP-3000 User Manuals

3.0 DESIGN DESCRIPTION

3.1 FUNCTIONAL ALLOCATION

The five major functions outlined in the FORTFORM Requirements Specification are allocated to individual software modules.

Chapter 12
COMPREHENSIVE EXAMPLE

Page 12-12

SOFTWARE
ENGINEERING
HANDBOOK

3.1.1 Line Fetch Function

The Line Fetch Function will be comprised of three modules:

—A module to read one statement of code from the input source file (SCOOP).

—A module to eliminate blanks from the input source statements (SQUASH).

—A module to parse source statements (PARSE).

SCOOP reads a statement from the user source file into a buffer (LINEBUF see Section 5.2.2). A copy of the statement is then made available to SQUASH which removes all blanks from the statement. The statement is then prepared for parsing. The PARSE module passes information to the Declarative and Body modules.

3.1.2 Declarative Function

The Declarative Function consists of a control module and three major subordinate modules:

—A control module distributes processing to the other three modules (DCL).

—A module to create a variable name symbol table (SYMTAB).

—A module to sort the variable names in the symbol table (SYMSRT).

—A module to recreate declarative statements using variable names from the symbol table (DECREC).

The input to the Declarative Function comes from the Line Fetch Function. This information is processed by SYMTAB to create the symbol table of variable names. After the symbol table is complete, the variable names are sorted alphabetically within declarative statement types. Declarative statements are reconstructed from variable names in the symbol table.

3.1.3 Body Function

The Body Function consists of a major module and one subordinate module.

—A major module identifies the flow-of-control structure of the user source program and eliminates redundant "CONTINUE" statements (BODY).

—The indent module indents statements according to the logical levels (INDENT).

Input to the Body Function comes from the Line Fetch Function. The logic levels and redundant CONTINUEs are identified in the BODY module. The source lines are made available to the INDENT module for line shifting.

3.1.4 Box Function

The Box Function is comprised of one major module and a subordinate module.

—The major module boxes groups of 3 or more comment lines (BOX).

—The star check module checks for comment lines completely filled with stars, previously generated by FORTFORM or otherwise, for boxing purposes (STRCHK).

The Box Function receives source lines from the Line Fetch Function. It first identifies comment lines. BOX then calls STRCHK to determine whether a particular comment line is filled with asterisks. This is done in order to avoid re-boxing of comments.

3.1.5 Line And Error Store Functions

This function is comprised of two separate modules:

—The error module receives error codes and outputs corresponding error messages (ERROR).

—The line store module outputs processed source lines to the output file (FLUSH).

3.2 DATA FLOW

A data flow diagram shown in Figure 1, illustrates top level flow of data through FORTFORM.

In the diagram, three file names are input from the user. Name legality is checked for all three file names first. Next, the input file is checked for its existence. Finally, the output and error files are checked to verify that they do not exist. If there is any deviation to the file specifications above, the user is shown the invalid file name and asked to respecify it. Otherwise, the input, SCRTCH, output and error files are opened and processing begins.

One statement at a time is input from the user source file. Physical lines are counted. If some limits are exceeded (see Requirements Specification, Design Considerations), an error code is sent to an error message generator and the remaining source code is written straight to SCRTCH with no further processing. If no errors are found, selected information needed for further processing is acquired by the parsing process.

Declarative statement types are determined and variable names and their corresponding types are selected. If the number of variables found exceed the 300 limit, an error is sent to the error message generator. Otherwise, the variables are stored in a symbol table (see Section 5.0) by type. When all declarative statements have been read, the stored variable

SOFTWARE
ENGINEERING
HANDBOOK

Chapter 12
COMPREHENSIVE EXAMPLE

Page 12-13

names are alphabetized within types. New declarative statements are constructed from these reordered variables and written to SCRTCH. Any comment lines discovered to be embedded within declarative statements are written directly to the top of SCRTCH.

Then the rest of program body statements are processed. Any statements found within a "DO" loop structure are indented according to FORTFORM Requirements (see Design Considerations). Redundant CONTINUEs are eliminated. At this point, comment lines are passed to the SCRTCH file as they appear. Any other statements not to be reformatted are also written to SCRTCH. If the number of nested "DO" logic levels exceeds the allowed 5, an error code is passed to the error generator. Note that this is not clearly designated in the diagram.

When one entire pass of the user's input file has been made, the partially modified version written in SCRTCH becomes input to the remaining FORTFORM processing.

The partially reformatted source will again be input one statement at a time. Comment lines will be selected out. Non-comment lines will be directly written to the user output file. Consecutive lines of comments will be counted. Only three or more consecutive lines of comments will be boxed before being written to the output file.

3.3 SOFTWARE STRUCTURE

Top level FORTFORM software structure shown in Figure 2, depicts a function oriented design. It has the following overall characteristics:

1. The user interaction is accomplished through the FORTFORM CONTROL(FORCON) with assistance from the FILE VALIDATION (FILVAL) module.

2. Input of the user's source file is achieved by PARSE and its subordinate modules SQUASH and SCOOP. This combination of modules in effect constitutes the Line Fetch Function.

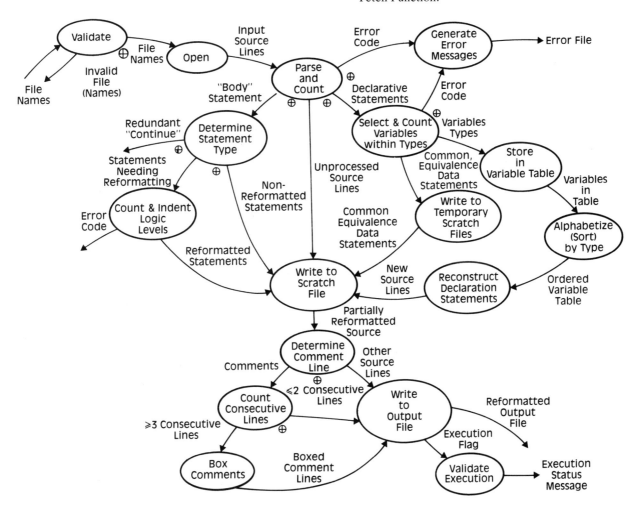

Figure 1. Fortform Data Flow Graph

Page 12-14

Chapter 12
COMPREHENSIVE EXAMPLE

**SOFTWARE
ENGINEERING
HANDBOOK**

3. The reformatting of declarative statement is processed by the DCL branch. The three major subordinate modules to DCL are:

   SYMTAB for creating a symbol table

   SYMSRT for sorting variables within the symbol table

   DECREC for recreating declarative statements

4. The Program Body Reformatting is done by the BODY modules and its subordinate module INDENT. The latter shifts lines according to the program logic levels.

5. The boxing of comments is accomplished by the BOX and its subordinate module STRCHK. STRCHK checks for comment lines completely filled with asterisks to ensure that already boxed comments are not boxed again. BOX gets its input from SCOOP.

6. The output is achieved by two independent modules, FLUSH and ERROR. Module FLUSH is used for writing into the output file and ERROR converts error codes into their corresponding error messages writing these messages into the output error file.

Further breakdown of the functional software structure can be seen in Figures 2A-2D.

4.0 MODULES

4.1 FORTFORM CONTROL MODULES

4.1.1 FORCON

FORCON serves as the control module for the FORTFORM software package. FORCON prompts the user for file names, calls FILVAL to validate the names, passes control between DCL, BODY, and BOX, and finally writes messages to the user indicating success or failure of the FORTFORM run.

4.1.2 INTERFACE DESCRIPTION

FORCON is activated by typing RUN FORTFORM after a system prompt is issued on the terminal. The user is prompted for file names to be entered as follows:

   ifn,ofn,enf

where

   ifn is the user input file name
   ofn is the user output file name
   efn is the user error file name

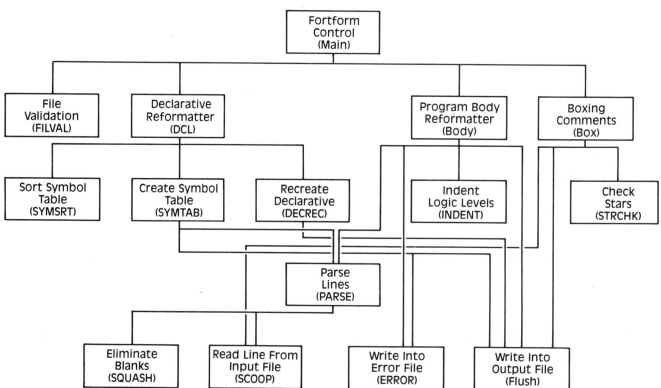

Figure 2. Fortform Software Structure

**SOFTWARE
ENGINEERING
HANDBOOK**

**Chapter 12
COMPREHENSIVE EXAMPLE**

Page 12-15

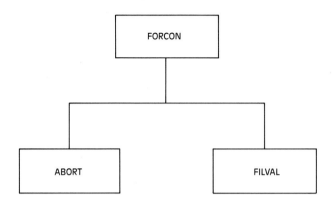

Figure 2A. Fortform Controller Function

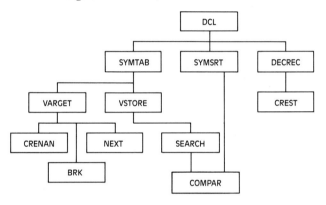

Figure 2B. Declarative Reformatting Function (DCL)

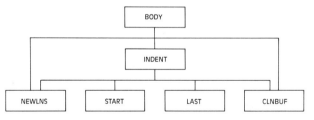

Figure 2C. Body Reformatting Function (BODY)

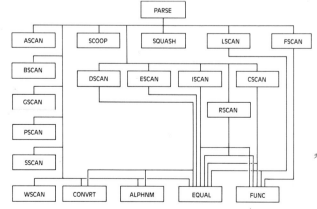

Figure 2D. Line Fetch Function (FETCH)

FILVAL is called by FORCON as follows:

CALL FILVAL (IFN,OFN,EFN, IFG, OFG, EFG)

    IFN - input file name
    OFN - output file name
    EFN - error file name
    IFG - input file flag
    OFG - output file flag
    EFG - error file flag
    IFG,OFG,EFG = 0 valid file name
        = 1 invalid file name

4.1.3 DESIGN LANGUAGE DESCRIPTION

See Appendix I Detailed Design for FORTFORM Control Modules.

4.1.4 SUBROUTINES USED

FORCON calls the following routines:

FILVAL (IFN,OFN,EFN,IFG,OFG,EFG)
DCL (PRGSCT,STTYPE,STNUMB,STBEGN,
STTERM,DONUMB)
BODY (PRGSCT,STTYPE,STNUMB,STBEGN,
STTERM,DONUMB
BOX

FCLOSE HP3000 operating system intrinsic
TERMINATE HP3000 operating system intrinsic
FSET HP3000 FORTRAN system routine

4.1.5 COMMENTS

FORCON—The user is allowed 3 attempts to input valid file names before FORCON aborts. FORCON supplies messages to the user indicating the outcome of FORTFORM processing.

FILVAL—file names must conform to the HP3000 description of file names (see HP3000 User Manual).

4.2 LINE FETCH MODULES

4.2.1 PARSE

PARSE selects information about source statements supplied by SCOOP. It calls SQUASH to get a blank-free statement. Then PARSE searches this blank-free statement for ANSI-66 FORTRAN keywords and statement numbers. PARSE sets parameters to be used by DCL and BODY according to statement type. PARSE also counts source lines; upon exceeding a limit of 500 lines PARSE sets an error flag LINLIM and returns to the calling module.

Page 12-16

Chapter 12
COMPREHENSIVE EXAMPLE

SOFTWARE
ENGINEERING
HANDBOOK

4.2.2 INTERFACE DESCRIPTION

PARSE is called by SYMTAB of DCL, and by BODY using the following calling sequence:

CALL   PARSE(PRGSCT,STTYPE,STNUMB,STBEGN, STTERM,DONUMB)

where PRGSCT is a program section indicator

=1 DCL section
=2 BODY section
=3 End of file

STTYPE indicates statement type of the current statement in LINBUF

=1 Integer
=2 Real
=3 Double Precision
=4 Complex
=5 Logical
=6 Non-ANSI Declarative
=7 Dimension
=8 Common
=9 Equivalence
=10 External
=11 Data
=12 Do
=13 Continue
=14 Comment Line
=15 Other Executable Statement
=16 End

STNUMB is set equal to FORTRAN statement labels when found.

STBEGN is the position of the first character in the statement.

STTERM is the position of the final character in the statement.

DONUMB is set equal to the terminating label of a DO statement when found.

4.2.3 DESIGN LANGUAGE DESCRIPTION

See Appendix II Detailed Design for Line Fetch Modules.

4.2.4 SUBROUTINES USED

PARSE calls the following subroutines:
SCOOP(ENDFIL)
SQUASH(STBEGN,STTERM,NUMLIN)

4.2.5 COMMENTS

PARSE counts lines and checks to see if the source size exceeds the maximum number of lines allowed (see Requirements Specification—Design Considerations for source input limitations). When the limit is exceeded, PARSE sets LINLIM to 1.

4.3 DECLARATION REFORMATTING MODULES

4.3.1 DCL

DCL is the central controller over the Declaration Reformatting (DEC) modules. It is also responsible for opening and closing DEC internal scratch files (see comments). Procedural flow is illustrated in Figure 3A,B.

4.3.2 INTERFACE DESCRIPTION

DCL is called by the FORTFORM controller, FORCON, immediately after file validation has been completed.

CALL   DCL(PRGSCT,STTYPE,STNUMB,STBEGN, STTERM,DONUMB)

"STTERM", and "DONUMB" will not be used by DCL but will be passed on to the submodule SYMTAB. They are the communication interface for those modules which must communicate with the PARSE module (see Section 4.2.4 PARSE Interface Description).

4.3.3 DESIGN LANGUAGE DESCRIPTION

See Appendix III, Detailed Design for Declaration Reformatting Modules.

4.3.4 SUBROUTINES USED

DCL calls the following modules:

SYMTAB(PRGSCT,STTYPE,STNUMB,STBEGN, STTERM,DONUMB)

SYMSRT

DECREC

FOPEN—This an an HP3000 MPE III Operating System intrinsic routine

FCLOSE—This is an HP3000 MPE III Operating System intrinsic routine

FCHECK—This is an HP3000 MPE III Operating System intrinsic routine

FSET— This is an HP3000 FORTRAN system call.

4.3.5 COMMENTS

There are four Declaration Reformatting scratch files that will be used. These files are used to hold those statements that are not going to be processed by FORTFORM.

COMSCR: This file will contain all "COMMON" statements found.

EQUSCR: This file will contain all "EQUIVALENCE" statements found.

DATSCR: This file will contain all "DATA" statements found.

NASCR: This file will contain all NON-ANSI statements found.

For information on the 'SYMBOL TABLE STRUCTURE', see Section 5.3.

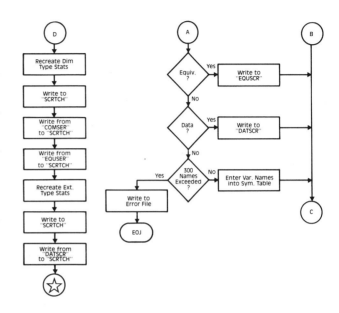

Figure 3B. Procedural Diagram – DCL

5.0 FILE STRUCTURE AND GLOBAL DATA

The organization of this section has been modified to indicate relationship between each module and external/global data.

5.1 EXTERNAL FILE DESCRIPTION

5.1.1 FORCON

FORCON will access four files. They are:

User Input File— Source file for FORTFORM;
User Output File— Destination file for FORTFORM;
User Error file— File for FORTFORM error messages; and
SCRTCH— general scratch file used by FORTFORM.

These files will be sequentially accessed and will be handled by the MPE III file manager. FORCON has no data structures. FORCON uses a global error flag STAFLG for determining the outcome of processing.

5.1.2 PARSE

PARSE accesses no files but uses three data structures, LB(80), SQBUF(1320) and LINBUF(20,80). These structures are all global and are discussed in Sections 5.2.1 and 5.2.2.

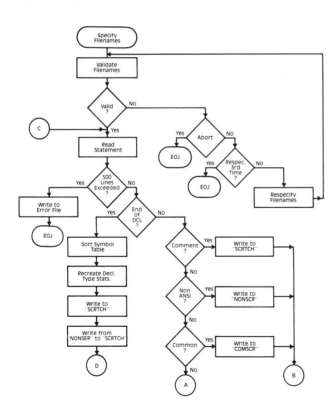

Figure 3A. Procedural Diagram – DCL

Page 12-18

Chapter 12
COMPREHENSIVE EXAMPLE

**SOFTWARE
ENGINEERING
HANDBOOK**

5.2 GLOBAL DATA

5.2.1 SYMBOL TABLE STRUCTURE

The following set of arrays from a symbol table used for storing variable names and other needed information for reformatting the declarative statements.

INTEGER SRTTAB (601)

This array ("SORT TABLE") is dimensioned by twice the maximum number of variables allowed +1. The extra position in the symbol table is reserved for temporary storage of variables during transition from the buffer to permanent positioning within the table. This array contains indices to the remaining arrays of the symbol table structure. These indices are the only elements to be rearranged during the sorting phase (see SYMSRT).

CHARACTER VARTAB (601,7)

This array ("VARIABLE NAME TABLE") is dimensioned twice the maximum number of variables allowed +1 (see SRTTAB) by 7 (or maximum character length +1). The second dimension allows storage of the maximum number of characters allowed each variable name (6) and type indicator in the first column. Placing the type indicator in the first character position allows SYMSRT to easily gather and alphabetize within type, the variable names in the symbol structure.

INTEGER VALEN (601)

This array ("VARIABLE NAME LENGTHS") contains the corresponding length of each variable name found in VARTAB.

INTEGER VARDIM (601)

This array ("NUMBER OF VARIABLE DIMENSIONS") contains a 0,1,2 or 3 to indicate the number of dimensions corresponding to the appropriate variable name in VARTAB.

CHARACTER DIMENS (601, 3, 6)

This array ("DIMENSIONS") is dimensioned twice the maximum number of variables allowed +1 (see SRTTAB), by the maximum number of dimensions per variable, by the maximum length of a dimension. The maximum length of any dimension can mean two things here. If the dimension is represented by a variable name, the maximum length is 6 characters. If the dimension is a numeric constant, the maximum length is 6 digits. This array contains the dimensions(s) of the corresponding variables found in VARTAB.

INTEGER DIMLEN (601, 3)

This array contains the corresponding lengths of the appropriate dimension(s) representation(s) found in DIMENS.

5.3.2 INTERNAL SCRATCH FILES.

There are four declaration reformatting scratch files that will be used to hold those declaration statements that are not going to be processed by FORTFORM. They will be sequentially stored and accessed.

COMSCR: This file will contain all COMMON statements found.

EQUSCR: This file will contain all EQUIVALENCE statements found.

DATSCR: This file will contain all DATA statements found.

NASCR: This file will contain all NON-ANSI statements found.

All four files above will be purged at the end of Declaration Reformatting Processing.

5.2.2 LINE BUFFER

The Declaration Reformatting Section will store unprocessable statements (see 5.3.2) from a global buffer LINBUF. For more information see Section 5.2).

5.2.3 STATEMENT CREATION BUFFER

A buffer called CREBUF will be used for reconstructing the declaration statements. It will be one line long as follows:

CHARACTER CREBUF (80)

6.0 REQUIREMENTS CROSS REFERENCE

See Figure 4 for the Requirements Cross Reference.

7.0 TEST PROVISIONS

Details of the test specifications for FORTFORM will be provided in separate Integration and Validation Test Documents. FORTFORM design will be reviewed. Code walkthroughs will be conducted for each module and each module will be unit tested before any integration testing starts.

8.0 PACKAGING

There are no special internal packaging provisions. However, the FORTFORM SOFTWARE PACKAGE will be transported by 800 B.P.I., 9-track tape.

SOFTWARE
ENGINEERING
HANDBOOK

Chapter 12
COMPREHENSIVE EXAMPLE

Page 12-19

Requirements	FORTFORM CONTROL	FILE VALIDATION	DECLARATIVE REFORMATTER	CREATE SYMBOL TABLE	SYMBOL SORT	RECREATE DECLARATIVES	BODY REFORMATTER	INDENT LOGIC FLOW	COMMENT BOXING	STARS CHECK	READ INPUT FILE	PARSER	SQUASHER	WRITE OUTPUT FILE	WRITE ERROR FILE
Group Similiar Type Declarative Statements	X		X	X		X									
Reorder Variable Names Within Declarative Types	X		X		X	X									
Indent Flow-of-Control Structure	X							X							
Eliminate Redundant "Continue's"	X						X								
Box Comments	X								X	X					
Error Detection	X	X	X				X					X			
Line Fetch	X										X	X	X		
Line & Error Store	X													X	X

Figure 4. Requirements Cross Reference

APPENDIX I
DETAILED DESIGN FOR FORTFORM

DEVELOPED BY MICHAEL JONES AND ANNE BOOM
AUGUST 1980
PURPOSE: THIS PROGRAM IS THE CONTROL PROGRAM OF THE FORTFORM SOFTWARE PACKAGE. IT PROMPTS THE USER FOR FILENAMES, PASSES CONTROL TO THE DCL, BODY, AND BOX MODULES. FORCON CHECKS ERROR FLAGS FOR TERMINAL ERRORS. IT CLOSES ALL USER FILES AND REPORTS THE PROGRAM STATUS TO THE USER UPON COMPLETION.

THE TARGET LANGUAGE IS ANSI FORTRAN '66.

THIS MODULE OF FORTFORM IS SYSTEM DEPENDENT.

INTEGER IFNUM, OFNUM
INTEGER STAFLG, LINLIM
INTEGER IFG, OFG, EFG, SCR
INTEGER NUM, OLNUM

INTEGER PRGSCT, STTYPE, STBEGN, STTERM
INTEGER TIMES, ENDFIL
INTEGER OLDNM, CHANCE

IFNUM AND OFNUM ARE USED IN COMMON TO INDICATE THE CURRENT INPUT AND OUTPUT FILE NUMBERS.
STAFLG AND LINLIM ARE IN COMMON AND STAFLG IS USED AS A STATUS FLAG WHILE LINLIM IS NOT USED IN THIS ROUTINE.
IFG, OFG, AND EFG ARE USED AS FLAGS TO INDICATE THE STATUS OF FILE VALIDATION.
SCR AND OLDNM ARE USED WITH THE FSET ROUTINE. SCR IS THE NEW LOGICAL UNIT NUMBER AND OLDNM IS THE OLD LOGICAL UNIT NUMBER.
CHANCE IS USED AS A COUNTER FOR FILE NAME ENTRY; PRGSCT, STTYPE, STBEGN, STTERM, STNUMB, AND DONUMB ARE VALUES SET BY PARSE; and TIMES IS A COUNTER USED BY FORCON.

REAL STNUMB, DONUMB

Page 12-20

Chapter 12
COMPREHENSIVE EXAMPLE

**SOFTWARE
ENGINEERING
HANDBOOK**

CHARACTER*30 IFN, OFN, EFN, SCRTCH, CLEAR

THE ABOVE ARE FILE NAMES RESPECTIVELY WHERE SCRTCH HOLDS THE NAME OF THE GENERAL SCRATCH FILE AND CLEAR HOLDS AN ARRAY OF 30 BLANKS USED TO CLEAR OLD FILE NAMES

COMMON/FCMAIN/IFNUM,OFNUM
COMMON/SYSCOM/STAFLG,LINLIM
OFNUM CONTAINS THE CURRENT FILE REFERENCE NUMBERS

SYSCOM IS THE SYSTEM ERROR FLAG COMMON

INITIALIZE THE FILE STATUS FLAGS
DATA IFG,OFG,EFG/3*0/
DATA CLEAR/'

SET FILE REFERENCE NUMBERS

IFNUM=10
OFNUM=11

CLEAR FILE NAMES AND INITIALIZE CHANCE

IFN=CLEAR
OFN=CLEAR
EFN=CLEAR

GET INPUT FILE NAMES

DISPLAY MESSAGE
  ENTER INPUT FILE NAME
ACCEPT IFN
DISPLAY MESSAGE
  ENTER OUTPUT FILE NAME
ACCEPT OFN
DISPLAY MESSAGE
  ENTER ERROR FILE NAME
ACCEPT EFN

CHECK FILE NAMES FOR THE WORD ABORT. IF YES, TERMINATE; IF NO, CALL FILVAL FOR FILE NAME VALIDATION.

IF ABORT(IFN,OFN,EFN)
  TERMINATE
  ENDIF
CALL FILVAL(IFN,OFN,EFN,EFG,IFG,OFG,EFG)

INITIALIZE TIMES AND GO INTO LOOP TO CHECK BAD FILE NAME. IF A BAD FILE NAME IS FOUND ALLOW THE USER TO ENTER ANOTHER, ALLOWING THREE CHANCES TO ENTER A BLANK FILE NAME ACCIDENTALLY. IF ALL FILE NAMES OKAY, CONTINUE.
IF ONE OR MORE FILE NAMES ARE BAD, REVALIDATE USING FILVAL AND STAY IN LOOP

THIS LOOP IS DESIGNED TO GIVE THE USER A TOTAL OF THREE TIMES TO VALIDATE FILE NAMES. IF ALL ARE BAD, THEN TERMINATE. BEFORE FILVAL IS CALLED THE FUNCTION ABORT MUST BE CHECKED.

TIMES=1
DO WHILE(IFG=O OR OFG=O OR EFG=O)
CHECK THE NUMBER OF TIMES THE USER HAS TRIED TO SPECIFY FILE NAMES IF MORE THAN 3 THEN TERMINATE THE PROGRAM
  IF TIMES=3
    TERMINATE
  ENDIF

IF IFG=O THEN OLD NAME WAS BAD ASK FOR NEW NAME AND CONTINUE
  IF IFG=O
    DISPLAY IFN,'INPUT FILE DOES NOT EXIST'
    IFN=CLEAR

    DISPLAY'PLEASE ENTER NEW NAME'
    ACCEPT IFN
  ENDIF
IF OFG=O THEN OLD NAME WAS BAD, ASK FOR NEW OUTPUT FILE NAME AND CONTINUE
  IF OFG=O
    DISPLAY OFN,'OUTPUT FILE ALREADY EXISTS'
    OFN=CLEAR
    DISPLAY'PLEASE ENTER NEW NAME'
    ACCEPT OFN
  ENDIF
IF EFG=O THEN OLD NAME WAS BAD, ASK FOR NEW NAME.
CALL ABORT TO CHECK FOR USER ABORT THEN CALL FILVAL TO VALIDATE FILE NAMES.
  IF EFG=O
    DISPLAY EFN,'ERROR FILE ALREADY EXISTS'
    EFN=CLEAR
    DISPLAY 'PLEASE ENTER NEW NAME
    ACCEPT EFN
  ENDIF
  TIMES=TIMES+1
  IF ABORT(IFN,OFN,EFN) ‹›O
    TERMINATE
  ENDIF
  CALL FILVAL(IFN,OFN,EFN,IFG,OFG,EFG)
ENDDO

AFTER THE FILE NAMES ARE VALIDATED, OPEN THE SCRATCH FILE (SCRTCH). IF THE NAME ALREADY EXISTS IN THE DIRECTORY AS A PERMANENT FILE, THE SYSTEM WILL USE IT AS A TEMPORARY FILE. THIS IS OKAY BECAUSE WE DELETE THE FILE ON EXIT FROM FORTFORM ANYWAY.

SCRTCH='SCRTCH'
OPEN SCRATCH FILE USING "SCRTCH" AS THE FILE NAME

AFTER OPENING THE SCRATCH FILE SET THE LOGICAL UNIT NUMBER AND CALL SCOOP TO SET THE BUFFER FOR THE FIRST TIME. CHECK FOR AN EOF CONDITION, IF SO SEND AN ERROR MESSAGE AND TERMINATE ELSE CONTINUE.

```
SET LOGICAL UNIT NUMBER=11
CALL SCOOP(ENDFIL)
IF ENDFIL=1
  CALL ERROR(8)
  CLOSE AND SAVE ERROR FILE
  DISPLAY'FORTFORM ABNORMALLY TERMIN-
  ATED—LIST ERROR
    FILE',EFN
  TERMINATE
ENDIF
```

IF THE FILE IS NOT EMPTY CALL DCL, UPON RETURN CHECK THE STATUS FLAG. IF IT IS 2 THERE WAS A TERMINAL ERROR SO CLOSE THE ERROR FILE AND TERMINATE, ELSE CONTINUE.

```
CALL   DCL(PRGSCT,STTYPE,STNUMB,STBEGN,
SITERM,DONUMB)
IF STAFLG=2
  DISPLAY'FORTFORM ABNORMALLY TERMIN-
  ATED—LIST ERROR
    FILE',EFN
  CLOSE AND SAVE ERROR FILE

  TERMINATE
ENDIF
```

CHECK FOR PROGRAM SECTION OF 2. THE ONLY TIME THIS SHOULD NOT HAPPEN IS WHEN THERE IS A BLOCK DATA ROUTINE, THEN SKIP BODY AND GO TO BOX. IF THE FLAG WAS A 2, THEN CALL BODY CHECK THE STATUS FLAG ON RETURN AND TERMINATE IF FLAG = 2.

```
IF PRGSCT=2
  CALL BODY(PRGSCT,STTYPE,STNUMB,
  STBEGN,STTERM,DONUMB)
  IF STAFLG=2
  DISPLAY'FORTFORM ABNORMALLY TERMIN-
  ATED—LIST ERROR
    FILE',EFN
      CALL FCLOSE(EFG,1,O)
      CALL TERMINATE
  ENDIF
ENDIF
```

IF THE FLAG WAS NOT A 2 THEN CONTINUE. FIRST CLOSE THE INPUT FILE, THEN REWIND THE SCRATCH FILE AND RESET THE INPUT AND OUTPUT FILE NUMBERS AND CALL BOX

```
CLOSE AND SAVE USER INPUT FILE
REWIND 11
```

```
IFNUM=11
OFNUM=12
CALL BOX
```

UPON RETURN FROM BOX, CHECK THE STATUS FLAG FOR A 1. IF YES, SAVE THE ERROR FILE AND DISPLAY MESSAGE.

```
IF STAFLG=1
  DISPLAY'FORTFORM ABNORMALLY TERMIN-
  ATED—LIST ERROR
    FILE', EFN
      CLOSE AND SAVE THE ERROR FILE
ENDIF
```

IF STAFLG ◇ 1 THEN DELETE ERROR FILE AND DISPLAY MESSAGE.

```
ELSE
    DISPLAY'FORTFORM NORMALLY
    TERMINATED'
    CLOSE AND DELETE THE ERROR FILE
ENDELSE
```

```
CLOSE ALL FILES AND END FORTFORM
  CLOSE AND SAVE THE USER OUTPUT FILE
  CLOSE AND DELETE THE SCRATCH FILE
  END
```

```
  SUBROUTINE FILVAL(IFN,OFN,EFN,IFG,OFG,EFG)
DEVELOPED BY MICHAEL JONES AND ANNE BOOM,
AUGUST 1980
PURPOSE: THIS ROUTINE VALIDATES AND OPENS
THE USER FILES

  INTEGER IFG,OFG,EFG,NUM,OLNUM
```

IFG IS THE INPUT FILE FLAG
OFG IS THE OUTPUT FILE FLAG
EFG IS THE ERROR FILE FLAG
NUM IS THE SYSTEM FILE NUMBER SET BY FOPEN
OLNUM IS THE OLD FILE NUMBER RETURNED BY FSET

THIS ROUTINE IS SYSTEM DEPENDENT

```
  CHARACTER*30 IFN,OFN,EFN
```

IFN CONTAINS THE INPUT FILE NAME
OFN CONTAINS THE OUTPUT FILE NAME
IFN CONTAINS THE ERROR FILE NAME

```
IF IFG=O
  CHECK INPUT FILE NAME
  IF VALID
    OPEN FILE
    SET LOGICAL UNIT NUMBER=10
    SET INPUT FLAG IFG
```

```
    ENDIF
  ENDIF
  IF OFG=O
    CHECK OUTPUT FILE NAME
    IF VALID
       OPEN FILE
       SET LOGICAL UNIT NUMBER=12
       SET OUTPUT FLAG OFG
    ENDIF
  ENDIF
  IF EFG=O
    CHECK ERROR FILE NAME
    IF VALID
       OPEN FILE
       SET LOGICAL UNIT NUMBER=13
       SET ERROR FLAB EFG
    ENDIF
  ENDIF
  RETURN
```

FUNCTION ABORT(IFN,OFN,EFN)

DEVELOPED BY MICHAEL JONES, AUGUST 1980
PURPOSE: THIS ROUTINE CHECKS FOR THE WORD
ABORT IN THE FILENAMES

THIS ROUTINE CONTAINS NON-ANSI '66 FORTRAN
STATEMENTS. THESE STATEMENTS DEAL WITH THE
CHARACTER STRINGS IFN,OFN,EFN, AND ABRT. ALSO
THE CHARACTER*30 IS NON-ANSI

   CHARA*30 IFN,OFN,EFN,ABRT

IFN IS THE INPUT FNAME
OFN IS THE OUTPUT FNAME
EFN IS THE ERROR FNAME
ANY OF THESE COULD CONTAIN THE WORD ABORT
ABRT IS A CONSTANT THAT CONTAINS ABORT

INITIALIZE ABRT

   DATA ABRT/'ABORT'/
CHECK FOR THE WORD ABORT IN ALL THREE OF
THE FILENAMES. IF THE WORD IS FOUND, THEN SET
THE FUNCTION EQUAL TO 1   ABORT=O
   IF IFN OR OFN OR EFN = ABRT
     ABORT=1
   ENDIF
   RETURN

   SUBROUTINE PARSE(PRGSCT,STTYPE,STNUMB,
STBEGN,STTERM,DONUMB);   DEVELOPED   BY
MICHAEL JONES, AUGUST 1980
PURPOSE: THE PARSE MODULE IS USED TO DETER-
MINE STATEMENT TYPE FOR THE DCL AND BODY
MODULES. PARSE BREAKS DOWN A STATEMENT AND
LOOKS FOR SPECIFIC KEY WORDS. THESE WORDS

ARE ASSIGN, BACKSPACE, BLOCKDATA, CALL,
COMMOM, COMPLEX, CONTINUE, C FOR COMMENT,
DATA, DIMENSION, DO, DOUBLEPRECISION, END,
ENDFILE, EQUIVALENCE, EXTERNAL, FORMAT,
FUNCTION, GOTO, IF INTEGER, LOGICAL, PAUSE,
READ, REAL, RETURN, REWIND, STOP, SUBROUTINE,
AND WRITE. IF PARSE DOES NOT FIND ONE OF THESE
KEY WORDS THEN IT CHECKS FOR AN '='. IF PARSE
CAN'T FIND ANY OF THE ABOVE, THE STATEMENT
IS ASSUMED TO BE A NON-ANSI DECLARATIVE.

SUBROUTINES CALLED: SCOOP(ENDFIL)
                        SQUASH(STBEGN,
                        STTERM,NUMLIN)
                        EQUAL(STTYPE)
                        CONVRT(DIGIT)
                        ALPHNM
                        ASCAN(STTYPE)
                        BSCAN(STTYPE)
                        CSCAN(STTYPE)
                        DSCAN(STTYPE,DONUMB)
                        ESCAN(STTYPE)
                        FSCAN(STTYPE)
                        GSCAN(STTYPE)
                        ISCAN(STTYPE)
                        LSCAN(STTYPE)
                        PSCAN(STTYPE)
                        RSCAN(STTYPE)
                        SSCAN(STTYPE)
                        WSCAN(STTYPE)

   INTEGER PRGSCT,STTYPE,STBEGN,STTERM
   REAL STNUMB,DONUMB
THESE ARE THE PARAMETERS TO PARSE. THEY CAN
HAVE THE FOLLOWING VALUES:
   PRGSCT IS THE PROGRAM SECTION.
   1—DECLARATIVE
   2—BODY
   3—END

   STTYPE IS STATEMENT TYPE.
    1—INTEGER
    2—REAL
    3—DOUBLE PRECISION
    4—COMPLEX
    5—LOGICAL
    6—NON-ANSI DECLARATIVE
    7—DIMENSION
    8—COMMON
    9—EQUIVALENCE
   10—EXTERNAL
   11—DATA
   12—DO
   13—CONTINUE
   14—COMMENT LINE
   15—OTHER EXECUTABLE STATEMENT
   16—END

STNUMB IS STATEMENT NUMBER.

SOFTWARE
ENGINEERING
HANDBOOK

Chapter 12
COMPREHENSIVE EXAMPLE

Page 12-23

STBEGN IS THE POSITION OF THE FIRST CHARACTER IN THE CURRENT STATEMENT

STTERM IS THE POSITION OF THE LAST CHARACTER IN THE CURRENT STATEMENT.

DONUMB IS THE STATEMENT LABEL ASSOCIATED WITH THE DO STATEMENT. INTEGER NUMLIN,ENDFIL,LINLIM,COUNT,LINE,MAXLIN,I,J

MAXLIN IS SET BY A BLOCK DATA ROUTINE CALLED BY FORCON. LINE IS AN INTERNAL COUNTER AS ARE I AND J. SQTERM IS USED BY SQUASH AS A POINTER TO THE LAST CHARACTER IN THE SQUASH BUFFER SQBUF.

CHARACTER   LINBUF(20,80),CREBUF(80),LB(80), SQBUF(1320),DIGGIT(5)

CHARACTER BLANK LINBUF IS THE GENERAL STATEMENT BUFFER WHICH CAN HOLD 1 INITIAL LINE AND UP TO 19 CONTINUATION LINES; LB IS THE INPUT LINE BUFFER USED BY SCOOP TO GET INFO TO PARSE; SQBUF IS A BUFFER THAT IS USED BY SQUASH AS OUTPUT FROM THE PACKING ROUTINE IN SQUASH; DIGIT IS A BUFFER USED BY CONVRT; IT HOLDS A 5 DIGIT NUMBER IN ASCII FORMAT TO BE CONVERTED TO AN INTEGER.

THESE ARE THE COMMON AREAS USED BY PARSE. SQASH IS COMMON TO SQUASH, PARSE, AND DCL
    COMMON/SQASH/SQBUF,SQTERM
    COMMON/SYSCOM/STAFLG,LINLIM
    COMMON/CNVRT/DIGIT
    COMMON/SCOO/LB
    COMMON/BUFCOM/LINBUF,CREBUF
    COMMON/PRSFLG/COUNT,ENDFLG,EXCFLG

CONVRT IS A FUNCTION THAT CONVERTS ASCII TO DECIMAL
    EXTERNAL CONVRT
INITIALIZE VARIABLES
    MAXLIN=501
    BLANK="
    STTYPE=O
    STNUMB=O
    DONUMB=O
    IF EXCFLG=1
        PRGSCT=2
    ELSE
        PRGSCT=1
    ENDELSE
CHECK FOR EOF IF YES SET PARAMETERS AND RETURN
    IF ENDFLG=1
        PRGSCT=3
        STTYPE=0
        STNUMB=0

        STBEGN=0
        STTERM=0
        DONUMB=0
        RETURN
    ENDIF
GET STATEMENT AND CHECK FOR MAXIMUM NUMBER OF LINES
    NUMLIN=0
    DO NUMLIN=1,20
        DO LINE=1,80
            LINBUF(NUMLIN,LINE)=LB(LINE)
        ENDDO
        COUNT=COUNT+1
        IF COUNT=MAXLIN
            LINLIM=1
            UNDO
        ENDIF
        CALL SCOOP(ENDFIL)
        IF ENDFIL=1
            ENDFLG=1
            UNDO
        ENDIF
        IF LB(1)='C'
            UNDO
        ENDIF
        IF LB(6)=BLANK
            UNDO
        ENDIF
        IF LB(6)='O'
            UNDO
        ENDIF
    ENDDO
CHECK FOR COMMENT LINE SET STTYPE ACCORDINGLY   IF LINBUF(1,1)='C'
        STTYPE=14
    ELSE
        CALL SQUASH(STBEGN,STTERM.NUMLIN)
NOW CHECK THE FIRST LETTERS OF THE SQUASH BUFFER AND CALL THE APPROPRIATE ROUTINE
        IF SQBUF(1)='A'
            CALL ASCAN(STTYPE)
        ELSEIF SQBUF(1)='B'
            CALL BSCAN(STTYPE)
        ELSEIF SQBUF(1)='C'
            CALL SCAN(STTYPE)
        ELSEIF SQBUF(1)='D'
            CALL DSCAN(STTYPE,DONUMB)
        ELSEIF SQBUF(1)='E'
            CALL ESCAN(STTYPE)
        ELSEIF SQBUF(1)='F'
            CALL FSCAN(STTYPE)
        ELSEIF SQBUF(1)='G'
            CALL GSCAB(STTYPE)
        ELSEIF SQBUF(1)='I'
            CALL ISCAN(STTYPE)
        ELSEIF SQBUF(1)='L'
            CALL LSCAN(STTYPE)
        ELSEIF SQBUF(1)='P'

Page 12-24

Chapter 12
COMPREHENSIVE EXAMPLE

**SOFTWARE
ENGINEERING
HANDBOOK**

```
      CALL PSCAN(STTYPE)
   ELSEIF SQBUF(1)='R'
      CALL RSCAN(STTYPE)
   ELSEIF SQBUF(1)='S'
      CALL SSCAN(STTYPE)
   ELSEIF SQBUF(1)='W'
      CAKK WSCAN(STTYPE)
   ENDELSE
 ENDELSE
 ENDIF
```
IF THE FIRST LETTER WAS NOT ONE OF THE ABOVE
THEN CALL EQUAL
```
   IF STTYPE=0
      CALL EQUAL(STTYPE)
   ENDIF
```
IF STTYPE IS STILL NOT SET ASSUME STATEMENT IS
NON-ANSI
DECLARATIVE
```
   IF STTYPE=0
      STTYPE=6
   ENDIF
```
CHECK FOR A STATEMENT NUMBER IF ONE IS FOUND
PUT IT IN DIGIT AND CALL CONVRT TO CONVERT
ASCII STRING TO REAL NUMBER.
```
   POINT=5
   FOR(I=5,I › 0,I=I-1)
     IF LINBUF(1,I)‹› BLANK
        CHAR=ALPHNM(LINBUF(1,I)
        IF CHAR ‹› 2
          POINT=5
          BREAK
        ENDIF
        DIGIT(POINT)=LINBUF(1,I)
        POINT=POINT-1
     ENDIF
   NEXT
   IF POINT ‹ 5
     FOR(I=POINT,I › 0,I=I-1)
        DIGIT(I)='O'
     NEXT
     STNUMB=CONVER(DIGIT)
   ENDIF
```
CHECK FOR EXECUTABLE STATEMENT IF YES SET
EXCFLG AND PRGSCT
```
   IF EXCFLF=0
     IF STTYPE=12 OR 13 OR 15
        EXCFLG=1
        PRGSCT=2
     ENDIF
   ENDIF
```

CHECK FOR END STATEMENT IF YES SET END FLAG
```
   IF STTYPE=16
     ENDFLG=1
   ENDIF
   RETURN
```


   SUBROUTINE SQUASH(STBEGN,STTERM,NUMLIN)
DEVELOPED BY MICHAEL JONES

WRITTEN BY ANNE BOOM
AUGUST 1980
PURPOSE: THIS ROUTINE FILLS SQBUF WITH A
PACKED VERSION OF LINBUF. SQUASH REMOVES ALL
THE BLANKS FROM THE DATA FOUND BETWEEN
COLS 7 AND 72 INCLUSIVE. THIS IS DONE TO MAKE
PARSING FASTER.

NO SUBROUTINES ARE CALLED

   INTEGER STBEGN,STTERN,NUMLIN,LINCNT,
PSNCNT
   INTEGER LLINE,LPSN,FLINE,FPSN,SQTERM,LINE
STBEGN CONTAINS THE POSITION OF THE FIRST
CHARACTER IN THE BUFFER.
STTERM CONTAINS THE POSITION OF THE LAST
CHARACTER IN THE BUFFER.
NUMLIN CONTAINS THE NUMBER OF LINES IN
LINBUF;
LINCNT IS USED AS AN INDEX TO THE LINES;
PSNCNT IS USED AS AN INDEX TO THE POSITION
WITHIN A LINE; AND
LLINE IS THE LAST LINE.

SUBROUTINE   DCL(PRGSCT,STTYPE,STNUMB,
STBEGN,STTERM,DONUMB)

DEVELOPED BY: ANNE M. BOOM

DATE: AUGUST 1980

PURPOSE: DCL IS THE CENTRAL CONTROLLER OVER
THE   DECLARATIVE   REFORMATTING   (DEC)
MODULES. IT IS RESPONSIBLE FOR OPENING AND
CLOSING DEC INTERNAL SCRATCH FILES (SEE FILES
BELOW). DCL IS CALLED BY THE FORTFORM CON-
TROLLER, FORCON, IMMEDIATELY AFTER FILE VAL-
IDATION HAS BEEN COMPLETED.

MODULES CALLED:
   SYMTAB(PRGSCT,STTYPE,STNUMB,STBEGN,
STTERM,DONUMB)
   SYMSRT
   DECREC

INPUTS: THE PARAMETERS: "PRGSCT","STTYPE",
"STNUMB","STBEGN", "STTERM", AND "DONUMB"
WILL NOT BE USED BY DCL BUT WILL BE PASSED ON
TO THE SUBMODULE SYMTAB. "STAFLG", STATUS
FLAG WILL BE SET BY ONE OF THE PROCESSING
MODULES TO INDICATE TO DCL(HERE) AND
FORCON(AFTER RETURN) IF PROCESSING HAS GONE
BAD.

OUTPUTS: THERE ARE NO OUTPUTS CREATED BY
THIS MODULE ALONE. IT WILL ONLY DIRECT CON-
TROL OVER THE OTHER MODULES WITHIN THE
DECLARACTIVE REFORMATTING SECTION OF
FORTFORM.

SOFTWARE
ENGINEERING
HANDBOOK

Chapter 12
COMPREHENSIVE EXAMPLE

Page 12-25

PARAMETERS: THE SIX PARAMETERS PASSED TO THIS MODULE WILL NOT BE DESCRIBED HERE. THEY ARE NOT USED BY DCL. RATHER, THEY ARE PASSED ON TO SYMTAB. BASICALLY, THEY ARE THE COMMUNICATION INTERFACE FOR THOSE MODULES WHICH MUST COMMUNICATE WITH THE "PARSE" MODULE. WHEN THE FIRST EXECUTABLE STATEMENT OF THE BODY OF THE USER'S INPUT SOURCE FILE IS ENCOUNTERED. THESE PARAMETERS WILL CARRY INFORMATION ABOUT THIS STATEMENT BACK FROM THE DECLARATION REFORMATTING SECTION.

FILES: FOUR DECLARATION REFORMATTING SCRATCH FILES ARE USED:
    COMSCR: THIS FILE WILL CONTAIN ALL "COMMON" STATEMENTS FOUND
    EQUSCR: THIS FILE WILL CONTAIN ALL "EQUIVALENCE" STATEMENTS FOUND
    DATSCR: THIS FILE WILL CONTAIN ALL "DATA" STATEMENTS FOUND
    NASCR: THIS FILE WILL CONTAIN ALL NON-ANSI STATEMENTS FOUND
    THESE FILES ARE USED TO HOLD THOSE STATEMENTS THAT ARE NOT GOING TO BE PROCESSED BY FORTFORM.

    SUBROUTINE   DCL(PRGSCT,STTYPE,STNUMB,
STGEBGN,STTERM,DONUMB)

DECLARE THE USE OF SYSTEM INTRINSIC (SYSTEM-DEPENDENT) ROUTINES
    SYSTEM INTRINSIC FOPEN
    SYSTEM INTRINSIC FCLOSE
COMMON VARIABLES
    COMMON/SYSCOM/STAFLG,LINLIM
    COMMON/BUFCOM/LINBUF(20,80),CREBUF(80)
    COMMON/SQASH/SQBUF(1 320),SQTERM
    COMMON/TABLE/SRTTAB(601),VARTAB(601,7),
    VARLEN(601),

    VARDIM(601),DIMENS(601,3,6),DIMLEN(601,3),
    TABROW,
        VARCNT,TYPES(11),DOUMAX,   TAGCOL,
    TYPTAG,TYPIND MAXLEN,MAXDIM,MAXVAR

    COMMON/CREATE/TYPTAB(11,16),TYPLEN(11),
    BLANK,LMARG,LPAREN
        RPAREN,COMMA,MAXCOL,LINE

    COMMON/TYPCON,INT,RE,DP,CPX,LOG,NA,DIM,
    COM,EQU,EXT,DAT,COMM

        INTCOL,RECOL,DPCOL,CPXCOL,LOGCOL,
    DIMCOL,COMCOL. EQUCOL,EXTCOL,DATCOL
    INTEGER STAFLG,LINLIM
    INTEGER   SRTTAB,VARLEN,VARDIM,DIMLEN,
    TABROW,VARCNT,DOUMAX,
        TAGCOL,TYPIND,MAXLEN,MADXIM,MAXVAR
    INTEGER SQRTERM

    INTEGER TYPLEN,LMARG,MAXCOL,LINE
    INTEGER   INT,RE,DP,CPX,LOG,NA,DIM,COM,
    EQU,EXT,DAT,COMM,
        INCOL,RECOL,DPCOL,CPXCOL,LOGCOL,
    DIMCOL,COMCOL
        EQUCOL,EXTCOL,DATCOL
    CHARACTER LINBUF, CREBUG
    CHARACTER SQBUF
    CHARACTER VARTAB,DIMENS,TYPES,TYPTAG
    CHARACTER   TYPTAB,BLANK,LPAREN,RPAREN,
    COMMA

PARAMETERS
    INTEGER PRGSCT,STTYPE,STBEGN,STTERM
    REAL STNUMB,DONUMB

LOCAL VARIABLES
    INTEGER FIL(4)
    INTEGER OLDCOM,OLDEQU,OLDDAT,OLDNA
    CHARACTER*6 COMSCR,EQUSCR,DATSCR,NASCR

OPEN THE "COMMON","EQUIVALENCE","DATA", AND NON-ANSI SCRATCH FILES

    OPEN FILES COMSCR,EQUSCR,DATSCR,NASCR

CREATE THE SYMBOL STRUCTURE
    CALL   SYMTAB(PRGSCT,STTYPE,STNUMB,
STBEGN,STTERM,DONUMB)

IF SOMETHING WENT BAD, RETURN
    IF (STAFLG=2)
        RETURN

SORT THE VARIABLE INDICES
    CALL SYMSRT

RE-SET THE SCRATCH FILES FOR OUTPUTTING
    REWIND 1
    REWIND 2
    REWIND 3
    REWIND 4
RECREATE THE DECLARATIVE STATEMENTS
    CALL DECREC

CLOSE AND PURGE THE SCRATCH FILES
    CLOSE FILES COMSCR,EQUSCR,DATSCR,NASCR
    RETURN
    END

NOTE: The rest of the PDL description has been omitted.

Page 12-26

Chapter 12
COMPREHENSIVE EXAMPLE

SOFTWARE
ENGINEERING
HANDBOOK

EXAMPLE MDF COVER SHEETS

The following pages contain examples of Module Development Folder cover sheets for the FORTFORM system.

MODULE DEVELOPMENT FOLDER

COVER SHEET   PAGE _1_ OF _3_

PROJECT: _FORTRAN FORMATTER_ REVISION: _0_ DATE: _9/79_
MODULE NAME: _DECLARATION REFORMATTING_ ISSUE DATE: _____
PROGRAMMER: _ANNE PATH_ BUDGET: _____
DESIGN SECTION: _4.3_   SOURCE LINES: _____
                              OBJ. MOD. SIZE: _____

ROUTINE NAME	DCL	SYMTAB	SYMSRT	DECREC	VARGET
DESIGN SUBSECTION	4.3.1	4.3.2	4.3.3	4.3.4	
DESCRIPTION	DECLARATION REFORMATTING CONTROLLER	SYMBOL TABLE CREATION CONTROLLER	SYMBOL TABLE SORTER	STATEMENT RECREATOR CONTROLLER	VARIABLE SELECTOR
CODE TO DESIGN					
SCHED START	8/05/79	8/05/79	8/05/79	8/05/79	8/05/79
ACTUAL START	8/10/79	8/10/79	8/10/79	8/10/79	8/10/79
SCHED COMPL	8/12/79	8/12/79	8/12/79	8/12/79	8/12/79
ACTUAL COMPL	8/27/79	8/27/79	8/27/79	8/27/79	8/27/79
CODE/UNIT TEST					
SCHED START	8/12/79	8/12/79	8/12/79	8/12/79	8/12/79
ACTUAL START	9/01/79				→
SCHED COMPL	8/22/79				→
ACTUAL COMPL	9/10/79				→
INTEGRATION					
SCHED START	8/24/79	8/24/79	8/24/79	8/24/79	8/24/79
ACTUAL START	9/01/79				→
SCHED COMPL	8/27/79				→
ACTUAL COMPL	9/10/79				→
CODE REVIEW DATE/INITIALS					
LISTING DATE					
SOURCE LINES	RATFOR / FORTRAN	RATFOR / FORTRAN	RATFOR / FORTRAN	RATFOR / FORTRAN	RATFOR / FORTRAN
BUDGET					
ACTUAL	50 / 51	88 / /21	20 /	.39 /	/23 /
OBJ. MOD. SIZE					
BUDGET					
ACTUAL					
CHIEF PROGR. APPROVAL					

MDF Cover Sheet

SOFTWARE
ENGINEERING
HANDBOOK

Chapter 12
COMPREHENSIVE EXAMPLE

Page 12-27

MODULE DEVELOPMENT FOLDER

COVER SHEET   PAGE ___ OF ___

PROJECT: _Fortran Formatter_   REVISION: _∅_ DATE: _9/27/79_

MODULE NAME: _Line Fetch_   ISSUE DATE: _9/26/79_

PROGRAMMER: _M. Warren_   BUDGET:

DESIGN SECTION: _4.2_   SOURCE LINES: _RAT-563 FOR-860_

                                      OBJ. MOD. SIZE: _606_

ROUTINE NAME	PARSE	SQUASH	SCOOP		
DESIGN SUBSECTION	4.2.3	4.2.2	4.2.1		
DESCRIPTION	Determine Fortran statement Type	Remove blanks from statement for Parsing	Get line of Fortran Source		
CODE TO DESIGN					
SCHED START	8/6	8/6	8/6		
ACTUAL START	8/7	8/7	8/7		
SCHED COMPL	8/13	8/13	8/13		
ACTUAL COMPL	8/27	8/27	8/27		
CODE/UNIT TEST					
SCHED START	8/13	8/13	8/13		
ACTUAL START	8/27	8/27	8/27		
SCHED COMPL	8/22	8/22	8/22		
ACTUAL COMPL	9/3	9/3	9/3		
INTEGRATION					
SCHED START	8/23	8/23	8/23		
ACTUAL START	9/4	9/4	9/4		
SCHED COMPL	8/27	8/27	8/27		
ACTUAL COMPL	9/21	9/21	9/21		
CODE REVIEW DATE/INITIALS					
LISTING DATE	9/27	9/27	9/27		
SOURCE LINES	RAT 525 FOR 810	RAT 25 FOR 35	RAT 13 FOR 15		
BUDGET ACTUAL					
MOD. SIZE	468	78	60		
BUDGET ACTUAL					
CHIEF PROGR. APPROVAL					

MDF Cover Sheet

Page 12-28

Chapter 12
COMPREHENSIVE EXAMPLE

SOFTWARE
ENGINEERING
HANDBOOK

INTEGRATION TEST SPECIFICATION
FORTRAN FORMATTER

1.0 SCOPE

This document contains a description of the management plan and technical procedure for integration testing of the Fortran Formatter (FORTFORM).

2.0 APPLICABLE DOCUMENTS

FORTFORM Software Plan SEP004P.0-79/7

FORTFORM Requirements Specification SEP004R.0-79/8

FORTFORM Design Document SEP004D.0-79/9

3.0 TEST PLAN

3.1 TEST PHASES

The integration test will be divided into three phases. Phase I will test the Declaration Reformatting Function modules (DCL) and the Line and Error Store Function modules (STORE). Phase II will test the Body Reformatting Function modules (BODY) with the FETCH, the STORE, and the previously tested DCL modules. Phase III will test the Boxing Function modules (BOX) with the FETCH, STORE, DCL and BODY modules. The FORTFORM controller, FORCON, will serve as a test driver in all three phases, having been previously unit tested and integrated with its three sub-modules.

3.1.1 PHASE I

The Phase I testing structure will appear as in Figure 1A. The following modules will be included in the test:

FORTFORM Controller modules

FORCON	UDC
ABORT	FILVAL

Declaration Reformatting Function Modules

DCL	SYMTAB
VARGET	CRENAN
BRK	NEX
VSTORE	SEARCH
SUMSRT	COMPAR
DECREC	CREST
GET	PUT

Line Fetch Function Module

PARSE	SQUASH
SCOOP	FUNC
EQUAL	ALPHNM
CONVRT	ASCAN
BSCAN	CSCAN
DSCAN	ESCAN
FSCAN	GSCAN
ISCAN	LSCAN
PSCAN	RSCAN
SSCAN	WSCAN

Line and Error Store Function Modules

FLUSH	ERROR

Two stubs must be written for this phase. One will simulate the Body Reformatting modules. The other will simulate the Boxing modules. It is assumed that all modules will have been unit tested and reviewed prior to initiation of Phase I integration.

3.1.2 PHASE II

The Phase II testing structure will appear as in Figure 1B. The modules used in Phase I plus the following modules will be included in the test:

Body Reformatting Function Modules

BODY	INDENT
CLNBUF	MEWLNS
START	LAST

The Box stub will be utilized.

3.1.3 PHASE III

The Phase III testing structure will appear as in Figure 1C. The modules used in Phases I and II plus the following modules will be included in the test:

Box Function Modules

BOX	STRCHK

3.2 TEST SCHEDULE

The test phases described in Paragraphs 3.1 will be performed according to the schedule shown in Figure 2. The testing of the three phases will occur sequentially, with regression testing conducted at each new phase.

3.3 TEST SOFTWARE

The unit tested FORTFORM controller, FORCON, will be used as the main driver in all three integration testing phases. No other drivers are necessary. Two stubs will be written to perform the following:

BODY Stub: This stub will echo-check the call to the BODY module.

BOX Stub: This stub will echo-check the call to the BOX module.

4.0 TEST PROCEDURE

The technical procedure for testing of each of the three test phases in Section 3 is described.

4.1 PHASE I–TEST PROCEDURE

Phase I testing verifies that the Fetch modules are passing the correct information to the DCL modules about each source statement read in from the user's file. It also verifies that FORCON receives certain flagged information set by DCL during error situations.

4.1.1 PHASE I–PURPOSE

Phase I testing is done because it is essential that the DCL moduels receive the correct statement type information for proper declaration reformatting. For proper FORTFORM control it is necessary for the DCL modules to communicate any problems encountered during execution. This constitutes the need to check the appropriate flag setting and interaction between the FORCON and DCL modules.

4.1.2 PHASE I–TECHNIQUE

Phase I testing will proceed in the following manner:

1. Before testing, a dummy user source file (see Section 4.1.4) will be created containing a program having delcarative and executable statements as well as comments. At FORTFORM execution, the SCOOP module of the FETCH function will read in data from this file to be processed.

2. In response to FORTFORM's file information request at the beginning of the FORTFORM execution, the above dummy file will be specified as user input file. Two other valid file names for error and output will be specified.

3. The FLUSH module of the Line and Error Store function will write all reformatted output to the output file specified in 2 above.

4.1.3 PHASE I–TEST SOFTWARE

The two stubs described in Section 3.3 will be used during this phase.

4.1.4 PHASE I–TEST/RESULTS

See Appendix A.1 (in this chapter).

4.1 PHASE II–TEST PROCEDURE

Phase II testing verifies that the FETCH modules are passing the correct information to the Body modules about each source statement read in from the user's file. It also verifies that FORCON receives certain flagged information set by Body during error situations.

4.2.1 PHASE II–PURPOSE

Phase II testing is done because it is essential that the Body modules receive the correct statement description information for proper reformatting. As in Phase I, it is necessary for error flag communication to work correctly so that FORCON can direct proper control over FORTFORM execution.

4.2.2 PHASE II–TECHNIQUE

See Section 4.1.2

4.2.3 PHASE II–TEST SOFTWARE

The only stub necessary is the Box stub described in Section 3.3.

4.2.4 PHASE II–TEST DATA/RESULTS

See Appendix A.2 (in this chapter).

4.3 PHASE III–TEST PROCEDURE

Phase III testing verifies that a special character string of '$$$$$' is placed after the 150th executable statement or 500th line of the source code (see FORTFORM Requirements) in order for the Box module to know when to terminate processing.

Page 12-30

Chapter 12
COMPREHENSIVE EXAMPLE

SOFTWARE
ENGINEERING
HANDBOOK

4.3.1 PHASE III–PURPOSE

Phase III testing is done because it is necessary to assure that the Box modules are able to recognize the special marker mentioned in Section 4.3.

4.3.2 PHASE III–TECHNIQUE

See Section 4.1.2.

4.3.3 PHASE III–TEST SOFTWARE

There is no extra test software for this phase.

4.3.4 PHASE III–TEST DATA/RESULTS

See Appendix A.3 (in this chapter).

APPENDIX A.1

PHASE I–Test Data/Results

TEST 1: Check for proper execution.

INPUT FILE: (see Listing 1A)

All data is within limits. Only declarative section of the source program is used. No error file should be created.

300 variable names.

All syntactically correct.

All variables ANSI Standard.

All statements ANSI Standard.

OUTPUT FILE: (see Listing 1B)

Alphabetized variables and rearranged statements as required. (See Design Document SEP004D.0-79/8).

ERROR FILE:

Empty.

TEST 2: Check for 'VARIABLE LIMIT EXCEEDED'.

INPUT FILE: (see Listing 2A)

Same as Test 1, plus one more variable name in line 6.

OUTPUT FILE:

Not created.

ERROR FILE:

See below.

VARIABLE LIMIT EXCEEDED

TEST 3: Check for 'LINE LIMIT EXCEEDED' in the declarative section.

INPUT FILE: (see Listing 3A)

Same declarative section as in Test 1, plus a large number of lines containing 'C's in the first column. The file reaches the 501 line limit.

OUTPUT FILE:

Not created.

ERROR FILE:

See below.

SOURCE SIZE EXCEEDED

TEST 4: Check for 'SYNTACTICALLY INCORRECT VARIABLES' in the declarative section.

INPUT FILE: (see Listing 4A)

Same as Test 1, plus a syntactically incorrect variable in line 8.

OUTPUT FILE:

Not created.

ERROR FILE:

See below.

DECLARATIVE SECTION SYNTACTICALLY INCORRECT

TEST 5: Check for 'NON-ANSI VARIABLES' in the declarative section.

INPUT FILE: (see Listing 5A)

Same as in Test 1, plus two non-ANSI variables in lines 9 and 10.

OUTPUT FILE: (see Listing 5B)

Alphabetized and rearranged as required.

ERROR FILE:

NON-ANSI FORTRAN '66 VARIABLE NAMES USED

**SOFTWARE
ENGINEERING
HANDBOOK**

**Chapter 12
COMPREHENSIVE EXAMPLE**

Page 12-31

TEST 6: Check for 'NON-ANSI STATEMENTS' in the declarative section.

INPUT FILE: (see Listing 6A)

Same as Test 1, plus a non-ANSI statement in line 7.

OUTPUT FILE: (see Listing 6B)

Alphabetized and rearranged as required.

ERROR FILE:

NON-ANSI FORTRAN 66 DECLARATIVE STATEMENTS USED

APPENDIX A.2

PHASE II—Test Data/Results

TEST 7: Check for proper execution.

INPUT FILE: (see Listing 7A)

All data is within the limits. Declarative and program body sections are used. No error file should be created.

Declarative section as in Test 1.

150 executable statements

500 lines

Maximum of 5 nested 'DO-LOOPS'

19 completely filled line continuations

OUTPUT FILE: (see Listing 7B)

Indented and rearranged as required. (See Design Documentation SEP004D.0-79/8).

ERROR FILE:

Empty.

INTEGRATION TEST LISTINGS

Integration test inputs (1A-7A) have been deleted to conserve space. Expected results have also been deleted.

VALIDATION TEST SPECIFICATION FORTRAN FORMATTER (FORTFORM)

1.0 SCOPE

This document describes the management plan and test procedure to fully validate the FORTRAN FORMATTER (FORTFORM). All software requirements are directly traceable to the FORTFORM Requirements Specification SEP004R.0-79/8.

2.0 APPLICABLE DOCUMENTS

FORTFORM Software Plan SEP004P.0-79/7

FORTFORM Requirements Specification SEP004R.0-79/8

FORTFORM Design Document SEP004D.0-79/9

FORTFORM User Manual SEP004U.2-79/9

3.0 TEST PLAN

3.1 VALIDATION TEST CRITERIA

The validation test will be divided into three segments:

1. Error Message Test

All error logic will be tested and appropriate error message generation exercised.

2. Bounds Test

All out-of-bounds tests are accomplished by 1 above. Various combinations of within-bounds testing will be performed.

3. Parallel Logic Test

The results of FORTFORM will be compared to the results of the original programs to assure that original logic was not modified by FORTFORM processing.

3.2 TEST SCHEDULE

Validation testing will take place in one day. Test segment 3, the Parallel Logic Test, will be conducted in parallel with each of the tests in test segment 1 and 2.

3.3 TEST SOFTWARE

No special test harness or driver is required for validation testing.

Page 12-32

Chapter 12
COMPREHENSIVE EXAMPLE

SOFTWARE
ENGINEERING
HANDBOOK

4.0 PROCEDURE

The technical procedure for validation test is described in the following paragraphs.

4.1 ERROR MESSAGE TEST

The following tests will validate all error logic. To assure that any one of the following tests is testing only one aspect, all other restrictions will remain in-bounds.

4.1.1 FILE ALREADY EXISTS

FORTFORM will be run specifying an output or error file that already exists. The message: file name FILE ALREADY EXISTS; and a prompt for the user to respecify the file should appear on the terminal.

4.1.2 FILE DOES NOT EXIST

FORTFORM will be run specifying an input file that does not exist. The message: file name FILE DOES NOT EXIST and a prompt for the user to respecify the file should appear on the terminal.

4.1.3 SOURCE SIZE EXCEEDED

Two source files containing 501 lines each will be used as input to FORTFORM. One file will consist of only declarative statements and comments. The other file will have executable statements in addition to declarative statements and comments. In the case of the first file, FORTFORM should terminate processing and no output file should have been created. Only the error message: SOURCE SIZE EXCEEDED should appear in the error file. In the case of the second file, the limit of 500 source lines should be processed. The rest of the input file should be placed in the output file with no further processing. Once again, the only message in the error file should be the message mentioned above.

4.1.5 EXECUTABLE STATEMENT LIMIT EXCEEDED

A source file containing 151 executable statements will be input to FORTFORM. The limit of 150 executable statements should be processed and found in the output file. However, the remaining input file should be written to the output file without further processing. The only error message that should appear in the error file is the following: EXECUTABLE STATEMENT LIMIT EXCEEDED.

4.1.6 STATEMENT CONTINUATION LIMIT EXCEEDED

A source file containing a statement with 20 continuation lines in the second logic level will be input to FORTFORM. No processing should occur. FORTFORM should terminate.

The error message: STATEMENT CONTINUATION LIMIT EXCEEDED should appear in the error file.

4.1.7 VARIABLE LIMIT EXCEEDED

A source file containing 301 variables in the declarative statements will be used as input to FORTFORM. The error message: VARIABLE LIMIT EXCEEDED should appear in the error file. No processing should occur. FORTFORM should terminate. No reformatted source code should be placed in the output file. The reformatted source output file should not be created.

4.1.7 EMPTY INPUT FILE

An empty input file will be specified as input to FORTFORM. No processing should take place.

4.1.8 NESTING LIMIT EXCEEDED

A source file with "DO" loops nested 6 deep will be used as input to FORTFORM. Only 5 levels of indentations should be made. FORTFORM should continue execution.

4.1.9 NON-ANSI FORTRAN '66 DECLARATIVE STATEMENTS USED

A source file with non-ANSI declarative statements will be used as input to FORTFORM. All occurrences of these should be grouped and placed after ANSI FORTRAN '66 data type statements. No variable alphabetizing should occur. FORTFORM execution continues.

4.1.10 DECLARATIVE SECTION SYNTACTICALLY INCORRECT

A source file with syntactically incorrect variables in the declarative section will be used as input to FORTFORM. No processing should occur and FORTFORM should terminate. No reformatted source should be placed in the user output file.

4.1.11 NON-ANSI FORTRAN '66 VARIABLE NAME USED

A source file with non-ANSI '66 variable names will be used as input to FORTFORM. These variable names should be used as input to FORTFORM. These variable names should be put in a newly created statement and added to the non-ANSI declarative section. FORTFORM execution continues.

4.2 BOUNDS TEST

The following tests will validate the correct processing of all limits. A first test will be made using a file which contains all maximum limits. Four additional tests will be made using different combinations of these limits. The above tests will be made using files with the following characteristics: (See Appendix A for file listings).

500 source lines

150 executable statements

300 variable names

a statement with 19 continuations

"DO" loops nested 4 deep

---

500 source lines

145 executable statements

295 variable names

a statement with 19 continuations

"DO" loops nested 4 deep

---

495 source lines

150 executable statements

295 variable names

a statement with 1 continuation

"DO" loops nested 5 deep

---

495 source lines

145 executable statements

300 variable names

a statement with 1 continuation

"DO" loops nested 5 deep

---

4 declarative statements

1 "END"

4.3 PARALLEL LOGIC TEST

The Parallel Logic Test (see Appendix A) will be conducted as described in Section 3.1 number 3 for each of the previously described tests.

5.0 VALIDATION CRITERIA/VARIANCE BOUNDS

All validation tests must produce results as defined in Section 4.0. All software requirements must be satisfied without variance.

6.0 SPECIAL PROVISIONS

No special provisions are required for FORTFORM validation.

APPENDIX A.1

PHASE I—Test Data/Results

TEST 1: Check for proper execution.

INPUT FILE: (see Listing 1A)

All data is within limits. Only declarative section of the source program is used. No error file should be created.

300 variable names

All syntactically correct

All variables ANSI Standard

All statements ANSI Standard

OUTPUT FILE: (see Listing 1B)

Alphabetized variables and rearranged statements as required. (See Design Document SEP004D.0-79/8)

ERROR FILE:

Empty.

USER MANUAL
FORTRAN FORMATTER
(FORTFORM)
DOCUMENT CONTROL NO. SEP004U.0-79/9

FORTFORM is a tool to aid the FORTRAN programmer in documenting ANSI FORTRAN '66 source programs. The following types of functions are performed by FORTFORM.

-Alphabetically sorting variables in FORTRAN Declarative Type statements and grouping Declarative statements by type.

-Indentation of Flow-of-Control structures.

-Elimination of redundant "CONTINUE" statements.

-Boxing of Comments.

Page 12-34

Chapter 12
COMPREHENSIVE EXAMPLE

SOFTWARE
ENGINEERING
HANDBOOK

1.0 USER INTERFACE

After logging on, to use FORTFORM, type:

:FORTFORM, ‹cr›

The user will then be prompted for file names:

PLEASE ENTER INPUT FILE NAME? ifn ‹cr›

PLEASE ENTER OUTPUT FILE NAME? ofn ‹cr›

PLEASE ENTER ERROR FILE NAME? efn ‹cr›

When FORTFORM has finished processing the user's file (see HUMAN Section 2.3), the user will receive a message indicating the status of the program execution. Execution is either successful or unsuccessful and one of the following messages will appear on the terminal:

"FORTFORM NORMALLY TERMINATED"

or

"FORTFORM ABNORMALLY TERMINATED-LIST ERROR FILE", efn

Two files will have been created. One will contain the reformatted ANSI FORTRAN '66 source code and the other will contain error messsages (see ERROR MESSAGES Section 4).

2.0 FILES

2.1 FILES NAMES

A file name is a designator which contains 1 to 8 alphanumeric characters, beginning with a letter (see HP MPE Commands Reference Manual).

2.2 INPUT FILE

To use FORTFORM, the user is required to specify a file containing the ANSI FORTRAN '66 source code to be reformatted. If the file does not exist, the user will be prompted for another input file name, i.e.,

ifn, INPUT FILE DOES NOT EXIST

PLEASE ENTER NEW NAME? new ifn ‹cr›

The following limitations are imposed on the input file:

-The user's ANSI FORTRAN '66 source code should be compiler error free.

-The user's input file must be one program segment: one main program, one subroutine, one function or one block data subprogram.

-It may not exceed 500 lines of source code. Of these, 150 executable statements will be the upper limit.

-The number of variable names appearing in the Declarative block may not exceed 300. This includes "EXTERNAL" subroutine names, but excludes "COMMON", "EQUIVALENCE", and "DATA" statements.

-Line-length of 72 characters will be accepted by FORTFORM.

-All statements, excluding comment statements and continuation lines must start after column 6.

-Comments will begin in column 1 with a "C".

-Line continuations will begin in column 6 according to ANSI FORTRAN '66.

-A "DO" statement must be contained on one line.

-Nesting of up to five levels of 'DO" loops will be processed.

-Any FORTRAN sequence numbers in the user's source file will be eliminated.

OUTPUT FILE

The user is responsible for specifying an output file in which the reformatted source code is to be placed. If the user attempts to specify an already existing file, the user will be asked to respecify the output file as follows:

ofn OUTPUT FILE ALREADY EXISTS

PLEASE ENTER NEW NAME? new ofn ‹cr›

The user should check both program execution status and the error file, before assuming output file completeness.

2.4 ERROR FILE

The user is responsible for specifying an error file in which generated error messages are to be placed, If the user attempts to specify an already existing file, the user will be asked to respecify the error file as follows:

efn ERROR FILE ALREADY EXISTS

PLEASE ENTER NEW NAME: new efn ‹cr›

For further explanation of errors, see ERROR MESSAGES in Section 4.

SOFTWARE
ENGINEERING
HANDBOOK

**Chapter 12
COMPREHENSIVE EXAMPLE**

Page 12-35

2.5 COMMENTS

FORTFORM allows the user a certain amount of error recovery. It allows the user three attempts to enter a valid file name. Since the HP3000 allows blank file names and an accidental carriage return could cause this, FORTFORM checks for blank file names and reprompts the user in this case. Entry of a blank file name is not counted as a valid file name entry and is not counted as an entry attempt. The user is allowed three blank file name entries per valid file name entry. To terminate FORTFORM, the user can enter the word ABORT as a file name and FORTFORM will be terminated.

3.0 PROCESSING

3.1 DECLARATION REFORMATTING

The Declaration Reformatting Function will group together declarative type statements in the following order:

INTEGER

REAL

DOUBLE PRECISION

COMPLEX

LOGICAL

After the above data type statements have been grouped, variable names within the type statements will be alphabetized. If more than 300 variable names, including "EXTERNAL" subroutine names appear in the declarative block, FORTFORM will terminate and an error message will appear in the error file. The output file will remain empty.

Any non-ANSI FORTRAN '66 declarative statements found will be grouped together and placed after the above data type statements. Variable names will not be alphabetized in these statements.

The remaining declarative statements will be arranged in the following order:

DIMENSION

COMMON

EQUIVALENCE

EXTERNAL

DATA

Variable names will not be alphabetized in "COMMON", "EQUIVALENCE" and "DATA" statements.

EXAMPLE 1

```
INPUT    DIMENSION Z(1),Y(5),A(7),I(10)
         INTEGER M,L,Q(7),B(10)
         DOUBLE PRECISION D
         REAL F, H(5),G


OUTPUT   INTEGER, B.L.M.Q
         REAL F,G,H
         DOUBLE PRECISION D
         DIMENSION A(7),B(10),H(5),I(10),
         Q(7),Y(5),Z(1)
```

3.2 PROGRAM BODY REFORMATTING

The Program Body Reformatting Function identifies logical levels. "DO" structure indentation will be three spaces per logical level. Previously indented logic will be rearranged according to the FORTFORM indentation specifications. If indenting causes a line overflow, line continuations will be generated. Processing will also delete redundant "CONTINUE" statements. Redundant "CONTINUE" statements are those "CONTINUE" statements that have no statement number.

Executable statements will be counted to check the 150 statement limit.

EXAMPLE 1

```
INPUT
   DO 10 I=1,10
   DO 20 J=1,20
   DO 30 K=1,30
   L=I+J+K
30 CONTINUE
20 CONTINUE
10 CONTINUE


OUTPUT
   DO 10 I=1,10
      DO 20 J=1,20
         DO 30 K=1,20
            L=I+J+K
30 CONTINUE
20 CONTINUE
10 CONTINUE
```

3.3 BOX COMMENTS

Comments which are three or more consecutive lines will be boxed. Comments already boxed in the FORTFORM specified fashion will not be reprocessed. The following is an example.

Page 12-36

Chapter 12
COMPREHENSIVE EXAMPLE

SOFTWARE
ENGINEERING
HANDBOOK

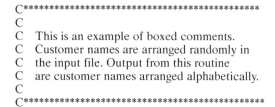

```
C**********************************************
C
C   This is an example of boxed comments.
C   Customer names are arranged randomly in
C   the input file. Output from this routine
C   are customer names arranged alphabetically.
C
C**********************************************
```

4.0 ERROR MESSAGES

The following is a list of error messages generated by FORTFORM. Below each is an explanation of the error.

1. file name FILE ALREADY EXISTS

The user has specified an output or error file that is already in existence. The user will be asked to specify the file.

2. file name FILE DOES NOT EXIST

The user has specified an input file that is not in existence. The user will be asked to respecify the file.

3. SOURCE SIZE EXCEEDED

The source input file contains too many lines. The limit of 500 lines will be processed. The rest of the input file will be placed in the output file with no further processing. However, if the 500 line limit is exceeded within the declarative section, FORTFORM will terminate processing and no output file will be created.

4. EXECUTABLE STATEMENT LIMIT EXCEEDED

The source input file contains too many executable statements. The limit of 150 executable statements will be processed. However, the remaining input file will be written to the output file without further processing.

5. STATEMENT CONTINUATION LIMIT EXCEEDED

The source input file contains a statement that has too many continuations. The limit is 19 continuations. No processing will occur. FORTFORM will terminate.

6. VARIABLE LIMIT EXCEEDED

The input source file contains too many variable names in the declarative section. The limit is 300 variable names. No processing will occur. FORTFORM will terminate. No reformatted source code will be placed in the output file. The reformatted source output file will not be created.

7. EMPTY INPUT FILE file name

The user specified input file was found empty. No processing could be done.

8. NESTING LIMIT EXCEEDED

The input source file contains a nested "DO" loop structure that exceeds the five level depth limit. Only five levels of indentations will occur. FORTFORM will continue execution.

9. NON-ANSI FORTRAN '66 DECLARATIVE STATEMENTS USED

The input source file conains non-ANSI FORTRAN '66 declarative statements. All occurrences of these will be grouped and placed after ANSI FORTRAN '66 data type statements. No variable alphabetizing will occur. FORTFORM execution continues.

10. DECLARATIVE SECTION SYNTACTICALLY INCORRECT

The input source file contains syntactically incorrect variables in the declarative section of the program. No processing will occur. FORTFORM will terminate. No reformatted source will be placed in the user output file.

11. NON-ANSI FORTRAN '66 VARIABLE NAME USED

The input source file contains non-ANSI FORTRAN '66 variable names in the declarative section. These variable names will be put in a newly created statement and added to the non-ANSI declarative section. FORTFORM execution continues.

GLOSSARY

This Glossary defines key terms and phrases used in the Software Engineering Handbook. Where appropriate, a definition includes a parenthesized section reference to an expanded discussion of the topic that uses that term or phrase. Items without a sectional reference are used only in other Glossary definitions.

afferent data—incoming data; data moving along an afferent data flow (input) path of a Data Flow Diagram (5.3.3).

afferent data flow—a data flow in a Data-Flow Diagram that is moving inward from the system boundary; i.e., a data flow that is being transformed to less resemble a system input.

analyst—a person who defines problems and develops algorithms and procedures for their solution.

as-built design—the final design after validation and acceptance tests are completed and signed off. This is represented in the updated design document that becomes the basis for software maintenance. (2.2.5)

baseline—a baseline is defined as that point in the software life cycle at which configuration control is applied to a specific deliverable (8.2).

binding time—the time at which interconnections between modules becomes final (5.3.4).

black-box testing—a testing strategy that derives test data solely from the requirements specification. Specifically, no use is made of knowledge of the program's internal structure (7.7.2).

box diagram—a graphic alternative to the flowchart, that by its construction rules, only permits use of structured control-flow constructs; also called Nassi-Schneiderman or Chapin charts (5.8.1).

boundary-value testing—a testing strategy that derives test data from boundary conditions; i.e., situations directly on, just above and just below the boundaries of input and output equivalence classes (7.7.2).

build—a combining of unit-tested modules through the process of integration testing. Builds are used to functionally partition systems for more convenient integration and/or validation testing. In large systems, some builds represent major system functions; as a result, these builds are formally defined and monitored (2.2.4).

CASE—a structured control-flow construct that selects one of n alternative actions (6.1.2).

cause-effect graphing—a testing strategy that uses a graphic technique to derive test data. It has a side-effect that points out specification ambiguities and incompleteness (7.7.2).

Change Control Authority (CCA)—a software maintenance organization that establishes priority, preliminary schedule, evaluates the global impact of a software change, and then initiates the maintenance, reviewing all changes before distribution occurs. (9.3.1)

coding—the translation of a detailed design representation to the appropriate programming language (2.2.3).

cohesion—a measure of the integral unity of the task performed by a module; a measure of the single-mindedness of a module, since an ideal module performs a single well-defined task. (5.3.5)

coupling—a measure of the strength of module interconnection that considers modules with strong interconnections to be highly-coupled, those with weak interconnections to be loosely-coupled. (5.3.4)

Data Flow Diagram (DFD)—a graphic representation of the flows of data through a system and the data transformations that take place. (5.4.1)

data structure—a set of data items considered to form a single entity. Vectors and matrices are examples of data structures composed of scalar elements of the same type; a record is an example of a data structure composed of nonhomogenous elements not necessarily scalar.

debugging—the art of isolating and correcting error causes (7.1.2).

definition—the first phase of the software life cycle—it includes system analysis, planning and requirements. Analysis development—the second phase of the software life cycle.

deliverable—documentation associated with each step in the software engineering process.

design inspection—a formal evaluation of the design involving three or four people, including a trained moderator; rigorous formatted inspection of the design providing a reliable mechanism for error detection (2.2.2).

design walkthrough—an informal design evaluation by an independent reviewer, usually another programmer familiar with the project (2.2.2).

detailed design—the resulting expansion of preliminary design; the internal procedure associated with a given design (2.2.2)

Detailed Design Review (DDR)—a review for correctness and maintainability of the complete descriptions of each module in the software system (5.9, 5.10).

DO-WHILE—a structured control flow construct that repeats a sequence of statements while a specific initial condition is true. Note that the sequence of statements is not executed if the specific condition is initially false (6.1.2).

driver—a temporary testing procedure used to test subordinate procedures. Contrast with stub (7.4).

efferent data—outgoing data; information that moves from the internal to the external (output) path (5.3.3).

efferent data flow—a data flow in a Data-Flow Diagram that is moving outward toward the system boundary size; a data flow that is being transformed to more closely resemble a system output.

equivalence class—a set of data so defined that a test using any member of the set can reasonably be assumed will yield the same test result.

equivalence partitioning—a test strategy that derives test cases that have these two properties: (a) the test case reduces, by a count of more than one, the number of other cases required to obtain an established level of testing; (b) the test replaces a large set of other possible test cases by use of equivalence class analysis (7.7.2).

gray-box testing—a testing strategy that derives test data by combining elements of black-box and white-box testing (7.7.2).

Higher-Order Language (HOL)—English-like user-oriented languages oriented towards problem soliving rather than detailing the work of the machine.

IF-THEN-ELSE—a control structure that implements conditional instruction execution (6.1.2).

integration test—the process of testing several unit-tested modules as a whole, to assure compliance with the design specification (2.2.4).

language processing tools—aids such as macroprocessors and special compilers used to extend non-structured languages without modifying the native compiler to support and enhance the programmer's environment (6.6.2).

lines of code—the actual number of instructions at the source code level of a programming language that collectively perform a software function (3.4.1).

Machine-Oriented Language (MOL)—assembly language (3.7).

maintenance—the last phase of the software life cycle that begins when software is operational and released to one or more users; includes the supervision of the software configuration as well as the physical modification of the software (2.3).

Manufacturing Facilities Control System (MFCS)—an example used to illustrate the software engineering design methodology (5.4).

modularity—a measure of the number of individual modules defined to implement a software system (5.3.6).

module—also called "routine", "procedure" and "subprogram" is executable code that implements a functional requirement or part of a functional requirement; normally, the smallest segment of code known and controlled by the operating system (2.2).

Module Development Folder (MDF)—a convenient, readily accessible repository for documentation during development; the folder contains all development material for one or more modules (2.2.2).

morphology—shape of a software structure that is measured in terms of depth, width, fan-out and fan-in (5.3.7).

operating system—software that controls the execution of computer programs and that may provide scheduling, debugging, input-output control, accounting compilation, storage assignment, data management, and related services.

preliminary design document—this document concentrates on a definition of software structure, data flow/structure, interface characteristics and the processing narrative for each module in the software system (5.8).

Preliminary Design Review (PDR)—a formal, technical and management review of the software development effort that concentrates on the top level structural design and its traceability to the requirements (5.7).

Preliminary User's Manual—a beginning document, reviewed by the requestor, that provides a direct description of the user interface and is invaluable during requirements review (4.2.7).

Program Design Language (PDL)—a language that describes a design using a combination of structured programming constructs and English prose (6.6.4).

program evaluation aids—tools used to support programming standards compliance and to provide documentation data (6.6.3).

programming system—a set of basic programs (program products) integrated and tested as a single program to perform a set of predefined functions (3.3.1).

program product—a program intended for use by persons other than its author; hence, it must be supported and maintained (3.3.1).

REPEAT UNTIL—a control structure that causes a SEQUENCE to be repeated until a specific condition is true. Note that the SEQUENCE of actions will be performed at least once (6.1.2).

requirements review—a formal review of the Software Requirements Specification to determine if the SRS is acceptable to both developer and requestor and adheres to the System Specification and the Software Plan (4.2.8).

SEQUENCE—a control structure where procedural steps are executed unconditionally, one after another (6.1.2).

Software Configuration Management (SCM)—formal procedures established to control changes made to a software configuration (2.3.3).

software evaluation matrix—a method of itemizing specific software characteristics by importance and by vendor in order to evaluate vendor packages on a comparative basis (3.5.2).

Software Plan—a formal document for a software project describing the scope of the effort, the resources required, the cost of the effort, and the project schedule (3.2).

Software Quality Assurance (SQA)—a formal procedure used by large software development organizations where an independent test team takes responsibility for planning and executing the integration and validation tests in order to minimize residual errors and promote software quality (7.6).

software reliability—the probability that a program will operate without failure for a given period of time (7.1.1).

Software Requirements Specification (SRS)—a document that concentrates on four aspects of a software project: information flow and interfaces; functional requirements; design requirements and constraints and testing criteria to establish quality assurance (4).

structured control flow—control flow within a program such that each control flow construct has the property of having a single point of entry and a single point of exit. See: CASE, DO-WHILE, IF-THEN-ELSE, REPEAT-UNTIL, SEQUENCE.

stub—a dummy procedure used to test a superordinate procedure. Contrast with driver (7.4).

System Specification (SS)—the document that defines overall system requirements without a detailed regard for the implementation approach; the document specifies functional characteristics and performance objectives of the system, interface characteristics, environment, overall design concepts, reliability criteria, design constraints and predefined subsystems (3.1).

testing—a systematic process, planned in advance, used to explicitly verify software conformance to specification (7.1.2).

Test Plan—a document for integration and validation testing that defines segments or procedures to validate each software function, a schedule for testing each function, and any software that must be developed to simulate hardware or software not available to the developer (7.5.1).

transform flow—information flow that occurs at the transition point of incoming and outgoing data (5.3.3.).

unit test—individual testing of each module by its implementing programmer to verify its correctness (7.3).

validation testing—a formal testing and evaluation of the software to demonstrate its conformance to the requirements specification (2.2.5).

white-box testing—a testing strategy that derives test data from knowledge of the program's internal structure (7.7.2).

SOFTWARE
ENGINEERING
HANDBOOK

Appendix A
DOCUMENT FORMATS

Page A-1

Appendix A.1: SYSTEM SPECIFICATION INTRODUCTION

Software is often an integral part of a larger configuration that includes hardware, facilities, and personnel. This configuration, called a "system", must be carefully specified prior to commencement of software planning and development.

The SYSTEM SPECIFICATION indicates the overall functional, operational, and performance characteristics of a system. In it both hardware and software elements are described and the requirements for each are specified.

The software organization is normally not responsible for the generation of the SYSTEM SPECIFICATION. However, because the system document serves as a baseline for all software documents, software personnel should participate in its development.

A recommended format for the SYSTEM SPECIFICATION is presented in this Appendix.

SYSTEM SPECIFICATION

1.0 SCOPE

This section provides an overview of the system and defines scope for performance, design, development and test requirements. In addition, system objectives and characteristics are discussed.

2.0 APPLICABLE DOCUMENTS

This section lists all documents which apply (in whole or in part) to the specification.

3.0 REQUIREMENTS

This section contains a descriptive and quantitative definition of all system requirements. The following topics are considered:

1. The performance and design requirements for the system.

2. The requirements related to operating, maintaining, and supporting the system, to the extent these requirements define or constrain design of the system.

3. The design constraints and standards necessary to assure compatibility of system items.

4. The definition of the principal interfaces between the system being specified and other systems with which it must be compatible.

5. The functions of the system, and the principal interfaces between and within each function.

6. The allocation of functional performance and the definition of specific design constraints.

7. The identification and use of existing equipment, computer programs or operating procedures.

Unless purely descriptive by nature, requirements are stated in quantitative physical terms with tolerances that can be verified by subsequent tests, demonstrations or inspection. Requirements stated in this section are the basis for the tests specified in Section 4 of the specification.

3.1 System Definition

This paragraph lists the elements to be developed or included as part of the system. Elements include hardware, software and operating procedures. A graphical representation (block diagram) of these items should also be shown if appropriate.

Page A-2

Appendix A
DOCUMENT FORMATS

SOFTWARE
ENGINEERING
HANDBOOK

3.1.1 Functional Description

This paragraph contains a brief description of the system including a list of all functions. The intended use of the system is described to the extent necessary for an overview understanding.

3.1.2 System Diagrams

This paragraph incorporates the system level functional schematic diagrams and includes the top-level functional control and data flow of the system. The level of detail that is required must identify all system functions and their relationship with system elements.

3.1.3 Interface Definition

This paragraph describes the functional and physical interface: 1) between the system and other systems with which it must be compatible; and 2) between all functions within the system.

3.1.4 Existing Resources and Procedures

This paragraph lists existing elements which the system is to be designed to incorporate. This list identifies the elements (e.g., hardware, software) by reference to nomenclature, specification number and/or part or model number. If the list is extensive, it may be included in an appendix which can be referenced in this paragraph.

3.1.5 Operation and Organization

This paragraph includes an overview description of the intended operation of the system. Also, the anticipated deployment of the system both geographically and organizationally (e.g., the number and location of installations) is described.

3.2 Characteristics

System characteristics are described in detail in the paragraphs that follow.

3.2.1 Performance Characteristics

This paragraph contains system performance characteristics and provides sufficient guidance for technical development. It describes what the system should accomplish and specifies both upper and lower performance limits. The following considerations are included:

1. Quantitative criteria covering endurance capabilities of the equipment that are required to meet the user needs under stipulated environmental and other conditions. Minimum total life expectancy is stated.

2. Quantitative expected performance for each operational mode (e.g., average rates, peak rates, quantity of inputs).

3. Programming language requirements (for software), if language is dictated by other system elements.

4. Other essential aspects of system performance which cannot be more appropriately located under another heading.

3.2.2 Physical Characteristics

This paragraph considers the following topics (as required):

1. Weight limits, electrical and equipment heat generation specifications.

2. Dimensional limitations, space, operator station layout, and access for maintenance.

3. Requirements for transport and storage, such as tie down, pallets, packaging, and containers.

4. Durability factors to indicate degree of ruggedness.

5. Health and safety criteria, including consideration of adverse explosive, mechanical, and biological effects.

6. Security criteria.

7. Media format for delivered software.

3.2.3 Reliability

Reliability is stated in quantitative terms. The conditions under which the reliability requirements must be met are explicitly defined.

3.2.4 Maintainability

This paragraph specifies maintainability requirements. The requirements apply to maintenance in a planned maintenance and support environment and are stated in quantitative terms. Examples are:

1. Time (e.g., mean and maximum downtime, mean time between failures, reaction time, turnaround time, mean and maximum time to repair, mean time between maintenance).

2. Rate (e.g., maintenance man-hours per specific maintenance action, maintenance hours per operating hour, frequency of preventive maintenance).

3. Maintenance complexity (e.g., number of people and skill levels, variety of support equipment).

SOFTWARE
ENGINEERING
HANDBOOK

Appendix A
DOCUMENT FORMATS

Page A-3

3.2.5 Availability

The degree to which the system is available, e.g., 24 hours per day, 7 days per week.

3.2.6 Environmental Conditions

This paragraph includes environmental conditions to be encountered during operation and/or storage of the system equipment. The following subjects should be considered: natural environment (wind, rain, temperature, etc.); induced environment (motion, shock, noise, etc.); electromagnetic signal environment.

3.2.7 Transportability

This paragraph includes requirements for transportability which are common to all system equipment to permit installation and logistic support. All system equipment that will be unsuitable (due to operational or functional characteristics) for normal transportation methods is identified.

3.3 Allocation of System Functions

This paragraph allocates the system functions described above to hardware, software or other system elements. Minimum system design and construction standards are also specified.

3.3.1 Division of Hardware and Software

This paragraph contains a list of all system functions and the allocation of either hardware or software.

3.3.2 Materials, Processes and Parts

This paragraph specifies requirements that govern the use of materials, parts, and processes. It contains specifications for particular materials and processes to be utilized in the design of system equipment. In addition, requirements for the use of standard components and parts for which a qualified products list has been established are specified.

3.3.3 Workmanship

This paragraph contains workmanship requirements for equipment to be produced during system development. Requirements for manufacture by specified production techniques are also discussed.

3.3.4 Interchangeability

This paragraph specifies the requirements for system elements that are interchangeable and replaceable. Entries in this paragraph are for the purpose of establishing a condition of design, and are not to define the conditions of interchangeability.

3.3.5 Safety

This paragraph specifies safety requirements that are basic to the design of the system. Equipment characteristics, methods of operation, and environmental influences are considered.

3.3.6 Human Engineering

Human engineering requirements for the system are specified and applicable documents (e.g., regulations) included by reference. Particular attention is paid to areas in which the effects of human error would be particularly serious.

3.4 Logistics

This paragraph considers the logistical characteristics that are required for the implementation, support and maintenance of the system.

3.4.1 Maintenance

This paragraph includes consideration of factors such as: 1) use of test equipment; 2) repair versus replacement criteria; 3) organizational levels of maintenance; 4) maintenance and repair cycles; 5) accessibility, and 6) distribution and location of spare parts.

3.4.2 Support

This paragraph specifies the support required for the system. Considerations include vendor hardware and software support and maintenance response requirements.

3.4.3 Facilities and Equipment

This paragraph specifies the impact of the system on existing facilities and facility equipment. It also describes requirements for new facilities, auxiliary equipment or software to support the system. Software development facilities and test facilities are also included.

3.5 Personnel, Training and Documentation

This paragraph specifies the training requirements for the system and includes: 1) how training is to be accomplished (e.g., school, on the job; 2) identification of equipment or software that will be required for training purposes; and 3) course material and training aids. Additionally, a training schedule and location are specified.

Page A-4

Appendix A
DOCUMENT FORMATS

SOFTWARE
ENGINEERING
HANDBOOK

3.5.3 Documentation

This paragraph specifies the documentation required for each system element. References to standards are acceptable.

4.0 QUALITY ASSURANCE

Provisions and criteria established in this section are used to verify functional and performance requirements specified in Section 3. Requirements for test/validation are defined. The following topics should be considered:

1. Collection and recording of data during all testing for use as part of the reliability analysis;

2. engineering evaluation and test requirements in direct support of design and development activity;

3. integration testing such as continuity checking, software/hardware interface mating, and function operation in the installed environment; support equipment compatibility and documentation verification;

4. formal test and validation of functional and performance characteristics.

5.0 NOTES

This section contains background information and other material pertinent to a complete description of the system.

6.0 APPENDIX

This section contains supplementary material that is part of the specification but has been appended for convenience in specification maintenance.

Appendix A.2:
SOFTWARE PLANNING

INTRODUCTION

The planning stage of the software engineering process considers the scope, operating environment and basic functional characteristics of all project software. These descriptive elements are related to a specific schedule and costs, resulting in the SOFTWARE PLAN—a management decision-making document.

Individual planning documents must be tailored to the size and complexity of the software project. However, certain core elements, listed in the following table, are required in every SOFTWARE PLAN.

ITEM	OBJECTIVES
Scope	Define and bound the work to be done.
Tasks and Deliverables	Specify all deliverables and summarize the tasks required to produce each.
Resources	Specify the number and type of resources required to perform the tasks.
Schedule	Present a schedule for tasks and deliverables.
Cost	Present estimated software costs.

A recommended format for the SOFTWARE PLAN is presented in this appendix.

SOFTWARE PLAN

1.0 SCOPE

The objective of this section is to provide an overview of the SOFTWARE PLAN and to define and bound the work to be done.

1.1 Objective

Each SOFTWARE PLAN should begin with an overview that provides the reader with: 1) the identity of the requestor; 2) a brief discussion or requirements; 3) background data such as the requestor's previous experiences (in the context of this application); 4) the intended use of the software, or perhaps, reasons for not using previously developed software. The key assumptions and restrictions used to develop the plan are also listed.

This subsection should also contain a brief description of the remainder of the document.

1.2 Functions and Bounds

This paragraph outlines the major software functions to be produced. It guides and limits the effort during later detailed data gathering required for requirements analysis. The statement of scope focuses on what is to be done, and should not focus on how a function is accomplished.

Each major function is described by a paragraph which presents a top level description of the function. This paragraph should reference a diagram which shows the data flow between the various functions.

It is appropriate to list subfunctions required to accomplish a major function. Enumerating subfunctions implies that some design has been done and although more accurate planning estimates can be achieved, design at this stage must be carefully managed.

The following topics may also be considered:

1. computer and operating system environment

2. a system block diagram (hardware and software)

1.3 Performance

This paragraph describes overall performance characteristics for the software including memory constraints, response or execution time considerations and special features.

1.4 Reliability

This paragraph discusses actions required to assure reliability and special considerations when reliability must be extraordinary (i.e., human-rated systems).

1.5 System Interfaces

This paragraph describes other system elements and their mode of interface with the software.

1.6 Schedule Constraints

This paragraph list scheduling dates that may effect software development:

1. Hardware availability dates;

2. Availability of software resources;

3. Availability of technical staff;

4. Pre-defined end-date of project.

2.0 TASKS AND DELIVERABLES

This section summarizes all tasks to be accomplished and deliverables to be produced. The order and relationship of tasks and deliverables is guided by the steps of the software engineering process.

2.1 Tasks

The tasks associated with software development have been discussed in the body of the Handbook. The major software engineering tasks are:

1. planning

2. requirements analysis

3. preliminary design

4. detailed design

5. unit code and test

6. integration test

7. validation

These tasks provide the framework for further refinement which may be used to specify subtasks within each of the above categories. The degree of refinement is dependent on the magnitude of the effort. However, sufficient detail must be provided so that valid schedule and cost estimates can be made.

2.2 Deliverables

Deliverables are associated with a specific task and are normally associated with the documents that evolve out of the software engineering process. The following deliverables are required for most software efforts:

1. Software Plan

2. Requirements Specification

3. Final (revised) Software Plan

4. Preliminary Design

Page A-6

Appendix A
DOCUMENT FORMATS

SOFTWARE
ENGINEERING
HANDBOOK

5. Detailed Design

6. Source Listings (entered in MDF)

7. Integration Test Plan/Procedure

8. Validation Test Plan/Procedure

9. Test Report/Results

10. User/Installation Manual(s)

In addition to the above deliverables, details on documentation, training and installation/operation may be contained in this section. For many projects, these items represent substantial cost and should be considered in detail.

NOTE:

Paragraphs 2.2.1, 2, and 3 may be omitted for small software efforts.

2.2.1 Documentation

This paragraph outlines the basic set of project documents and defines procedures and responsibilities for document publication. It is often necessary to define or reference publication procedures. The following outlines indicate those topics that should be addressed:

A. Preparation and approval
B. Typing
C. Proofing and Editing
D. Reproduction
   1. Routine
   2. Bulk
E. Distribution
   1. Within project
   2. To the client
   3. To other suppliers
   4. Management

2.2.2 Training

This paragraph defines the developer's training responsibilities. Two categories of training, internal training for the project team, and external training for the requestor and the requestor's customer, are described.

An outline for a detailed discussion of training follows:

I. Types of Training
  A. Internal Training
    1. Technical
      a. Programming language(s)
      b. Use of test tools
      c. Use of terminals
      d. The development system hardware

      e. Interfaces to related systems
      f. The scope of work
      g. The baseline design
    2. Non-technical
      a. Management procedures
      b. Change control procedures
      c. Documentation control
      d. Reporting requirements
      e. Clerical procedures
  B. External Training
    1. Installing the software system
    2. Using the system
    3. Maintaining and modifying the system

II. Resources
  For each type of training identified, show:
    training schedules;
    instructors required;
    training materials;
    facilities (classrooms, training aids, computers, etc.);
    number of trainees;
    special requirements

2.2.3 Installation

This paragraph defines responsibilities for installation and operation of the software as a system component.

The following outline describes topics that may be discussed:

I. Installation
  A. Responsibility for installation
  B. Installation schedule
  C. Transition plan
    1. Method—parallel operation, immediate replacement, etc.
    2. Cutover criteria—how the decision is made to stop use of the old system and to rely upon the new system.
    3. Who makes the cutover decision?
    4. Backup positions should the system fail.
  D. Data Base Generation
  E. Multiple Site considerations
II. Operation
  A. Responsibility for operation
  B. Responsibility for tuning and enhancement
  C. Duration of responsibilities

3.0 RESOURCES

Before a schedule and cost can be estimated, resources must be associated with the tasks outlined in the preceding section. Resources include any tangible or measurable item that must be used to accomplish planning or development tasks.

SOFTWARE
ENGINEERING
HANDBOOK

**Appendix A
DOCUMENT FORMATS**

Page A-7

3.1 People

People are the most important resources in any software development effort. Requirements must be specified by considering the following:

1. number of people required

2. skill level of each person

3. duration of dedicated effort

A chart may be provided showing the manpower loading profile planned for the entire project by monthly interval. The chart indicates two categories of manpower: programming and non-programming. The first category includes software designers, programmers, their immediate managers, and programmer technicians. The second category includes all other people.

Some projects will require application of skills not available in-house (e.g., microprocessor expertise, telecommunications skills). Therefore, it will be necessary either to hire a qualified individual or retain an external consultant. In either case, there will be expenses that should be specified in the cost section of the plan.

3.2 Hardware

This paragraph contains a detailed estimate of the type, quantity and point of application of all hardware required for planning and development.

A chart showing a hardware requirements profile planned for the total project by monthly interval may be provided.

In addition to computer hardware, other resources that may be considered include: special test equipment; prototype system element (e.g., mechanical components) and support hardware (e.g., a word processing system for document preparation).

3.3 Software

This paragraph describes support and utility software that will be used to aide in the development of the planned software, or will be included as part of the planned software. Resources include:

1. operating systems

2. compilers

3. test tools

4. application packages

5. data base packages

Each software resource must be described with reference to availability, documentation and applicability.

4.0 COST

The objective of this section is to present an estimate of the project cost to the requestor. The cost statement may be presented in several ways. Cost can be equated to estimated lines of code or to tasks to be accomplished or to deliverables. Cost may also be shown as a function of time. A detailed discussion of software costing methods is presented in Chapter 3 of the Handbook.

Project cost estimates must include the following components:

I. Labor
   A. Requirements Specification
   B. Design Specification
   C. Code and Unit Test
      Under this heading show the major function modules each with its associated cost (see Section 4.1.1)
   D. Integration Test
   E. System and Acceptance Test
   F. Test Support Software
   G. User Documentation
   H. Site Support
II. Computer Time
III. Equipment Procurement
IV. Travel and Living

5.0 SCHEDULE

This section presents a schedule for the tasks, deliverables and resources described above. Good planning techniques demand subdivision and scheduling of the work to be done.

As planning develops, high level functions can be broken down into more detailed subfunctions. During each step of this top-down planning, more detailed scheduling is completed to give management better control and insight.

5.1 Allocation of Resources

A schedule for the allocation of all resources described in Section 3 is derived. People, hardware, software and deliverables must be scheduled so that the project flows smoothly.

6.0 PERSONNEL ORGANIZATION

This section is primarily applicable to large projects or to projects where a new organization is being used, e.g., a chief programmer team is being used for the first time. This section clarifies job assignments, minimizes interactions, establishes points of responsibility, and provides a handy written reference for each project member.

Page A-8

Appendix A
DOCUMENT FORMATS

SOFTWARE
ENGINEERING
HANDBOOK

Appendix A.3:
SOFTWARE REQUIREMENTS SPECIFICATION

The SOFTWARE REQUIREMENTS SPECIFICATION (SRS) establishes detailed requirements for design and test of a software system. Functions are refined in detail; interfaces are described; design constraints and performance characteristics are established; data base characteristics are identified; test and validation criteria are defined.

A recommended format for the SRS is presented in this appendix.

SOFTWARE REQUIREMENTS SPECIFICATION

1.0 SCOPE

This section contains a summary and brief description of software requirements.

2.0 APPLICABLE DOCUMENTS

This section contains a list of documents that apply (in whole or in part) to the specification.

3.0 INTERFACES

This section specifies the functional relationship of the software to other hardware, software, and people. General and/or descriptive material is included in Section 3.1.

3.1 Interface Description

This paragraph specifies, either directly or by reference, constraints imposed on the design of the software because of its relationship to other hardware, software, or human interfaces. Where applicable, it also includes detailed interface definition resulting from analysis and requirements contained in the SYSTEM SPECIFICATION. Quantitative requirements are included in the following subparagraphs. A separate interface document may be generated on large projects for purposes of better control.

3.1.1 Hardware

This paragraph contains a description of all hardware interfaces relevant to the software described by the SRS. Interfaces defined in this paragraph include all relevant characteristics of the computer, such as memory size, word size, access and instruction times, interrupt capabilities, and special hardware capabilities. The computer characteristics may be described by references to applicable documents. Each document is listed in Section 2.

In addition, special hardware designed to test software or required as part of a prototype implementation is described. Reference to appropriate documentation is essential.

3.1.2 Software

This paragraph contains a description of all software resources and/or functional software required to complete development of the software described herein.

Typical software interfaces described in this paragraph and referenced in Section 2 are:

1. Operating System
   characteristics
   I/O capabilities
   drivers
   special features

2. Applications Software (existing)

3. Data Base Software

4. General System Utilities and Support

5. Compilers, Editors, Special Tools

6. Acquired Software

**SOFTWARE
ENGINEERING
HANDBOOK**

**Appendix A
DOCUMENT FORMATS**

Page A-9

3.1.3 Human

This paragraph describes the human interfaces to the software. User characteristics and training are established; human engineering of the interface is discussed; special features (e.g., audio response, computer graphics) are established.

3.1.4 Packaging

This paragraph describes software packaging considerations such as transportation media; documentation shipped with software when released; special features required to satisfy varied interfaces (e.g., different I/O drivers for different hardware configurations).

3.2 Interface Diagram

The relationship of the software to other system elements is graphically represented. The paragraph incorporates, in subparagraphs as appropriate, a functional block diagram or equivalent representation of the interface requirements for the software.

3.3 Data Flow Diagrams

The overall relationship of the data flowing throughout the system is presented. This information should be presented at a fairly high level without getting too involved in the design aspects of the software. The data should particularly point out the input data and its sources external to the software being designed, the data required for each of the major functions listed in the Software Plan and the expected output data from the software to be designed.

4.0 FUNCTIONS

This section specifies the functional requirements of the software. Requirements are stated in quantitative terms, with tolerances where applicable. General and descriptive material may be included in an introduction that normally makes reference to the functional block diagram or equivalent representation of the software (Section 7).

4.n Description of Function N

The basic paragraph for each function begins with descriptive and introductory material that defines the function and its relationship to other functions. The following four subparagraphs specify quantitative requirements.

4.n.1 Inputs

This paragraph specifies (either directly or by reference to another part of the specification) the source(s) and type(s) of input information associated with a function. Included are a description of the information, its source(s) in quantitative terms, e.g., units of measure; limits and/or ranges of units of measure; accuracy/precision requirements, and frequency of input information arrival.

4.n.2 Processing

This paragraph provides a description of each of the processing requirements for the function. Presentation of these descriptions under each function include:

1. Purpose—The purpose describes the exact intent of the function. This involves a definition of the specific input and output parameters and the processing required.

2. Approach—The approach presents a processing narrative that identifies accuracies required, sequence and timing of events, and relevant restrictions or limitations, when applicable, equations and/or diagrams, and an appropriate legend defining mathematical or control symbology.

4.n.3 Outputs

This paragraph specifies, (either directly or by reference to another part of this specification) the destination(s) and type(s) of output information associated with a function as a result of the processing described in Paragraph 4.n.2. This includes a description of the information; its destination(s); and, in quantitative terms, units of measure, accuracy/precision requirements and frequency of output information, where applicable.

4.n.4 Design Requirements

This paragraph specifies, in appropriate subparagraphs, requirements which affect the design of the software. These requirements may include:

1. The specification of a programming language(s) to be used. The use of a specific language may be related to a functional element of the software or blanket use of a single language may be dictated.

2. The use of programming standards to assure compatibility among software modules.

3. Program organization, such as overall program segmentation. In addition, for modules that contain or process proprietary information, special attention shall be given to the requirements for protecting this information.

4. Program design resulting from consideration or modifications to the software during operation (e.g., on-site modification requirements and the permissible amount of operational degradation allowed during installation of modification may be specified).

Page A-10

Appendix A
DOCUMENT FORMATS

SOFTWARE
ENGINEERING
HANDBOOK

5. Special features to facilitate testing of the software. For example, special procedures for the design of interfaces, requirements for intermediate printouts, and commentary on the program listing may be required.

6. Expandability (growth potential) to facilitate modifications and additions.

5.0 DATA BASE

This section specifies all software data requirements in descriptive and quantitative terms. The data configuration invariably affects the design of the software and must be carefully considered in the requirements document.

5.1 Characteristics

This paragraph is included 1) when a formal structured data base must be developed as part of the software system or 2) when an existing data base is to be used. Data base hierarchical structure and methods for data acquisition are discussed. Support software may be referenced.

In addition a description of capacity requirements is presented. Parameters such as total simultaneous message handling, total number of simultaneous machines controlled, total number of simultaneous displays and operator station requests, number and types of inputs processed are described. The system capacities are directly related to computer storage capacities, interfacing subsystem timing rates, and interfacing equipment capacities.

5.2 Discrete Data Items

All global data items are described in this paragraph. Included in the data description is a discussion of file structure and format (where applicable); content and quantity of each data item; relationship of software functions to data, and data limits or constraints.

5.3 Access

This paragraph describes data base access characteristics for all global data items. The data "environment" is also discussed, i.e., the frequency and method of change (update) for individual data items.

6.0 QUALITY ASSURANCE

In this section, requirements for formal validation of software performance and functionality are specified. Because this section serves as the basis for the validation test specification, two important issues must be addressed:

1. What functional/performance requirements are to be tested?

2. What are the limits of each test?

The above questions imply that testing must be bounded. It is impossible to "exhaustively" test most software systems; therefore, the quality assurance procedure must be specified to produce acceptable confidence that the software is "correct".

Validation requirements and methods specified in this section must be related to performance and design requirements. Requirements must be specified to a level of detail necessary to clearly establish the scope and accuracy of the test method. Validation methods include inspection of the software, review of analytical data, automated demonstration tests and review of test results. Requirements specified herein shall be the basic for preparation and validation of such documents.

6.1 Validation Requirements

This paragraph specifies the requirements that form the basis of the validation test plan and procedure. Through reference to Section 4, each function to be validated is discussed.

6.2 Validation Tests

This paragraph contains a high level discussion of the types of tests to be performed. Techniques are outlined, but specific procedures are reserved for inclusion in a test specification.

6.3 Resources

The resources (manpower, computer time, additional software) required during validation testing are outlined. Each resource should be associated with one or more of the tests indicated in Paragraph 4.2.

6.4 Integration

This paragraph identifies requirements that cannot be verified until system integration testing (or equivalent).

7.0 SOFTWARE BLOCK DIAGRAM

This section contains a block diagram that depicts software functions and their relationship to other system elements. Interfaces may also be shown.

The intent of this section is to illustrate in pictorial fashion software functions, interfaces and interrelationships.

SOFTWARE
ENGINEERING
HANDBOOK

Appendix A
DOCUMENT FORMATS

Page A-11

8.0 NOTES

This section presents information that is included here for convenience only, e.g., background information that will be of assistance in understanding the specification or the software are included.

9.0 APPENDIX

This section contains requirements which for convenience in specification maintenance are incorporated separately. Appendices may be bound as separate documents for convenience in handling (e.g., when parts of the program are classified or proprietary). When data are placed in an appendix, the paragraph of Section 9 is referenced in the main body of the specification.

The SRS appendix often includes a PRELIMINARY USERS MANUAL (which may be bound separately). See Chapter 4 of the Handbook for discussion and Chapter 12 for an example.

10.0 GLOSSARY

This section contains a glossary of important terms used in the specification.

APPENDIX A.4:
DESIGN DOCUMENTATION

INTRODUCTION

The Design Document is the most critical of all software development documentation. The design serves as a guide for implementation and test, as a critical review tool, and as an essential maintenance document.

The Design Document evolves throughout the development process. Portions of the document are completed during the preliminary design step. Detailed design results in the completion of remaining sections. Finally, after code and testing are complete, changes are reflected as the As-Built Design.

The Design Document establishes the relationship between functional details and the software structure. It addresses data flow and structure, procedural details for each module of a software system, data base characteristics, and certain test and packaging provisions.

DESIGN DOCUMENT

1.0 SCOPE

This section contains an overall description of the software. The following topics are addressed:

1. hardware, software and human interfaces

2. major functions and related processing

3. externally defined data bases

4. major design constraints, limitations

Appropriate nomenclature for the software should be identified and reference to the Requirements Specification should be made.

Page A-12

**Appendix A
DOCUMENT FORMATS**

SOFTWARE
ENGINEERING
HANDBOOK

2.0 APPLICABLE DOCUMENTS

This section contains a list of specifications (document control numbers should be included), manuals, texts, standards, etc., that are referenced in the body of the Design Document and/or contain supplementary information to the design.

3.0 DESIGN DESCRIPTION

The design description is a top-level definition of the software structure and data flow/structure determined during the Preliminary Design step.

3.1 Functional Allocation

The relationship between major software functions (described in the Requirements Specification) and the software structure is addressed in this paragraph. Each function is described with reference to both data flow or structure (Paragraph 3.2) and software structure (Paragraph 3.3).

3.2 Data Flow/Structure

Depending upon the nature of the software, this paragraph contains:

1. a written and graphical description of important data flow paths or

2. a written and graphical description of the data structure

In some cases, both of the above topics may be addressed.

3.2.1 Description of Flow Paths/Structural Elements

This subparagraph contains a detailed description of data flow and the transforms applied during data flow [see Chapter 5 of the Handbook for technical descriptions of these terms]. Flow of control is also considered when necessary. If the structured design methodology (Chapter 5) is used, afferent, transform, transaction and efferent flow paths are identified and discussed.

As an alternative, or in addition, to the data flow description, data structure is described. The logical and hierarchical organization of data is discussed and the physical data configuration (e.g., tabular, linked list) is presented.

3.2.2 Graphical Representation of Flow/Structure

Data Flow Graphs (Chapter 5) and/or a schematic graphical representation of data structure is presented. This mode of data description should complement subparagraph 3.2.1.

3.3 Software Structure

The complete software structure is described in this paragraph. Using one or more structure diagrams (Chapter 5) each major software function described in Paragraph 3.1 is presented in terms of the modules that will accomplish the function. The primary goal is to show the relationship among modules and the hierarchy of control and processing.

4.0 MODULES

This section contains a detailed description of each module in the software system. Parts of the section are completed during preliminary design, others during detailed design and Paragraph 4.2 is added only after code and unit test is complete.

NOTE: All section 4.0 paragraphs are repeated for each module.

4.x Description of Module X

A complete procedural description of Module X is presented in the paragraphs that follow.

4.x.1 Processing Narrative

An explicit description of the inputs, processing, and outputs is presented. The primary goal is clarity and completeness. Detailed algorithms and/or mathematical analysis is normally referenced as an Appendix.

The design description can evolve in two stages:

1. during preliminary design a top-level description (e.g., a flowchart, box diagram or design language) of the module is developed;

2. during detailed design a complete description of procedure is developed; design language is recommended (see Paragraph 4.x.3).

Both the preliminary (if it has been developed) and detailed description are retained as part of the document.

The detailed description should contain: 1) a definition of all important local identifiers and all global data; 2) a processing description that can be translated directly to code; 3) design notes regarding procedural details.

4.x.2 Interface Description

A detailed description of the external interfaces to the module is presented. These interfaces include:

**SOFTWARE
ENGINEERING
HANDBOOK**

**Appendix A
DOCUMENT FORMATS**

Page A-13

1. A subprogram "argument list" in which each data/control item is defined. Definition should include argument identifier, data type, input/output indicator, data bounds (if any).

2. All file I/O including READs and WRITEs to standard I/O devices, parts and secondary storage devices.

3. All modules called by Module X.

4.x.3 Design Language Description

If a design language (see Chapter 5) is used for detailed design, the listing is included here.

4.x.4 Modules Used

This paragraph contains a list of all modules used by Module X.

4.x.5 Comments

This paragraph contains all supplementary information including: restrictions/limitations, performance characteristics, error-handling, etc.

4.x.6 Data Organization

This paragraph expands upon information presented in Paragraph 3.2 when such data relates to Module X. The use of global data and buffers; data organization internal to Module X, and file handling are considered.

A compiler-generated data dictionary for Module X may also be included. The data dictionary normally contains identifier memory assignment, various cross reference maps and other tabular data.

NOTE: Paragraph 4.x.6 is optional. On large projects, listings and data dictionaries may be separated from the design document so that a reasonably sized document can be maintained.

5.0 FILE STRUCTURE AND GLOBAL DATA

This section contains a detailed discussion of the files and related global data that comprise the data base used by the software.

5.1 External File Description

All files that exist prior to execution of the software or are retained after termination are considered "external" and are described. The following descriptive information is provided for each file:

1. title

2. length in words or bytes

3. access method

In addition, the static or dynamic nature of each file is noted. Interrelationships between files are described.

5.1.1 File Structure

The hierarchical or tabular structure of each file is described. Associative elements are noted, pointers and list characteristics are defined, and a graphical description is presented, if required.

5.1.2 Logical Record Description

The logical record for each file is described. Record format and individual data items are presented.

5.2 Global Data

A description of all global data (e.g., FORTRAN COMMON) is presented. If global data is blocked, the purpose of the block is noted; each item is described and equivalent masking of data is noted.

5.3 Cross Reference

This paragraph contains two cross reference matrices that relate file access by individual module, and global data reference by individual modules. The matrix format is illustrated by Figure A.4-1.

6.0 REQUIREMENTS CROSS REFERENCE

This section indicates traceability to the Requirements Specification. A Requirements Cross Reference Matrix is used to relate satisfaction of a requirement with one or more software modules. This section should be completed during preliminary design.

7.0 TEST PROVISIONS

This section contains guidelines for unit testing, overall strategy for software integration, and special capabilities required for testing. It does not replace formal test plans and procedures.

Page A-14

**Appendix A
DOCUMENT FORMATS**

**SOFTWARE
ENGINEERING
HANDBOOK**

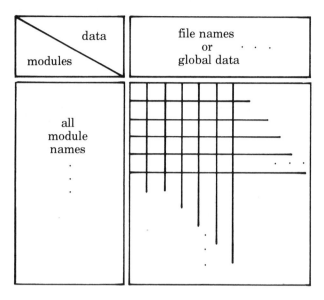

Figure A.4-1 Module-File Cross Reference

7.1 Unit Test Guidelines

Unit test is addressed for each module described in Section 4.0. The following topics are considered:

1. overview of unit test procedure

2. driving software, if required

3. special data bounds checking

4. error handling tests

7.2 Integration Strategy

This paragraph presents an overview of the order and method of integrating individual modules into the software system. Builds (clusters of modules tested as a unit) are identified.

7.3 Special Considerations

Special test tools (e.g., automated data generation) or capabilities (e.g., hardware simulator) are described. Major software drivers (test software) are discussed.

8.0 PACKAGING

Two types of packaging are discussed in this section: 1) internal program organization (e.g., module overlay) that is dictated by memory constraints or other factors; 2) external shipping requirements for transportation of the software from development to requestor site.

8.1 Special Program Overlay Provisions

Program overlay structure is defined in this paragraph. Overlay tree structures are included and special features and requirements (e.g., multiple copies of the same module) are discussed.

8.2 Criteria for Software Transfer

Mode and format of software transfer (e.g., "three ASCII files on RK05 cartridge disk") are identified. All utilities, operating system command files and installation instructions are discussed in detail.

9.0 SPECIAL NOTES

This section contains general comments and notes that may be referenced from other sections of the document. Among the possible topics included are:

1. special design conventions

2. design alternatives and rationale

3. notes on algorithms

4. suggestions for future modifications

In addition, a subparagraph on Maintenance Notes is recommended. The designer indicates special consideration for maintenance.

10.0 APPENDICES

The appendices contain information that supplements the design document. Typical contents might include: excerpts from vendor manuals, standards, large tables, algorithm derivations, listings (after code and test) hardware descriptions, scheduling data.

APPENDIX A.5:
TEST SPECIFICATION

INTRODUCTION

The development process culminates with a series of formalized test techniques that aid in the assembly of a software system and verify the functional and operational characteristics of the software. In this appendix, a general outline for the content and format of a test specification is presented.

By incorporating the applicable paragraphs, the outline may be used for both integration and validation testing. It should be noted that integration testing is procedurally oriented, requiring not only test information but also guidelines for the incorporation of modules or builds. Validation testing is generally not concerned with internal program elements. Rather, the validation test evaluates the functional characteristics and requirements of the software.

The following outline summarizes the content and format that are recommended for a test specification. Paragraphs labeled (IT) or (VT) are included only for integration and validation testing, respectively.

TEST SPECIFICATION

1.0 SCOPE

This section describes the scope of the tests to be undertaken. The software to be tested is identified and other system elements involved in testing are described. The types of tests to be conducted; the expected results, and the overall procedure for conducting the tests are described. The goal of the tests is also stated.

2.0 APPLICABLE DOCUMENTS

This section lists other planning and development documents (specifications, standards, bulletins, manuals, etc.) which are applicable to paragraphs within other sections of the specification.

3.0 TEST PLAN

A detailed description of the test approach is presented in this section. Test phases, schedule, software and environment are described in the following paragraphs.

3.1 Test Phases

This paragraph contains a description of each major element or phase of testing. Order of integration (IT), schedule, test data and approach are described in overview fashion.

3.1.n Description of Test Phase N

An abstract of each test phase is presented in the paragraph. Dependencies on other tests, scheduling constraints and other requirements are also discussed.

3.2 Test Schedule

This paragraph contains a complete schedule for testing. The order and dependencies of all tests are described in detail, availability windows for testing resources are specified.

3.2.1 Integration Test Schedule (IT)

This paragraph contains a complete schedule for integration tests. The integration and testing of individual builds, is scheduled to coincide with completion of unit code and test for modules according to the availability of equipment and personnel. When test drivers or test data must be generated, schedules must also be defined to coincide with test resource availability.

3.2.2 Validation Test Schedule (VT)

This paragraph describes each of the validation tests and their order of execution.

3.3 Test Software

This paragraph presents an overview of all test software including drivers, test monitors, simulation packages and related software tools. Test software is described in detail in Section 4.0.

3.4 Test Environment (optional)

This section contains a complete description of the computer operating environment that is required for testing. The computer model, memory requirements, peripheral devices, media, and terminals are described. The relevant operating system, with any required modifications, is also specified.

4.0 TEST PROCEDURE

This section specifies a specific test procedure for each testing phase described in Section 3.0.

Page A-16

Appendix A
DOCUMENT FORMATS

SOFTWARE
ENGINEERING
HANDBOOK

4.n Description of Test Phase N

Tests applied during test phase n are described in the following paragraphs.

4.n.1 Purpose

The purpose of the test is described. Reference is made to the design or requirements documentation. Typical test "purpose" include:

1. test module function

2. test interface validity

3. test data structure/file access

4. test timing

5. test design constraints or bounds

4.n.2 Technique

The approach to be used in performing the test is described in this paragraph. Special methods or resources are described in detail.

4.n.3 Test Software

This paragraph describes all test drivers and other test software required for phase n testing. If test software is extensive, reference may be made either to an appendix or to a separate test software document.

4.n.4 Test Data/Results

Test data and expected results are explicitly defined. Test cases are described or referenced. Input techniques, expected processing, and output format are considered.

4.n.5 Special Tools (optional)

All special software (or hardware) tools that apply to test phase n are described.

4.n.6 Allowable Variance (VT)

This paragraph specifies and bounds the functional and performance characteristics that are to be expected during validation test phase n. Tolerances are indicated and bounds for performance are set. "Acceptable" and "unacceptable" characteristics are defined before tests commence.

5.0 APPENDICES

The appendix of the test specification includes all test related information that is required to qualify the above paragraphs. Data that is too voluminous for inclusion in a paragraph may be included in the appendix.

A listing of all test cases is normally included in an Appendix. Each case must be uniquely identified and each data item must be defined. A listing of all test drivers is also included.

6.0 NOTES

Any information that is related to testing but is not covered in the above paragraphs is included in this section. Information might include statistical justification for variance criteria; mathematical models; notes on computer hardware or operating system addenda to scheduling data.

APPENDIX A.6:
MODULE DEVELOPMENT FOLDER

1.0 INTRODUCTION

The Module Development Folder (MDF) is a readily accessible repository for documentation that is generated during the development process. The MDF is created at the conclusion of the preliminary design review and is the source for all information related to a specific module.

In addition, the MDF provides a number of important benefits during software development:

1. identifies the status of low level (routine) development schedules

2. provides a common collection point for all development information

3. provides management training for the programmer by requiring him (her) to set and maintain completion dates

4. enables easy review of development

5. provides extremely useful data for the software maintenance period

Recalling the definition of the software hierarchy (Chapter 2, Figure 2.5), an MDF may contain information on one or more modules associated with a given software function. Information includes both design and test related data.

The MDF is a folder or notebook with a standardized cover sheet (Figure A.6.1). All MDFs for a software system are stored in a central location. This appendix outlines the recommended contents and format of the Module Development Folder.

2.0 CONTENTS OF THE MODULE DEVELOPMENT FOLDER

The contents of the MDF provides technical documentation for use by development, and later, maintenance personnel. The MDF is also a source of management information regarding the history of development for the routines associated with a module.

The development folder contains the following data:

1. MDF Cover Sheet

2. Requirements Cross Reference

3. Design Description—Preliminary Design

4. Design Description—Code to Design

5. Unit Code

6. Functional Capabilities List

7. Test Description(s)

8. Test Results(s)

9. Design Description—As-Built Design

Each topic is discussed in the following paragraphs.

2.1 MDF Cover Sheet

Upon completion of a module the MDF cover sheet should contain all information illustrated in Figure A.6.1. The scheduled start/completion date, and actual start/completion date for each routine are entered. The total budgeted number of source lines and the object module size for the module are entered as well as the actual number of lines and object size for each of the routines. The MDF Cover Sheet is divided into two portions, a header and a body.

2.1.1 HEADER ENTRIES

The entry for project contains the assigned project identification, and the entry for module name should contain a descriptive name for the module. If more than one module is to be included in the folder, functional identification is substituted for the module name. Programmer entry contains the name of the person assigned responsibility for development of the module. The design documentation section indicates the design document paragraph satisfied by this module.

Budget information includes source lines and object module size. For most projects these are estimates, but in some cases these values are specified in the requirements specification. The revision entry is updated as changes are made to schedule entries in the body of the MDF. The date appearing to the right of the revision entry is the date of the revision. The issue date indicates when a copy of the MDF is made for circulation and review.

2.1.2 Body Entries

Each column in the body provides a development history for a module. The design document subsection number identifies in greater detail that portion of the design whose function is met. The routine name is the name used in calling the module in the code itself. The description is a brief, one line description of the function performed by the routine. The three entries for each column are the original planned date for completion, the currently scheduled date for completion, and the actual date for completion. Code review is performed upon completion of code and unit test. Review date approval is indicated by the initials of the chief programmer or his designate. The listing date is the date for the current listing found in the Module Development Folder.

If the MDF contains multiple modules associated with a given function each of the modules has a budget and an actual value for number of source lines and object size. These are indicated in the appropriate column.

Lead Software Engineer approval is indicated by the signature (initials) at the bottom of the cover sheet. The date of completion for the Module Development Folder is also included.

2.2 Requirements Cross Reference

This section refers to the SOFTWARE REQUIREMENTS SPECIFICATION. Either the paragraph number or a statement of the requirements implemented by the module is given.

2.3 Design Description—Preliminary Design

This section contains the design document module design description. It is reviewed during the Preliminary Design Review.

2.4 Design Description—Code to Design

This section contains the detailed design description of each module in the folder. The description may be duplicated from the design document and provides necessary detail for direct generation of source code.

Page A-18

Appendix A
DOCUMENT FORMATS

**SOFTWARE
ENGINEERING
HANDBOOK**

MODULE DEVELOPMENT FOLDER

COVER SHEET

PAGE _____ OF _____

PROJECT: _____ REVISION: _____ DATE: _____

MODULE NAME: _____ ISSUE DATE: _____

PROGRAMMER: _____ BUDGET: _____

DESIGN SECTION: _____ SOURCE LINES: _____

OBJ. MOD. SIZE: _____

(MODULE OR ROUTINE NAMES IF APPLICABLE)

DESIGN SUBSECTION				
DESCRIPTION				
CODE TO DESIGN				
SCHED START				
ACTUAL START				
SCHED COMPL				
ACTUAL COMPL				
CODE/UNIT TEST				
SCHED START				
ACTUAL START				
SCHED COMPL				
ACTUAL COMPL				
INTEGRATION				
SCHED START				
ACTUAL START				
SCHED COMPL				
ACTUAL COMPL				
CODE REVIEW DATE/INITIALS				
LISTING DATE				
SOURCE LINES				
BUDGET				
ACTUAL				
OBJ. MOD. SIZE				
BUDGET				
ACTUAL				
CHIEF PROGR. APPROVAL				

Figure A.6.1 Module Development Folder Cover Sheet

2.5 Unit Code

This section initially contains a listing of the first error-free compilation. The listing will remain in the folder; however, subsequent updates periodically replace previous listings in order to provide current coding/test status.

2.6 Functional Capabilities List

A Functional Capability List is extracted from the preliminary design and serves as a checklist and guide in the preparation of test cases. The list indicates the functional capabilities that are associated with each module contained in the MDF.

2.7 Test Description

This section contains a description of each test applicable to the module. The description defines the objectives of each test to a level of detail that clearly shows which capabilities are being tested. The description includes, for each test, the test tools required, test inputs, and expected test results.

2.8 Test Results

This section contains all test results and analyses necessary to demonstrate that the code meets design specification and that unit testing is complete. Outputs are identified by test number and are clearly annotated to facilitate review.

2.9 Design Description – As-Built

This section contains the validated design after all tests have been successfully completed.

3.0 MDF DEVELOPMENT CHRONOLOGY

The MDF is established after the preliminary design has been reviewed and approved. It is the primary management tool for assessing software development progress.

Initially, the chief programmer establishes desired integration dates for each module and the assigned programmer then prepares schedule dates and budget estimates. These entries are reviewed by the chief programmer.

The responsible programmer receives the capabilities list established at preliminary design time and uses it during the detailed design to assure completeness. The programmer uses the capabilities list again to prepare test case descriptions after completion of detailed design and before completion of coding. The test case results are collected during unit and integration testing.

The as-built design is entered into the MDF upon completion of the integration of the module with other modules of the software system. As the MDF evolves, it is necessary to periodically review and update the MDF cover sheet. A weekly review is recommended.

The chief programmer reviews progress with the responsible programmer and notes actual completion of tasks by filling in the appropriate date. Periodic review may require revision of planned completion dates or budget items. Whenever a change is made the revision level and revision date for the MDF cover sheet are modified. The MDF cover sheet should be issued weekly by the chief programmer and distributed to both the responsible programmer and the responsible manager. In summary, the MDF cover sheet is a useful tool for tracking and measuring the progress of program development.

4.0 MDF DEVELOPMENT RESPONSIBILITIES

Because the MDF serves as both a management and technical source of information, great care should be taken to assure that:

1. The cover sheet (Figure A.6.1) is kept up to date and accurately reflects the status of the module;

2. The contents of the folder are arranged in a manner that can be clearly understood by a reader unfamiliar with the module.

Responsibility for maintenance of the MDF is assigned to the chief programmer, and except for the cover sheet, is performed by the responsible manager.

APPENDIX A.7: MAINTENANCE DOCUMENTS

INTRODUCTION

Software maintenance requires specific documents for management control and technical evaluation. In this appendix, the Software Problem Report (SPR) and Software Change Report (SCR) are discussed. In addition, types of commonly encountered software errors are categorized for use in reporting.

1.0 SOFTWARE PROBLEM REPORT (SPR)

The SPR, shown in Figure A.7.1, is completed by the individual who uncovers a program error. The SPR is used by the maintenance organization to evaluate the criticality of an error. Each entry of the SPR is described in this appendix.

Page A-20

**Appendix A
DOCUMENT FORMATS**

SOFTWARE
ENGINEERING
HANDBOOK

PARAMETER	KEY	PARAMETER DESCRIPTION
LOG NO	A	A unique SPR number assigned by a configuration control authority (CCA). This number may have an alpha prefix to denote additional information. (e.g., a development prefix to distinguish these SPRs from problems documented during a parallel maintenance phase of an earlier version of the same software). Numbers are sequential.
LOG DATE	B	The date the problem is logged by CCA.
TIME	C	This is the date and time of day the problem was discovered.
ACTIVITY	D	Test phase during which the problem was discovered. DEV—development test INTEG—integration test VAL—validation test SYS—system test SITE—operational problem
STATUS	E	Status is a dynamic indicator maintained in the configuration records. It appears on the SPR for use by developers and testers in tracking and reporting latest status to the CCA. Codes indicate the following: 1—SPR is being reviewed to determine appropriate action. 2—SPR has been assigned to a developer for correction. 3—Fix is available. It has been tested, and is ready for delivery to master program library. 4—Master program library has been updated; retest of fix on master program library not complete. 5—Test rerun, problem still exists, SCR rejected. 6—Test rerun, fix works, SPR closed. 7—Hold for future closure. Problem is not reproducible, or is product improvement, or is very low priority, etc.

ORIGINATOR	F	Name, address and telephone number of author of SPR.
PROBLEM WITH	G	Identification of whether the problem is in a routine, the data base, a document, or some combination of these.
ROUTINE/ELEMENT/SS	H	Name of the routine exhibiting the problem. If the routine is not known, identify the element or subsystem (i.e., provide the maximum amount of detail possible).
REV	I	Revision level of routine exhibiting the problem, if known.
TAPE	J	Tape ID of Master Program Library tape containing the offending routine.
DATA BASE	K	ID of data base used when the problem was discovered.
DOCUMENTS	L	Document number(s) of document(s) exhibiting errors.
TEST CASE	M	ID of the principal test case which demonstrated the error.
HARDWARE UNIT	N	ID of the computer system being operated when the problem was discovered.
PROBLEM DESCRIPTION IMPACT	O	Detailed description of the symptoms of the problem and, if possible a description of the actual problem. Impact of the problem on future testing, on interfacing software, documentation, etc., should also be provided.
NOTES	P	Working area for status keeping additional information, etc.

2.0 SOFTWARE CHANGE REPORT (SCR)

The SCR, shown in Figure A.7.2, is completed by the maintenance organization after an SPR has been processed. The SCR indicates error category, repair strategy and repair status. It is the request for authorization to proceed with the change(s) to effect the repair.

PARAMETER	KEY	PARAMETER DESCRIPTION
LOG ON	A	A unique SCR number assigned by CCA upon receipt of the modification.

**SOFTWARE
ENGINEERING
HANDBOOK**

**Appendix A
DOCUMENT FORMATS**

Page A-21

S	OFTWARE		LOG NO: Ⓐ
P	ROBLEM		LOG DATE: Ⓑ
R	EPORT		TIME: Ⓒ

| Ⓓ DEV ☐ INTEG ☐ VAL ☐ SYS ☐ | STATUS: Ⓔ | 1 | 2 | 3 | 4 | 5 | 6 | 7 |

ORIGINATOR: NAME
ADDRESS   Ⓕ   TELEPHONE

PROBLEM WITH: Ⓖ   ROUTINE ☐   DATA BASE ☐   DOCUMENT ☐

ROUTINE/ELEMENT/SS: Ⓗ	REV. Ⓘ	TAPE Ⓙ
DATA BASE: Ⓚ	DOCUMENTS: Ⓛ
TEST CASE: Ⓜ	HARDWARE UNIT: Ⓝ

PROBLEM DESCRIPTION/IMPACT: Ⓞ

NOTES:

Ⓟ

Figure A.7.1 Software Problem Report

Page A-22

Appendix A
DOCUMENT FORMATS

SOFTWARE
ENGINEERING
HANDBOOK

S	OFTWARE	ERROR CATEGORY ⊗	LOG NO: Ⓐ
C	HANGE		LOG DATE: Ⓑ
R	EPORT		TIME: Ⓒ

ORIGINATOR Ⓓ		SS: Ⓔ	ROUTINE: Ⓕ
RESPONSE TO SPRS: Ⓖ			

Ⓗ RESPONSE INCLUDES:
ROUTINE MOD ☐   DOC. UPDATE ☐   DATA BASE CHG ☐   EXPLANATION ☐

RESPONSE: Ⓘ

APPROVAL: _____ Ⓙ

CHANGE:

CODE TYPE: Ⓚ   I/O ☐   COMP ☐   LOGICAL ☐   DATA HAND ☐

ROUTINE: Ⓛ	OLD MOD: Ⓜ	NEW MOD: Ⓝ
REF DATA BASE: Ⓞ	DBCR Ⓟ	REF DOCUMENT Ⓠ	DUT: Ⓡ

HAS FIX BEEN TESTED? Ⓢ	YES NO NA	YES NO NA	YES NO NA	YES NO NA	YES NO NA
REMARKS:	ELEMENT	SS	SS INTEG.	VALID.	OPERATIONS

WAS PROBLEM CORRECTLY STATED ON SPR? Ⓣ   YES ☐   NO ☐

REMARKS: Ⓤ

PROBLEM SOURCE: Ⓥ   SYS SPEC ☐   REQ SPEC ☐   DES SPEC ☐   DB ☐   CODE ☐

ESTIMATES RESOURCES: Ⓦ   MANHOURS _____ COMPUTER TIME _____

Figure A.7.2 Software Change Report

LOG DATE	B	Date the SCR is logged by CCA.
TIME	C	Time the SCE and the delivered modification are available to CCA and logged.
ORIGINATOR	D	Author of the modification (generally the closer of the SPR(s)).
SS	E	Subsystem affected by the modification being delivered.
ROUTINE	F	Name of the routine for which the modification is being delivered. (This field is a repeat of field L).
RESPONSE TO SPRs	G	SPR number(s) being totally or partially closed by the delivery. If an SCR partially closes a problem, a P is appended to the SPR number (e.g., 1234(P)).
RESPONSE INCLUDES	H	Identification of elements in the delivery; e.g., a routine modification, document update or data base change or a combination of these. If the SCR closes an SPR by supplying an amplifying explanation this is indicated. Most explanations involve user documentation deficiencies and should also result in a user document update.
RESPONSE	I	Detailed description of the correction being made to the software. In the case of a document update or data base change the Document Update Transmittal (DUT) and Data Base Change Request (DBCR) numbers, respectively, are referenced with the description of the necessary change in P and R.
APPROVAL	J	Signature of appropriate manager. This is the indication of formal approval to proceed with the repair.
CODE TYPE	K	Type(s) of source code involved in the routine modification.

I/O—input, output, or formatting statements, etc.
COMP—computational code.
LOGICAL—code that establishes branches in the program.
DATA HANDS—code that moves data from place to place, stores data, etc. That is, data handling code. |

ROUTINE	L	Name of routine being modified, document being changed, or data base being altered. In the case of an explanatory SCR the name given on the SPR is repeated.
OLD MOD	M	Revision level identification of current.
NEW MOD	N	Revision to be revision altered and superseded to produce the new revision level.
REF DATA BASE DBCR	O P	If a data base change is in order, this supplies the data base identifier to which the changes delivered by the data base change request are to be applied.
REF DOCUMENT DUT	Q R	If corrective action also requires a change to a document, the title of the document to be changed is given and the document update transmittal (DUT) delivering the change is referenced by number.
HAS THE FIX BEEN TESTED?	S	Testing of a modification made to a routine must be completed at appropriate predetermined levels prior to delivery of a modification. Element, subsystem, integration, validation, and operational testing, if applicable, will be indicated. Remarks indicating test success are required.
WAS PROBLEM CORRECTLY STATED ON SPR?	T U	Indication of accuracy of the problem statement is to be given. An accurate restatement of the problem is to be given in the remarks section.
PROBLEM SOURCE	V	Identification of the source of the Problem.

1. System Specification

2. Requirements Specification—requirements baseline document

3. As-coded Design Specification

4. DB—data base

5. CODE—source code only |

Page A-24

Appendix A
DOCUMENT FORMATS

SOFTWARE
ENGINEERING
HANDBOOK

ESTIMATED
RESOURCES   W   Resources required to close the problem in man-hours of work and cost of computer time.

ERROR
CATEGORY   X   The error category code for the problem. To be assigned by person making the required fix. See Section 3.0 for a discussion of error categories.

3.0 ERROR CATEGORIES

The source materials used in categorizing an error are the Software Problem Report and the Software Change Report. Both documents are used for management decision making.

A standardized method for the classification of errors is necessary so that the overall nature of the problem may be quickly evaluated and categorized. The following aspects of software problem categorization are considered: 1) generation of categories; 2) assignment of categories to problem reports, and 3) analysis of results.

3.1 Generation of Error Categories

The approach taken in defining the error categories (failure categories, error codes, or defect categories) was to base results on an analysis of actual SPRs and SCRs as reported by TRW ('Software Reliability Study', G. R. Craig, et.al., NTIS Report AD 787 784, October 1974).

One hundred sixty nine error categories under 15 major groups are presented in that publication. A brief description of each of the major groups discussed follows.

3.1.1 Computation Errors

Computation errors result from coded equations. These equations fall generally into two categories: 1) those that produce values directly related to the physical problem being solved by the software (e.g., algorithms, vector algebra, modeling code), and 2) equations used in a bookkeeping sense (e.g., computation of indices, record numbers, table entry numbers).

3.1.2 Logic Errors

The logic error categories tie errors to existing logical code or the need for logical code.

3.1.3 I/O Errors

Categories in this group are limited to errors resulting from I/O code. An attempt should be made to distinguish them from interface or other error categories. This categorization is very difficult since the physical manifestations that are usually labeled I/O are generally symptomatic of other errors. For example, CC020 (an indicator from Craig's report pointing to output missing data entries) could be symptomatic of a loop processing or logic error. The intent is to establish categories relating to output format, position, completeness, field size, and control.

Also included in this group is the unexplainable program halt (again from Craig, FF030) which is not covered by the paragraph above. This category is assigned to non-repeatable halts.

3.1.4 Interface Errors

Interface errors are grouped into five major categories:

1. Routine/routing interface errors—This group includes error categories at the interfaces between applications software routines.

2. Routine/system software interface errors—These are errors resulting at the interface between an applications routine and an operating system or system utility routine.

3. File processing interface errors—These are errors in handling files.

4. User interface errors—This group includes errors at the user interface, including the machine operator, manual or data card inputs, tape inputs, etc. In this group the term "input data" is used to include all sources at the user level.

5. Data base interface errors—This group includes categories which describe incompatibilities between the data base structure and an interface/access routine.

3.1.5 Data Handling Errors

This group of categories covers errors made in reading, writing, moving, storing, and modifying data. These categories apply only to those errors occurring wholly within a routine and not those occurring across an interface.

SOFTWARE
ENGINEERING
HANDBOOK

Appendix A
DOCUMENT FORMATS

Page A-25

3.1.6 Operating System/System Support Software Errors

These categories include errors discovered in the operating system (OS) software, the compiler, the assembler, and the system support or specialized utility software.

3.1.7 Configuration Errors

Configuration errors are the catastrophic problems encountered when the software, after undergoing some sort of modification (usually to fix a problem), fails to be compatible with the operating system or remaining applications software. In the majority of cases, these errors are the product of tight schedules and failure to adhere to rigorous configuration management techniques.

3.1.8 User Requested Changes

This group of categories is established to record requested changes and enhancements of capability based on usage of the delivered software.

3.1.9 Preset Data Base Errors

These categories are assigned to SCRs written directly against present or constant data in the data base.

(Note: Preset data is generated by the user and remains constant or serves as an initial setting to be updated or modified by a routine.)

3.1.10 Global Variable Definition Errors

This group includes categories defining errors in the specification of global variables or constants, i.e., data defined for use by interfacing routines. These variables are to be distinguished from internal or local variables used only within a single routine.

3.1.11 Recurrent Errors

This group includes problems that are reopened (the fix did not work when tested on site in the master configuration), and duplicates of previous SPRs.

3.1.12 Documentation Errors

The SPR can be used to flag documentation problems. The approved (code-to) design document user manual and implementation documents are part of the deliverable product and are maintained rigorously.

3.1.13 Requirements Compliance Errors

These categories include cases where the software failed to provide a capability specified by the requirements specification. This does not imply that the design overlooked the requirements. These categories point to the fact that supposed "full capability" code was not in compliance with the requirements at the time the SPR was written.

3.1.14 Unidentified Errors

This group provides a category for closing SPRs that do not supply sufficient information for analysis. SPRs in this group provide so little information that no other error category can be assigned.

3.1.15 Operator Errors

Operator errors are assigned whenever a problem is due to machine operator, developer, or tester error. Do not confuse these errors with those where the error is due to a problem with the user interface, i.e., an error in the user interface design.

3.2 Notes on Category Generation

Error categories fall into two groups, symptomatic categories and categories which identify the cause of the error. For example, I/O error CC020 (Output missing data entries) is a symptom which could have been caused by improper definition of a loop variable, a table initialization error, etc. Computational error AA080 (Sign convention error) points to the cause of the error. Symptoms are generally well documented in the SPR.

3.3 Assignment of Error Categories

Assignment of error categories is something of an art, even when a problem is well documented. It is important to note that all problem reports are assigned to a category, regardless of whether the problem is a real one or not. The following guidelines should be used when error categories are assigned:

Page A-26

Appendix A
DOCUMENT FORMATS

**SOFTWARE
ENGINEERING
HANDBOOK**

1. The individual who corrects the problem should be the source of the code level error category assignment. That person alone is close enough to the problem to define it in non-symptomatic terms.

2. Error categorization should be done at the time the problem is closed.

3. Assignment of categories should be based on the Software Problem Report and the Software Change Report.

4. Long lists of error categories are difficult to use effectively. However, time spent in precisely defining the error often leads to more rapid resolution of the problem.

3.4 Analysis of Error Category Results

In analyzing the results of the error categorization for a project, five general questions should be asked:

1. What is the error?

2. Why did the error occur?

3. When was the error introduced?

4. When and how was the error found?

5. What can be done on future projects to prevent the error or locate it sooner?

APPENDIX A.8: INSTALLATION MANUAL AND USER GUIDE

INTRODUCTION

Unlike the majority of software documentation that is written by software professionals for software professionals, user documentation must be written at a level that the ultimate user of the software can easily comprehend. Because these documents must communicate with the user, great care must be taken in their preparation.

The style, format and content of user documentation depends upon the software application, the sophistication of the user and the software category (e.g., a product). Two documents are normally generated—the Installation Manual and User Guide. These documents may be combined, or they may be published separately.

INSTALLATION MANUAL

INSTALLATION MANUAL

1.0 INTRODUCTION

This section provides a description of the operating characteristics of the software. Functions and objectives, performance levels and operating environment should be clearly described. Only information relevant to the normal use of installation of the software is included.

1.1 Applicable Documents

A complete bibliography of documents that are available to the user of the program should be included in this section. Document control numbers and publication dates must be provided.

SOFTWARE
ENGINEERING
HANDBOOK

**Appendix A
DOCUMENT FORMATS**

Page A-27

1.2 Functional Description

This section presents a functional description of the software. A top level block diagram showing the interrelationships of program modules is provided. Accompanying text presents a concise outline of the program flow, processing algorithm(s) and any intermodular communication.

1.3 Performance

This section defines the elements of software performance. Items discussed include timing within certain tolerance levels, file capacities and any limitations on I/O rates. Quantitative, physical terms (max/min values) should be specified for parameters or tolerance ranges.

1.4 Environment

Computers, equipment configurations and operating systems must be defined in this section. Any unusual requirements or specialized equipment should be specifically described with model numbers and physical limitations (e.g., cable lengths) clearly defined.

2.0 SOFTWARE INSTALLATION

This section describes the installation procedure for the software. A complete description of software distribution media is presented and all source files are described. Required operating system utilities are identified and special installation software is described.

2.1 System Definitions

System terminology and parameters are defined in this section. Also, installation information associated with operating system priority schemes, checkpoint, or common data areas is included in this section.

2.2 Software Installation

The procedures that are necessary to install the software package are specified in this section. Techniques for the manipulation of distribution media are outlined and the procedure for the operator-console interface is described.

A description of the installation commands and corresponding console messages must be spelled out in "cookbook" fashion. The structure of all commands, messages and user responses to those messages are included in this section. Recovery procedures (if included) must be explicit with regard to user action in response to specific error conditions. References to appendices which contain information pertinent to user installation should be inserted in this section.

2.3 Installation Example

This section includes an example of an installation with output from the operator's console to act as a visual guide for the user. Examples of correct (and incorrect) procedures should be included with appropriate system response.

3.0 TEST CASES AND RESULTS

Once installation has been successfully accomplished, a number of validation test cases are executed to verify that the software is operating correctly. This section contains a description of pertinent test cases and the expected results.

USER GUIDE

1.0 INTRODUCTION

This section provides the reader with an abstract of the function and operation of the software. All requirements for usage should be discussed and all important software limitations must be described.

The introduction must provide enough information so that the reader will be able to determine:

1. the scope of the software;
2. the operational characteristics of the software;
3. preliminary requirements for operation;
4. functional limitations

1.1 Applicable Documents

Complete bibliography of documents that are available to the user of the program should be included in this section. Document control numbers and publication dates must be provided.

1.2 Functional Description

An overview of the software functional description is presented in this section. Important analyses and models are outlined; logical flow is discussed; analysis options are considered, and references for in-depth expansion of the previous topics are given.

Page A-28

Appendix A
DOCUMENT FORMATS

SOFTWARE
ENGINEERING
HANDBOOK

2.0 DETAILED PHYSICAL DESCRIPTION

In the paragraphs and subparagraphs that follow, the physical attributes of the software are described. Section 2 normally comprises the bulk of the User Guide.

2.1 Data Files and Data Description

The purpose, content and organization of data files are defined in this section. The following file characteristics are considered:

1. Storage medium and code type

2. Organization (random, ISAM, sequential, etc.)

3. Size

4. Record type/description

5. Number of records per file

6. Protection levels

7. File growth potential

A brief description of the contents, purpose, and accessibility of the data files is presented. Methods for creation, update, protection, and retention are considered. All interrelationships between files should be stated.

2.1.1 Variable Descriptions

In addition to file descriptions, detailed descriptions of the applicable variables accessible by the user are outlined. Information about format, data type with examples of each may be included in this subsection. Any special considerations such as required use of leading zeroes and justification must also be stated. This subsection is often relegated to an appendix.

2.2 Input Requirements

The contents of the Input Requirements section are highly dependent on the function of the software. In general, however, three types of information are provided:

1. input source and description

2. input format

3. examples

It is critically important that no ambiguity be introduced in this section. Units must be specified and optional input must be qualified.

2.2.1 Input Source and Description

Each input item is described with respect to its source and purpose. A description of the origin of the data input as well as the purpose for which it is intended should be included.

2.2.2 Input Format

This section describes the data field length, the data type (numeric, ASCII, binary, octal, etc.) and any other aspect that might further clarify the format to the user.

2.2.3 Examples

Examples of each data input should be included either here or in an appendix referred to by this subsection. Examples of values outside the range should be included along with the result of the input of each erroneous datum.

2.3 Output

This section provides a description of the output produced by the software under normal use conditions. Messages for operators/users and output-related error conditions should be described here or in an appendix which is referred to by this section.

2.3.1 Output Format and Description

Each output item is described in this subsection. First, the output hierarchy is defined, i.e., blocks of data and their meaning are described, followed by individual data elements. All output messages (except error messages) are also discussed.

2.3.2 Example

Examples of program output under various processing options and error conditions is presented in this subsection or referenced in an appendix.

3.0 ERROR CONDITIONS AND DIAGNOSTICS

This section discusses all levels of error control inherent in the software. It specifies the procedures for:

1. invalid data field conditions

2. invalid combinations of data

3. analysis errors

4. accuracy tolerances

5. rounding and truncating conditions

SOFTWARE
ENGINEERING
HANDBOOK

Appendix A
DOCUMENT FORMATS

Page A-29

In addition, this section describes the response to the above conditions and specifies the meaning of any special diagnostic codes and flags. Methods for isolating errors are also included.

4.0 GLOSSARY

This section, which is generally included only in large documents, clearly defines all terms, mnemonics and acronyms used with the User Guide.

5.0 APPENDICES

The appendices contained with the User Guide provide a supplement to the information given in the above sections. Often, an abridged version of design documentation is included.

5.1 Top-Level Flow Diagrams

A description of the top level functional flow of the software is presented. Emphasis is placed on information relevant to the user.

5.2 Input/Outout Processing

A description of software interaction with I/O is presented. Guidelines for modification of input/output format may also be given.

5.3 Notes

Miscellaneous information not presented above may be included in one or more appendices under this section.

**SOFTWARE
ENGINEERING
HANDBOOK**

**Appendix B
SOFTWARE METHODOLOGIES AND TOOLS**

Page B-1

APPENDIX B.1: DATA STRUCTURE ORIENTED DESIGN

1.0 INTRODUCTION

Two general approaches to software design have evolved during the past decade. Data flow oriented design, discussed in Chapter 5 of the Handbook, has its origins in the concepts of program modularity and functional decomposition. Data structure oriented design, discussed briefly in this Appendix, requires a hierarchical data structure from which software structure and procedure are derived.

Design methods developed by Michael Jackson and Jean-Dominique Warnier are the most common data structure oriented approaches. An overview and comparison of each technique is presented in this Appendix; however, further reading and study are essential before a complete understanding of the strengths and weaknesses of these methods can be achieved.

2.0 THE JACKSON METHODOLOGY

The Jackson Methodology for software design was developed during the early 1970s and has been formalized in the text, *Principles of Program Design* (Academic Press, 1975) by Michael Jackson. Unlike the data flow oriented approach developed from the work of Myers, Constantine and Yourdon, Jackson's approach does not place great emphasis on module definition. Rather, Jackson concentrates on transforming the problem data structure into a structured procedural specification for software.

Jackson's emphasis on the importance of data structure is explained in Section 2.1. An outline of important technical steps is presented in Section 2.2. Both segments contain excerpts from The Jackson Design Methodology (IEEE Software Design Tutorial, 2nd edition, 1977) by Michael Jackson.

2.1 ON THE IMPORTANCE OF DATA STRUCTURE

There are important underlying reasons for basing program structure on data structure. The essential aim in design is to make the program fit the problem. A failure in achieving this objective creates the familiar difficulties in maintaining most data processing systems. Everything therefore depends on a full understanding of the problem structure, and this is best obtained from a consideration of the data structures. The general idea that data structures are a model of the problem (or more properly, of the problem environment) will be familiar to anyone who has worked on a data base system. We can go further:

1. The problem environment is modeled in the data structures which are hierarchical (for certain models, e.g., networks, we need to impose different structures on the data at

different times). Imposition of different structures can be achieved by versatile data base software, but it can also be achieved by simpler methods such as sorting.

2. The task to be carried out by the program must be expressible in elementary executable operations of the computer-based system, operating on elementary components of the data.

3. In addition to these primary operations, a need also arises for such secondary operations as reading and writing, in order to find our way about the data structures. Even in a data base system there is a pervasive need to process serial subfiles.

4. In order to obtain a correct program, we must ensure that each operation is allocated to an appropriate program component.

5. For an intelligible and maintainable program, we must use a structure that corresponds to the data structure.

6 The executable operations, both primary and secondary, must fit perfectly into such a structure: each operation, of either type, is naturally related to a component of the data structure.

We therefore arrive at the following design procedure:

1. Define the data structures.

2. Create the program structure from the data structures.

3. Express the program task in executable operations, and allocate each one to a program component.

Where a program processes more than one data structure, and almost every useful program must have at least one input and one output data structure, the program structure must be based on all of the data structures. In simple cases, accounting for a high proportion of data processing problems, the data structures fit together quite simply. Essentially, we seek correspondences between the components of one structure and the components of another. For example, suppose that we have a file or records containing information about issues and receipts of parts in a factory store. We wish to produce a summary showing the net movement for each part. The data structures are as shown in Figure B.1

Clearly, we have these correspondences:

1. Input file corresponds to output report; there is one of each, and the report is produced from the file;

2. Part group corresponds to net movement line; there is the same number of each, and they are so ordered that they correspond pairwise.

We can therefore create the program structure shown in Figure B.2 and the design proceeds without difficulty.

Page B-2

Appendix B
SOFTWARE METHODOLOGIES AND TOOLS

**SOFTWARE
ENGINEERING
HANDBOOK**

It should be noted from Figure B.1.1 that Jackson defines a simple notation to indicate repetition (*) and selection (o) in each element of the data or program structure. For example, Input File in Figure B.1.1 is made up of multiple part groups (denoted by *) that are comprised of one or more movement records, each of which has either an "issue" or a "receipt" (denoted by o).

An important distinction must be made between Jackson's representation of "program structure" shown in Figure B.1.2 and modular structure discussed in Chapter 5 of the Handbook. Jackson's structure does not explicitly identify software modules. Instead, procedural "structure" is described.

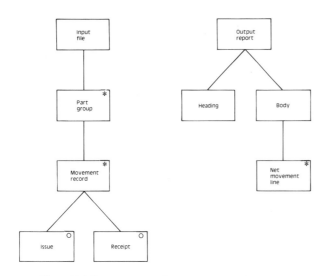

Figure B.1 Data structures for parts movement program

2.2 TECHNICAL ELEMENTS OF THE METHOD

Jackson has developed a number of techniques to deal with situations where input and output data structures do not correspond directly or data structure complexity requires special attention. The following paragraphs briefly explain some of the more important techniques.

2.2.1 STRUCTURE CLASHES

In many cases there is no direct correspondence between input and output data structures. Jackson terms such cases as "structure clash". To mitigate a structure clash an intermediate data structure is constructed, allowing a mapping or transformation between input and output. One program element is developed to map input to the intermediate structure, and a second element is designed to transform the intermediate structure to output.

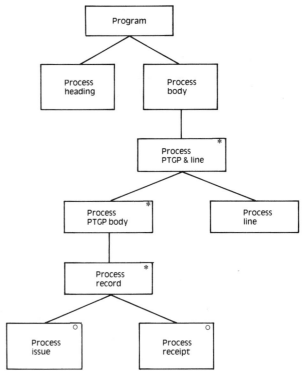

**Figure B.2 Program structure based on data
structure in Figure B.1**

2.2.2 PROGRAM INVERSION

The two program elements that must be developed to solve a structure clash may be executed as separate jobs, executed in parallel, or executed as subroutines. Program inversion is used to create a subroutine, callable from one program element, that will provide data from the intermediate file.

2.2.3 BACKTRACKING

To quote Jackson:

"In a simple program we can find our way about the input data structure by reading one record ahead: at any moment we can inspect the next record to be processed, and so determine whether there is a further occurrence of the iterated part in an iteration and which part is to be executed in a selection.

Sometimes, however, we need to read more than one record ahead; more significantly, we are sometimes unable to solve the problem by reading any predetermined number of records ahead."

To solve these difficulties the following backtracking techniques are used:

Stage 1

Structure the problem as a simple selection, ignoring the impossibility of evaluating the condition.

Stage 2

Recognizing that the selection is really an assumption, introduce into the program text the statements that correspond to abandoning the assumption when it has proved untenable. These are "quite" statements, and are implemented as conditional transfers to the else-clause.

Stage 3

Consider the side-effects which result from partial execution of the now abandoned part of the selection.

The virtue of this technique is that it allows us to consider one aspect of the problem at a time. At stage 1, we imagine that the selection is possible, and design the program accordingly. At stage 2, we consider only the question of "what evidence would lead us to abandon the choice which we have assumed?" At stage 3, we consider the side-effects, having already created the program text in which they are unambiguously visible.

2.2.4 MULTI-THREADING

Some structure clashes require the development of multiple intermediate data structures (files). Multi-threading is a design technique for developing the program elements to handle these multiple files.

2.3 SUMMARY

The Jackson Methodology is an important design approach for problems with distinct data structures. Jackson moves directly from data structure to procedure, thereby requiring additional analysis for the definition of modules.

3.0 LOGICAL CONSTRUCTION OF PROGRAMS

Logical Construction of Programs (LCP) is a software design technique developed by J. D. Warnier (*Logical Construction of Programs,* Van Nostrand, 1974). Like Jackson, Warnier makes extensive use of data structure to lead to a structured procedural specification of software.

The LCP method can be summarized as follows:

1. Describe the input/output data structure using a hierarchical notation called the Warnier diagram.

2. Represent "repetitive" and "alternative" data as required by the application.

3. Develop the procedural "structure" of the program from steps 1 and 2.

4. Define the "detailed organization" of the program by isolating classes of instructions for each logical process described in step 3.

5. Validate the program using the output Warnier diagram.

The above steps are illustrated with a simple example taken from Warnier's text.

3.1 A WARNIER DESIGN EXAMPLE—PRELIMINARY DEFINITION

As an example of the LCP approach consider a requirement for a reporting system on salary paid to employees within a work unit at one of several plants. The desired report format is shown in Figure B.3 and the corresponding Warnier diagram is shown in Figure B.4. Finally, a Warnier diagram for input is shown in Figure B.5.

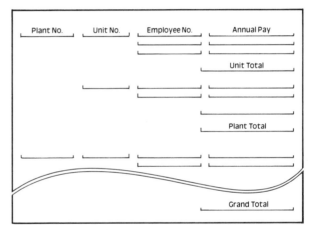

Figure B.3: Report Format—Warnier Example

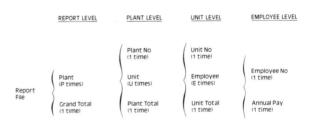

Figure B.4: Corresponding Warnier Diagram

Figure B.5: Warnier Input File Structure

Page B-4

Appendix B
SOFTWARE METHODOLOGIES AND TOOLS

**SOFTWARE
ENGINEERING
HANDBOOK**

Using a set of "rules" (e.g., If an input data subset has a repetitive structure, so does the program sub-set), the program structure is specified (Figure B.6A, B). At this point, steps 1, 2, and 3 of the LCP approach are complete.

3.2 A WARNIER DESIGN EXAMPLE – DETAILED ORGANIZATION

The following excerpt from Warnier's text describes the approach to detailed organization:

For the detailed organization, the sequences must be numbered and lists of instructions by type must be drawn up:

1. input (read) instructions

2. branch and preparation of branch instructions

3. calculations and preparation of calculations instructions

4. output and preparation of output instructions

5. subroutine call instructions

The relations between each sub-set of instructions and the set of logical sequences is then studied. The relation is defined by the property:

An instruction is related to a sequence (element of the set of logical sequences) if it is executed the same number of times at the same place of the program.

If an instruction is related to several logical sequences, it must be programmed several times: once in each sequence. Thus the mapping between the instruction set (domain) and the logical sequence set (range) is validated.

If a group of instructions is related to several logical sequences, it should be made into a subroutine. The subroutine is constructed and programmed once only and is called as many times as there are sequences in which it should be executed. The case of subroutines in a program is analogous to that of tables in input data sets: physically present once only, these subsets are called several times at different instants of time.

The detailed organization is terminated by merging the list of instructions by type into one complete list of instructions, sorted, sequence by sequence, into the order in which they should be executed. Here, as an example, is the detailed organization of the program of annual payments studied earlier.

Example: the starting point is the flowchart of logical sequences to which the sequence numbers have been added Figure B.6(b). The numbering is 10 by 10 to leave gaps to add sequences for later program amendments.

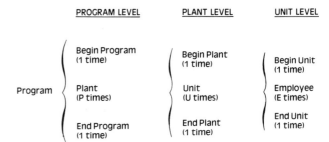

Figure B.6(a): Corresponding Program Structure

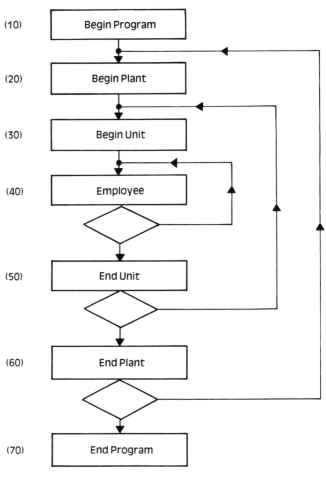

Figure B.6(b): Procedural Representation

3.2.1 INPUT INSTRUCTIONS

First, write down the list of input instructions. Here, initially, this list contains one element only since there is only one physical input file. The instruction is READ A RECORD FROM THE FILE (READ FILE). The answer to the questions "how many times?" and "when do we have to read a record" is, in the case of standard sequential files, "As many times as there are records in the file plus one". Indeed, the End of File record must also be read when the file is sequential.

**SOFTWARE
ENGINEERING
HANDBOOK**

**Appendix B
SOFTWARE METHODOLOGIES AND TOOLS**

Page B-5

To ensure the correct allocation of the input instructions, it suffices to execute 1 read in sequence 10 and another in sequence 40. The problem of the input instructions has been solved by using 2 instructions for the same file:

1. one in sequence 10: read the first record of the file

2. another in sequence 40: read another record of the file or the end-of-file record.

3.2.2 BRANCH INSTRUCTIONS

Secondly, write down the list of branch instructions. This is easy, since each branch instruction is identified on the flow-chart by the diamonds attached to the rectangles of the logical sequences. Note that the diamond is attached to the rectangle to show clearly that the branch instruction is the last element of the sequence. Indeed, the branch is executed the same number of times as the sequence that it terminates.

In a repetitive program set, there is exactly one branch instruction. This instruction is always in the same place: it is the last instruction of the repetitive sub-set.

Example: in the problem under review, the branches are listed by reading the flowchart and noting their conditions:

Sequence	Instruction	Next Sequence
.40	-if identifier of Unit read= identifier of Unit processed	40
.50	-if identifier of Plant read= identifier of Plant processed	30
.60	-if NOT end of file (EOF)	20

The list must be completed by adding the preparation of branch instructions.

3.2.3 CALCULATIONS

In the example, the list of calculations is easy to draw up. The totals of the annual payments have to be obtained by units, and by plant. A grand total for the whole enterprise must appear at the end of report. For each type of accumulation, fields must be cleared.

The relation between the instructions and the sequences is always the same. Here is the list of the calculations and their preparation:

.10—Clear Grand Total
.20—Clear Plant Total
.30—Clear Unit Total
.40—Add Annual Payment of Unit Test
.50—Add Unit Total to Plant Total
.60—Add Plant Total to Grand Total

3.2.4 OUTPUT INSTRUCTIONS

To complete this example, there remain only the editing and output instructions. Each output instruction is followed by a restoration of the output field.

If the various elements of a line must be transferred to the output area under different conditions, then the editing of the elements should be detailed. Here, adhering to the same relation for the mapping, is the list of the editing instructions and the outputs:

.20—Edit Plant Number
.30—Edit Unit Number
.40—Edit Employee Number
.40—Output and restore print line
.50—Edit Unit Total
.50—Output and restore print line
.60—Edit Plant Total
.60—Output and restore print line
.70—Edit Grand Total
.70—Output and restore print line

The instructions are now all allocated to the sequences. What remains is to compile the list of the sequences after having sorted the instructions in each sequence. On completion, all the fields of core memory for the program are defined and thus the memory layout is prepared: input areas, reference fields, calculation fields and output areas.

3.2.5 INSTRUCTION LIST

From the 4 lists obtained (5 if there were any sub-routine calls), which have been reproduced below, the detailed instruction list can be drawn up for coding the program in the appropriate language. This list is written, sequence by sequence, in ascending order of the sequence numbers.

Within a sequence, the order of the instructions is usually the following:

1. preparation of branches

2. preparation of calculations and calculations

3. preparation of output and outputs

4. inputs

5. branches

Recapitulation of Lists already obtained:

10—Read 1st Record
40—Read another Record or EOF

40—If iden. Unit = ident. Ref Unit 40
50—If ident. Plant = iden. Ref. Plant 30
60—If EOF 20

Page B-6

Appendix B
SOFTWARE METHODOLOGIES AND TOOLS

SOFTWARE
ENGINEERING
HANDBOOK

20—Transfer Plant N read to Ref Plant N
30—Transfer Unit N read to Ref Unit N

10—Clear Grand Total
20—Clear Plant Total
30—Clear Unit Total
40—Add Annual Pay. to Unit Total
50—Add Unit Total to Plant Total
60—Add Plant Total to Grand Total

20—Edit Plant N
30—Edit Unit N
40—Edit Employee N
40—Output and Restore Print line
50—Edit Unit Total
50—Output and Restore Print line
60—Edit Plant Total
60—Output and Restore Print line
70—Edit Grand Total
70—Output and Restore Print line

Sorted List of the instructions of the program

10—Clear Grand Total
    Read 1st Record
20—Transfer Plant N to Ref Plant N
    Clear Plant Total
    Edit Plant N
30—Transfer Unit N to Ref Unit N
    Clear Unit Total
    Edit Unit N

40—Add Annual pay. to Unit total
    Edit Employee N
    Output and Restore Print line
    Read another record or EOF
    If ident. Unit = ident. Ref. Unit 40

50—Add Unit total Plant Total
    Edit Unit Total
    Output and Restore Print line
    If ident. Plant = ident. Ref. Plant 30

60—Add Plant Total to Grand Total
    Edit Plant Total
    Output and Restore Print line
    If EOF 20
70—Edit Grand Total
    Output and Restore Print line

Note sequence 40 in this example. This sequence begins with a calculation, then there is an output. At the end of the sequence the following record is made available by an input instruction, then it is tested by a branch-instruction.

The program is now completely determined. There is not a single instruction in the preceding detailed list that is dependent upon a particular type of computer. The solution just described can easily be translated into any language for any machine.

4.0 SUMMARY

Data structure oriented software design provides an alternative to the data flow oriented approach presented in the body of the Handbook. The Jackson and Warnier methodologies provide an approach to design that is procedural in nature. Each technique ultimately results in the definition of detailed design specification.

For further information on these methodologies, the reader is urged to study the texts referenced in this Appendix.

APPENDIX B.2: SOFTWARE TOOLS

1.0 INTRODUCTION

Software tools are a valuable aid in satisfying the growing demand for computer-based products and services. Effective tools "amplify" the raw capabilities of a person. When moving a boulder, a lever provides mechanical advantage. So it can be with software tools. A wood chisel can be used to produce beautiful woodwork. It can also be used to pry open a can of paint—a very inappropriate use of the tool. Similarly, a software tool can be misused. It is essential that the various software tools be used by a person trained in their use and that the correct tool for the job at hand be chosen.

Properly chosen and properly used, software tools can effectively address all of the following key software issues:

1. Productivity of Software People

2. Software Quality

3. Transportability of Software

4. Software Maintenance

5. Shortage of Software Professionals

The tools provided to the software manager and the software engineering staff must be consistent with the chosen methodology. Where practical, these tools should automate some portion of the software activities. Planning is required to assure a smoothly integrated set of tools that encourage a smooth work flow with minimum overlap in function. For example, the output of a design language processor should be directly usable as the input to a compiler without editing or conversion. An editor should be "knowledgeable" of the compiler language being used to eliminate a large number of source program errors by not permitting them to be made.

2.0 CLASSIFICATION OF SOFTWARE TOOLS

Software tools are divided into two classes: tools that assist in the management of software and tools that assist the performance of technical work. As suggested earlier, there must be a smooth integration of these tools. The tools must be integrated both within each class and across each class. Further, the two classes of tools must be integrated with direct relationships established between deliverables and project management.

2.1 MANAGEMENT TOOLS

Traditionally, software project management tools have been limited to actual versus planned cost charts or to critical path charts. While both of these uses are necessary to efficient project management, they are definitely not sufficient. Use of these tools as the only measure of progress lead in one case to the "90% complete syndrome". That is to say "since 90% of the budget is spent, the project is 90% complete". In the other case, the obvious solution is to apply more people to the critical path. This is the time-honored but grossly counterproductive "human wave approach to programming".

A well-trained, knowledgeable technical manager uses tools effectively but is not totally dependent upon them to be an effective technical manager. This person must have technical and administrative skills as well. One cannot manage a software project by analyzing "production reports". A successful software manager uses tools to help identify areas of management concern. It takes expert knowledge to evaluate alternatives, to make sound technical judgements, and to formulate practical solutions.

2.2 TECHNICAL TOOLS

Technical tools are used to help the software engineer design and implement software for an application. These technical tools must support the chosen methodology. Even more importantly, they must be integrated with the kit of management tools.

Another attribute of technical tools is that they be automated and interactive. These attributes are particularly important for tools used in the early phases of the development cycle. Traditionally, these early activities consume large volumes of effort, much of which is devoted to producing documentation manually. The fact that this essential documentation of requirements and design is so time consuming has been and continues to be the principal deterrent to achieving high quality documentation. Automated tools that address these two areas have substantial advantages. First, each tool forces a certain degree of formalism that can eliminate ambiguity. Second, use of such tools allow the computer professional to apply a primary tool of his profession, the computer, to eliminate much high-cost manual labor. Job enrichment applies to software development. Elimination of most of the drudgery associated with high quality documentation helps maintain the enthusiasm needed to produce it and, more importantly, keep it up to date.

3.0 CURRENT SITUATION

Today, the number of technical tools far exceeds the number of management tools available. Although planning phase technical tools do exist, wide application does not exist. The situation seems to be generally recognized and a great deal of potentially valuable work is underway at universities and within industry.

APPENDIX B.3: PROGRAM DESIGN LANGUAGE

1.0 INTRODUCTION

There are a variety of methods used to describe a software design. Among the more frequent are flowcharts (both structured and unstructured), box diagrams, Hierarchical Input, Output, Process (HIPO) charts,, and English prose descriptions. Some of these methods were introduced in Section 5.8 of this Handbook. That section also introduces the Program Design Language (PDL) as a design description tool.

This portion of Appendix B amplifies the discussion of PDL as a design description tool. A specific PDL is discussed. PDL is recommended for use just as various "standard" document formats have been recommended within the Handbook. The principal value of this standardization is improved communication.

Although there are other ways to present a software design, use of a PDL seems to be the most effective means for many software designers. Table 5.1 presents a comparison of various detail design tools.

2.0 PROGRAM DESIGN LANGUAGE DEFINITION

A Program Design Language is a tool to describe the design of software using what is sometimes called "structured English" or pseudo-code. This design description is people oriented. It is not a programming language. A PDL provides a set of well defined structures that allow the writing of software designs in a form that is both easy to understand and can easily be translated into a computer source program.

A PDL provides a means for representing both procedure and data in a formal, constrained manner. There is a formal syntax. However, outside of a limited set of constructs, ordinary English prose is used. For example:

```
IF you understand English
    you understand the meaning of this example
ELSE
    this PDL statement example is nonsense
END IF
```

The example just given was a PDL if statement. The capitalized words were PDL "reserved" words. Everything else, including the indentation, was user defined prose.

The PDL described in this Appendix contains a variety of statement types divided into two categories: Procedural Description and Data Description. In turn, Procedural Description statements can be split into four sub-categories: Sequence, Selection, Repetition and Miscellaneous. The procedural language described was originally defined by a General Electric component. The data description statements described in this Appendix are an extension and formalization of ideas considered by that organization. The following paragraphs provide a summary description of the PDL.

2.1 SEQUENCE STATEMENTS

The simplest PDL procedural statements are the Sequence statements. These are nothing more than a sequence of one or more English sentences or complete PDL statements. To ease discussion of more complicated statements, one or more Sequence statements will be represented by "block". In the description of other PDL statements, such a sequence will be denoted by "block".

2.2 SELECTION STATEMENTS

Selection statements provide a means for stating a choice of alternatives. The IF statement previously shown in a selection statement. It allows the choice of one or two alternatives.

2.3 IF STATEMENT

This procedural statement has a form as follows:

```
IF condition-1
    block
[ELSE IF condition-2]
    block
ELSE
    block
END IF
```

The notation used above involves brackets ([ ]) and braces ( ). This notation along with block will be used in each of the statement descriptions. An element of a PDL statement that appears in brackets may appear zero or more times as part of the statement. An element of a PDL statement enclosed by braces is optional. If it does occur, it may occur only once.

The IF statement described can be seen to have any of the following forms:

```
IF condition
    block
END IF
```

```
IF condition
    block
ELSE
    block
END IF
```

```
IF condition-1
    block
ELSE IF condition-2
    block
ELSE IF condition-3
    block
END IF
```

2.3.1 CASE STATEMENT

This procedural statement is used to select one of several alternative cases of a single condition. The value of "variable" is evaluated once and the resulting action depends upon this value. The case statement has the following form:

```
CASE OF variable
CASE value [, value]
    block
[CASE value [, value]
    block]
CASE ELSE
    block
END CASE
```

Note that the CASE statement can have a wide variety of specific examples. This statement is a notational convenience. The same effect can be obtained with an appropriately written IF statement. However, the intent of this IF statement will not be as apparent to the reader. Since the purpose of a PDL is to improve human understanding of a design, the redundance of function seems justified.

2.3 REPETITION STATEMENTS

Repetition statements provide a means for representing a variety of repeated actions. Three types of repetitive action frequently occur. Stepping completely through a table in a regular fashion; repeating an action while a given side condition is true; and repeating an action until some termination condition is met are the most frequently encountered program actions and a good PDL should provide for each of these cases.

2.3.1 DO STATEMENT

This procedural statement is used to repeat an action starting at some initial point, stepping to a new point, and terminating after some fixed number of steps. Stepping through a table of values is a good example of the use of this PDL statement. The statement has the form:

SOFTWARE
ENGINEERING
HANDBOOK

Appendix B
SOFTWARE METHODOLOGIES AND TOOLS

Page B-9

```
DO step
   block
END DO
```

In this statement, "step" is text representing an initial value, an increment value, and a final value. The Fortran DO statement is a common occurrence of this type of construct in a programming language.

2.3.2 DO WHILE STATEMENT

This procedural statement is used to repeat the action while the condition is true. The DO WHILE statement has the following format:

```
DO WHILE condition
   block
END WHILE
```

2.3.3 REPEAT STATEMENT

This procedural statement is used to repeat the action until the terminating condition is true. There is a distinct difference in meaning between the REPEAT statement and the DO WHILE statement. The action of the REPEAT statement will be performed at least once. On the other hand, the action of a DO WHILE statement will be skipped completely if the termination condition is initially true. The REPEAT statement has the following format:

```
REPEAT
   block
UNTIL condition
```

2.4 MISCELLANEOUS PROCEDURAL STATEMENTS

There are a variety of other frequently occurring procedural actions that are useful but do not fit the previous categories.

2.4.1 ESCAPE STATEMENT

This statement is related to the repetitive statement, DO WHILE, and REPEAT. Quite often there is a need for an escape from a repetitive action before the terminating condition is normally met. The form of the escape statement is:

```
ESCAPE
```

To better explain the use of the ESCAPE statement, examples of its use are shown below.

```
DO i=1, step=3, done at i=10
   block
   IF entry not valid
      ESCAPE
```

```
   END IF
   block
END DO
```

```
DO WHILE there is another item in the linked list
   block
   IF current list element is a valid type
      block
   ELSE
      set error flag
      ESCAPE
   END IF
   block
END WHILE
REPEAT
   block
   DO WHILE other processor busy
   run next job in this processor
   IF there is a new job
      run new job in this processor
   ELSE
      set flag
      ESCAPE
   END IF
   block
   END WHILE
   block
UNTIL signaled to quit
```

2.4.2 RETURN STATEMENT

This statement is used to show a point in a description of a process where processing breaks off and returns to a higher level process. It is analogous to the escape from loop processing provided by the ESCAPE statement. The RETURN statement has the following format:

```
RETURN
```

2.4.3 EXIT STATEMENT

This statement is used to show a point where further processing ceases. It is analogous to a RETURN from the highest level process of the described design. Again, although the function is in some sense redundant, the gain in clarity of description justifies the definition of a new PDL statement. The EXIT statement has the following format:

```
EXIT
```

2.5 DATA DESCRIPTION STATEMENTS

A design is not complete until the significant data are described. What data are significant is largely a subjective decision. The PDL description is not a computer program; PDL is not a programming language. It is not appropriate to describe each scalar, array, or data structure. These categories are, however, useful in ordering the descriptions.

Page B-10

Appendix B
SOFTWARE METHODOLOGIES AND TOOLS

**SOFTWARE
ENGINEERING
HANDBOOK**

In each data description statement, the format provides for both the name and description of the item. An effort should be made to choose self-describing names for data elements. Often, a descriptive name will do away with any need for a description. This is a desirable goal since the reader of the design will understand the purpose and use of data from the name alone. The undesirable alternative forces the design reader to constantly check the "glossary" (data descriptions).

2.5.1 SCALAR STATEMENT

This data description statement is used to define the name and purpose of scalar data. The form of this statement is:

SCALAR |name, purpose;| name, purpose

2.5.2 ARRAY STATEMENT

This data description statement is used to define the name and purpose of array data. The form of this statement is:

ARRAY |name, purpose;| name, purpose

2.5.3 STRUCTURE STATEMENT

This data description statement is used to define the name and purpose of a data structure. A data structure is a non-homogeneous conglomeration of other types of data including sub-structures. By contrast, vector and array types of data have homogeneous elements. The form of this statement is:

STRUCTURE |name, structure, purpose;| name, structure, purpose

3.0 PROGRAM DESIGN LANGUAGE EXAMPLE

The Program Design Language example in this section should clarify the use and intent of a PDL. This example has been adapted from an internal General Electric document. It demonstrates the use of a PDL to develop a program that inserts or deletes macros from a library.

Example:

Name: Macro Library Editor

Function: Inserts or deletes macro definitions from a library of macro definitions.

Data Description

SCALAR new library flag
ARRAY editor command line (80 characters)
ARRAY library directory buffer (256 structures)

STRUCTURE
    Scalar flag, values are "added"
    "deleted"
    "copy old macro"
    ARRAY macro name (13 characters)

Process Description

Process Edit Input File
Write Updated Macro Library File
EXIT

Process Edit Input File:

```
clear new library flag
open input file containing editor commands and
macro definitions
open old macro library file
IF old macro library file does not exist
    create new macro library file
    open new macro library file
    set new library flag (error exists if try to delete
    from this library)
END IF

clear library directory buffer
IF this is an old library
    read the library directory from old macro
        library file into library directory buffer
END IF

REPEAT
    read next line from input file
    parse editor command line
    CASE of editor command

    CASE "old macro"
    add macro name to library directory buffer
    mark library directory buffer "added"
    add macro definition to macro library

    CASE "delete macro"
    IF this is a new library
        write error message
    ELSE
        mark library directory buffer
        entry "deleted"
    END IF

    CASE "end-of-edit"
    CASE ELSE
        write error message
        close all files
        EXIT

    END CASE
UNTIL end of edit
RETURN
```

**SOFTWARE
ENGINEERING
HANDBOOK**

**Appendix B
SOFTWARE METHODOLOGIES AND TOOLS**

Page B-11

Write Updated Macro Library File:

```
REPEAT
    get next library directory entry flag
    CASE of flag

    CASE "added"
    CASE "deleted"
        read over macro definition on old library

    CASE "copy old macro"
        copy macro definition from old library to new
        library

    CASE ELSE
        write error message

    END CASE
UNTIL all library directory entries processed

rewind new library file
write updated directory to head of new library file
close all files
RETURN
```

3.1 DISCUSSION OF EXAMPLE

The PDL example is a description of an editor for a macro library. The editor has been described as a main process and two sub-processes. The main process describes the two actions of the editor: first, it reads an input file which contains command lines and may contain macro definitions to be added to the library; second, it writes an updated version of the macro library. Each of these lines may be considered to be an invocation of a subordinate process. Whether in fact the coding implementation packages this librarian as three routines or one is not an issue at this point in the design.

Next, the two subordinate processes are described. One is called "Process Edit Input File"; the other "Write Updated Macro Library File". The names match those named in the superordinate process. How can somebody look at a "Process Edit Input File" and know that it is a reference to a subordinate process? How can one know that "clear new library flag" (the first line of Process Edit Input File) is not a subordinate process? There is no way to know, unless some convention is used. The convention used in the example is that a description is written in lower case only. PDL is too new to take a position that this convention is "part of the language". since it does improve communication of the design, it is certainly in the spirit of PDL. A principal intent of the example was to show PDL in use. The example does show that PDL is people oriented. It is "structured English". It can be understood by the non-programmer. Although the design is not complete, a casual review shows this to be the case. That, in itself, suggests that PDL is a good way to describe design. The example bears a very superficial resemblance to a program. This is as it should be.

4.0 SUMMARY

This portion of Appendix B has discussed a Program Design Language in some detail. The rationale for this design description tool was explained and types of PDL statements were defined. An example of a PDL design description was presented and discussed.

**SOFTWARE
ENGINEERING
HANDBOOK**

**Appendix C
SOFTWARE ENGINEERING
BIBLIOGRAPHY**

Page C-1

INTRODUCTION

An annotated software engineering bibliography is presented in this Appendix. An attempt has been made to group references in the following categories:

1. Management Topics

2. System/Requirements Analysis

3. Software Design

4. Coding

5. Testing

6. Maintenance

7. General Software Engineering

However, many references (particularly textbooks) cover a wide range of topics and have been listed only under category of major emphasis.

The bibliography has been kept relatively brief. It should be noted that each reference cited contains its own bibliography, thereby providing relatively comprehensive coverage of software engineering.

1. MANAGEMENT TOPICS

1.1 Baker, F. T., "Chief Programmer Team Management of Production Programming," *IBM System Journal,* Vol. 11, No. 1, 1972.

A complete discussion of the CPT concept.

1.2 Boehm, B., *Software Engineering Economics,* Prentice-Hall, 1981.

Contains much good material. An excellent reference for a widely used software cost model, COCOMO.

1.3 Brooks, F. P., *The Mythical Man-Month,* Addison-Wesley, 1975.

A landmark text of the management of large software development projects. Highly recommended.

1.4 DeMarco, T., *Controlling Software Projects Management, Measurement & Evaluation,* Yourdon Press, 1982.

Covers measurement throughout the software development process.

1.5 Donaldson, H. A., *A Guide to the Successful Management of Computer Projects,* Wiley, 1978.

Covers project management in the "commercial d.p." environment

1.6 Gunther, R. C., *Management Methodology for Software Product Engineering,* Wiley, 1978.

A complete guide for managers responsible for the development of software "products." All phases of product development covered.

1.7 Jones, C., *Tutorial: Programming Productivity: Issues For the Eighties,* IEEE, 1981.

An excellent set of tutorial materials on a topic of major management concern.

1.8 Lientz, B., Swanson, E., *Software Maintenance Management,* Addison-Wesley, 1980.

Speaks effectively to the issues and concerns of maintenance managers.

1.9 Penny, G., *Managing Computers: Data Processing Case Histories,* Hayden, 1974.

A brief anthology of computer project case histories. Heavy emphasis on business applications.

1.10 Putnam, L. and Fitzsimmons, A., *Estimating Software Costs,* Datamation (three-part series), Sept., Oct., Nov., 1979.

Practical guidelines for software cost and schedule estimating. Based on Rayleigh curve model of effort on software tasks.

1.11 Shooman, M., *Software Engineering Design, Reliability, and Management,* McGraw-Hill, 1983.

Thorough treatment of software testing and reliability. Placed here because of management concerns with reliability.

1.12 Walston, C. and Felix, C., "A Method of Programming Measurement and Estimation," *IBM Syst. Journal,* No. 1, 1977.

Productivity results for a major study of over 60 software projects. Highly recommended.

1.13 Weinberg, G., *The Psychology of Computer Programming,* Van Nostrand, 1971.

A classic text on the human aspects of software development. Highly recommended.

1.14 Wolverton, R. W., "The Cost of Developing Large Scale Software," *IEEE Trans. on Computers,* June, 1974, pp. 615–36.

A discussion of cost related factors and cost data. Insights still valid for the 1980s.

1.15 Yourdon, E., *Managing the Structured Techniques,* 2d ed., Prentice-Hall, 1979.

A manager's overview of planning and development techniques. Worthwhile annotated bibliography.

Page C-2

**Appendix C
SOFTWARE ENGINEERING
BIBLIOGRAPHY**

**SOFTWARE
ENGINEERING
HANDBOOK**

1.16 Yourdon, E., *Structured Walkthroughs,* 2d ed., Yourdon Press, 1978.

An overview of software review procedures. Worthwhile discussion of the manager's role. Recommended.

2. SYSTEM/REQUIREMENTS ANALYSIS

2.1 Atwood, J., *The Systems Analyst,* Hayden, 1977.

Coverage of requirements analysis for the commercial computing environment.

2.2 DeMarco, T., *Structured Analysis and System Specification,* Prentice-Hall, 1979.

A complete treatment of "system analysis" using the DFG approach. Highly recommended.

2.3 Gane, C. and Sarson, T., *Structured Systems Analysis: Tools and Techniques,* Improved Systems Technologies, 1977.

2.4 Orr, K., *Structured Systems Development,* Yourdon Press, 1977.

A generalized approach to systems analysis using the Warnier notation.

2.5 Ross, D. T., and Schoman, K. E., "Structured Analysis for Requirements Specification," *IEEE Transactions Software Engineering,* Jan. 1977, pp. 6–15.

An overview of the SADT approach.

2.6 "Specifications for Reliable Software," *ACM Software Engineering Notes (SIGSOFT),* Vol. 3, No. 4, July 1979.

A report on recent experiences with software specification tools. Five different techniques are reviewed.

2.7 *Systems Development Management,* Auerbach Publishers, 1979.

A collection of independently authored pamphlets on system analysis and development. One volume in the Auerbach Information Management Series.

2.8 Teichroew, D. and Hershey, E., PSL/PSA: "A Computer Aided Technique for Structured Documentation and Analysis of Information Systems," *IEEE Transactions Software Engineering,* Vol. 3, No. 1, 1977, pp. 41–8.

An overview of PSL/PSA, and a review of current techniques for software requirements analysis.

2.9 Wetherbee, M., *Systems Analysis for Computer-Based Information Systems,* West Publishing Co., 1979.

Another view of systems analysis oriented toward the commercial environment.

3. SOFTWARE DESIGN

3.1 Freeman, P. and Wasserman, A., *Tutorial: Software Design Techniques,* 4th ed., IEEE, 1977.

An anthology of important papers in the area of software design. Recommended.

3.2 Gomaa, H., "A Software Design Method for Real-Time Systems," *Communications of the ACM,* Vol. 27, No. 9, Sept. 1984.

Describes an excellent extension of data flow driven design to deal with real-time issues. Builds on research of many others.

3.3 Jackson, M. A., *Principles of Program Design,* Academic Press, 1975.

A fundamental treatise on the Jackson design method. Numerous examples taken from commercial and other applications.

3.4 Marca, D., "A Method for Specifying Structured Programs," *ACM Software Engineering Notes (SIGSOFT),* Vol. 4, No. 3, July 1979, pp. 22–31.

A review of box-diagram techniques for detailed design specification. Bibliographic references to Nassi/Sniederman and Chapin.

3.5 Montalbano, M., *Decision Tables,* SRA, 1974.

A comprehensive treatment of the theory and practice of design tables.

3.6 Myers, G., *Composite/Structured Design,* Van Nostrand, 1978.

Clear explanations of design characteristics and techniques. Recommended.

3.7 Page-Jones, M., *The Practical Guide to Structured Systems Design,* Yourdon Press, 1980.

A good in-depth treatment of the transition from analysis to design. Recommended.

3.8 Warnier, J. D., *Logical Construction of Programs,* Van Nostrand, 1974.

A fundamental treatise on LCP. Examples are clear and illustrate the utility of Warnier's approach.

3.9 Yourdon, E. and Constantine, L., *Structured Design,* Prentice-Hall, 1979.

A primary source for the design methodology presented in Chapter 5 of the *Handbook.* Highly recommended.

3.10 Zelkowitz, M., Shaw, A., and Gannon, J., *Principles of Software Engineering and Design,* Prentice-Hall, 1979.

SOFTWARE
ENGINEERING
HANDBOOK

Appendix C
SOFTWARE ENGINEERING
BIBLIOGRAPHY

Page C-3

Majority of text spent on detailed design considerations. A number of worthwhile case studies.

4. CODING

4.1   Basili, V. and Baker, T., *Tutorial: Structured Programming: Integrated Practices,* IEEE, 1981.

A collection of invited lectures on structured programming. Both technical and management considerations are presented.

4.2   Dijkstra, E., *A Discipline of Programming,* Prentice-Hall, 1976.

A guide for the uninitiated by the "father" of structured programming.

4.3   Kernighan, B. and Plauger, P., *Software Tools,* Addison-Wesley, 1976.

To quote the authors: "good programming is not learned from generalities, but by seeing . . . significant programs. . . ." A text that contains usable tools as examples. Recommended.

4.4   Kernighan, B. and Plauger, P., *The Elements of Programming Style,* McGraw-Hill, 1974.

A landmark text on the characteristics of "good" code practices. Highly recommended.

4.5   Knuth, D., *The Art of Computer Programming* (a multi-volume set), Addison-Wesley.

A mix of theory and practice that has become a classic series on programming, algorithm design, and related topics. Recommended.

4.6   Van Tassel, D., *Program Style, Design, Efficiency, Debugging, and Testing,* 2d ed., Prentice-Hall, 1978.

An in-depth consideration of detailed design and coding practices. Test guidelines are worthwhile.

5. TESTING

5.1   Anderson, R., *Proving Programs Correct,* Wiley, 1979.

A mildly theoretical treatment of program correctness and program proofs.

5.2   Beizer, B., *Software Testing Techniques,* Van Nostrand Reinhold, 1983.

Very thorough treatment of software testing.

5.3   McCabe, T., *Tutorial: Structured Testing,* IEEE, 1982.

Comprehensive view of unit level testing. Builds on author's previous work measuring software complexity.

5.4   Myers, G., *The Art of Software Testing,* Wiley, 1979.

A complete technical treatment of software testing. Highly recommended.

5.5   "Proc. Software Quality Assurance Workshop," *ACM Software Engineering Notes,* special issue, Vol. 3, No. 5, Nov. 1978.

A collection of papers on software testing and quality assurance.

5.6   *Program Test Methods,* W. Hetzel, Prentice-Hall, 1973.

A collection of papers on software testing and verification.

5.7   Miller, E., *Tutorial: Program Testing Techniques,* 2d ed., IEEE, 1981.

A collection of invited papers reprinted on test methods, automated tools, and theory. Recommended.

6. MAINTENANCE

6.1   Cashman, P. and Holt, A., "A Communication Oriented Approach to Structuring the Software Maintenance Environment," *ACM Software Engineering Notes,* Vol. 5, No. 1, Jan. 1980.

A general discussion of software maintenance with a description of MONSTR, an automated tool for software maintenance.

6.2   Gelperin, D., "Testing Maintainability," *ACM Software Engineering Notes (SIGSOFT),* Vol. 4, No. 2, April 1979.

Provides guidelines for describing and evaluating maintainability.

6.3   Gilb, T., "Comment on Testing Maintainability," *ACM Software Engineering Notes (SIGSOFT),* Vol. 4, No. 3, July 1979.

Presents ten quantitative measures (factors) for maintainability. Recommended.

6.4   Lientz, B., Swanson, E., and Tompkins, G., "Characteristics of Application Software Maintenance," *CACM,* Vol. 21, No. 6, June 1978, pp. 466–71.

Guidelines for the specification of maintenance characteristics. Experiences for large systems.

6.5   Swanson, E., "The Dimensions of Maintenance," *Proc. 2d International Conference Software Engineering,* IEEE, 1976.

Presents worthwhile "measures" of software maintenance. Recommended.

Page C-4

**Appendix C
SOFTWARE ENGINEERING
BIBLIOGRAPHY**

**SOFTWARE
ENGINEERING
HANDBOOK**

7. GENERAL SOFTWARE ENGINEERING

Text and Articles

7.1   DeMarco, T., *Concise Notes on Software Engineering,* Yourdon Press, 1979.

7.2   Jensen, R. and Tonies, C., *Software Engineering,* Prentice-Hall, 1979.

7.3   Pressman, R., *Software Engineering: A Practitioner's Approach,* McGraw-Hill, 1982.

   One of the most widely used college-level software engineering texts. An excellent source of supplementary material. Strongly recommended.

7.4   Zelkowitz, M., "Perspectives on Software Engineering," *ACM Computing Surveys,* Vol. 10, No. 2, June 1978, pp. 197–216.

Conference Proceedings, Anthologies

7.5   *Proc. of Intl. Conference on Software Engineering,* IEEE 1st, 2d, 3d, and 4th (1975–9) available.

7.6   *Computer Software Engineering,* Polytechnic Press, New York, 1976.

7.7   *Research Directions in Software Technology,* P. Wegner, MIT Press, 1979.

General Information Sources

   Communications of the ACM (CACM)
   Computer (IEEE)
   Computing Surveys (ACM)
   Datamation
   IEEE Transactions Software Engineering
   SIGSOFT Software Engineering Notes
   Software — Practice and Experience

SOFTWARE
ENGINEERING
HANDBOOK

Appendix D
QUANTITATIVE METHODS FOR
SOFTWARE ENGINEERING

Page D-1

1.0 INTRODUCTION

Throughout the Software Engineering Handbook, qualitative techniques for management and technical control of the software development process are presented. However, few quantitative tools are described.

Over the past decade, researchers have proposed a set of quantitative measures for software and the process by which it is developed. These quantitative methods represent initial attempts to establish meaningful measures and models. This appendix presents an overview of quantitative methods for software engineering.

1.1 Quantitative Methods for Software Engineering

Quantitative methods for software engineering fall into two broad categories:

1. management models and measures that improve project planning and estimation, enhance record keeping, and provide a means by which the efficacy of new technical methods can be assessed;

2. metrics that can be used in the development of software and in the technical assessment of software quality and performance.

Management methods concentrate on evaluating data important to software planning (e.g., cost, effort and schedule estimation) and identifying data to be collected during software development. Metrics attempt to quantify software "intangibles" such as: complexity, reliability, and human factors.

The great physical scientist, Lord Kelvin, once said that if a phenomenom cannot be measured and/or described in a quantitative fashion, the phenomenom is not well understood. The quantitative methods presented in this appendix are a first step toward improved understanding of the software development process.

1.2 Management Methods and Tools

Quantitative methods and tools for software engineering management enhance planning, control and evaluation of tasks conducted during each phase of the software life cycle. During the planning phase, models based on empirical data can be used to estimate project cost, personnel allocation and scheduling. Additionally, these models can be used for risk analysis. Development phase metrics can assist in assessing software quality and reliability. Data collected and evaluated during the maintenance phase can help establish tracking and evaluation methods.

Section 2.0 of this appendix presents an introduction to quantitative methods for software management. Several empirical software cost estimation models are considered; models useful in conjunction with project scheduling are discussed; new automated tools for project planning are described; recent "software productivity" studies and data are assessed; recommendations for local data collection are made; and, other management related tools are presented.

1.3 Technical Methods and Tools

Quantitative methods and tools that assist the software engineer are being developed to provide a more rational basis for measuring activities during the development phase of the software life cycle. To date, work conducted in this area focuses primarily on the end product of development—the code representation of software.

Section 3.0 presents an overview of software metrics—a rapidly evolving area addressing technical measures of software. Both source code oriented measures and control/data structure oriented techniques are considered. Halsted's "software science" is discussed; various software complexity measures are introduced; models for software reliability are described; and, psychological/human factors models and data are considered.

1.4 Limitations of a Quantitative Approach

Quantitative models and metrics for software engineering are still in their formative years. Researchers frequently work with limited data, make simplifying assumptions not always reflecting a real world environment, or consider only a limited number of parameters where many parameters may apply. Today, validated models and metrics applicable to a wide range of software application areas and development environments do not exist.

However, models and metrics do exist that can guide local efforts in software engineering. Local data can be collected; local "coefficients" can be derived; and, practical modifications can make quantitative results locally meaningful. The models and metrics described here should be used only after careful study and calibration indicate validity for a specific software environment.

2.0 QUANTITATIVE METHODS FOR SOFTWARE MANAGEMENT

Chapter 3 of the Software Engineering Handbook describes management tasks associated with Software Planning. Key decisions involving resource allocation, cost and schedule estimation and overall project control occur during the planning step. The use of quantitative methods can greatly assist such decision makers.

Page D-2

Appendix D
QUANTITATIVE METHODS FOR
SOFTWARE ENGINEERING

SOFTWARE
ENGINEERING
HANDBOOK

2.1 Software Cost Modelling

Section 3.4.1 of the Handbook describes a costing technique which relys on historical data collected from past efforts of a development organization. Although such techniques can provide good results, the basis upon which it is founded is an implicit simplifying assumption that considers "average" conditions in all respects. The effects of changes in personnel, degree of project complexity, changes in programming language or development environment, or myriad other parameters are difficult to integrate into these "on average" cost estimating processes.

Quantitative costing models have been developed to reflect one or more of the above parameters. The following paragraphs present an overview of cost modelling.

2.1.1 Modelling the Software Development Process

Models of the software development process can be derived to predict different project characteristics:

*people required as a function of time;
*cost as a function of software characteristics (e.g., measure of complexity, size, staff experience, etc.);
*project duration as a function of number of people and programming environment;
*effort as a function of software characteristics; and
*software quality as a function of software characteristics.

During the software planning step, cost and schedule are the primary characteristics established. Therefore, models that predict cost or labor effort are most desirable.

2.1.2 Resource Models

Resource models are a series of empirically derived equations that predict effort (in person-months), project duration (in chronological months), or other pertinent project data. Basili (ref. 1) describes four classes of resource models: static, single variable models; static multivariable models; dynamic multivariable models, and theoretical models.

The static single variable model takes the form:

resource $= c_1$ * (estimated characteristics) * exp (c_2)

where the resource could be effort (E), project duration (D), staff size (S), or requisite lines of software documentation (DOC). The constants c_1 and c_2 are derived from data collected from past projects. The estimated characteristic is lines of source code, effort (if estimated) or other software characteristics.

Walston and Felix (ref. 2) derived a set of static, single variable models based on data collected from 60 software development projects ranging in size from 4,000 to 467,000 source lines and 12 to 11,758 person-months. The following resource models were developed:

$$E = 5.2L \exp(0.91)$$
$$D = 4.1L \exp(0.36)$$
$$D = 2.47E \exp(0.35)$$
$$S = 0.54E \exp(0.6)$$
$$DOC = 49L \exp(1.01)$$

Effort (in person-months), E; project duration (in calendar months), D; and pages of documentation, DOC, are modeled as a function of estimated number of source lines, L. Alternatively, project duration and staffing requirements (people), S, may be computed from derived or estimated effort.

The above equations are environment and application specific and may not be applied generally. However, simple models like those above can be derived for a local environment if sufficient historical data are available.

To illustrate the manner in which resource models do vary, consider models derived from another study conducted by Systems Engineering Laboratory (SEL) and cited by Basili (ref. 1):

$$E = 1.4L \exp(0.93)$$
$$D = 4.6L \exp(0.26)$$
$$D = 4.4E \exp(0.26)$$
$$S = 0.25E \exp(0.74)$$
$$DOC = 30.4L \exp(0.90)$$

The above equations were derived from a sample of fifteen projects. The variance in the Walston and Felix model and the SEL model can be attributed to variation in application environment.

Static multivariable models, like their single variable counterpart, use historical data to derive empirical relationships. A typical model in this category takes the form:

resource $= c_{11}$ * e1 exp(c_{12}) + c_{21} * e2 exp(c_{22}) +...

where ei is the ith software characteristic and c_{i1}, c_{i2} are empirically derived constants for the ith characteristic.

A dynamic multivariable model projects resource requirements as a function of time. For empirically derived models, resources are defined in a series of time steps that allocate some percentage of effort (or other resource) to each step in the software engineering process. Each step may be further subdivided into tasks. A theoretical approach to dynamic multivariable modelling hypothesizes a continuous "resource expenditure curve" (ref 1), and from it, derives equations that model the behavior of the resource. The Putnam Model, a theoretical dynamic multivariable model, is discussed in the next section.

Each of the previously discussed models takes a macroscopic view of software project development. The final resource model takes the microscopic viewpoint; that is, the characteristics of the source code (e.g., number of operators and operands). A number of theoretical models with this source code orientation are discussed in section 3.0.

SOFTWARE
ENGINEERING
HANDBOOK

Appendix D
QUANTITATIVE METHODS FOR
SOFTWARE ENGINEERING

Page D-3

2.1.3 Putnam Estimation Model

The Putnam Estimation Model (detailed in reference 3) is a dynamic multivariable model that assumes a specific distribution of effort over the life of a software development project. The model is derived from manpower distributions encountered on large projects (total effort of 30 person-years or more). Extrapolation to smaller software projects may be possible.

Effort distribution for large software projects can be characterized as shown in Figure D.1. The curves shown in the figure take on a shape first described analytically by Lord Rayleigh. Empirical data on system development, collected by Norden (ref. 4.5), has been used to validate use of the curves. Hence, Putnam calls the relationship shown in Figure D.1 the "Rayleigh-Norden Curve".

The Rayleigh-Norden Curve may be used to derive a "software equation" relating the number of delivered lines, L, of code (source statements) to effort and development time:

$$L = C_k K^{1/3} t_d^{4/3}$$

where C_k is a 'state of technology constant' and reflects "throughput constraints" that impede the progress of the programmer. Typical values might be: $C_k = 2500$ for a "poor" software development environment (e.g. no methodology, poor documentation and reviews, a batch execution mode); $C_k = 10,000$ for a "good" software development (e.g., methodology in place, adequate documentation/reviews, interactive execution mode); $Ck = 12,500$ for an "excellent" environment (e.g., automated tools and techniques). C_k should be derived for local conditions using historical data collected from past development efforts.

K is the total effort expended (in person years) over the life cycle for software development and maintenance. It should be noted that the Rayleigh-Norden Curve assumes that development effort is 40% of the total effort (0.4K). Rearranging the model by solving for development, effort, K, yields:

$$K = L^3 C_k^{-3} t_d^{-4}$$

Where:

t_d is the development time in years,

C_k is the state of technology constant, and

L is the number of delivered lines of code.

The equation for development effort can be related to development cost by the inclusion of a labor rate factor ($/person-year). Because of the negative cubed and fourth power terms in the model, a small change in lines of code, L, significantly reduces cost. For example, if software requirements are reduced such that a 10 percent reduction in estimated lines of code results, overall development cost will be reduced by 27 percent (according to the Putnam Model). Similar tradeoffs can be examined for changes in project completion date (t_d changes) or projected change in technology constant (C_k changes).

A detailed technical discussion of the Putnam Model and the empirical basis from which it has been derived is beyond the scope of the Handbook. The reader is urged to obtain the IEEE tutorial "Software Cost Estimating and Life Cycle Control" (L. Putnam, 1980) for further discussion of technical aspects of the model.

2.1.4 An Alternative Estimation Model

The Putnam Model described in the preceding section is a relatively elegant mathematical approach to cost and effort estimation. It has been shown (ref. 4) to be applicable to large projects. There is evidence that the Putnam approach may be useful for estimating medium scale (10,000 – 40,000 lines of source code) projects.

Aron (5) suggests a quantitative estimating procedure with good potential for smaller projects. Although not as elegant as the Putnam model, Aron's procedure is practical and permits local tuning as the results of previous estimates are evaluated and historical data are evaluated.

Aron proposes the following step by step estimation procedure:

*estimate the number of deliverable lines of code (LOC) for each major software function;
*estimate difficulty of each major function;
*estimate the duration of the project;
*determine person-months for software development; and
*adjust results based on other project parameters.

The key to Aron's procedure is a "Productivity Table", derived from local historical data. This table depicts LOC/unit-effort as a function of project duration and project difficulty. The difficulty categories—easy, medium and difficult—are subjective and can generally be related to familiarity with application area, interfaces with other system elements, and algorithm complexity. The degree to which major functions are decomposed will affect both the accuracy of the estimate and the effort required to generate the estimate.

To illustrate application of the technique, consider a software development project that has eight major functions, f1, f2, ..., f8. The project must be completed in nine months. The following table contains estimates of function size (in LOC) and difficulty.

Page D-4

Appendix D
QUANTITATIVE METHODS FOR
SOFTWARE ENGINEERING

SOFTWARE
ENGINEERING
HANDBOOK

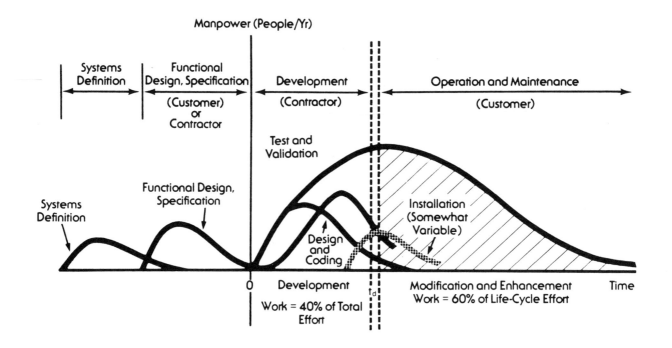

Figure D.1* Effort Distribution for Large Software Projects

*Putnam, L., Reference 3—©1980 IEEE

FUNCTION	SIZE(LOC)	(DIFFICULTY)
f1	500	easy
f2	300	medium
f3	300	medium
f4	400	easy
f5	700	medium
f6	200	difficult
f7	100	easy
f8	500	medium

Summing lines of code to be developed by difficulty cateogry, the above table yields 1000 LOC that are deemed 'easy' to develop; 1800 LOC that are 'medium'; 200 that are 'difficult'.

A productivity table is developed from the same historical data discussed in Chapter 3 of the Handbook. In fact, Aron's estimating procedure is quite similar to the Lines of Code technique (Section 3.4.1) presented in the Handbook. The major differences between the two approaches are: 1) the inclusion of a difficulty measure in Aron's technique, and 2) the use of a single LOC estimate in Aron's technique.

Using data contained in Aron's productivity table resource estimates (in man-months) can be developed for the example presented above.

LOC	CODE CATEOGRY	PRODUCTIVITY (from table)	EFFORT (person-days)
1000	easy	20 LOC/day	50
1800	medium	10 LOC/day	180
200	difficult	5 LOC/day	40

The project is estimated to require 270 person-days or (at 22 person-days per month) 12.3 person-months of effort.

Aron's estimating procedure combined with the lines of code technique can provide an additional cross-check for LOC based estimates. The productivity table can be refined

SOFTWARE
ENGINEERING
HANDBOOK

Appendix D
QUANTITATIVE METHODS FOR
SOFTWARE ENGINEERING

Page D-5

to include a wider spectrum of difficulty categories, a range of productivities derived from a range (i.e., the LOC costing technique) of LOC effort estimates by software engineering step (e.g., effort required for design or test), or a 'third dimension' that could represent productivity by application area.

2.2 Schedule Modelling

Quantitative approaches to software project scheduling are still in early stages of development. Rough guidelines for distribution of effort, such as the 40-20-40 Rule (40 percent of effort prior to coding, 20 percent for coding, 40 percent for test), have been proposed, and standard project management tools (e.g., PERT) are applicable.

This section presents a number of quantitative relationships that affect software project scheduling. The material will help supplement a manager's understanding of software scheduling.

2.2.1 People–Time–Productivity Relationships

There is a common myth that is still believed by many managers who are responsible for software development effort:

"...if we fall behind schedule, we can always add more programmers and catch up later in the project..."

Unfortunately, Brooks' Law (1.2 App. C) is probably closer to the truth: "Adding people to a late project will make it later!"

From a quantitative standpoint, the reason for this apparent anomaly lies in the complex communication paths that must be established among software development staff. Although communication is absolutely essential to successful software development, every new communication path requires additional effort and therefore additional time.

As an example, consider four software engineers, each capable of producing 5000 LOC/year when working on an individual project. When these four engineers are placed on a team project, six potential communication paths are possible. Each communication path requires time that could otherwise be spent 'developing code'; therefore, assume that team productivity (when measured in LOC) will be reduced by 250 LOC/year for each communication path. Team productivity is $20,000 - 250*6 = 18,500$ LOC/year.

The one-year project on which the above team is working falls behind schedule and with two months remaining, two additional people are added to the team. The number of communication paths escalates to 14. The productivity 'input' of the new staff is the equivalent of $840*2 = 1680$ LOC for the two months remaining before delivery. Team productivity now is $20,000 + 1680 - 250*14 = 18180$ LOC/year! The 250 LOC/year reduction for all paths was taken to reflect the learning curve required of new staff.

The above example is a gross oversimplification of real world circumstances. But, it does tend to validate Brooks' contention that the relationship between the number of people working on a software project and overall productivity is not intuitively obvious.

2.2.2 Scheduling Models

Scheduling of a software project often begins long before the Software Planning step (Handbook, Chapter 3). During system definition, an overall project completion date is established and specific completion dates for each system element are defined. The Putnam Model provides a quantitative method for determination of a realistic software completion date when the number of lines of code can be estimated reliably.

A "trade-off chart" for size, effort and time may be derived from the Putnam cost model described in section 2.1.2 of this appendix. Figure D.3 parameterizes the "software equation" and indicates feasible and infeasible combinations of effort and project duration for software development projects with size ranging from 20,000 to 1,000,000 LOC. The use of a trade-off chart like Figure D.2, tuned to a local environment (i.e., C_k computed for local data), can result in better completion date estimates.

The importance of establishing a reasonable completion date estimates cannot be overemphasized. If the completion date is unreasonably short, no amount of scheduling will be able to compensate. Schedule slippage will occur.

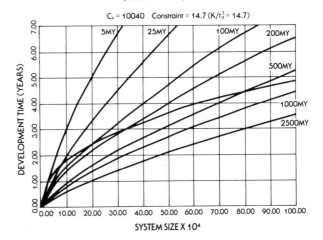

SIZE-EFFORT-TIME
(Trade-off Chart)

Figure D.2*

*Putnam, L., Reference 3—©1980 IEEE

Page D-6

Appendix D
QUANTITATIVE METHODS FOR
SOFTWARE ENGINEERING

**SOFTWARE
ENGINEERING
HANDBOOK**

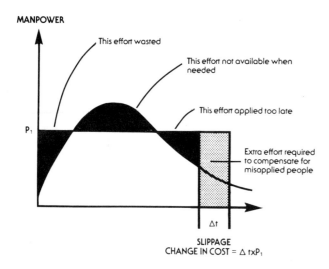

Figure D.3* Distribution of Effort

*Putnam, L., Reference 3—©1980 IEEE

The Rayleigh-Norden curve for large project development provides a guideline for distribution of effort throughout a software project. Figure D.3 (from Putnam, ref. 3) illustrates the difference between rectangular staff loading and a Rayleigh-Norden distribution.

Unfortunately, the Rayleigh-Norden resource distribution provides no information about intermediate project milestones, tasks and subtasks required to 'solve' a major system function, and the degree to which the schedule will be maintained. Tausworthe (ref. 6) addresses these issues by developing a quantitative evaluation of "work breakdown structure" (WBS) for software projects.

In generating a WBS, the software planner attempts to identify work tasks, necessary resources and other constraints that relate to a development project. A set of "equal effort" milestones is established during the course of development. As each milestone is met, measurable progress toward completion is made. The project manager also gets an indication of scheduling accuracy.

To illustrate the quantitative aspects of Tausworthe's approach, consider a project with M defined milestones that must be completed. Each milestone is defined so that it takes approximately the same amount of effort (e.g., 1 or 2 person-weeks). Milestones are reviewed at regular intervals. Each is comprised of an average of m tasks that must be accomplished. Tausworthe defines "s" as the standard deviation of the actual number of milestones completed during each review period and derives an expression for the deviation in time to reach milestone M:

$$s_M \cdot 1.48 \ s1 \ (R/rM) \ \exp(0.5)$$

where:
s_M is the standard deviation in time.

s1 is defined as s/(m exp(0.5)) and represents a normalized standard deviation of an individual milestone.

R is the total number of milestone reviews.

r is the number of the current milestone review, therefore, r/R gives an indication of percent completion (r = R at completion).

To illustrate the potential use of the above equation, the following examples from Tausworthe (ref. 6) are presented:

"As an example, suppose that a 10% end date prediction accuracy is required (i.e., $s_M = 0.1$) by the end of the first quarter (i.e., r/R = 0.25) of a project. Inverting the above equation and assuming s1 = 1, that is, the ability to maintain a given milestone is highly uncertain, the number of unit milestones is 876. If the project team is more confident of being able to maintain each milestone (e.g., s1 = 0.5), the number of unit milestones can be reduced to 220. A one person-year project with bi-weekly review (26 milestones) must attain a value of s1 = 0.17, a high degree of confidence."

The above example gives a manager an indication of the level of detail for the WBS and the relative specificity of the scheduling process.

There are practical limits to the degree to which a project can be subdivided into milestones. Reasonable scheduling accuracy is discussed in the paragraphs that follow:

"Practically speaking, a work plan (or schedule) with tasks shorter than one week in duration will usually require too much planning and management overhead to be worthwhile. On the other hand, a work plan with tasks longer than one or two weeks will probably suffer from a large s1. Thus a breakdown into 1 or 2 week tasks is probably the most reasonable target for planning purposes. A working year consists of about 47 actual weeks of work (excluding vacation, holidays, sick leave, etc.). Therefore, a project of w workers can reasonably accommodate only about 47 w/d tasks per year (including management tasks) each of duration d weeks; spread over y years. The total number of milestones can reach M = 47 wy/d, so the practical accuracy limit one may reasonably expect at the one-quarter point (r/R = 0.25) is approximately:

$$s_M \cdot = 0.432 \ s1 \ (d/wy) \ \exp(0.5)$$

Note that the schedule accuracy is related to the total person-year effort in a project, other things being equal. A 3 person-year project completing 1 task per person-week can expect to have $s_M = 0.216 \ s1$. With s1 = 0.4 (±2 days per weekly task), the end date estimation accuracy is within 10 percent."

The examples discussed above indicate a quantitative approach to work breakdown, the first step in software project scheduling. Tausworthe suggests the following algorithm for generating a WBS:

**SOFTWARE
ENGINEERING
HANDBOOK**

**Appendix D
QUANTITATIVE METHODS FOR
SOFTWARE ENGINEERING**

Page D-7

1. Start with a project statement of work (the 'software scope') and put the TASK on top of a "working stack".

2. Consider the task at the top of the working stack. Define technical performance objectives; end-item objectives; reliability and quality objectives; schedule constraints; and other appropriate factors. Define inputs and materials required for starting the task; accomplishments and outputs that signal completion of the task; known precedent tasks or milestones; known interfacing tasks; and resources required, if known. Determine whether this task can be accomplished within duration (or cost) accuracy goal.

3. If the goal has been achieved, skip to the next step; otherwise, partition the current TASK into a smaller number of comprehensive subtasks. Include interfacing tasks and other tasks whose output is a decision regarding substructuring of other subtasks. Mark the current TASK as a MILESTONE, pull its description off the working stack, push it onto a "finished stack", and push each of the subtask descriptions onto the working stack.

4. Repeat from step 2 until the working stack is empty.

5. Sequence through all items on the finished stack and accumulate durations (costs) into the proper milestones.

The work breakdown structure approach to software scheduling can provide a manager with a quantitative indication of "how things are going". The algorithm can be refined to provide a solid approach to the definition of milestones that form the basis of software project scheduling.

2.2.3 Scheduling Tools

Software project scheduling does not differ greatly from scheduling of any multi-task development effort. Therefore, generalized project scheduling tools and techniques can be applied to software with little modification.

PERT (Program Evaluation and Review Technique) and CPM (Critical Path Method) can be applied to software development. Both scheduling techniques develop a 'network' description of a project, that is, a pictorial or tabular representation of the sequences and interdependency of tasks that must be accomplished from beginning to end of a project. The network is defined by developing a list of all tasks associated with a specific project (e.g., the work breakdown structure described in the preceding section) and a list of orderings (sometimes called a restriction list) that indicates in what order tasks must be accomplished.

A typical network, illustrated schematically in Figure D.4, generally has a number of parallel paths (each containing one or more project tasks) that may be scheduled to occur concurrently. Both PERT and CPM provide quantitative tools that allow the software planner to:

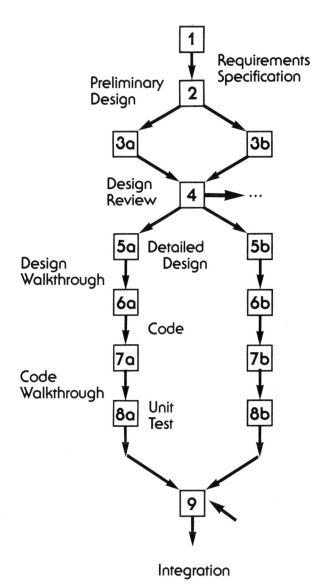

Figure D.4 Typical Network

1. determine the "critical path"—the chain of tasks that determines the duration of the project;
2. estimate "most likely" time estimates for individual tasks by applying statistical models;
3. calculate "boundary times" that define the time 'window' for a particular task.

Boundary time calculations can be very useful in software project scheduling. Slippage in the design of one function, for example, can retard further development of other functions. Among the boundary times that may be discerned from a PERT or CPM network are (ref. 7):

Page D-8

**Appendix D
QUANTITATIVE METHODS FOR
SOFTWARE ENGINEERING**

SOFTWARE
ENGINEERING
HANDBOOK

* earliest start (ES)—the earliest time a task can begin when all preceding tasks are completed as rapidly as possible.
* latest start (LS)—the latest time a task can be initiated without delaying the minimum project completion time.
* earliest finish (EF)—the sum of ES and the task duration, D.
* latest finish (LF)—the LS added to the task duration, D.
* total float (TF)—the amount of surplus time or leeway allowed in scheduling activities to avoid interference with any activity on the network critical path; the slack between the LS and ES times.

Techniques for calculation of ES, LS, EF, LF and TF are described in detail in references (ref. 7,8,9). Boundary time calculations lead to a determination of critical path and provide the manager with a quantitative method for evaluating progress as tasks are completed.

2.3 Automated Tools for Software Planning

Chapter 3 (section 3.4.3) of the Handbook describes the PRICE-S system for automated cost estimation. Automated cost/scheduling systems are not a substitute for thorough work breakdown and system definition. However, automated tools can provide insight and cross-checking capability difficult or impossible to achieve manually.

An overview of another automated tool for software cost/ schedule estimation is presented in this section. SLIM, an automated costing system, is based on the Rayleigh-Norden curve for the software life cycle. SLIM applies the Putnam software model, linear programming, statistical simulation and PERT techniques to derive software project estimates.

Developed by Quantitative Software Management, Inc., of McLean, Virginia, SLIM helps the software planner perform the following functions in an interactive terminal oriented session:

1. 'calibrate' the local software development environment by interpreting historical data supplied by the planner;
2. create an information model of the software to be developed by eliciting basic software characteristics, personnel attributes, and environmental considerations;
3. conduct software sizing—the approach used in SLIM is a more sophisticated, automated version of the lines-of-code costing technique described in Chapter 3 of the Handbook.

Once software size (i.e., LOC for each software function) has been established, SLIM computes size deviation—an indication of estimation uncertainty; a 'sensitivity profile' that indicates potential deviation of cost and effort; and a 'consistency check' with RADC (Rome Air Development Center, Rome, N.Y.) data collected for software systems of similar size.

The planner can invoke a linear programming analysis that considers development constraints on both cost and effort. SLIM determines all feasible solutions. Using the Rayleigh-Norden curve as a model, SLIM also provides a month-by-month distribution of effort and cost so that staffing and cash flow requirements can be projected.

In addition to the 'standard' estimating features described above, SLIM estimates the number of pages of software documentation (using an internal database); computer usage as a function of time; and a broad array of "what if" analysis features. The SLIM system is described in detail (with representative terminal output) in reference 3.

2.4 Software Productivity Data

Quantitative methods for software management must rely on historical data as a foundation for planning and evaluation. Productivity indicators (LOC/person-month) can be discerned from even the most simple management statistics. More detailed information correlating productivity with project, staff and environmental characteristics requires detailed, systematic data collection.

During the past decade, results of a number of studies that evaluate software productivity data have been published. Many of the models discussed earlier in this appendix are based on these data. However, the following maxim should be remembered:

"the best productivity data are the numbers you collect for your own organization"

In the sections that follow, an overview of important software productivity studies is presented and a recommended format for internal data collection is proposed.

2.4.1 An Overview of Recent Studies

Only a small percentage of software development organizations collect productivity data. Regrettably, only a small fraction of this group evaluate the data that is collected and publish results. In this section we present an overview of software productivity data published in the literature or maintained in a database accessible to interested parties.

Abstracts of important software productivity studies are presented as a guide to further research in quantitative methods for software engineering. It is important to note once again that data are affected by an extremely large number of project, staff and environmental parameters (see discussion of Walston and Felix, following). Therefore, comparisons of published results with local data should be conducted with care.

A landmark study of software productivity was published in 1974 by R. W. Wolverton (ref. 10). The Wolverton paper addresses an approach to software cost estimation and pres-

SOFTWARE
ENGINEERING
HANDBOOK

Appendix D
QUANTITATIVE METHODS FOR
SOFTWARE ENGINEERING

Page D-9

ents data collected from a number of large software projects conducted by TRW. A software cost database is described. The study synthesizes a number of important relationships, among them:

* cost per object instruction vs. relative degree of difficulty;
* cost per routine vs. relative size of routine;
* person-months vs. number of object instructions;
* productivity as a function of programmer experience; and
* allocation of resources during the planning and development phases.

Wolverton's study validates the 40-20-40 rule as a useful guideline for software development.

A more recent study of software productivity and the parameters that affect it was conducted by Walston and Felix (ref. 2). Based on a large database for software projects conducted by the IBM Federal Systems Division, the study provides one of the most comprehensive evaluations of software productivity and the factors that can cause variance are established. The effect of these variables on productivity is shown quantitatively.

In a paper on the characteristics of large software systems, Belady and Lehman (ref. 11) present a collection of productivity data from government and industry sources. Statistics for approximately 50 large software projects are presented. Data includes: program size (in LOC); person-months of effort; number of modules; number of programmers; project duration; and variation in project data.

Stephenson (ref. 12) presents a study of software productivity for the SAFEGUARD missle system. The study is important because it indicates the quantitative differences in productivity for 'applications' software, 'real time' software, and 'installation and maintenance' software. Allocation of resources for this 2 million instruction system corresponded closely to the 40-20-40 rule.

Basili and Zelkowitz (ref. 4) report on the Software Engineering Laboratory organized by the University of Maryland and NASA. The function of the laboratory is to collect software development data and correlate this data with various technologies and external parameters. In the referenced paper, the authors fit NASA project data to the Rayleigh-Norden model, showing a correspondence of the model with both large and medium sized projects.

Another important source of software productivity data is the Rome Air Development Center (RADC) database for software development projects. The RADC database contains final project statistics on hundreds of government sponsored software efforts.

2.5 The Software Project Report – A Format for Local Data Collection

Collection and evaluation of local historical software development data are important steps for a quantitative approach to software project management. A format for local data collection must accomplish a number of objectives:

1. provide a systematic method for collecting data on past projects;
2. incorporate a scheme for data collection that begins at the project level (gross numbers) and allows refinement by function, application area or software module;
3. establish a basis from which manual or automated data reduction can occur;
4. standardize the data collection approach for all software components in the organization.

2.6 Other Management Oriented Tools

The software engineering process is partitioned into a set of well-defined steps described throughout the Handbook. Each step has associated with it a set of 'tools' that aid the manager and software engineer alike. In an outstanding survey of automated tools for software engineering, Edward Miller (ref. 13) summarizes the importance of tools:

"Of all areas that impact computing professionals, software tools must rank highest. Virtually every activity that involves computing—whether it is a payroll system for a small firm or a complicated multidimensional differential equation solution running on a maxi-computer—must begin and end with some form of automated tool.

Tools are of all kinds. There are many tools in widespread use that have become essential to the use of computers in any application; an example of such a tool is a compiler or an assembler. Other tools are less widely used but are still crucially important..."

This section presents an overview of the "other tools". Managers with responsibility for software development must be aware of tools that can improve productivity, software quality, and ultimately maintainability of the released system.

2.6.1 An Index of Tools

Software tools fall into a number of predefined categories that closely parallel the steps of the software engineering process. One of the most comprehensive surveys of software tools is contained in an article by Reifer and Trattner (ref. 14). The authors define the following tool categories:

1. simulation
2. development
3. test and evaluation
4. operations and maintenance
5. performance measurement
6. programming support

Page D-10

Appendix D
QUANTITATIVE METHODS FOR
SOFTWARE ENGINEERING

SOFTWARE
ENGINEERING
HANDBOOK

The article examines and categorizes 70 tools.

An automated tool index has been published by Miller (ref. 13). Although by no means complete, it represents a relatively current (1979) listing of software tools and suppliers. Another comprehensive directory of software tools (1980) has been developed by Reifer Consultants (ref. 17).

2.6.2 Requirements Analysis Tools

In Chapter 4, section 4.6 of the Handbook, an automated tool for software requirements analysis—PSL/PSA—is discussed. General Electric has been involved in the implementation and evaluation of PSL/PSA over the past two years. The following paragraphs summarize some aspects of this work:

PSL/PSA provides a comprehensive computer-assist during requirements analysis. It will generate data flow diagrams and provide most of the facilities of the data dictionary described by DeMarco in his book, Structured Design. These capabilities extend PSL/PSA use into preliminary design. PSL also offers a Program Design Language facility that allows effective comuter-assists during both preliminary and detailed design.

Currently, PSL/PSA is supported on Digital Equipment Corporation's VAX-11/780, Honeywell Information Systems' L66 and the Hewlett-Packard 3000 computer by several components in General Electric.

A number of other automated requirements tools are in use throughout the industry, SADT (ref. 15), an analysis and design method developed by Softech, provides a graphical notation that enables the interrelationship among functions to be established and it also provides a formal method of ground rules for specifying a system. TRW's SREM (ref. 16) provides an automated approach for specification of requirements using a structured language, RSL, and a set of computer assisted tools, REVS, that insure completeness and consistency of requirements. Reprints of these references may be found in Miller (ref. 13).

2.6.3 Quality Assurance Tools

An overview of generic categories of automated testing tools is presented in Chapter 7, section 7.8 of the Handbook. This section provides references to a number of specific automated test tools.

An excellent survey of automated quality assurance tools is presented by Miller (ref. 13). In his IEEE tutorial, Miller reviews and presents reprints of several papers on the following test and quality assurance tools:

AVE—is an automated system for analyzing FORTRAN programs to detect classes of errors. The DAVE system uses data flow analysis to uncover structural inconsistency in a software system.

FAST—uses a 'scanner/parser' to create a program database that is queried and analyzed in an interactive approach to software quality assurance. The FAST system enables study of specific software constructs and traces their use throughout the program.

DISSECT—applies symbolic evaluation of a user defined path through a program. The DISSECT system allows a user to break the program into a number of predefined paths to examine the behavior of each path.

ATLAS—applies a concept called 'model-oriented testing' to develop a series of test cases that will verify that the program corresponds to an idealized model.

The quality assurance tools noted above represent only a few of many tools and techniques developed over the past few years. Because quality assurance often requires 40 percent of overall project effort/cost, time and effort reduction derived through the use of automated tools can have an important impact on improved productivity.

2.6.4 Maintenance Tools

The maintenance task, discussed in Chapter 9 of the Handbook, accounts for the majority of all effort expended during the software life cycle. Automated tools that reduce maintenance effort can dramatically reduce software life cycle costs.

Miller (ref. 13) identifies the following categories for maintenance tools:

* source code control programs—control the current versions of full source texts for software systems;
* data dictionaries—keep complete sets of definitions for software variables and other information items;
* cross reference generators—obtain various cross reference listings for entire programs or individual modules;
* flow generators—develop flow charts using the source code of 'old' undocumented programs;
* automatic interface analyzers—check the consistency of software interfaces;
*file managers—maintain system files in large scale operating environments; and
* decompiling programs—document object level programs that otherwise have no source listing.

Maintenance tools serve to enhance configuration management, provide documentation when (regrettably) none has existed, and provide some guidance in error diagnosis and correction.

2.7 Summary

A quantitative approach to the management and development of computer software is beginning to evolve. Techniques for software planning encompass empirical models of the

SOFTWARE
ENGINEERING
HANDBOOK

**Appendix D
QUANTITATIVE METHODS FOR
SOFTWARE ENGINEERING**

Page D-11

development process; scheduling techniques for project planning; automated tools for cost/effort estimation, and a growing collection of software productivity data that serve as a historical basis for estimating.

The key to an effective quantitative approach is collection and evaluation of 'local' software productivity data. A data collection approach that views overall project variables followed by specific software characteristics has been proposed.

This section of Appendix D has presented an overview of a rapidly evolving area in software engineering. It is incumbent upon the software manager to regularly evaluate progress in this area and apply methods, tools and techniques when applicable to the local environment.

3.0 SOFTWARE METRICS

Software engineering has spawned a need for a family of "metrics" that assign quantitative measure to computer software at each step in the life cycle. In this section of the appendix, an overview of metrics that can be applied during the development phase of the life cycle is presented.

A number of pertinent questions arise during software design, coding and test:

* Can the quality of the design be assessed using some quantitative measure?
* Is the design correct and has it been developed at a level of complexity that will result in ease of implementation?
* Are there characteristics of the detailed design and code that might provide guidance with regard to testing effort required, number of latent errors, and overall software reliability and quality?

Current research in software metrics is attempting to develop answers for these questions.

The current state of the art for software metrics is summarized by Browne and Shaw (ref. 18):

A great deal of energy is regularly invested in making measurements of computer software. The techniques of description, measurement and evaluation are largely ad hoc. Most of the analysis and even the measurement techniques have not been generalized...

In other words, present metric techniques are not readily extended to new kinds of systems, new kinds of questions, and new development environments. As a result, there is no quantitative basis for comparing programs or software engineering methodologies...

At present, software engineering is a technical activity for which we have developed a large set of ad hoc engineering techniques without corresponding scientific foundation...

The above assessment of software metrics is undeniably harsh. New and better metrics must be developed, but until such metrics are available, managers and technical staff should be aware of current (and potentially valuable) work that has already emerged. The remainder of this section should serve as a starting point for further evaluation of the practically and applicability of software metrics.

3.1 Software Metrics Categories

Although many software metrics have been proposed, all can be divided into three broad categories: design metrics, code metrics and quality/reliability metrics. Measures within each of these categories are often interrelated with metrics in another category, making clear distinctions somewhat difficult.

Design metrics focus on qualifiable attributes associated with software structure and procedure (see Chapter 5 of the Handbook). The number of modules and the degree of module interconnection have been used as a basis for structurally oriented software models (ref. 19). The characteristics of logical flow in program procedure are used as the basis of McCabe's metric—one of the most widely used measures of software complexity.

Code metrics define measurable attributes of program source code and attempt to devise models of complexity and reliability as well as derived indices of merit. Halstead's (ref. 21) metrics are preeminent in this category.

Software quality/reliability metrics run the gamut from generalized measure of software completeness to empirically derived reliability models. Both design and code metrics have been used to predict the number of latent errors in a program, the "testability" of a program. Independently derived reliability models attempt to predict failure rates for computer software.

It is important to note that the use of software metrics requires a commitment to collect and evaluate software engineering data for current and future projects. Once sufficient data has been collected, metrics can be correlated to local design, code and test effort (in resource units such as person-days) and/or the number of errors encountered during reviews and testing. Once well-correlated models have been established, software metrics may be used as predictors for future work.

3.1.1 A Design Metric—McCabe's Complexity Measure

The McCabe complexity measure is a software metric that may be applied after detailed software design is complete. A measure of complexity is developed using the number of linearly independent control paths in a program. The complexity metric $V(G)$, is actually the "cyclo-

Page D-12

**Appendix D
QUANTITATIVE METHODS FOR
SOFTWARE ENGINEERING**

**SOFTWARE
ENGINEERING
HANDBOOK**

matic number" of a control flow graph developed from classical graph theory. In practice, however, V(G) for a module may be computed simply by determining the number of decision points (conditional representations and loops) plus one.

In its simplest form, V(G) may be approximated by:

$$V(G) = ITE + DW + RU + CC + 1$$

where ITE is the number of if-then else constructs; DW and RU are the number of do-while and repeat-until constructs, respectively; and CC is the number of case conditions.

The higher the value of V(G), the greater the complexity of software procedure. Experimental evidence indicates that the amount of test effort and the number of latent errors is directly proportional to V(G). It can be seen from the above equation that any extraneous branches (i.e., violations of the structure constructs) serve to increase the value of V(G). This provides quantitative confirmation of the benefits of structured programming.

The McCabe metric has been shown (ref. 22) to have a good correlation with software attributes such as: detailed design time; design review time; test effort (time), and design and coding errors uncovered during testing. It follows that computation of V(G) could be used as a predictor for scheduling of reviews and test effort as well as an indicator of software quality (as reflected in the number of errors).

3.1.2 Halstead's Software Metrics

Halstead's (ref. 21) work in the development of source language level complexity measure is among the most widely known and it studies software metrics. Halstead's theory, which he calls Software Science, proposes the first analytical "laws" for computer software. To develop a source code oriented complexity measure, software science uses a set of primative measure that may be derived after code is generated or estimated once design is complete. These are:

n1—the number of distinct operators that appear in a program
n2—the number of distinct operands that appear in a program
N1—the total number of operator occurances
N2—the total number of operand occurances

To illustrate how these primitive measures are obtained, consider the simple sort program shown below:

```
SUBROUTINE SORT (X,N)
DIMENSION X (N)
IF (N.LT.2) RETURN
DO 20 I = 2,N
DO 10 J = 1,I
IF (X(I).GE.X(J)) GO TO 10
SAVE = X(I)
```

```
X(I) = X(J)
X(J) = SAVE
10 CONTINUE
20 CONTINUE
RETURN
END
```

Among the distinct operators for the above program are: .GE., =, DO, array subscript, etc. There are ten distinct operators (n1 = 10) and 28 occurrences of operators (N1 = 28). Operands for the program are all variable names and constants. Therefore, n2 = 7 and N2 = 22.

Halstead uses this primitive measure to develop expressions for the overall program length; potential minimum volume for an algorithm; the actual volume (number of bits required to specify a program); the program level (a measure of software complexity); language level (a constant for a given language); and other features such as predicted development effort, development time and even projected number of faults in the software.

Halstead shows that length, N, can be estimated

$$N = n1 \log n1 + n2 \log n2$$

and program volume may be defined:

$$V = N \log (n1 + n2)$$

It should be noted that V will vary with programming language and represents the volume of information (in bits) required to specify a program. The volume for the FORTRAN version of the SORT Module shown above can be shown to be 204. Volume for an equivalent assembler language version would be 328. Volume is directly related to the mental effort required to develop a program. As we would suspect, it takes more effort to specify a program in assembler language.

Halstead proposes that each language may be categorized by language level, L, that will vary among languages. Halstead theorized that language level is constant for a given language but recent work indicates that language level is a function of both language and programmer. The following language level values have been empirically derived for common languages:

Language	mean L
English prose	2.16
PL/1	1.53
ALGOL /68	1.21
FORTRAN	1.14
assembler	0.88

It appears that language level implies a level of abstraction in the specification of procedure. High level languages allow specification of code at a higher level of abstraction than assembler (machine-oriented) language.

SOFTWARE
ENGINEERING
HANDBOOK

Appendix D
QUANTITATIVE METHODS FOR
SOFTWARE ENGINEERING

Page D-13

Halstead's work is amenable to experimental verification. A large body of research has been conducted to investigate Software Science. A discussion of this work is beyond the scope of this Appendix. However, software science shows promise as a quantitative technique for the prediction of software testing effort and software reliability, software development effort estimation, software maintenance effort estimation, and as a formal measure of complexity and modularity.

3.2 Software Quality Metrics

Software quality is a difficult attribute to measure quantitatively. However, important measures of quality do exist and have been proposed in the literature. This section of Appendix D contains edited excerpts of reference 22, "Software Quality Metrics, Concepts and Their Application."

The sections that follow (adapted from that publication) describe a set of software quality metrics that may be used by the requester as a measure of developer compliance to a predefined quality baseline, and by the developer as an internal quality auditing procedure. For the most part, the metrics described are required subjective evaluation. However, each provides a valuable means by which software quality may be assessed.

Little control of total software quality has been introduced in-line to the software development process. Unlike the manufacturing of hardware there is little in-line calibration to identify components which need rework. There are few checks for tolerence to insure parts will fit well until integration and test. Little consideration is given during design to the economies associated with operation and maintenance effort. The result is that most poor quality is found too late, during testing or operation and maintenance, when the costs to correct the situation are extremely high.

Standards and conventions provide one technique to provide a means of quality control. The introduction of modern programming techniques, especially walk-throughs, code inspection, and program support libraries, have added discipline and visibility to the programming process and therefore some additional means of control. However, none of these techniques provide consistency or quantification in their application; most rely on subjective analysis.

This material discusses further steps toward a more disciplined engineering approach to software quality management—the use of software quality metrics.

3.2.1 The Life Cycle Implications of Software Quality

Life Cycle Management of large-scale software systems has been increasingly emphasized in recent years. This emphasis is due primarily to the unexpected high costs that have been experienced during the life of most systems. These unexpected high costs have not necessarily been related to the systems' inability to perform their intended functions, but instead can be attributed to the high costs of maintenance, transferring the systems to another environment, interfacing the systems to other systems, and upgrading the systems.

These high costs result from characteristics of the software that do not necessarily relate to the correctness of the implementation of a function or how reliably the function operates, but instead relate to "how well" the software is designed, coded, and documented with respect to maintaining, transferring, modifying, etc., the software. This "how well" is a major aspect of the software quality.

This situation identifies a weakness in how the requirements of software system developments currently are defined. Emphasis is placed on the functions that must be performed, the schedule in which the system must be produced and the cost of producing the system. Little or no attention is given to identifying what qualities over the life cycle the software system should exemplify. There are two major reasons for this focus. First, the initial operation of the system, how correctly and reliably the system performs, is always important to the sponsor of a development. It provides the first test of not only how well the developer has done but also how well the sponsor has done in specifying, monitoring and controlling the development. Cost and schedule are obvious concerns since the system usually must be developed in a constrained period of time and within a constrained budget. Second, no standard definition or identification of what qualities the acquisition manager should consider has been available. No mechanism has existed which would allow an acquisition manager to quantitatively specify the quality desired and then to measure how well the development is progressing toward the desired quality. The little consideration given quality to date generally has been very subjective and not followed by measurement or assurance activities.

The illusiveness of a concise definition of software quality in part can be attributed to the fact that software production is still in its infancy. Until the last few years, the production of software was viewed as an art rather than an engineering discipline. The fact that software was viewed as an art rather than an abstraction, having no physical presence to measure, contributes to this black box approach. Modern programming practices have greatly impacted this point of view introducing significantly more management understanding and visibility into the software production process.

The potential life cycle cost savings of a standardized concept of software quality and a mechanism for specifying and measuring software quality are substantial considering the large portion of life cycle costs attributed to the qualities mentioned previously.

3.2.2 The Concept of Software Quality

The concept of software quality described in this section is based on eleven quality factors grouped according to three orientations or viewpoints with which the requester interacts

Page D-14

Appendix D
QUANTITATIVE METHODS FOR
SOFTWARE ENGINEERING

SOFTWARE
ENGINEERING
HANDBOOK

with a delivered software product. These three orientations are: product operation, product revision, and product transition. The factors are conditions or characteristics which actively contribute to the quality of the software. These characteristics have been defined so they can be related to a cost to perform the activity characterized by the factor or to operate with a specified degree of quality. The relationship of the factors to the three orientations or product activities is shown in Figure D.5. The questions in parenthesis provide a relevancy or brief interpretation of the factors. The formal definitions of the factors are provided in Table D.1.

This conceptualization of factors in software quality provides a framework for the requester or the developer to quantify concerns for the longer life-cycle implications of a software product. For example, if the requester is sponsoring the development of a system in an environment in which there is a high rate of technical breakthroughs in hardware design, the portability of the software should take on an added significance. If the expected life cycle of a system is long, finding and fixing errors as effectively as possible (maintainability) become a cost critical consideration. If the system is an experimental system where the software specifications will have a high rate of change, flexibility in the software product is highly desirable. If the functions of the system are expected to be required for a long time, while the system itself may change considerably from time to time, reusability is of prime importance in those modules which implement the major functions of the system. With the advent of more networks and communication capabilities, more systems are being required to interface with other systems and the concept of interoperability is extremely important. All of these considerations can be accommodated in the framework established.

TABLE D.1 Definition of Software Quality Factors*

Correctness	Extent to which a program satisfies its specifications and fulfills the user's mission objectives.
Reliability	Extent to which a program can be expected to perform its intended function with required precision.
Efficiency	The amount of computing resources and code required by a program to perform a function.
Integrity	Extent to which access to software or data by unauthorized persons can be controlled.
Maintainability	Effort required to locate and fix an error in an operational program.
Testability	Effort required to test a program to insure it performs its intended function.
Flexibility	Effort required to modify an operational program.
Portability	Effort required to transfer a program from one hardware configuration and/or software system environment to another.
Reusability	Extent to which a program can be used in other applications—related to the packaging and scope of the functions that programs perform.
Interoperability	Effort required to couple one system with another.

3.2.3 Software Quality Metrics

These quality factors represent a management-oriented view of software quality. To introduce a dimension of quantification, this management-oriented view was translated to a software-related viewpoint. This translation was accomplished by a set of criteria for each factor. These criteria further define the quality factor and help describe the relationships between factors as a criterion can be related to more than one factor. The criteria are independent attributes of the software or software production process by which the quality factors can be judged, defined and measured. These attributes are shown in Figure D.6. The factors are identified in ellipses and the criteria are identified in rectangles. The definitions of these criteria are provided in Table D.2.

Quality metrics can be established to provide a quantitative measure of the attributes represented by the criteria. The hierarchical nature of the framework established, involving the factors, criteria and metrics, allows for expansion and

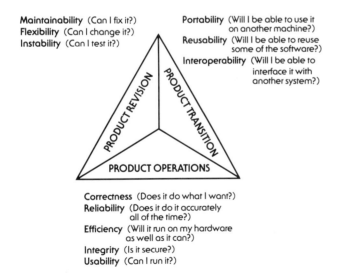

Maintainability (Can I fix it?)
Flexibility (Can I change it?)
Instability (Can I test it?)

Portability (Will I be able to use it on another machine?)
Reusability (Will I be able to reuse some of the software?)
Interoperability (Will I be able to interface it with another system?)

Correctness (Does it do what I want?)
Reliability (Does it do it accurately all of the time?)
Efficiency (Will it run on my hardware as well as it can?)
Integrity (Is it secure?)
Usability (Can I run it?)

Figure D.5 Allocation of Software Quality Factors to Product Activity

*McCall, J. and Walters, G., References 22 and 34.

**SOFTWARE
ENGINEERING
HANDBOOK**

**Appendix D
QUANTITATIVE METHODS FOR
SOFTWARE ENGINEERING**

Page D-15

refinement as further experience with these concepts is gained and as software engineering technology advances. New metrics, criteria and even factors may be identified as relevant to the needs of project management. This hierarchy is depicted in Figure D.7.

3.2.4 Examples of Metrics

The most accurate assessment of the qualities of a software product is its operational history. If after two years of operation a software product must be converted to a new hardware system and the cost to accomplish this is 100 percent of the initial development cost, it can be stated that from a portability aspect, this product was of poor quality. Testing provides a quantitative measure of the qualities of software product also. However, the completeness of the testing has always been a concern. Most testing is oriented toward insuring the software product runs as efficiently as necessary, performs functionally well (correctness) and does not fail (reliability). Extensive testing usually reveals the usability and testability of the product although not often with the people who will be using the system or testing changes to it. Under special circumstances, tests may be oriented toward evaluating the integrity of a product. In most cases, with the pressures of tight budgets and schedules, testing is never as thorough as desired. Even when testing reveals problems, the costs to correct those problems (often involving redesign as well as recording and retesting) are very high.

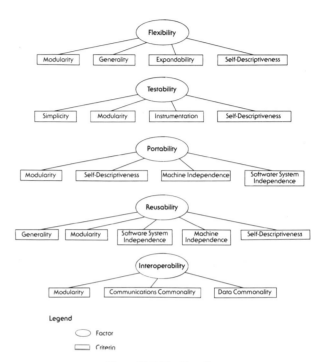

Figure D.7 (Continued)

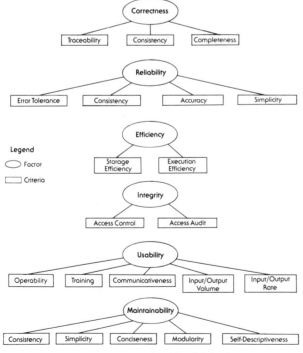

**Figure D.7 Relationship of Criteria
to Software Quality Factors***

Figure D.8 Software Quality Framework*

*McCall, J. and Walters, G., Op. Cit.

**Appendix D
QUANTITATIVE METHODS FOR
SOFTWARE ENGINEERING**

**SOFTWARE
ENGINEERING
HANDBOOK**

Criterion	Definition	Related Factors
Traceability	Those attributes of the software that provide a thread from the requirements to the implementation with respect to the specific development and operational environment.	Correctnesss
Completeness	Those attributes of the software that provide full implementation of the functions required.	Correctness
Consistency	Those attributes of the software that provide uniform design and implementation techniques and notation.	Correctness Reliability Maintainability
Accuracy	Those attributes of the software that provide the required precision in calculations and outputs.	Reliability
Error Tolerance	Those attributes of the software that provide continuity of operation under nonnominal conditions.	Reliability
Simplicity	Those attributes of the software that provide implementation of functions in the most understandable manner. (Usually avoidance of practices which increase complexity).	Reliability Maintainability Testability
Modularity	Those attributes of the software that provide a structure of highly independent modules.	Maintainability Flexibility Testability Portability Reusability Interoperability
Generality	Those attributes of the software that provide breadth to the functions performed.	Flexibility Reusability
Expandability	Those attributes of the software that provide for expansion of data storage requirements or computational functions.	Flexibility
Instrumentation	Those attributes of the software that provide for the measurement of usage or identification of errors.	Testability
Self-Descriptiveness	Those attributes of the software that provide explanation of the implementation of a function.	Flexibility Maintainability Testability Portability Reusability

Table D.2 Criteria Definitions for Software Quality Factors*

*McCall, J. and Walters, G., Op. Cit.

SOFTWARE
ENGINEERING
HANDBOOK

Appendix D
QUANTITATIVE METHODS FOR
SOFTWARE ENGINEERING

Page D-17

Criterion	Definition	Related Factors
Execution Efficiency	Those attributes of the software that provide for minimum processing time.	Efficiency
Storage Efficiency	Those attributes of the software that provide for minimum storage requirements during operation.	Efficiency
Access Control	Those attributes of the software that provide for control of the access of software and data.	Integrity
Access Audit	Those attributes of the software that provide for an audit of the access of software and data.	Integrity
Operability	Those attributes of the software that determine operation and procedures concerned with the operation of the software.	Usability
Training	Those attributes of the software that provide transition from current operation or initial familiarization.	Usability
Communicativeness	Those attributes of the software that provide useful inputs and outputs which can be assimilated.	Usability
Software System Independence	Those attributes of the software that determine its dependency on the software environment (operating systems, utilities, input/output routines, etc).	Portability Reusability
Machine Independence	Those attributes of the software that determine dependency on the hardware system.	Portability Reusability
Communications Commonality	Those attributes of the software that provide the use of standard protocols and interface routines.	Interoperability
Data Commonality	Those attributes of the software that provide the use of standard data representations.	Interoperability
Conciseness	Those attributes of the software that provide for implementation of a function with a minimum amount of code.	Maintainability

Table D.2 Criteria Definitions for
Software Quality Factors (Continued)*

*McCall, J. and Walters, G., Op. Cit.

Page D-18

Appendix D
QUANTITATIVE METHODS FOR
SOFTWARE ENGINEERING

SOFTWARE
ENGINEERING
HANDBOOK

The measurements represented by quality metrics are applied during the early phases of the development. They provide an indication of the progression (quality growth) toward the desired product quality. The earlier in the life cycle the metrics are applied, the more "indicative only" these metrics will be. Obviously, if a design specification has high quality, but is poorly implemented, the resulting software product will not have high quality. Successive application of metrics during the development helps prevent that situation. This overall concept is shown in Figure D.8.

The relationship between predictive and acceptance type metrics is not clearly established yet. Acceptance type metrics can be viewed as a validation of the predictive metrics. Additional research and experience in this area is required to formally establish the relationships.

Predictive metrics are oriented toward available tangible items during development. These tangible items include source code, documentation including requirements specifications, design specifications, manuals, test plans, problem reports and correction reports, and review reports. Since the documents generated vary between projects, metrics related to documents are based on the existence of certain information regardless of the document in which it exists.

There are essentially two types of predictive metric. The first type, like a ruler, is a relative quantity measure. The second type is a binary measure of the existence/absence of an attribute. The metrics, desribed here were chosen to be language-independent. The units of a metric are important to avoid ambiguity and to obtain a meaningful metric. The following rule was used in choosing the units of a metric: *the units of the metric will be the ratio of actual occurrences to the possible number of occurrences.* Once stated, this rule is obvious, yet many studies have failed because they did not comply with this rule, resulting in poor correlation between the criterion and the factor.

An example of a relative quantity metric is a complexity measure which is applied during design to a design (e.g. a flow chart) and during implementation to the source code. The metric (ref. 23) is based on path flow analysis and variable set/use information along each path. A variable is considered to be "live" at a node if it can be used again along that path in the program. The measure is calculated by summing the "liveness" of all paths in the program. The units rule is applied by dividing this measure by the maximum possible complexity of the program; i.e., all variables live along all paths.

Figure D.8 Example Metrics*

*McCall, J. and Walters, G., Op. Cit.

SOFTWARE
ENGINEERING
HANDBOOK

Appendix D
QUANTITATIVE METHODS FOR
SOFTWARE ENGINEERING

Page D-19

An example of a binary measure is a checklist used to assess if a design document is complete. Each item in the checklist requires a score be given depending on the existence (1) or absence (0) of specific information. The metric is a normalized summation of scores for the checklist items.

These two examples are shown in Figure D.9, a metric data collection worksheet used to record measurements. The worksheet identifies the phase or phases during which the measurement is taken and whether it is a relative quantity measure (value column on worksheet) or a binary measure (yes/no column on worksheet). The metrics can be applied manually utilizing the worksheet and the corresponding narrative descriptions of the measures or, in many cases, can be applied automatically with appropriate support software.

In establishing the metrics discussed here, every attempt was made to utilize the work and experience of others. The first published effort formally establishing metrics appears to have occurred in 1978 (ref 24). Seven major attributes, related to the quality factors in this chapter, were identified, further defined by other attributes, and a few metrics were established. The metrics and attributes were specifically oriented toward aerospace applications. More recent efforts have expanded the number of quality factors or attributes (refs 25, 26, 27) and the applications to which the concepts apply (refs 23, 29, 30, 31). Many detailed studies into specific qualities and metrics have also been pursued (refs 31, 32, 33). A more exhaustive list of references can be found in reference 34. Each of these efforts dealt with source code metrics. Other efforts described design and code inspections (ref 35). Concepts described are extensions of these previous efforts. The extensions provide a management oriented view of software quality, quantifying the metrics even at the early phases of development, establishing metrics which specifically relate to the various quality factors, and applying automation to the metric collection even at the early phases of development.

The other trade-offs that should be considered are the interrelationships among the factors. Table 2 can be used as a guide in determining the relationship among factors. Some factors are synergistic; others conflict. The following examples show how the factors relate.

Maintainability vs. Efficiency – optimized code, incorporating intricate techniques and assembly language, usually causes problems for the maintainer. Using modular high-level code to improve maintainability of a system usually increases overhead, resulting in less efficient operation.

Integrity vs. Efficiency – the additional code and processing required to control access to the software or data usually lengthen the run time and require additional storage.

Interoperability vs. Integrity – coupled systems allow for more avenues of access and different users who can access the system. The potential for accidental access of sensitive data is increased as well as the opportunities for deliberate access. Often, coupled systems share data or software compounding the security problem as well.

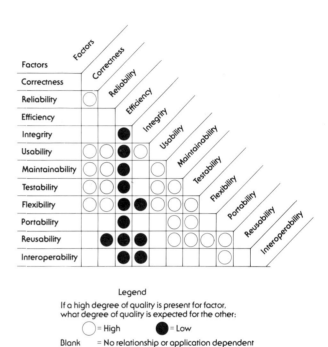

Legend
If a high degree of quality is present for factor,
what degree of quality is expected for the other:

◯ = High   ● = Low

Blank   = No relationship or application dependent

Figure D.10 Relationships between Software Quality Factors*

*McCall, J. and Walters, G., Op. Cit.

3.2.5 Steps for Quality

The steps listed in this section provide a formal approach to the specification of software quality:

1.a   **Identify and Assign Relative Importance to Factors** – In preparing a request for proposal (RFP) or system requirements specification (SRS), the requester should identify and assign a relative importance to each critical quality factor.

1.b   **Cost-to-Implement vs Life Cycle Cost Savings Trade-Off** – The requester should evaluate the cost to implement the quality versus the resulting expected cost saving in later phases of the program. Based upon this trade-off for each factor, the relative importance should be revised if necessary.

1.c   **Trade-Off Among Factors** – The impact of the interrelationships among the critical quality factors should be examined (Figure D.10) and the relative importance of the critical factors re-evaluated. The resultant set of critical factors at this step will be those stressed in the requirements.

1.d   **Provide Definitions of Factors** – Once critical qualities are identified and priorities assigned, they should be included in the RFP or SRS along with a definition of each factor. The developer should be required to respond to how the software to be developed will exhibit the qualities specified.

Page D-20

**Appendix D
QUANTITATIVE METHODS FOR
SOFTWARE ENGINEERING**

**SOFTWARE
ENGINEERING
HANDBOOK**

1.e Provide Detailed Description of Factor Related to Application – Wherever possible, detailed explanation of the reason(s) for specifying the factor should be included with the definition for each quality factor. For example, if portability is a major concern to the requestor as precise a description as possible should be included. The types of environments to which the system might be transported should be specified.

2.a Identify Critical Software Attributes Required – Having identified the critical quality factors, the requester then identifies the related critical software attributes required. For example, to stress the importance of maintainability, the following software attributes would be identified as required in the RFP or SRS: consistency, simplicity, conciseness, modularity and self-descriptiveness. The precise definitions would be included in the RFP or SRS.

2.b Request Developer to Provide Plan to Achieve Attributes – The requester should request the software developer to define in the software plan exactly how each required software attribute for each quality factor will be achieved.

A refinement of the approach would specify the particular metric(s) to be applied. This requires precise statements of the level of quality acceptable for the software. Currently, the underlying mathematical relationships which allow measurement with this precision do not exist for all the quality factors. The mechanism for making a precise statement for any quality factor is a rating of that factor. The dependent variable for each rating is the effort/cost required to perform a function such as correcting or modifying the design or program. To apply this refinement, the Acquisition Manager would follow these additional steps:

3.a Specify Rating for Each Quality Factor – After identifying each critical quality factor, specific performance levels or ratings required for it should be specified. For example, a rating for maintainability might be that the average time to fix a problem should be five person-days or that 90% of the problem fixes should take less than six person-days. This rating would be specified in the RFP. To comply with this specification, the software would have to exhibit characteristics which, when present, give an indication that the software will meet this requirement. These characteristics are measured by metrics which are inserted into a mathematical relationship to obtain the predicted rating.

3.b Identify Specific Metrics To Be Applied – The specific metrics should be identified which will be applied to various software tangible items during development to indicate progress toward achieving the required level of quality.

Since metrics have had limited application at this time and little data has been gathered to validate metrics in such areas as portability, interoperability and reusability, the requester is advised not to levy requirements for meeting specified quality levels. Instead, he should specify the relative importance of the quality factor as development guidelines.

3.2.6 Applying Software Metrics During Development

In applying metrics, it is important to use existing control mechanisms; i.e., reviews, status reports, documentation delivered during development and the source code. The current emphasis of these controls is existing schedule and cost performance and determing functional correctness of the software being developed. The quality metrics are applied to these same control vehicles to provide an indication of the quality of the software product being developed.

Corresponding to the three levels of specifying software quality, the measurement can be performed at three levels of detail. The first level of software quality measurement involves applying the metrics to software products as they are produced. Different sets of metrics are applicable to products developed during the requirements analysis, design and coding phases. Use of metrics in this manner ensures a formal and consistent review of each of the software products. The steps to be followed for this level of measurement are:

1.a Apply The Subsets of Metrics That Apply at Each Phase – The subset of metrics which relate to the identified critical quality factors and software attributes and are applicable to the phase of development should be applied to the available software products. For example, during the design phase, metrics could be applied to design specifications interface control documents, test plans, minutes and materials prepared for reviews, etc.

1.b Overall Subjective Evaluation – A subjective evaluation of how well the software is being developed with respect to the specific quality factors can be made based on the inspection of the software products using the metrics.

The second level of detail uses experience gained through application of metrics and accumulation of historical information to take advantage of the quantitative nature of the metrics. Measurement values are used as indicators of the progress toward a high quality product. The additional steps for this level of detail are described in the following steps:

2.a Evaluate Low Metric Scores – After the metrics are applied to the available software products, the values are obtained and evaluated. If a particular module receives low metric scores, it can be individually evaluated for potential problems. If low metric scores are realized across the system, an evaluation should be made to identify the cause. It may be that a design or implementation technique used widely by the development team is the cause. Corrective action such as the enforcement of a development standard can then be introduced.

2.b Analyze The Variance of Scores – Further analysis can be conducted. An examination of the metric scores of each module in a system will reveal such metrics vary widely. Further examination will reveal whether this variation correlates with the number of problem reports or with historical variances in performance. This sensitivity analysis identifies characteristics of the software, represented by the metrics, which are critical to the quality of the product. Quality assurance personnel should place increased emphasis on these characteristics of the software product.

SOFTWARE
ENGINEERING
HANDBOOK

Appendix D
QUANTITATIVE METHODS FOR
SOFTWARE ENGINEERING

Page D-21

2.c   **Evaluate Scores Against Thresholds** – Threshold values may be required. A simple example is the percent of comments per line of source code. Certainly code exhibiting only one or two percent measurements would be identified for corrective action. It may be that ten percent is a minimum acceptable level.

The most detailed metrics approach uses predictive equations. Currently, generally applicable predictive equations are not available. However, as more project data is gathered to derive valid local equations, the following steps would be appropriate.

3.a   **Apply Normalization Function** – To illustrate the procedure, assume a normalization function has been developed for the factor, flexibility. The normalization function, applicable during the design phase, relates degree of modular implementation to the flexibility of the software. The predicted rating of flexibility is in terms of the average time to implement a change in specifications. The normalization function is shown in Figure D.10. The measurements associated with modular implementation are taken from design documents which reveal if input, output and processing functions are mixed in the same module, if application and machine-dependent functions are mixed in the same module and if processing is data volume or data value limited. As an example, assume the measurements were applied during the design phase and a value of 0.65 was measured. Inserting this value in the normalization function results in a predicted rating for flexibility of 0.33 as identified by point A in Figure D.10. If the requester had specified a rating of 0.2 (identified by point B), he has an indication that software development is progressing well with respect to this quality. By analyzing the variance associated with this normalization function, Figure D.11 shows that the requester has an 86 percent level of confidence that system flexibility will be better than required.

3.b   **Determine Corrective Action to be Taken** – Comparison of the predicted rating to the specified rating provides a more quantitative indication, with an associated level of confidence, of how well software development is progressing toward the specified levels of quality.

Corrective action based upon further analysis would be in order if the predicted rating was lower than the specified rating.

Even though steps 3a and 3b are not currently appropriate for the requester to apply, the developer can certainly use them as another technique in his quality assurance program.

4.0 SUMMARY

Management and technical control of software development are predicated on solid data. Quantitative methods in software engineering have been proposed as a first step toward the development of predictive models for program cost, schedule, and resources, and technical models for software complexity, quality and reliability.

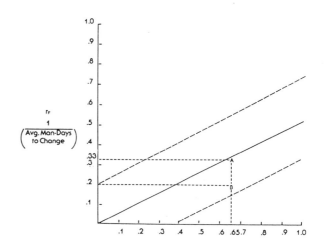

MO. 2 Modular Implementation Measure/Design Phase

Figure D.10 Normalization Function for Flexibility During Design*

*McCall, J. and Walters, G., Op. Cit.

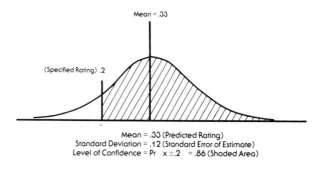

Mean = .33 (Predicted Rating)
Standard Deviation = .12 (Standard Error of Estimate)
Level of Confidence = Pr   x ±.2   = .86 (Shaded Area)

Figure D.11 Determination of Level of Confidence*

*McCall, J. and Walters, G., Op. Cit.

Appendix D has presented an overview of quantitative methods in software engineering. It should serve as a starting point for managers who desire a more precise approach to project estimating and control. The appendix also serves as a guide for software engineers who are developing systems that demand quantitative measure for the quality of design, code and testing.

5.0 REFERENCES

1. Basili, V., Models and Metrics for Software Management and Engineering, IEEE, No. E40-167-7, 1980.

2. Walston, C. and Felix, C., A Method of Programming Measurement and Estimation, IBM Systems Journal, 16, 1, 1977, pp. 54-73.

Page D-22

Appendix D
QUANTITATIVE METHODS FOR
SOFTWARE ENGINEERING

SOFTWARE
ENGINEERING
HANDBOOK

3. Putnam, L., Software Cost Estimating and Life Cycle Control, IEEE, No. EH0-165-1, 1980.

4. Basili, V. and Zelkowitz, M., Analyzing Medium Scale Software Development, Proc. 3rd, Intl, Conf. Sofware Engineering, 1978, pp. — 116-123.

5. Aron, J., Estimating Resources for Large Programming Systems, in Software Engineering: Concepts and Techniques, ed. J. Buxton, Van — Hostrand Reinhold, 1976.

6. Tausworthe, R., The Work Breakdown Structure in Software Project Management, Journal of Systems and Software, 1, 1980.

7. Riggs, J., Production Systems: Planning, Analysis and Control, 3rd, ec., Wiley, 1981, pp. 214-218.

8. Mader, J. and Phillips, C., Project Management with CPM AND PERT 2nd ed., Reinhold, 1970.

9. Wiest, J. and Levy, F., A Management Guide to PERT/CPM, 2nd ed., Prentice-Hall, 1977.

10. Wolverton, R. W., The Cost of Developing Large-Scale Software, IEEE on Computers, June, 1974.

11. Balady, L and Lehman, M., The Characteristics of large Systems, in Research Directions in Software Technology, MIT Press, 1979, pp. — 106-138.

12. Stephenson, W., An Analysis of Resources Used in SAFEGUARD System Software Development, Proc. 2nd Intl. Conference Software Engineering, IEE, 1976.

13. Miller, E., Automated Tools for Software Engineering, IEEE, No. E40-150-3, 1979, p. 1.

14. Reifer, D. and Trattner, S., A Glossary of Software Tools and Techniques, Computer, July 1977.

15. Ross, D., and Schoman, K., Structure Analysis for Requirements Definition, IEEE, Trans. Software Engineering, January, 1977.

16. Alfred, M. W., A Requirements Engineering Methodology For Real-Time Requirements, IEEE Trans. Software Engineering, January, 1977.

17. Software Tools Directory, Reifer Consultants, Inc., 2733 Pacific Coast Hwy, Suite 203, Torrance, CA. 90595, 1980.

18. Browne, J.C. and Shaw, M., Toward A Scientific Basis For Software Evaluation, Software Metrics Panel Final Report, A.J. Perlis, et al editors, Research Report #182/80, Yale University, June 1980.

19. Gilb, T., Software Metrics, Winthrop Publishers, 1977.

20. McCabe, T., A Complexity Measure, IEEE Trans. Software Engineering, vol. 1, no. 4, December 1976.

21. Halstead, M., Elements of Software Science, Elsevier, 1977.

22. McCall, J. and Walters, G., Software Quality Metrics: Concepts and Their Application, TIS-78CIS015, Command and Information Systems, General Electric Co., Sunnyvale, CA. 1978.

23. Richard, P. and Chang, P., Localization of Variables: A Measure of Complexity, GE TIS 76CIS07, December 1976.

24. Rubey, R., Hartwick, R, "Quantitative Measurement of Program Quality", Proceedings of 23RD National Conference, ACM, 1968.

25. Boehm, B., et al, Characteristics of Software Quality, North Holland Publishing Co., New York, 1978.

26. Halstead, M., Elements of Software Science, Elsevier Computer Science Library, New York 1977.

27. Kosarjo, S. R., Ledgard, H.F., "Concepts in Quality Software Design", NBS Technical Note 842, August 1974.

28. PATHWAY PROGRAM — Program Quality Assurance for Shipboard Installed Computer Programs, Naval Sea Systems Command, April 1976.

29. Myers, G. J., Reliable Software Through Composite Design, Petrocelli/Charter, 1975.

30. Abernathy, D. H., et al, "Survey of Design Goals for Operating Systems", Georgia Tech, GITIS-72-04, 1972.

31. Elshoff, J., "Measuring Commercial PL/1 Programs Using Halstead's Criteria", SIGPLAN Notices, May 1976.

32. Bell, D.E., Sullivan, J.E., "Further Investigation into the Complexity of Software", Mitre, MTR-2874, June 1974

33. Dunsmore, H., Gann, J., "Experimental Investigation of Programming Complexity", Proceedings of ACM/NBS Sixteenth Annual Technical Symposium, June 1977,

34. McCall, J., Richard, P., Walters, G., "Factors in Software Quality", 3 vols, NTIS AD-AO49-014, AD-AO49-015, AD-AO49-055, November 1977. (Produced under contract F30602-87-C0417 with the Air Force Systems Command Electronics Systems Division and Rome Air Development Center).

35. Fagan, M., "Design and Code Inspections and Process Control in the Development of Programs", IBM TR 00-2763, June 1976.